CONCEPTS OF CULTURE

CONCEPTS OF CULTURE
art, politics, and society

**Edited by Adam Muller,
University of Manitoba**

UNIVERSITY OF CALGARY PRESS

Published by the
University of Calgary Press
2500 University Drive NW
Calgary, Alberta, Canada T2N 1N4
www.uofcpress.com

We acknowledge the financial support of
the Government of Canada, through the
Book Publishing Industry Development
Program (bpidp), and the Alberta Foundation for the Arts for our publishing
activities. We acknowledge the support
of the Canada Council for the Arts for
our publishing program.

Library and Archives Canada
Cataloguing in Publication

Concepts of culture : art, politics and
society / edited by Adam Muller.

Includes bibliographical references
and index.
ISBN 1-55238-167-6

1. Culture – Textbooks.   I. Muller,
Adam, 1968–

HM621.C645 2005   306
C2005-905878-1

Cover design, Meika West.
Cover photograph, Getty Images.
Internal design & typesetting,
zijn digital.

Canada

The Alberta
Foundation
for the Arts   Alberta

Canada Council   Conseil des Arts
for the Arts   du Canada

CONTENTS

ACKNOWLEDGMENTS

I would like to thank my contributors for their durable commitment to the ideas at the heart of this project, and for their kindness, patience, and support as it has, sometimes rather gradually, unfolded. I would also like to thank the Faculty of Arts and the Department of English at the University of Manitoba for their financial support both of the production and of the publication of this anthology. Matt Hildebrand's assistance as my RA during the earlier stages of the anthology's development was invaluable, and his keen eye and ability to type tirelessly proved absolutely vital to the production of the first manuscript draft. I am also grateful to Victoria Newell for her efficient and generous editorial assistance as I worked to assemble the anthology's final draft. This last draft, which involved some pretty fundamental alterations to the one that preceded it, took the shape it did principally as a result of the constructive criticisms of two superb external assessors provided by the University of Calgary Press. Without their feedback there is no question that this anthology would have remained in some fundamental ways impoverished and incomplete, and my thanks to them is profound. Although I take full responsibility for any limitations of this book as a whole, I am only too happy to share with them whatever credit might happen to come my way. I first conceived of this project in 1998 during my tenure as a Visiting Scholar at the interdisciplinary School for Post-graduate Research on Interculturalism and Transnationality (SPIRIT) at Aalborg University in Denmark. There, I was fortunate enough to be surrounded by a group of scholars drawn from across the humanities and the social sciences who proved only too willing to share their views with me and, when the time came, to comment helpfully on mine. I remain profoundly grateful for this experience, one that I still regard as decisively formative. I therefore wish to express my sincerest thanks to SPIRIT's director, Ulf Hedetoft, as well as to its faculty, students, and support staff. Lastly, I wish to thank my wife, Emily, without whose love and support this project never would have reached fruition. Her encouragement and judicious criticisms have made perhaps the biggest positive difference not merely to this anthology, but to every other aspect of my life as well.

introduction
UNITY IN DIVERSITY

ADAM MULLER

Wenn ich Kultur höre ... entsichere ich meinen Browning – Hanns Johst,
Schlageter[1]

Clearly, we are involved with one of those terms that have a way of
touching off controversies. – Harry Levin, "Semantics of Culture"

Although the first recognizably modern English usage of "culture"
occurs towards the end of the nineteenth century, the conceptual
roots of the term extend much deeper, travelling past John Locke's *An
Essay Concerning Human Understanding* (1690) and the writings of the
fourteenth-century Arab historian Ibn Khaldûn[2] to come to rest in the
histories of Herodotus and Tacitus. Etymologically, the Latin root of
the term is "colere," meaning anything from cultivating to inhabiting,
protecting, or worshipping, the latter a term connoting both divinity
and transcendence, aspects of which inform the influential Ciceronian
notion of "cultura animi" or cultivation of the soul. We thus find in its
early English usage associations with husbandry, natural growth, and
refinement, associations exploited by Thomas More in 1510 with reference to "the culture and profit of theyr [*sic*] minds,"[3] and by Francis
Bacon in *The Advancement of Learning* (1605) in which he writes that

"the culture and manurance of minds in youth hath such a forcible, though unseen, operation, as hardly any length of time or contention of labour can countervail it afterwards."[4] Despite its lengthy and varied aetiology, the concept of culture really only received its first clear European articulation in Anne Robert Jacques Turgot's *On the Historical Progress of the Human Mind* (1750), in which Turgot says of man that as "Possessor of a treasure of signs which he has the faculty of multiplying to infinity, he is able to assure the retention of his acquired ideas, to communicate them to other men, and to transmit them to his successors as a constantly expanding heritage."[5] Turgot's insights emerged at roughly the same time thinkers like Rousseau were attempting to systematize the terms of humankind's transition from nature to culture, attempts which by the early nineteenth century were becoming more widely understood as the first steps towards a comprehensive "science of man." The perceived necessity of such a science may be attributed to several related concerns, including the social and moral disruptions accompanying the Industrial Revolution then redrawing the environmental, political, and economic face of Europe. Writing in the 1970s, Ernest Becker observes that the "science of man, let it be emphasized once and for all, had the solution of this moral crisis as its central and abiding purpose. Why build a science of man in society? In order to have a sound basis for a new moral creed, an agreed, factual body of knowledge that men of good will could use to lay down laws for a new social order."[6] Explicitly *moral* concerns, however, were not the only source of Europeans' desire for a science of mankind and a clearly delineated culture concept. Also significant in the development of "culture" were a cluster of vigorous scientific debates (including those over the age of the earth and, eventually, over biological evolution) as well as the ongoing and more general consequences of ethnocultural contact and (sometimes violent) exchange accompanying Europe's so-called Age of Exploration.

Anything like our contemporary understanding of culture would not have arisen without communities of experts first settling such matters as the age of the earth and the length of time human beings have been living together socially on it, creating significant patterns of behaviour, artefacts, and so on. Geology, which initially arose as a science in response to commercial concerns linked to the resource needs of emerging industrial economies, developed rapidly throughout the late eighteenth and early nineteenth centuries, along the way raising many questions as to the significance of fossils, the answers to which threatened to undermine standardly accepted accounts both of the earth's age and of human history. In the middle of the seventeenth century, Archbishop James Ussher had proposed a Biblical chronology according to which the six days of creation had taken place in 4004 BC, but in 1830 Charles Lyell, one of the pre-eminent scientists of his day, claimed that the stratification of fossil remains proved that human beings were much more recent additions to the earth than were plants, fish, and reptiles. Lyell's claims were roughly consistent with those of the Frenchman Jacques Boucher de Perthes, who argued in the 1830s that based on the fossil record man must have been contemporaneous with extinct mammals, and who in 1838 unearthed stone axes which he took as evidence of human creativity and craftsmanship in the Pleistocene, a period which was popularly held to antedate human creation. The severe religious backlash against Boucher de Perthes' conclusions served for some time to retard theoretical advances by geologists who feared alienating religious authorities, but by the mid-1850s the last major obstacles to the widespread acceptance of Boucher de Perthes' views were removed. Notwithstanding the subsequent popularity of such texts as Philip Henry Gosse's *Omphalos* (1857), in which the author proposed that although God had indeed created the world in six days he made it *seem* as though it had taken longer for man to appear, the publication of Charles Darwin's *Origin of Species* in 1859 decisively cemented the gains of the epistemological and theological revolution which preceded it, in the process legitimating a notion of biological evolution which dramatically affected the ways in which "culture" was subsequently used and understood.

In addition to advances in geology, archaeology, and biology, European exploration and colonization proved hugely influential in determining the nature and scope of the culture concept. The resultant discovery of many new species of primates including orangutans, chimpanzees, and gorillas served to complicate the European understanding of humanity, and when people were discovered in hitherto unexplored parts of the globe there was some question as to whether or not they were really human. By the sixteenth century, European exploration of Africa, Asia, and the Americas had substantially undermined the argument made by Augustine in *The City of God* that men could not inhabit the far corners of the earth, a claim less important as a statement of empirical fact than as a philosophical principle ensuring that when indigenous people were encountered elsewhere, Europeans felt no moral obligation to grant them an essential (and common) humanity. Nonetheless a variety of confusions clouded Europeans' attempts to understand their world in light of the new information filtering into it from abroad. These attempts were at times quite bizarre, like Sir William Petty's in the 1670s claiming that the second rung of Nature's ladder was occupied by elephants (since they showed more intelligence, warmth, and sympathy than apes).

As more became known about strangers in strange lands, attention turned from whether or not they were human toward the development of schemes to account for differences between distinct human populations. At least since Paracelsus in 1520, a "polygenist" alternative to Augustine had been on the table which held that human beings appeared in many different places at once, and it was out of concern with the origins of non-Europeans that the science of anthropology really began to take shape. In 1800, there was created in Revolutionary France the Société des Observateurs de l'Homme which, although only lasting until Napoleon withdrew his support in 1804, nonetheless aimed for a "comprehensive classification of races, a complete comparative anatomy, a comparative dictionary of all languages, a complete anthropological topography of France, and a museum of comparative ethnography."[7] Although responsible for redirecting French scientific attention towards the systematic classification of human interactions and affairs, and as a result possessing the potential to ameliorate the worst of European colonialism's effects, the members of this group alas shared many of the moral and observational biases of their time. Hence Louis François Jauffret's proposal for a cruel experiment involving an artificially maintained feral child, and the Société's ill-fated expedition to Australia, which led at least one of the researchers involved, a young medical student and self-styled "anthropologist" named François

Péron, to conclude that the Malayans he observed were less moral as well as physically weaker than Europeans.

Péron's views remain historically noteworthy for their connection to a paradox which first emerged late in the seventeenth century, and which concerned diametrically opposed assessments of primitive "savages": by some they were held to be barbaric, wild, and grotesque non-humans, immoral and disgusting; and yet by others like Rousseau they were understood as so-called "noble savages," children of nature free from the debilitating and dehumanizing cares of a civilized world. Péron's work is significant because it marks the start of the decline in the popularity of the concept of the noble savage,[8] although his most substantial contribution to the study of mankind lies in his suggestion that the differences between peoples are most properly attributable to "race." Prior to the fifteenth century, when people were thought of by Europeans either as Christians or non-Christians, race had not been employed as an analytical or descriptive category. By the nineteenth century, though, race became increasingly important in explanations of cultural difference, and the culture concept itself emerged both against the backdrop of this prevailing usage, and in no small way as an alternative to it.

Many early anthropologists, including Péron, were influenced in one way or another by evolutionary theory. Montesquieu (1748), A.R.J. Turgot (1750) and Adam Ferguson (1789) are typically referred to as evolutionists because of their commitment to a developmental model of human evolution, one which aimed to account for humans' transition from savagery to civilization, and one which was underpinned by the measurement of different societies in terms of their varying levels of technological or material development. It remained problematic for early evolutionists that their view of cultures as amenable to technological differentiation was underwritten by a reductive historical outlook which proposed the separation of the world into an "us" (humans or people) and a "them" (nonhumans and nonpeople). This proposal was itself substantially informed by a strand of Christian thought which, partly via its endorsement of a vertically arranged chain of being at the top of which sat God, lent support to the view that if humans were indeed all the same sorts of beings-in-the-world, then evolutionary distinctions might legitimately be made because of the human family's fragmentation resulting from the immoral behaviour of some subset(s) of its members. One consequence of this view was that over time there emerged a hierarchically organized sense of human moral and material development, the terms of which specified that "savages" might be found located at the bottom of the hierarchy, "barbarians" somewhere above them, and the "civilized" at the top and therefore nearest to God.[9]

Evolutionism in various forms strongly marked thinking about culture throughout the nineteenth century, and indeed thanks to the politically charged legacy of critics like Matthew Arnold (1822–1888) it remains a force in contemporary cultural studies as well. Relevant differences between prominent Victorian students of culture should not be obscured, however, not least because they reveal in evolutionary approaches a conceptual richness highly relevant to a more nuanced understanding of the historical development of the culture concept, as well as deep human sympathy by the observer for the subjects of his analysis. So, for example, Henry Lewis Morgan (1818–1881), referred to by Darwin as the New World's first social scientist, drew on his early experiences working with the Iroquois, and more specifically his long-time study of what he termed Subsistence, Government, Language, the Family, Religion, House Life, and Architecture to propose a "grand design" to human affairs. Morgan's proposal aimed to show that, for example, subsistence evolved through five successive and increasingly materially and technically complex stages of development,[10] much as did the family.[11] Indeed Morgan regarded family as the most important element in the evolution of a society, and while he may be criticized for failing to understand kinship as related to anything other than marriage, for being overly paternalistic and romantic, and for the fact that his "grand design" clearly works better for describing some peoples than for others, his contributions to our understanding of culture remain significant. His most lasting of these was his theory of social organization, and his realization that the important issue in social evolution was the change of kinship-based societies into territorial or politically based ones. His insights profoundly influenced a large number of important nineteenth-century thinkers, most notably

Engels and Marx, who gave prominence to the family in their critical analysis of modern industrialization.

Like Morgan, Edward Burnett Tylor (1832–1917) studied aboriginal societies, though in his case those located in Mexico and Cuba. He later became keeper of the University Museum at Oxford, and Reader and then Chair of Anthropology at Oxford, and it is Tylor whom we must thank for the first comprehensive English-language definition of the culture concept. In his two volume study entitled *Primitive Culture* (1871) he writes: "Culture, or civilization, taken in its wide ethnographic sense, is that complex whole which includes knowledge, belief, art, morals, law, custom, and any other capabilities and habits acquired by man as a member of society."[12] It is important to note that Tylor thinks of "culture" and "civilization" synonymously here, revealing thereby his indebtedness to Matthew Arnold, whose influential *Culture and Anarchy* had appeared in 1869 and proffered the view that culture, the cultivation of which requires the "study of perfection," is "the best which has been thought and said in the world."[13] This notion of culture's inherent excellence, while durable (it is often still appealed to in discussions of the educational system and its reform), would subsequently come under stress from many quarters, but most consistently from twentieth-century Marxist social historians and sociologists amongst whom E. P. Thompson, Richard Hoggart and Raymond Williams – founders of what would later come to be known as "British cultural studies" – figure prominently. For these thinkers, each of whom was in some way motivated by a deep appreciation of the richness and complexity of English working-class life, culture was nothing if not inescapably and fascinatingly *ordinary*. Acknowledging and theorizing this ordinariness allowed Thompson and his colleagues, like the Fabians and the *Annales* historians before them, to reject any conception of culture which limited its reference solely to bourgeois tastes and values.

Culture for Tylor, however, as for Arnold, was coextensive with the notion of civilized "refinement," which implied for the first time that even primitive societies could eventually attain the civilized state long thought to be the exclusive domain of Europeans. Despite the progressive sympathy such an implication, if acknowledged, might be expected to elicit from those otherwise content to view indigenous peoples as irredeemably condemned to their primitivism, it should be noted that by the time James Frazer published his extremely influential *The Golden Bough* (1890), a study of magic and religion indebted on many levels to Tylor's research and fieldwork, "culture," thought of as "civilization," was understood entirely in the singular. Only one "culture" was believed to exist, although various peoples might evince differing developmental orientations towards it. Viewed hierarchically, as it typically was, European societies were thought to represent culture's apex, and consequently the primary concerns for nineteenth-century scholars became locating the mechanism whereby peoples become "civilized," and classifying and interpreting the vast quantities of information accumulating from Europe's far-flung colonies.

By the late nineteenth century, however, a number of problems with evolutionary accounts were becoming widely acknowledged. Firstly, evolutionary accounts have a great deal of difficulty specifying precisely when one period or stage begins and another ends. Tylor attempted to address this concern by developing the notion of what he termed "survivals," or "processes, customs, opinions, and so forth which have been carried on by force of habit into a new state of society different from that in which they had their original home, and they thus remain as proofs and examples of an older condition of culture out of which a newer has been evolved."[14] Survivals allowed evolutionists to explain the persistence in European societies of practices like magic and superstitions which would otherwise seem at odds with their advanced modernity, but additional problems with evolutionary theories remained. One of the more troubling of these concerned the ordering of the various evolutionary stages, questions about which revealed great inconsistencies among the evolutionists themselves: Could a society bypass a stage altogether? Do all societies evolve through all the same stages and in the same way? Is there therefore only one (i.e., "unilineal") evolution?

From their equivocations as they grappled with these questions there arose two main evolutionist orientations, the *monogenic* (the view that mankind descended from a single point of origin), and the *polygenic* (the view that mankind's origins were many). And yet despite their differences, evolutionists were all committed, however implicitly, to the notion of progress. That is, they all assumed not simply that things change, but that they change in a particular direction, and that such change is good. Complicating this commitment to progress was anthropologists' inherent comparativism, which for many consisted in the belief that some cultures of the present resemble cultures of the past much more directly than do others. In order to reveal the specifics of human evolution, it therefore became necessary to arrange contemporary cultures along a continuum from the least to the most advanced. This arrangement or patterning of cultures lent support to the view that some present-day cultures were more "ancient" than others in virtue of their enduring dependence on such things as stone tools, and, as Lewis Langness points out, "since paleontologists had likewise shown that may extinct animals could be understood only through a knowledge of contemporary animals found in distant parts of the globe, the equation of savages with ancestors came to be widely accepted and firmly held."[15] Notwithstanding the romantic appeal of this proposed equivalence, the comparativism required to sustain it was hindered both by the paucity of available empirically solid information on non-Western peoples, as well as by the blatant racism and ethnocentrism of many anthropologists.[16]

Although evolutionists failed in crucial ways to address a number of potentially damaging issues and questions, evolutionism itself exercised a strong influence not only in the domain of anthropology, but also in psychology, psychoanalytic theory, criminology, aesthetics, medicine, and the popular imagination. So, for example, G. Stanley Hall's (1844–1924) influential research into child psychology, which not only represented the first attempt by a psychologist to give explicit content to such stages as infancy, childhood, and adolescence – stages which he felt must be traversed in order, each one the stimulus for the next – but which also revealed an apparent equivalence between "savage" thought and the thought of children. It is from Hall's work that we first derive the idea that such things as memory traces of temperament and conduct exist in the human species, throughout our lives linking us with our ancestors in a myriad of unconscious ways. As Hall himself puts it in his study entitled *Adolescence*, "Our souls are echo-chambers in which [the] whispers [of our ancestors] reverberate.... We have to deal with the archaeology of mind, with zones or strata which precede consciousness as we know it, compared to which even it, and especially cultured intellect, is an upstart novelty."[17] Hall's ideas profoundly influenced a large number of psychologists, but most notably Freud, Jung, and Piaget. All three of these thinkers demonstrate a strong evolutionary bias in their work as well as, like Hall, an acceptance of the embryologist Ernst Haeckel's "biogenetic law": the observation that the features present in the developmental stages of individual organisms sometimes resemble those of adult individuals of earlier zoological forms. Haeckel's biogenetic law is often discussed in terms of the so-called "recapitulation hypothesis" – the claim that *ontogeny* (the individual's development) repeats *phylogeny* (the development of the species) – and this idea has deeply influenced not just our thinking about the development of children but, thanks to anthropologists' extension of the hypothesis to a host of non-biological phenomena, to our understanding of other (and particularly aboriginal) cultures as well. The idea of surviving aboriginal people as "primitive" is in fact at least partly indebted to the recapitulation hypothesis insofar as it has been assumed that aboriginals represent "arrested stages of cultural development that the more advanced races had passed through."[18]

Evolutionists, then, together gave shape to a scheme within which culture was held to evolve according to a more or less uniform pattern. When archaeological or anthropological fieldwork revealed an object or a belief in similar form in more than one place, it was explained in terms of the idea of "parallel" evolution, the view that the process of human evolution was the same everywhere. No matter their place of origin, all humans were thought to be tied to the same evolutionary process, their own particular level of development notwithstanding, and this belief, and the assumption of basic intellectual equality upon which it rests, were viewed as indicative of the fundamental "psychic unity" of mankind. And yet the reconciliation of such an ostensibly egalitarian view with the patently racist beliefs not just of many anthropologists but of the nineteenth-century European public at large remains surprisingly difficult to obtain. One should remember, however, that this seeming paradox didn't bother evolutionists particularly much since they held that intellectual capacity and cultural evolution unfolded simultaneously. The view of many evolutionists was that human beings at the same stage of cultural development would indeed possess the same intellectual capacity. Hence the so-called "progressivism" of someone like Tylor, who followed Arnold in rejecting the separation of the scientific and humanistic conceptions of culture,[19] and for whom putative "savages" could therefore be thought of as recognizably moral (religious, etc.), if not quite as much so as Europeans.

This humanistic conception of "culture" continued in many ways to be a more progressive and inclusive understanding of human populations than that employed and defended by Tylor, mostly because the late-nineteenth century humanists tended to view "culture" as something like a "way of life." Tylor's view in contrast is much more fragmentary and materialistic, and unlike Arnold he was indifferent to the faults of the culture around him and unconcerned with ascertaining the prescription for a better way of life.[20] Instead, like most anthropologists, Tylor desired to understand how values come about and how others become able to attain them, although his speculations on these matters remained problematically undersupported by reliable available fieldwork.

It is in virtue of his advocacy of the "scientific" study of culture, one that depended heavily on extensive and empirically verifiable fieldwork, that Franz Boas (1858–1942) is perhaps best remembered. Known as the father of historical particularism – the view that everyone and everything must be understood on his or its own terms, without reference to more general functions or relations – as well as of American anthropology, Boas and his students together transformed not just the study of culture but our understanding of the culture concept itself. Rejecting Tylor's Arnoldian "absolutism" in favour of a much more nuanced cultural "relativism," Boas hesitated to make generalizations about individual cultures before all the data concerning each culture had been gathered. His approach was thus principally *ideographic* (dealing with specific cases) and not *nomothetic* (proffering generalizations based on examination of a number of cases), marking a signal departure from the orientation to culture structuring the practice of most of his nineteenth-century colleagues, one consistent both with his more general belief in the futility of the search for a grand theory capable of unifying all aspects of people's lives,[21] and with his conception of anthropology as a kind of historiography.[22]

Although Boas achieved his fame in America, where he ended up lecturing for thirty-seven years as Columbia University's first professor of anthropology, he was born and received his university education in Germany, where he was steeped in an intellectual tradition that included the works of Immanuel Kant, Gottfried Herder, G.W.F. Hegel, Friedrich Schleiermacher and Wilhelm Dilthey. The connection between Boas and Herder and Dilthey is particularly strong, thus linking Boas to German Romanticism and Idealism, although a comprehensive account of these relationships exceeds the scope of this introduction.[23] It is, however, worthwhile noting that Boas derived from Herder (1744–1803) his plural conception of "cultures" and from Dilthey (1833–1911) his understanding of anthropology as history as well as his recognizably "hermeneutic" sense of cross-cultural "understanding," or *verstehen*.[24] Boas may thus be understood as the inheritor of a system of thought quite distinct from that exemplified by the work of Frenchmen like Montesquieu and Turgot. As Frank Manuel puts it:

In the French system a closed or isolated culture is in continuous peril of stultification; the rut of sameness is mortal. The multiplication of communications, the creation of new relationships is the key to new perceptions, hence to new ideas. Endless novelty invites new impressions and discoveries. The French look upon cross-fertilization as the highest good, productive of science, technology, and ultimately moral perfectibility. The Germans, on the other hand, tend to view cross-fertilization as destructive of values, style, identity, structure, growth. The intrusion from the outside is alien, unnatural, inimical to form and cohesiveness.[25]

For the French, change could be accelerated by disciplining (rationally organizing) the wills of men; progress could actually be accelerated through reform. "The French *philosophes* from Turgot on down, with their geometric pattern of enlightenment – blocks of darkness that presented danger and of light that in time would penetrate the black – expected this conversion of superstition to scientism to take place as painlessly and as fast as possible."[26] German philosophers, on the other hand, were bound to a much slower sense of time and viewed progress itself as both discontinuous and unalterable by force of will: "For each being, each Volk, for mankind itself, there was an ordained time-span of growth and decay, and there was no way that organized wills could affect this biological life process."[27]

Herder radically altered the way in which "culture" was understood by attacking both its synonymity with "civilization" and its association with a secular notion of progressive human development which assumed European "civilized" or "cultivated" completeness. Writing in *Yet Another Philosophy of History* (1774) he argues that:

> Those who have so far undertaken to explain the progress of the centuries have mostly cherished the idea that such progress must lead towards greater virtue and individual happiness. In support of this idea they have embellished or invented facts; minimized or suppressed contrary facts, and in this way invented the fiction of the "general, progressive amelioration of the world" which few believed, least of all the true student of history and the human heart.[28]

Herder's objections, which Terry Eagleton notes are themselves consistent with a more generally Romantic and anti-colonialist fetishization of suppressed "exotic" societies,[29] come with a number of relevant methodological entailments, not the least of which is that the student of culture attend systematically and comprehensively to the vast totality of objects and experiences comprising the spirit of a people, or its "volkgeist." The relativism implicit in this approach to different societies comes through clearly in the following passage, also from *Yet Another Philosophy of History*, which I quote by way of emphasizing its sublimation in Boas's ideographic conception of proper anthropological practice:

> Do not limit your response to a word, but penetrate deeply into this century, this region, this entire history, plunge yourself into it all and feel it all inside yourself – then only will you be in a position to understand; then only will you give up the idea of comparing everything, in general or in particular, with yourself. For it would be manifest stupidity to consider yourself to be the quintessence of all times and all peoples.[30]

By way of avoiding this stupidity, Herder not only rejects anything like the assumption of a universal history and uniform cultural development, he also proposes that we conceive of "culture" only in the plural, or as what Raymond Williams terms "the specific and variable cultures of different nations and periods, but also the specific and variable cultures of social and economic groups within a nation."[31] This cultural pluralism was later used by critics such as those associated with Frankfurt University's Institut für Sozialforschung[32] to attack the mechanical character of the European civilization emerging under industrialism, a new socio-ethical and economic order vulnerable to criticism in virtue of its reliance upon abstract rationalism, and because of its indifference to the dehumanizing effects of industrial modernization.

Dilthey accepted much of Herder's view of the complexity of human life, as well as his pluralistic conception of culture. Indeed the central question of Dilthey's philosophy[33] became how to discern a meaning or pattern in the complex diversity of human life in the absence of absolutes or universals grounding the philosopher's perception of it. He answered this question by claiming that life was not, in fact, a series of disconnected facts but rather, when encountered everywhere, encountered as always-already organized, interpreted, and therefore meaningful. Indeed, Dilthey goes so far as to follow Hegel's suggestion that "culture" represents a "second centre" capable of unifying "all that happens to man, what he creates and does, the systems of purposes through which he lives and the outer organization of society in which individuals congregate."[34] On this view culture is that which holds experience, expression, and understanding together, providing an autonomous sphere within which the "common experience" takes shape:

Every word, every sentence, every gesture or polite formula, every work of art, and every political deed is intelligible because the people who expressed themselves through them and those who understood them have something in common; the individual always experiences, thinks, and acts in a common sphere and only there does he understand. Everything that is understood carries, as it were, the hallmarks of familiarity derived from such common features. We live in this atmosphere, it surrounds us constantly. We are immersed in it. We are at home everywhere in this historical and understood world; we understand the sense and meaning of it all; we ourselves are woven into this common sphere.[35]

This "atmospheric" and autonomous culture for Dilthey thus constitutes what Charles Taylor in *The Malaise of Modernity* refers to as our "horizons of significance," the framework within which our actions and material and social productions come to mean something to us, at the same time identifying us as "us." The study of culture, the "science of man," therefore requires that we focus our critical attention on something that is a part of us, and for Dilthey it begins with our coming to terms with the meanings that humans have assigned to the world.[36] The study of culture is thus properly conceived of as part of the *Geisteswissenschaften*, or sciences of the spirit (human sciences), as opposed to the *Naturwissenschaften* or natural sciences, which require more detached modes of observation and analysis. The force of this distinction helps to reveal Dilthey's understanding of culture as that which marks our separation from the animals, as something divorced from our essential, "natural," selves. As taken up by Boas, this distinction helped pave the way for the elimination or discrediting of prevailing views of racial and geographical determinism, as well as of the more general racism characterizing the work of many of his peers.

Although he was responsible for the first really serious questioning of the foundations of evolutionary explanations of culture, questioning which resulted in the emergence of distinctions between "convergent" and "parallel" evolution, as well as of concepts like "independent invention" and "diffusion" in response to concern over how the same item or practice came to appear in two or more geographically distinct areas, Boas actually never formally announced the specifics of a new conception of culture. However, that said, the concept of culture which he implicitly accepted was clearly quite different from that advanced by Tylor, not least because Boas, in virtue of his substantial experience in the field, understood that there wasn't only one culture, there were many. Notwithstanding their dissimilarity, though, Boas's understanding and use of "culture" shared many of the properties of Tylor's, most notably the latter's particularism. It was not until A.L. Kroeber's ideas on the "superorganicism" of culture were published in 1917 that a significantly new way of thinking about culture appeared.

Despite the contributions of British and German[37] diffusionists to refining our understanding of the meaning of different concentrations of similar artefacts (or "culture traits") in different areas, it was

Kroeber (1876–1960) who most systematically advanced and defended a view of culture unlike that of his teacher Boas. Whereas Boas believed that the individual was an important unit in the study of culture, Kroeber argued that individuals were subordinate to culture. Hence in his paper "The Superorganic" we find Kroeber arguing that "the social substance – or unsubstantial fabric, if one prefers the phrase – the existence that we call civilization [culture], transcends [mind and body] utterly for all its being forever rooted in life."[38] Noting that "civilization is not mental action but a body or stream of products of mental exercise," Kroeber insisted that "Civilization, as such, begins only where the individual ends."[39] What Kroeber means by this, and indeed what is more generally understood as "superorganicism," is that each culture should be understood as a totality, the specific character of which derives not from the racial or other characteristics of each of its members, but rather from certain shared ideas and values. Kroeber's research into art, religion, and fashion helped him to show how the patterns recognizable within each of these domains kept evolving independently of specific actors. Thus cultural and "organic" evolution could be distinguished (culture supervenes on nature and is therefore "superorganic"), and psychological explanations came to be viewed as misplaced in anthropological analysis.[40]

The issue of whether or not the individual is irrelevant to our understanding of culture proved extremely contentious, even amongst Boas's students. Paul Radin (1883–1959), for one, distrusted Kroeber's statistical and distributive approach to culture, and like Boas thought that it was only by spending long periods of time with another culture, thoroughly mastering its rituals and language, that an anthropologist might come to really understand another way of life. Radin was the first anthropologist to publish an informant's life history, and as his interest in the individual evolved it influenced a number of thinkers, including Edward Sapir (1884–1939), who later helped to create the important school of Culture-and-Personality Studies. Boas himself felt that classifications of the sort favoured by diffusionists should not precede enthnography, since there was a danger in classifications built on what Langness terms "analogies of outward appearance,"[41] and since only in the context of a whole could the significance of individual parts be comprehended. Although Boas and many of his students suggested in their work that cultures possessed a sort of unity or wholeness, their concern with traits, elements, and (for some) even individuals prevented them from fully refining the idea of unity. Another student, Robert Lowie (1883–1957), actually defended the idea of culture as inherently fragmentary, referring in his *Primitive Society* (1920) to "that thing of shreds and patches called civilization."[42] But Lowie, like Boas before him, also believed in the autonomy of culture. For him, culture must always be understood as a reality in and of itself, and any explanation aiming to account for the causes of culture would only succeed to the extent that it located those causes *within* culture.

Against this view of culture as independent of its specific contexts of emergence and interpretation we may begin to understand the desire of many thinkers concerned with the subject to attend more closely to the material "base" structuring modes of actual human social interaction, and possibly culture itself. Talcott Parsons (1902–79), for instance, conceived of the relationship between culture and material force not simply in terms of the dichotomy of inner experience/outer determination, but "as analytical levels of a unified empirical world."[43] Parsons is one of the main exponents of what has become known as functionalism, a heterogeneous school of thought so-named because of its adherents' strict belief in the principle that cultural facts may only be properly understood in their current relationship to one another, and not historically or in an evolutionary perspective. Thus Parsons and Edward Shils (1910–95) proffer the view of an actor enmeshed in a "system of orientations" within which objects, "by the significances and cathexes attached to them, become organized."[44] Actions occur within "constellations" or "systems," three of which in virtue of their interrelationship possess singular importance: social systems, personalities, and cultural systems. Social systems are comprised of political and economic institutions, the former being the means through which power is exerted in a society and the latter the means through which goods and services are produced and distributed. Personality, on the other hand, is comprised of systems of motivated action specific to the organic body which is the individual. Cultural systems, finally, are made up of systems of symbolic patterns – values and ideas, mostly (and most problematically) those contained within the sacred texts of the world's great religions. One consequence of the interrelationship of these systems is that actors internalize cultural systems which are much more general than social systems, the latter composed as they are of real social interactions. Parsons thus recommends that functionalist analyses concentrate on making sense of what he terms the "institutionalization" of culture, with the way in which culture, through agency, becomes part of the real structure of social systems. Explaining what this means for our understanding of values, Jeffrey Alexander writes that "Actors must make choices between real alternatives; when they do so, normative, or value, standards are evoked. Institutionalization means that one standard or another has become an intrinsic feature of the actor's role."[45]

Parsons' and Shil's functionalism bears a strong resemblance to the so-called "pure" functionalism of Bronislaw Malinowski (1884–1942). As a result of his extensive fieldwork with the Trobriand islanders, Malinowski developed the theory that there exist seven basic human "needs,"[46] and "culture" is that mechanism through which they are respectively met. Needs moreover can be distinguished as either "individual" or "group" needs, the level of attention paid to each subsequently becoming the main point of contention between structural and psychological functionalists. Malinowski, clearly a psychological functionalist given his analytical emphasis on the individual's psychology, claims that "The functionalist includes in his analysis not merely the emotional as well as intellectual side of mental processes, but also insists that man in his full biological reality has to be drawn into our analysis of culture. The bodily needs and environmental influences, and the cultural relation to them, have thus to be studied side by side."[47] In a marked rejection of Lowie's view of culture as existing in "shreds and patches," Malinowski set about showing how the disparate elements of culture nonetheless combine or coexist in such a way as to allow us to understand culture as a unified whole. In order to do this he proposed that an individual's activities may always be correlated with the whole, and that institutions, beliefs, and customs should therefore always be viewed, not in isolation, but in their broad cultural context even as it must be shown that they meet specific human needs (i.e., their functionality must be ascertained).[48] But note the methodological cal entailment here: for Malinowski a huge, potentially debilitatingly huge, amount of material must be sifted through and sorted prior to any generalizations about culture being made. Most students of culture rejected this entailment and instead occupied themselves analyzing one of culture's important features (typically its social structure), which they then tried to claim as anthropology's only legitimate interest. In Lewis Langness' words, "Malinowsky and his pupils were considered to have collected too many facts of too many kinds to make simple comparative work possible."[49]

The main alternative to Malinowski's functionalism came from the work of A.R. Radcliffe-Brown (1881–1955), who followed Emile Durkheim (1858–1917)[50] in advocating a kind of structural functionalism eventually referred to as "social anthropology," and, later and in a somewhat different form, "sociology." Radcliffe-Brown rejects culture *per se* and asserts in *A Natural Science of Society* (1957) that "You cannot have a science of culture. You can study culture only as a characteristic of a social system."[51] Whereas Boas rejected a "science" of culture as impossible given the complexity of the historical processes involved in culture formation, Radcliffe-Brown tried to show how "culture" was simply a less meaningful concept than "social systems"; indeed for him it remained little more than what he termed a "logical fiction," "a convenient concept whereby we can describe a certain type of physical phenomena."[52] Anthropology, understood by Radcliffe-Brown as the "natural science of society," was thus most properly directed towards ascertaining the structure of the social world and particularly with determining how each part of the whole functions in relation to the system.

And yet it is by no means always clear what Radcliffe-Brown means by "culture." At times he intends for it to refer to the set of rules governing the terms on which human beings fit together in a social system; at other times he uses "culture" to refer to common symbols and the meanings most usually attached to them; at still other times he seems to be meaning a shared set of ways of thinking and feeling. Since, however, it is impossible for something to be shared or held in common independently of actual beings capable of and disposed to doing the sharing, Radcliffe-Brown was forced to acknowledge the utility of studying the individual, although he claimed that all an investigator could do was study specific acts of behaviour:

Culture cannot exist of itself even for a moment; certainly it cannot continue.... You cannot have coaptation without culture and you cannot have the continuity of culture without continuity of the social structure. The social structure consists of the social behaviour of actual individual human beings, who are *a priori* to the existence of culture. Therefore if you study culture, you are always studying the acts of behaviour of a specific set of persons who are linked together in a social structure.[53]

By studying social structure, itself an abstraction derived from behaviour, Radcliffe-Brown believed it was possible to ascertain the function of any behaviour by determining how it served to facilitate the well-being of the group.

Radcliffe-Brown is noteworthy in virtue of the force of his rejection of psychology and of the culture concept. He prohibited his students from studying both, and indeed used "culture" as a sort of pejorative wastebasket in which to discard all the facts and ideas in which the anthropologist was not, at the moment, interested. His rejection of psychology arose from his conviction that it was a mode of study limited entirely to the individual, whereas anthropology on his view, *contra* Malinowski, maintained a primary interest in the relationship linking the individual to the social system. For him the function of a social institution can therefore only be seen in its effects on individuals, and the only data of interest to the social anthropologist must be observations of the acts of behaviour of individuals (including speech), or the products of such acts. In a marked rejection of Boasian historical particularism,[54] history for Radcliffe-Brown was understood to be ideographic, while anthropology was more properly thought of as nomothetic.[55]

Notwithstanding their many substantial differences both Malinowski and Radcliffe-Brown believed in evolutionism, Malinowski even more so than Radcliffe-Brown, with the consequence that both became vulnerable to the criticism that they accepted all of evolutionism's implicit promotion of inferiority-superiority dichotomies. Functionalism also ultimately proved unable to explain change within social systems, since functionalists, in virtue of their historical agnosticism, viewed cultures as though they were timeless. Nor could functionalists adequately distinguish between motives and functions, so that they could not satisfactorily account for the differences between, for example, a ritual which inadvertently served to do something (say, channel social emotion in a particular way) and one explicitly designed to achieve that same thing. And, finally, in functionalist theory the move to differentiate culture and society was accompanied by a critical preference for values over symbols as objects of analysis, with the result that functionalism, as Jeffrey Alexander has noted, has very little to say about such purely symbolic phenomena as ritual, sacralization, pollution, metaphor, myth, narrative, metaphysics, and code.[56]

The work of Leslie White (1900–75) proves instructive in placing functionalism in relation to materialism, the view derived from Karl Marx (1818–1883)[57] that technological and economic factors exert a disproportionately large influence on the structure of a society. For Marx, a "dialectical" materialist, "the mode of production in material life determines the general character of the social, political, and spiritual processes of life. It is not the consciousness of men that determines their existence, but on the contrary, their social existence determines their consciousness."[58] "Dialectic" is the term used to describe the interplay of *base* (the availability and allocation of resources), *structure* (kinship systems, modes of political and religious organization), and *superstructure* (ideologies, religious beliefs, superstitions), an interrelationship which on Marx's view revealed the extreme dependence of structure and superstructure on a society's base or material infrastructure.

Like Malinowski and Radcliffe-Brown, White desired to make the study of mankind a science. Unlike Radcliffe-Brown he refused to give up the culture concept, acknowledged the importance of symbols,[59] and eventually adopted a position similar to Kroeber's superorganicism known as "culturology." Put most simply, culturology is the view that culture has an existence independent of human beings, and therefore those wishing to account for some aspect of culture must do so only in terms of some other aspect. Under no circumstances should reference be made to concepts or theoretical approaches particular to other disciplines such as psychology, biology, sociology, or history; the explanations of culture for White lie squarely within culture itself. As he puts it in his 1969 study *The Science of Culture*, "Culture is a continuum of interacting elements [traits], and this process of interaction has its own principles and its own laws. To introduce the human organism into a consideration of cultural variations is therefore not only irrelevant but wrong; it involves a premise that is false. Culture must be explained in terms of culture."[60] Like Kroeber, White refuses to concede that human beings have anything to do with the cultural process *per se*. Hence his conviction that "Human beings are necessary as carriers of cultural traditions; they are not necessary for an explanation of changes in these cultural traditions."[61] Needless to say, this view of culture is an extreme one, and White (along with Kroeber) was criticized for "reifying" culture, making a material out of what is more properly understood as a mental thing. Take, for instance, the following excerpt from *The Science of Culture*:

Man is but a particular kind of material body who must do certain things to maintain his status in a cosmic material system. The means of adjustment and control, of security and survival, are of course technological. Culture thus becomes primarily a mechanism for harnessing energy and of putting it to work in the service of man, and secondarily, of channeling and regulating his behavior not directly concerned with subsistence and offense and defense. Social systems are therefore determined by technological systems, and philosophies and the arts express experience as it is defined by technology and refracted by social systems.[62]

Here culture is no longer an abstract or symbolic entity, but rather a real "mechanism" whereby two functions are performed: the reconciliation of man with his material world (through philosophy, conventions governing resource management, etc.), and structuring or otherwise ordering those "inessential" behaviours (artmaking, sport, etc.) vital to the ongoing health of the social whole.

Notwithstanding its critics, aspects of White's position remain influential, particularly his conception of "cultural evolution," the view that cultural changes occur gradually through the accumulation of small, quantitative increments which, upon reaching a tipping point, yield much larger qualitative transformations. Like a voyage plotted only a degree or two off course, cultural change for White only becomes qualitatively significant with the passing of time, after the agglomeration of a critical mass of quantitative alterations which then significantly impinge on the efficiency of a society's interactions with its material environment (i.e., its *instrumentality*). As he puts it in *The Science of Culture*, "Other factors remaining constant, culture evolves as the amount of energy harnessed per capita per year is increased, or as the efficiency of the instrumental means of putting the energy to work is increased."[63] Note that for White the technological system, or base, exerts the most influence in determining the ontology of the cultural system. This commitment to the ontic primacy of the base quite clearly links White to "cultural materialists"[64] like Marvin Harris, who argues that a direct causal relation obtains between the material base in a society and aspects of its culture, even to the extent that "thoughts about institutions are constrained by the institutions under which men do their thinking."[65] Such a strongly (over-) deterministic materialism marks the work of a number of more recent influential cultural commentators, including Michel Foucault and Jean-François Lyotard. Lyotard, for example, whose work has been taken up in many quarters,[66] echoes White when he argues in his explanation of postmodernism that the "objects and the thoughts which originate in scientific knowledge and the capitalist economy convey with them one of the rules which supports their possibility: the rule that there is no reality unless testified by a consensus between partners over a certain knowledge and certain commitments."[67] What we know, in other words, what we take to be constitutive of reality, comes to count as "knowledge" in virtue of its sanction by those with the right kind of institutional (i.e., disciplinary) power, power which for Lyotard accrues thanks to institutions' (including the university's) ever-deeper implication in market capitalism. Hence Lyotard's claim that "Knowledge is and will be produced in order to be sold, it is and will be consumed in order to be valorized in a new production: in both cases, the goal is exchange. Knowledge ceases to be an end in itself, it loses its 'use value.'"[68]

White's notion of a materially framed cultural evolution is also in significant respects consistent with the position of the Italian Marxist Antonio Gramsci (1891–1937), who likewise evinced a strong materialism in addition to his finely attuned normative conception of (r)evolutionary progress, the latter consisting in a change of state from lesser to greater autonomy. On Gramsci's view, all human societies can be shown to contain two basic groups: those who are privileged, and those who in various ways are not (oppressors and the oppressed, the dominant and the subordinate, etc.). The "ensemble" of those without social privileges includes women and minorities as well as the economically disadvantaged and criminals, and taken together they lack unity as well as in many cases what might be termed "uptake," an awareness of the extent of their own oppression. In Gramsci's words, "the active man-in-the-mass has a practical activity, but has no clear consciousness of his practical activity."[69] Gramsci's moral and explanatory project thus consists in his search for a means of reversing the distribution of power responsible for reinforcing the supremacy of the beliefs, values, and practices of those with power in a society, a project subsequently taken up and extended by scholars such as Fredric Jameson and Edward Said, both of whom cite Gramsci as a major influence on their work.

The power of those in charge is for Gramsci maintained in two ways: by force and coercion (i.e., by *domination*), and by something he terms "hegemony," the ideological triumph of the set of values and interests definitive of the dominant group. So, for example, respect for the laws of property might be a value shared by all or most in a society, but it is respect which explicitly works to further the interests of a property-owning elite, all the more powerfully given its endorsement by those with little or no claim to property themselves. In effect, hegemony refers to the willing acceptance by the disadvantaged of the norms and desires of the privileged; it delineates the terms of the subaltern's self-marginalization. Gramsci's analysis of culture is thus driven by his desire to delegitimate the belief sets of dominant groups and create a "counter-hegemony" under which the formerly disenfranchised might begin to recognize and legitimate their own beliefs, experiences, hopes, and desires. Since hegemonic values permeate every aspect of social life, the whole of civil society becomes for Gramsci a site within which the struggle for hegemony plays out. Given the ideological saturation of the social whole, Gramsci was famously forced to conclude in his *Prison Notebooks* that everything, all "action," is in fact and foremost *political.* What this politicization entails, of course, is that every possible public and private space and practice – including schools, religion, philosophy, home life, the workplace, art, and literature – is implicated in the struggle to achieve societal transformation.

Gramsci's Marxism departs from functionalism in a number of important respects, but chiefly in terms of the conception of "society" which undergirds it. His "cultural Marxism" proceeds from the view of society as a divided thing, so fractured by ideological and material differences that culture itself becomes hegemonic and thus part of the process of domination.[70]

It is within this fragmentary and divisive milieu that organic "quasi-intellectuals," themselves conditioned by the institutions and norms typical of the dominant modes of production, work creatively to reinterpret the relationships linking institutions to the masses, thereby eventually challenging the hegemony of the dominant culture by refining the "consciousness" of the oppressed. Real change can, for Gramsci, in the end only come about as a result of the transformation of consciousness. Gramsci's position may thus also be understood as a significant departure from functionalism in virtue of its normativity. For it should be remembered that Gramsci is not merely concerned with explaining or interpreting culture, but with achieving a revolutionary transformation of the status quo. The dominant culture is, for him, always eventually challenged, hence Alexander's conviction that he views society as "not primarily an economic or political order but a 'moral-political' bloc."[71]

In what seems to be a reflection of Boas's own methodological orientation towards culture, Gramsci termed his philosophical position "absolute historicism," thereby signifying the fact that on his view morals, truths, values, and even nature itself have no independent existence;

they are simply the by-products of forces specific to different historical epochs. Metaphysically, what this means is that Gramsci rejects transcendence in favour of immanence, and idealism in favour of materialism.[72] For him there are no universal standards of judgment independent of discrete historical contexts; even morality itself is understood to be a social construction. Claims concerning truth or "the good" may therefore be evaluated properly only within the context of some knowable, pre-existing historical reality,[73] one decisively marked by signs of its own contingency.

Reflecting back not just on Gramsci's outlook but on the many different theoretical approaches to culture discussed so far in this introduction, the issue of universals looms ever larger. There are a great many different ways to "cash out" this issue, a good sampling of which may be found in the excellent anthology assembled by Martin Hollis and Steven Lukes entitled *Rationality and Relativism*. For my purposes here, though, I propose following Ernest Gellner in that anthology and taking the problem of universals to be "in effect a concern with whether there is but one kind of man, or whether there are many kinds of men; or alternatively, what shared features unite all men or all human societies."[74] One is thus a universalist to the extent either that one accepts the view that there exists only one kind of person, or human subject, notwithstanding the great variety of cultural contexts and social and personal histories in which he or she might be enmeshed, or else that there exist some recognizably consistent sets of features which identify human beings and their societies as such, which allow us to acknowledge what Raimond Gaita calls our "common humanity"[75] regardless of the time or place in which it is organized and lived. It should be clear both from the above history of the culture concept and from even a cursory glance at what academics are publishing, here in this anthology and elsewhere in monographs and journals, that universalism has been far from unproblematically affirmed in those disciplines having something to do with culture, a by-product not so much of the Boasian turn in cultural theory as of the political and moral concerns which informed it. For as anti-universalists frequently point out, and not without cause, appeals to universals have throughout history underwritten invidious attempts by members of one culture to subjugate or otherwise oppress members of others, the latter deemed to depart too far (in principle or in practice) from the only universally "right" or the "true" way to live. Cultivated indifference to the precious singularity of cultures, viewed as both a moral and as a political problem, prompted cultural particularists like Herder, Tylor, Boas, and Gramsci, along with legions of their adherents, to reject talk of transcendental "universals" for more immanent modes of cultural analysis and critique.

The swing towards cultural particularism, although its conceptual roots lie firmly in the nineteenth century, became particularly noticeable in anthropology and the other human sciences from the middle of the twentieth century on. This was due, no doubt, to a variety of causes including the acknowledged success of the Boasian project and the widespread acceptance of its moral and procedural *a priori*, anxiety over homogenizing totalitarian ideologies (and their attendant political dispensations), the rise of postmodernism, and intensifying anti-colonial struggles in Africa, South Asia, Indochina, and the Middle East. Together these and related civil rights struggles required cultural commentators to take differences seriously, by which I mean that cultures rapidly came to be deemed comprehensible and amenable to judgment only on their own terms, without recourse to concepts, vocabularies, or values naively held to apply universally.[76] This kind of anti-universalism has often, and not unproblematically, been referred to as "relativism." In Satya Mohanty's words:

Opposing the imperial arrogance of the scholar who interprets aspects of other cultures in terms of the inflexible norms and categories of the scholar's own, the relativist insists on the fundamentally sound antipositivist idea that individual elements of a given culture must be interpreted primarily in terms of the culture, relative, that is, to its own unique system of meanings and values.[77]

What this means for the relativist is that something like witchcraft, for example, cannot be properly understood from a perspective external to the indigenous context – the shared beliefs, symbols and practices constitutive of a culture as such – in which it is practised and which therefore shapes its larger significance. On this view witchcraft as practiced by the Zande people of Sudan, to use one frequently cited example,[78] is neither evaluable nor even really comprehensible from a non-Zande perspective. Whatever claim it might have on an observer's attention thus derives principally, as any number of influential anthropologists including E. Evans-Pritchard and Ruth Benedict have suggested, from its salience within the religious, medical, and social schemes characteristic of (i.e., relative to) the Zande themselves. Failure to concede to the Zande the upper hand in determining the significance of the things nearest and dearest to them strikes the relativist as both condescending and risky, since whatever it is that makes the Zande practices typically Zande (and not Anlo-Ewen or Xhosan) risks receding from view as it becomes incorporated within culturally alien descriptive languages and cognitive and moral schemes.

A thorough treatment of cultural relativism and its discontents[79] exceeds my brief here, though consideration of relativism's challenges to the culture concept links several of the essays in this anthology. In her contribution, for example, Martha Nussbaum offers a provocative indictment of the kind of cultural relativism which insists that normative criteria must emerge from within the society to which they are applied. Against those inclined to insist that the (purportedly Western) values associated with feminism and democracy cannot be universalized, and that therefore attempts to promote them in non-Western contexts amounts to little more than cultural imperialism, Nussbaum cogently demonstrates how values, in order to have any instrumental power in a society, any society, depend on the human beings comprising that society being equipped to benefit from them in a number of important ways. People must, Nussbaum argues, be healthy and not die prematurely; they must have the security and integrity of their person guaranteed; they must be capable of forming emotional attachments to people and to things; and they must be able to engage in the free exercise of their reason. In the absence of a culture's at least minimally guaranteeing these apparently universal "capabilities," its inhabitants' rights to some very basic freedoms must be understood as fraudulent.

Although his technical vocabulary and philosophical starting points differ markedly from Nussbaum's, Geoffrey Hartman shares with her a desire for what he terms "a larger transpolitical perspective" from which disputes arising between disparate cultures might be resolved peacefully, a perspective which Nussbaum cashes out in terms of her capabilities approach. What Hartman lacks and what Nussbaum possesses, however, is the basic optimism that such a perspective will ever be available in some meaningful (i.e., actionable) form. One symptom of its inaccessibility is, for Hartman, the inherent difficulty of the academic language in which it is typically evaluated and discussed. Precisely in virtue of its technical demands, this language may be seen to necessitate the possession of a highly specialized intellectual competence or distinction markedly at odds with the requirements of accessibility and openness central to so inclusive a perspective. Whatever this language's virtues,[80] and Hartman concedes that it is singularly adept at resisting cooptation and containment by the powers that be (it is thus ideally suited to the work of opposition and resistance), it nonetheless remains the standard operating language of the intellectual elite upon whom responsibility for articulating the basic form of such a wholistic perspective rests. Hartman is concerned that members of this elite have historically tended to advance cultural claims in the name of universals which belie their more sectarian origins, much to the detriment of the culture concept which remains fundamentally bifurcated, negatively suspended between the universal and the particular and unable to assist with the coming-into-being or "embodiment" of those who, like Hartman himself, struggle to make sense, to themselves and to others, of who and of what they are.

Universalism also lies at the heart of Jim Parry's essay devoted to the analysis of modern Olympism, an ideology of sport often considered universal in virtue both of its transnational appeal and owing to its organization around a cluster of values such as "fair play," "respect," and "excellence" which are held to characterize the very best of sport no matter when, where, or by whom it is played. Parry, however, shows how Olympism's universalist ambitions are constantly threatened by a variety of particularisms, or what might broadly be construed as Olympism's historical contingency: its emergence from, and indebtedness to, a singularly nineteenth-century European interpretation of the practices and values of Ancient Greece; and its constant vulnerability to geopolitical forces and the pressures of economic globalization.Drawing on recent philosophical work designed to resolve a similar tension in political liberalism, Parry demonstrates how an "untidy" compromise might be reached enabling Olympism to function as simultaneously a universalist ideology upon which a plethora of idiosyncratic (local) interpretations and practices rest.

This compromise position is not, finally, unlike that reached by Robert Stecker who aims in his contribution to steer the middle position he terms "historical particularism" carefully between contending essentialisms and constructivisms, the former markedly universalist and the latter particularist in kind.[81] It also resonates in the context of Mette Hjort's pragmatic defence of consensus in the university, an institution vulnerable to multiculturalist (i.e., cultural-particularist) criticisms of what for some remains its "civilizing" mission: its responsibility for introducing students to their shared inheritance, the national and world cultures which they hold in common. What Hjort manages to show in her contribution, however, is that the university, understood as a *cultural* institution, actually serves at least two distinct purposes, namely the preservation of culture (via such practices as canonization) and its critique. Neither of these purposes is expendable, at least not pragmatically, the former because of the intellectual requirements of modern industrial nation states, the latter owing to the justice that might thereby be done. Nor are these purposes as incommensurable as they might at first seem, and Hjort presciently shows how in the rhetorically overheated context of the "culture wars" too little attention has been paid to what disputants hold in common – the beliefs, desires, and ambitions that they actually share. Thus one of the university's most important jobs, Hjort concludes, one undertaken in the name both of universal and of particular concerns, is to introduce students not just to the conflicts in and between cultures and their inhabitants but to the (pragmatic and other) advantages of consensus.

Hjort's argument draws attention to the issue of agreement, and thus opens the door to what remains a second important theme linking both the papers of this anthology and a great deal of the extant research on culture, namely the question of the fundamental unity of culture, sometimes referred to as the doctrine of cultural integration. Unlike the issue of universals, which revolves around claims concerning consistencies across cultures, the question of cultural integration addresses the boundedness of cultures, the degree to which a culture's internal coherence marks it as distinctly itself. The distinctiveness of cultures is clearly related to relativism insofar as judgments can be made relative to specific cultures only insofar as these cultures are indeed recognizably different from one another (or else judgments made about one culture would inevitably apply to another and no "relative" claims could obtain). This is the view of Michelle Moody-Adams, who argues that the "descriptive cultural relativism underwriting most meta-ethical relativisms ... presupposes the doctrine of cultural integration."[82] More significantly, for Moody-Adams the doctrine of cultural integration is typically linked to two other assumptions, the first being that "cultures are fully individuable, self-contained wholes," and the second being that the "capacity for moral agency is culturally determined."[83] Along with the doctrine of cultural integration, these two assumptions are addressed by nearly every contributor to this volume, albeit with different results.

Christoph Brumann, for instance, criticizes anthropologists such as Lila Abu-Lughod who fault the culture concept for providing homogenized representations of human affairs, emphasizing what unifies people at the expense of accounting fully for what makes them different, along with those subcultures, counter-cultures, and other sites of formal and informal resistance within which those differences find collective expression. In response, Brumann proffers a pragmatic defence of the culture concept, one which stresses the usefulness of conceiving of "culture" as a collective noun designating shared patterns of thought and action, but which nonetheless does not entail that such patterns go "all the way down" a culture, implicating every one of its members along the way. Culture, like other collective nouns including "forest" and "cutlery," can accurately and meaningfully designate clusters of items without requiring that those items be absolutely identical. "Culture" is what David Novitz in his contribution terms a "colligatory" concept, and Novitz like Brumann maintains that it has important explanatory work to do. For human affairs do exhibit important regularities and consistencies, as well as irregularities and discontinuities, the latter of which really only achieve explanatory salience against the background of what it finally is that human beings, however provisionally, share.

Cultural unity is, of course, not just a methodological or descriptive problem but a moral and a political one too, and several of the essays in this anthology tackle it explicitly as such. Jacques Barzun, for example, bemoans the disappearance of a truly "popular" American culture, a condition he argues follows from modernity's fragmentation of the social lifeword and the disappearance of a widely accepted set of symbols, values, and practices around which a culture might coalesce. One symptom of this disappearance, Barzun argues, is contemporary art's inability (or unwillingness) to express the hearts and minds of a whole people, from highbrows to lowbrows and everyone in between. For it should be remembered that one of art's signal political and moral responsibilities, one which on Barzun's view it is systematically failing to accept, is to generate in individuals the idea of themselves as vitally connected to other human beings. Hence the attention paid by thinkers like Martha Nussbaum[84] and Richard Etlin[85] to art's capacity for assisting in the cultivation and refinement of empathy, one of the most powerful preconditions for mutual intelligibility and, by extension, social solidarity. As Etlin puts it:

Year after year, and eventually century after century, countless people are transported by a Beethoven symphony, awed by a Gothic cathedral, and touched deeply by a Rembrandt self-portrait or a Shakespeare play, because these works of art speak directly to a deeply rooted understanding about the nature of being and of human relationships in a way that is indissolubly tied to aesthetic experience. This phenomenon is intimately related to questions of ethics, not in the sense that the beautiful is the good and vice versa, but rather that feelings of kindness, compassion, and love arise just as spontaneously in the human heart as does the response to great works of art.[86]

It is little wonder, then, that Barzun is as concerned as he is with the disappearance of the literary canon, and with the decline of the institutional power required to make claims concerning the greatness and universality of artworks stick. Both for him signify the degree to which contemporary society has become alienated from itself.

It is worth noting, however, that the kind of fragmentation and decline which worries Barzun is far from a matter of great anxiety for some of this anthology's other contributors. Imre Szeman, for one, while accepting some version of Barzun's argument concerning the dissolution of culture, finds in that dissolution, particularly within the context of a university "in ruins," as Bill Readings has famously termed it,[87] the opportunity for a new "critical" humanities to arise free from the heavy weight of a cultural tradition whose scope and merits had for generations been merely assumed, but which in reality had acted in its own way to constrain our understanding of "culture" by predetermining its primary terms of reference, thus ensuring its self-replication over time. Szeman concludes that the challenge to culture posed by globalization, a fraught term broadly designating the threat to local values and institutions (i.e., to the very essence of indigenity) of forces and actors tied to the global circulation of capital, is, finally, illusory, since "culture" has never really been as bounded and coherent as it has been claimed. Culture's purported unity, Szeman argues echoing and extending the position of Radcliffe-Brown, is no more than an ideologically convenient fiction designed to preserve the power and privileges of an economic and social elite, and it is the politically and morally praiseworthy responsibility of critical humanists to explain exactly how (and why) this fiction works.

Culture's inner workings also form the subject of Martin Roberts' contribution to this volume, which aims to provide a nuanced account of what exactly contemporary "film culture" is and how it works. Like Szeman, Roberts seems relatively untroubled by the fragmentary character of film culture, its constitution by disparate constellations of actors, forces, and institutions sometimes barely (if at all) coordinated and engaged. What Roberts manages to convey very successfully is how little film culture's disparateness and breadth really matter, except at the level of socio-historical description, how indeed the stresses and incommensurabilities at play in the cultural system comprised of all aspects of the production, distribution, and consumption of films actually lends to that system precisely the sort of dynamic energy upon which creative and technical innovation and originality depend.

The issue of incommensurability lies at the heart of the last essay in this collection, a collaboration by two philosophers of science who aim to clarify our understanding of what disagreements are and how they work, particularly with reference to scientific subcultures but, for a number of important reasons not the least of which is the strong formal correspondence between scientific and other disputes, in ways also highly illustrative of the inner workings of disagreements between larger cultures and their component parts. For incommensurability refers to the notion that there exists no neutral space within which disagreements may be rationally evaluated, and just as the question arises whether or not Kepler's (Copernican) and Fabricius' (Ptolemaic) astrononomical methods are comparable, and if so on what terms, analogous and often more politically charged cultural questions arise concerning, to use an example addressed by several contributors, whether or not international human rights are incommensurable with indigenous forms of moral governance. At issue here, of course, is the tension between universals and particulars, but the pragmatic approach to incommensurability Matheson and Martens advocate, like Stecker's historical contextualism, allows us to sidestep the facile reduction of this issue to one branch of the dichotomy or the other. For a nuanced and contextually attuned pragmatism encourages us to see individuals as anything but radically overdetermined by the cultures they inhabit, epistemologically or otherwise, and indeed to view cultures themselves as sites of ineluctable disputation and change. In Matheson's and Martens' words, "cultures should be seen as perpetually bubbling cauldrons of debate, in which the resolution of one difference is often followed by the creation of several more." Matheson's and Martens' pragmatism requires that the full complexity of these disputes be considered as part of the attempt by one party to understand, and then if possible to resolve, his or her conflict with others. In this regard, then, they may be taken to endorse precisely the sort of rigorous inquiry into the contradictory fullness of cultures that this anthology, taken as a whole, recommends.

It is in the spirit of rigorous interdisciplinary exchange and debate that the essays selected for inclusion in this anthology have been conjoined. Perhaps most significantly – partly in virtue of its commitment to interdisciplinarity and partly due to my own theoretical proclivities – this volume acknowledges, for what I believe is the first time, the importance of analytic philosophy and liberal political theory to the systematic and comprehensive study of culture. As Richard Rorty and others have shown, this importance rests on such features of analytic and liberal thought as the introduction of powerful new arguments against scientism and in defence of historicism, and its capacity for powerful self-criticism,[88] to which we might also add its articulation of a "thick" discourse on human rights. And yet analytic and liberal voices go virtually unnoticed in contemporary work in cultural studies, except perhaps for when they serve as objects of critical condescension and scorn, a response no doubt attributable to cultural studies' indebtedness to theoretical paradigms (Marxism, poststructuralism) traditionally inhospitable to work of this kind. Note that my claim here is not that cultural studies has no good formal or other reasons to be circumspect about the terms of its engagement with liberalism and analytic philosophy, but rather that the benefits to constructive engagement with work in these domains considerably outweighs any presumed costs (as I hope the essays in this volume show), and stands to benefit all those whose work touches on questions of culture by providing them with an enlarged, and perhaps also more technically precise, set of concepts and terms of reference with which to work.[89]

Principally in light of ongoing changes to the institutional lifeworld in which it is embedded, one marked by a powerful resurgent and dynamically complex disciplinarity,[90] cultural studies to my mind stands in particular need of updated and more cosmopolitan theoretical foundations if it is to survive as a discipline in its own right. This is the view of many engaged in the study of culture, including some of cultural studies' traditionally most vocal proponents. Thus the significance of Terry Eagleton's recent injunction that "cultural theory ... cannot afford simply to keep recounting the same narratives of class, race and gender.... It needs to chance its arm, break out of a rather stifling orthodoxy and explore new topics."[91] My hope is that this anthology will serve, both implicitly and explicitly (insofar as I have endeavoured to place some very fine poststructuralist and postmodern texts in conversation with some analytic philosophical and liberal-humanist ones drawn from across a diverse range of disciplines) to show how careful reference to work from hitherto functionally disparate intellectual traditions proves capable of producing extraordinarily suggestive interpretive resonances. It is ultimately upon the power of these resonances, given the crisis in the discipline represented by the recent closing of the University of Birmingham's famed Centre for Contemporary Cultural Studies, that the revivification of cultural studies depends.

Notes

1   "Whenever I hear the word 'culture' ... I release the safety-catch of my Browning pistol." Johst (1890–1978) was a playwright and president of the Reichsschrifttumskammer and Deutsche Akademie für Dichtung during the Nazi period. *Schlageter*, his most famous play, was first performed on Hitler's birthday in April, 1933.

2   Note the strikingly modern character of Khaldûn's definition of culture: "Culture is not an independent substance, but a property ... of another substance which is man. Hence the natural character of culture must have reference to what is natural to man, i.e. to his nature and what differentiates him from the rest of the animal world," quoted in L.L. Langness, *The Study of Culture* (Novato, CA: Chandler and Sharp, 1987), 2. Much of my subsequent discussion of the history of the culture concept is drawn from Lewis Langness's excellent history.

3   Thomas More et al., *The English Works of Sir Thomas More* (London: Eyre and Spottiswoode, 1931), 369. The reference is located in a passage of More's *Life of John Picus*.

4   Francis Bacon and G. W. Kitchin, *The Advancement of Learning* (London: Dent, 1973), XIX, 2.

5   Marvin Harris, *The Rise of Anthropological Theory* (New York: Thomas Y. Crowell, 1968), 14.

6   Ernest Becker, *The Lost Science of Man* (New York: Braziller, 1971), 11.

7   Langness, *The Study of Culture*, 8.

8   A concept which, following extended elaboration in literary and philosophical texts, including work by Blake, de Tocqueville, and John Stuart Mill, continued to be powerfully appealing at least through the Romantic period.

9   Ibn Khaldûn conceived of the same vertical arrangement from an Islamic perspective.

10 Natural Subsistence upon Fruits and Roots on a Restricted Habitat; Fish Subsistence; Farinaceous Subsistence through Cultivation; Meat and Milk Subsistence; and Unlimited Subsistence through Field Agriculture.

11 Morgan claims that the family evolved through five forms: Consanguine (intermarriage of brothers and sisters in a group); Panaluan (intermarriage of several brothers' wives in a group, and of several sisters to each other's husband's in a group); Syndasmian (pairing of a man and a woman in a marriage, but without exclusive cohabitation); Patriarchal (marriage of one man to several wives); and Monogamian (the family of "civilized" society).

12 Edward B. Tylor, *Primitive Culture: Researches into the Development of Mythology, Philosophy, Religion, Art and Custom* (London: John Murray, 1903), 1.

13 Matthew Arnold, *Culture and Anarchy: An Essay in Political and Social Criticism* (London: John Murray, 1869), 4.

14 Tylor, *Primitive Culture*, 16.

15 Langness, *The Study of Culture*, 34.

16 See Lord Avebury's *The Origin of Civilization and the Primitive Condition of Man* (1870). In this text, one in many respects paradigmatic of its place and time, Avebury claims that "savages" often only have "absurd" justifications for their actions, that they tell lies and are weak, and that they have no knowledge of true love and are therefore wanting a morality.

17 G. Stanley Hall, *Adolescence* (New York: Appleton, 1904), 61.

18 Langness, *The Study of Culture*, 37.

19 Essentially a distinction between culture understood as exogenous (i.e., as only knowable scientifically) and endogenous (i.e., as hard-wired to our conception of humanity).

20	See George Stocking's succinct enumeration of the relationship between Arnold's and Tylor's ideas in his article "Matthew Arnold, E. B. Tylor, and the Uses of Invention." Although Tylor thinks more in terms of evolutionary product and Arnold of individual process, Stocking writes that "both men conceived culture in normative humanist terms as a conscious 'cultivation' of the capacities which are most characteristically human. [...] Arnold's culture ... was, both for the individual and for society, an organic, integrative, holistic phenomenon. [...] Arnold's culture, like that of most modern anthropologists, was an inward ideational phenomenon. For Arnold, much more than for Tylor culture was a 'way of life'" (795).

21	Hence his claim in "The Aims of Anthropological Research" that "Cultural phenomena are of such complexity that it seems to me doubtful whether valid cultural laws can be found." Franz Boas, *Race, Language, and Culture* (Chicago: University of Chicago Press, 1982), 257.

22	See Boas's 1936 response to A. L. Kroeber in "History and Science in Anthropology: A Reply": "To understand a phenomenon we have to know not only what it is, but also how it came into being. Our problem is historical." Ibid., 305.

23	For a more complete account of the links between idealism, romanticism, and culture, see Frank Manuel's *Shapes of Philosophical History* (1965) and William Adams's *The Philosophical Roots of Anthropology* (1998).

24	For Dilthey understanding occurs when one mind "grasps" the mind of another. It is the process whereby we comprehend the lived human experience, the latter having been expressed in some way.

25	Frank Manuel, *Shapes of Philosophical History* (Stanford: Stanford University Press, 1965), 125.

26	Ibid., 126.

27	Ibid., 127.

28	Johann Gottfried Herder, "Yet Another Philosophy of History," in *Herder on Social and Political Culture*, ed. F.M. Barnard (Cambridge: Cambridge University Press, 1969), 187.

29	Ironically these societies were viewed by critics like Herder as possessing "culture," while the nations of industrializing Europe were not. Following Rousseau, von Humboldt, and others, culture thus became the basis for a moral critique of European civilization, several of the effects of which I have enumerated above.

30	Herder, "Yet Another Philosophy of History," 181–82.

31	Raymond Williams, *Keywords: A Vocabulary of Culture and Society* (Glasgow: Collins, 1989), 89.

32	Note, however, that in a recent essay on Theodor Adorno, Jürgen Habermas describes how, during the time of his student days in Frankfurt in the 1950s, Herder and the rest of the German hermeneutic tradition were criticized for being overly idealistic. Jürgen Habermas, "Dual-Layered Time: Personal Notes on Philosopher Theodor W. Adorno in the '50s," *Logos: A Journal of Modern Society and Culture* 2, no. 4 (2003): 52–57.

33	My understanding of Dilthey's social philosophy has been improved thanks to a number of sources, but particularly the lecture notes of Bruce Janz.

34	Wilhelm Dilthey, "The Human Studies," in *Culture and Society: Contemporary Debates*, ed. Jeffrey Alexander and Steven Seidman (Cambridge: Cambridge University Press, 1998), 32.

35	Ibid., 37.

36	See Dilthey: "Every fact is man-made and, therefore, historical; it is understood and, therefore, contains common features; it is known because understood, and it contains a classification of the manifold because every interpretation of an expression by the higher understanding rests on such a classification. The classifying of expressions is already rooted in the facts of the human studies." Ibid., 38.

37 Including Leo Frobenius, Fritz Graebner, and Wilhelm Schmidt of the Kuturkreis (Culture Circle) School.

38 A. L. Kroeber, "The Superorganic," *American Anthropologist* 19 (1917): 212.

39 Ibid., 192.

40 It should be remembered that Kroeber's superorganicism was an attempt both to define culture as an entity existing entirely in its own right, independently of individual men and women, and also an attempt to establish anthropology as a discrete science and therefore *not* psychology, biology, or sociology.

41 Langness, *The Study of Culture*, 61.

42 Robert Lowie, *Primitive Society* (New York: Boni and Liveright, 1920), 331.

43 Jeffrey C. Alexander, "Analytic Debates: Understanding the Relative Autonomy of Culture," in *Culture and Society: Contemporary Debates*, ed. Jeffrey Alexander and Stephen Seidman (Cambridge: Cambridge University Press, 1998), 4.

44 Talcott Parsons and Edward B. Shils, "Values and Social Systems," in *Culture and Society: Contemporary Debates*, ed. Jeffrey Alexander and Steven Seidman (Cambridge: Cambridge University Press, 1998), 39.

45 Alexander, "Analytic Debates: Understanding the Relative Autonomy of Culture," 5.

46 Nutrition, reproduction, bodily comforts, safety, relaxation, movement, and growth.

47 Bronislaw Malinowski, "The Group and the Individual in Functional Analysis," *American Journal of Sociology* 44 (1939): 939.

48 This ties in tightly with Malinowski's view of culture as a "vast instrumental reality." Langness, *The Study of Culture*, 81.

49 Ibid., 83.

50 Radcliffe-Brown actually borrowed his notion of "function" from Durkheim, but he defined it in such a way that it could only be applied to social structure, whereas Durkheim remained more sensitive to the historical concern for origins. Cf. Alexander on Durkheim: "until recently, Durkheimian cultural theory was taken to be a prototypically functionalist approach to interpretive understanding, explaining religious and symbolic classifications as reflections of social structure, a mechanistic reduction of cultural autonomy that goes well beyond the ambivalence of Parsonian value theory." Alexander, "Analytic Debates: Understanding the Relative Autonomy of Culture," 18.

51 A. R. Radcliffe-Brown, *A Natural Science of Society* (Glencoe, IL: Free Press, 1957), 86.

52 Ibid., 44. Other logical fictions for Radcliffe-Brown include language and social structure.

53 Ibid., 107–8.

54 What Radcliffe-Brown termed "pseudohistory."

55 "Ideographic" refers to the idea that an idea may be represented directly, in some sense independently of the medium of its expression. "Nomothetic" refers to concern with the general laws underlying something.

56 Alexander, "Analytic Debates: Understanding the Relative Autonomy of Culture," 6.

57 Materialism can of course be traced back much further than Marx, and certainly at least as far back as Hegel, but Marx is the first philosopher to apply materialism to human societies in anything like an anthropological way.

58 Harris, *The Rise of Anthropological Theory*, 55.

59 Culture, for White, depended crucially on humans' ability to symbolize.

60 Leslie White, *The Science of Culture* (New York: Farrar, 1969), 141.

61 Leslie White and Beth Dillingham, *The Concept of Culture* (Minneapolis: Burgess, 1973), 37.

62 White, *The Science of Culture*, 390–91.

63 Ibid., 368.

64 Also known as "vulgar" materialism because of its adherents' failure to distinguish adequately between superstructure and base.

65 Harris, *The Rise of Anthropological Theory*, 231.

66 And, particularly insofar as several contributions to this anthology are concerned, by Bill Readings in his criticism of the corporatization of the university in *The University in Ruins*.

67 Jean-François Lyotard, "What Is Postmodernism?" in *The Postmodern Condition: A Report on Knowledge*, trans. Geoff Bennington and Brian Massumi (Minneapolis: University of Minnesota Press, 1984), 77.

68 Ibid., 4–5.

69 Antonio Gramsci, "Culture and Ideological Hegemony," in *Culture and Society: Contemporary Debates*, ed. Jeffrey Alexander and Steven Seidman (Cambridge: Cambridge University Press, 1998), 53.

70 Hence Said's criticisms of the deployment of an invidiously reductive "we" in justifications of American nationalism and (neo-)colonialism. He writes that "For the record then, I have no patience with the position that 'we' should only or mainly be concerned with what is 'ours'.... American identity is too varied to be a unitary and homogenous thing; indeed the battle within it is between advocates of a unitary identity and those who see the whole as a complex but not reductively unified one. This opposition implies two different perspectives, two historiographies, one linear and subsuming, the other contrapuntal and often nomadic." Edward W. Said, *Culture and Imperialism* (New York: Knopf, 1993), 25.

71 Alexander, "Analytic Debates: Understanding the Relative Autonomy of Culture," 7.

72 Cf. Terry Eagleton's view of the developmental history of "culture" as singularly marked by a structuring tension between immanence and transcendence.

73 As Gramsci writes in his *Prison Notebooks*, the "process of historical development is a unity in time through which the present contains the entire past but realizes, in the present, only that much of the past that is 'fundamental,' leaving out the rest that is indiscernible and would be the real 'essence.'... What has been 'lost,' that is, what was dialectically not mediated in the historical process, was irrelevant in itself; it was random and contingent 'slag,' chronicle but not history, a superficial episode" (1971, 873).

74 Ernest Gellner, "Relativism and Universals," in *Rationality and Relativism*, ed. Martin Hollis and Steven Lukes (Cambridge, MA: MIT Press, 1982), 181–82.

75 Raimond Gaita, *A Common Humanity: Thinking about Love and Truth and Justice* (New York: Routledge, 2000).

76 But which in fact could be shown to be deeply "interested," saturated with cultural bias and thus indicative of more fundamentally parochial concerns.

77 Satya Mohanty, *Literary Theory and the Claims of History: Postmodernism, Objectivity, Multicultural Politics* (Ithaca, NY: Cornell University Press, 1997), 122. A full treatment of the many modalities of "relativism" exceeds the scope of this introduction. More comprehensive accounts may be found in work by Hollis and Lukes, Mohanty, and Moody-Adams.

78 See ibid. and Michelle Moody-Adams, *Fieldwork in Familiar Places: Morality, Culture, and Philosophy* (Cambridge, MA: Harvard University Press, 1997).

79 I am using the term "relativism" very loosely here in a way designed to highlight its markedly contextualist character, its privileging of the local or particular over and above the universal or general. There are, of course, many different kinds of relativism, including cultural relativism, moral relativism, and relativism about values.

80 For an expanded defence of the difficulty of contemporary academic discourse see the essays contained in Jonathan Culler and Kevin Lamb, eds., *Just Being Difficult? Academic Writing in the Public Arena* (Baltimore: Johns Hopkins University Press, 2003).

81 If a property of an artwork is held to be "essentially" of that artwork then it will be so regardless of place, time, or observer/interpreter. It may therefore be held to be at least in some significant sense universalistic, since it is a property universally held to obtain. Likewise most versions of constructivism, by claiming for the properties of artworks their existential dependence on the interpretive activity of different agents at different times, reveal a sensitivity to context reasonably explained in terms of a supervening particularism. Judgments made in the name of this particularism are thus *relative* judgments.

82 Moody-Adams, *Fieldwork in Familiar Places: Morality, Culture, and Philosophy*, 62.

83 Ibid.

84 Martha Nussbaum, *Poetic Justice: The Literary Imagination and Public Life* (Boston: Beacon Press, 1995).

85 Richard A. Etlin, *In Defense of Humanism: Value in the Arts and Letters* (Cambridge: Cambridge University Press, 1996).

86 Ibid., 8.

87 Bill Readings, *The University in Ruins* (Cambridge, MA: Harvard University Press, 1996).

88 Richard Rorty, "On Analytic Philosophy and Transformative Philosophy: The Relation of Contemporary Philosophy to Humanities." Paper delivered at the *Humanities in the Two Hemispheres Conference*, Brisbane, Australia, June 5–7, 1999.

89 This is essentially the argument I make in my contribution on contemporary American critical theory in the new *Johns Hopkins Guide to Literary Theory and Criticism*, and my views are shared by a number of leading scholars, including Richard Rorty, Richard Shusterman, Satya Mohanty, and (at least in his most recent work) Dominick LaCapra. See ibid.; Richard Shusterman, *Practicing Philosophy: Pragmatism and the Philosophical Life* (New York: Routledge, 1997); Mohanty, *Literary Theory and the Claims of History*; and Dominick LaCapra, *History in Transit: Experience, Identity, Critical Theory* (Ithaca, NY: Cornell University Press, 2004).

90 What we still consider "disciplines" (i.e., History, English, Philosophy) are increasingly internally methodologically cosmopolitan in ways that raise doubts about the necessity of dedicated interdisciplinary alternatives such as Women's Studies, Globalization Studies, and Cultural Studies.

91 Terry Eagleton, *After Theory* (New York: Basic Books, 2003), 11.

1 Christoph Brumann's contribution to this collection offers what he describes as a "pragmatic" defence of the culture concept in response to scholars like Lila Abu-Lughod, who have in their own work recommended abandoning the concept altogether. There are several reasons that have been given to justify this rejection of "culture," the most important of which involves a concern that the concept generates flattened or otherwise homogenized accounts of the profound diversity of the human experience – the heterogeneity, inconsistency, mutability, and idiosyncrasy of individuals and their practices, their beliefs, desires, and the values which arise from (and condition) their expectations of the world around them. Abu-Lughod and those like her argue that "culture" privileges commonality, coherence, and agreement over conflict, contingency, and inconsistency. When viewed historically, the term's application both in socio-political and academic discourses – particularly insofar as these discourses subsequently informed such homogenizing projects as European colonialism and the globalization of market capitalism – must thus be considered significantly less than successful, if not downright dangerous.

In response to these concerns, Brumann observes that what critics of the culture concept are actually objecting to, and reasonably so, are certain uses or misapplications of "culture" and not the concept itself. Indeed by retaining "culture" as a term appropriately and conveniently designating some of the shared consequences of human interaction (certain emotions, concepts, and practices, for example), and by consolidating and defending the morally, politically, and intellectually legitimate common ground which has arisen over centuries' worth of inquiry into what cultures are and how they work, Brumann contends that it will become possible to marshal decisive criticisms of precisely the distortions and abuses to which those "writing against culture" most strenuously object.

Brumann maintains that "culture" needs to be understood as an abstraction, or what he terms an "abstract aggregate." Much as the terms "forest" or "city" refer to no specific entities while nonetheless still remaining linguistically meaningful, "culture" on his view should be taken to refer to repeatedly occurring instances of thought and behaviour, the exact terms of corre-spondence between which will necessarily remain a matter of some debate. But the existence of such debates does not by itself invalidate the concept of "culture," any more than arguing over the precise ratio of pine trees to fir trees (or tall fir trees to short fir trees) negates the idea that both may be found in a forest. There will, in other words, always remain more than one way of defining and interpreting cultures with reference to the clusters of habits linking people's lives at particular times, but to dispense with a term like "culture" is to imply that human behaviour never exhibits regularities, patterns, and commonalities. This flies in the face both of the accumulated evidence of anthropological inquiry, and of the general reliability of human beings' own social-psychological heuristics when it comes to matters involv-ing, for example, the aggregate determinations we regularly make concern-ing others' "predictability" and "character."

Brumann further argues that nothing about "culture" prevents us from acknowledging arbitrariness and variation within cultures, and indeed dis-cussion continues with respect to specific cultures and subcultures over precisely where they begin and end, as well as how they should be accu-rately defined. Just as a glass may be considered half-empty, it may also be considered half-full, and Brumann argues that the best and most complete account of the condition of the glass is that which attempts to understand it as both.

WRITING FOR CULTURE
why a successful concept should not be discarded*

CHRISTOPH BRUMANN[1]

> There are times when we still need to be able to speak holistically of
> Japanese or Trobriand or Moroccan culture in the confidence that we are
> designating something real and differentially coherent. - James Clifford,
> *The Predicament of Culture*

For a long time, defining cultural/social anthropology as the study of
the cultural dimension of humans would have raised few objections
among the discipline's practitioners. Now the place of culture within
that definition is considerably less certain. Within the past decade or so
there has developed what Sahlins calls the "fashionable idea that there
is nothing usefully called 'a culture,'"[2] and one prominent voice even
advocates "writing against culture,"[3] giving a name to a whole "'writing against culture' movement," in Fernandez's observation.[4] Although
scepticism over the culture concept has its origins in deconstruction-
ist and poststructuralist thought, anthropologists sympathizing with it
come from an amazing range of theoretical positions that reaches far

* This article first appeared, along with responses to it and Christoph Brumann's
reply to them, in *Current Anthropology* 40 (February 1999).

beyond that specific vantage point. It will be worthwhile to document this disciplinary discourse at some length before contrasting it with standard anthropological formulations of culture. It turns out that what is being addressed by the critics is certain *usages* of the culture concept rather than the concept itself, and I argue that it is possible – and not very difficult – to disentangle the concept from such misapplications and to find historical precedents for this in anthropology. In a next step I will address what I consider to be the root of the confusion, namely the fact that the sharing of learned traits among humans is never perfect, and how this can be dealt with. Finally, I will present pragmatic reasons for retaining "culture" and also "cultures": the concept has been successful, and other scientific disciplines as well as the general public increasingly employ it in a way we should not be entirely unhappy about. Some of these uses are certainly problematic, but retaining the concept and the common ground it has created will bring us into a better position to challenge them.

The Critique

The major concern of the sceptical discourse on culture is that the concept suggests boundedness, homogeneity, coherence, stability, and structure whereas social reality is characterized by variability, inconsistencies, conflict, change, and individual agency:

The noun *culture* appears to privilege the sort of sharing, agreeing, and bounding that fly in the face of the facts of unequal knowledge and the differential prestige of lifestyles, and to discourage attention to the worldviews and agency of those who are marginalized or dominated.[5]

The classic vision of unique cultural patterns ... emphasizes shared patterns at the expense of processes of change and internal inconsistencies, conflicts, and contradictions.... From the classic perspective, cultural borderlands appear to be annoying exceptions rather than central areas for inquiry.... The broad rule of thumb under classic norms ... seems to have been that if it's moving it isn't cultural.[6]

Culture ... orders phenomena in ways that privilege the coherent, balanced, and "authentic" aspects of shared life.... Culture is enduring, traditional, structural (rather than contingent, syncretic, historical). Culture is a process of ordering, not of disruption.[7]

The most dangerously misleading quality of the notion of culture is that it literally flattens out the extremely varied ways in which the production of meaning occurs in the contested field of social existence.[8]

Applied in this way, culture – a mere "anthropological abstraction"[9] – is transformed into a thing, an essence, or even a living being or something developing like a living being:

"A culture" had a history, but it was the kind of history coral reefs have: the cumulated accretion of minute deposits, essentially unknowable, and irrelevant to the shapes they form.... [O]ur conception of culture almost irresistibly leads us into reification and essentialism.[10]

Much of the problem with the noun form [of culture] has to do with its implication that culture is some kind of object, thing, or substance, whether physical or metaphysical.[11]

Culture ... consists in transforming difference into essence. Culture ... generates an essentialization of the world[12]

A powerful structure of feeling continues to see culture, wherever it is found, as a coherent *body* that lives and dies.... It changes and develops like a living organism.[13]

This brings the concept of culture uncomfortably close to ideas such as race that originally it did a great deal to transcend:

Viewed as a physical substance, culture begins to smack of any variety of biologisms, including race, which we have certainly outgrown as scientific categories.[14]

Where difference can be attributed to demarcated populations we have culture or cultures. From here it is easy enough to convert difference into essence, race, text, paradigm, code, structure, without ever needing to examine the actual process by which specificity comes to be and is reproduced.[15]

Despite its anti-essentialist intent … the culture concept retains some of the tendencies to freeze difference possessed by concepts like race.[16]

As a result, the differences between the anthropologist and the people under study are exaggerated, and the latter are placed in a subordinate position. This increases the distance between the two parties to the ethnographic encounter while enhancing the anthropologist's privileged position as the expert and translator – or even the very creator – of such utter strangeness:

"Culture" operates in anthropological discourse to enforce separations that invariably carry a sense of hierarchy.… [I]t could be … argued that culture is important to anthropology because the anthropological distinction between self and other rests on it. Culture is the essential tool for making other. As a professional discourse that elaborates on the meaning of culture to account for, explain, and understand cultural difference, anthropology also helps construct, produce, and maintain it. Anthropological discourse gives cultural difference (and the separation between groups of people it implies) the air of the self-evident.… It would be worth thinking about the implications of the high stakes anthropology has in sustaining and perpetuating a belief in the existence of cultures that are identifiable as discrete, different, and separate from our own.[17]

In effect, the concept of culture operates as a distancing device, setting up a radical disjunction between *ourselves*, rational observers of the human condition, and those *other people*, enmeshed in their traditional patterns of belief and practice, whom we profess to observe and study.[18]

In global terms the culturalization of the world is about how a certain group of professionals located at central positions identify the larger world and order it according to a central scheme of things.[19]

The essentialism of our discourse is not only inherent in our conceptualizations of "culture," but it reflects as well our vested disciplinary interests in characterizing exotic otherness.[20]

Proceeding from the diagnosis to the cure, a number of writers suggest that a simple grammatical shift might help:

A view of the cultural (I avoid "culture" deliberately here, to avoid reification as best I can)[21]

I find myself frequently troubled by the word *culture* as a noun but centrally attached to the adjectival form of the word, that is, *cultural.*... If *culture* as a noun seems to carry associations with some sort of substance in ways that appear to conceal more than they reveal, *cultural* the adjective moves one into a realm of differences, contrasts, and comparisons that is more helpful.[22]

Nationalists were themselves using what looked very like anthropological arguments about culture.... One possible escape from this dilemma might be to abandon talk of different "cultures" altogether, because of its taint of essentialism, but to retain some use of the adjectival "cultural."[23]

Following Keesing ... I use the term "cultural" rather than "culture." The adjectival form downplays culture as some innate essence, as some living, material thing.[24]

Reformulating culture: return to the verb.[25]

Further, despite Moore's belief that "even if one wanted to, it would be impossible to trash the culture concept because it is so deeply rooted in the history of ideas and in the discipline of anthropology,"[26] some writers go so far as to envision an anthropology without it, albeit not in very strong terms:

It may be true that the culture concept has served its time.[27]

We need to be fully conscious of the varying boundaries, not so much of a culture but of cultural practices. A recognition of these features may make us wary of simplistic notions of cultural homogeneity.... It may indeed make us wary of ... even using the term "cultural" altogether.[28]

In its application, the concept of culture fragments the experiential continuity of being-in-the-world, isolating people both from the non-human environment (now conceived as "nature") and from one another.... Would it not be preferable to move in the opposite direction, to recover that foundational continuity, and from that basis to challenge the hegemony of an alienating discourse? If so, then the concept of culture, as a key term of that discourse, will have to go.[29]

Perhaps we would do best if we stopped privileging the representation of "culture," and instead focused on the level of events, acts, people, and processes.[30]

Perhaps anthropologists should consider strategies for writing against culture.[31]

In assembling the above collage I do not want to suggest that each of the quoted writers supports all of the ideas expressed. Nonetheless, there is a surprising degree of common ground among scholars who would not agree on very many other issues.[32] I am convinced that most readers of this article could easily furnish similar references from equally diverse sources. A profound doubt about the validity of the culture concept, justified in terms of the many misleading associations it is presumed to carry, has undoubtedly become an important trope in current anthropological discourse.

Historical and Optimal Usage

There is no denying that anthropologists in their ethnographic and theoretical work have committed the aforementioned sins in abundance, but I am not convinced that they have done so *because of the culture concept.* To demonstrate this, I will turn to anthropological definitions of culture, since the conception of that term ought to be most clearly expressed there. Modern textbooks define culture as follows:

A culture is the total socially acquired life-way or life-style of a group of people. It consists of the patterned, repetitive ways of thinking, feeling, and acting that are characteristic of the members of a particular society or segment of a society.[33]

Culture ... refers ... to learned, accumulated experience. A culture ... refers to those socially transmitted patterns for behavior characteristic of a particular social group.[34]

Culture is the socially transmitted knowledge and behavior shared by some group of people.[35]

Here and in other textbook definitions, no mention is made of boundaries, universal sharing, immunity to change, or culture's being a thing, an essence, or a living being. Since the negative tendencies identified by the culture sceptics are ascribed to a "classic perspective," however, one might expect them to be more present in older formulations. Here are some well-known examples:

Culture, or civilization ... is that complex whole which includes knowledge, belief, art, law, morals, custom, and any other capabilities and habits acquired by man as a member of society.[36]

Culture embraces all the manifestations of social habits of a community, the reactions of the individual as affected by the habits of the group in which he lives, and the products of human activities as determined by these habits.[37]

The culture of any society consists of the sum total of ideas, conditioned emotional responses, and patterns of habitual behavior which the members of that society have acquired through instruction or imitation and which they share to a greater or less degree.[38]

Culture means the whole complex of traditional behavior which has been developed by the human race and is successively learned by each generation. *A culture* is less precise. It can mean the forms of traditional behavior which are characteristic of a given society, or of a group of societies, or of a certain race, or of a certain area, or of a certain period of time.[39]

Except for the occasional use of an outmoded word (such as "race" or, arguably, "civilization") and for male bias, these definitions do not deviate fundamentally from the modern ones. Incidentally, most anthropological textbooks and encyclopedias I consulted quote Tylor's formulation, invariably with extensive comments[40] but often without giving any alternative definition.[41] This makes me wonder[42] whether there really is a significant gap between what modern and "classic" social/cultural anthropologists take to be the core meaning of the word "culture"; rather, they seem to have different theories about the same thing. And what applies to modern definitions of culture applies to the older ones as well: in the above quotations as well as in the other anthropological definitions in Kroeber and Kluckhohn's famous 1952 collection, there is none which explicitly denies that a culture has clear boundaries, is homogeneous, does not change, or is a thing or an organism. I find it significant, however, that none of them unambiguously says so either, leaving these aspects open for investigation instead. One might argue that many of the definitions postulate discrete cultures by attributing a culture to a specific "group," "society," or "area," but none of them says that these units are always clearly bounded or that they must be so to have a culture attributed to them. Most definitions are also mute on the evenness of distribution required for delimiting a culture. The few that mention it, however, speak of a "greater or less degree" of sharing[43] or even of every individual's being a representative of at least one subculture.[44]

The majority of the definitions in Kroeber and Kluckhohn's volume see culture as a set consisting of identifiable elements and use a noun followed by "of" and an enumeration of the elements to define it, as in the above "integral whole of" or "sum total of." Clearly, this additive notion of culture is only one way of conceiving it. But while the nouns used for this purpose tend toward either the abstract (e.g., "summation," "set," "system," "class," "organization") or the concrete (e.g., "mass," "pattern," "body," "total equipment"), even the latter ones are almost invariably employed in a clearly metaphorical way (which, it should be added, is hardly unconventional even with a word such as "body" – who has ever touched a "body of evidence"?). Some of the older formulations are indeed suspect of conceptual animism, as when Kroeber and Kluckhohn themselves muse on how "the fate of a culture depends on the fate of the society which bears it,"[45] or when Richard Thurnwald defines culture as "the totality of usages and adjustments which relate to family, political formation, economy, labor, morality, custom, law, and ways of thought. These are bound to the life of the social entities in which they are practiced and perish with these."[46] Apart from these exceptions, however, the most reifying and essentializing definitions in the Kroeber and Kluckhohn collection do not come from social/cultural anthropologists.[47] And when Leslie White characterizes culture as "an elaborate mechanism ... in the struggle for existence or survival,"[48] he puts this into a context in which it is obvious that no more than a metaphor is implied.

At the same time, however, one also comes across formulations such as the following:

We can observe the acts of behaviour of ... individuals, including ... their acts of speech, and the material products of past actions. We do not observe a "culture," since that word denotes, not any concrete reality, but an abstraction.[49]

Culture is essentially a construct that describes the total body of belief, behavior, knowledge, sanctions, values, and goals that mark the way of life of any people. That is, though a culture may be treated by the student as capable of objective description, in the final analysis it comprises the things that people have, the things they do, and what they think.[50]

A culture is invariably an artificial unit segregated for purposes of expediency.... There is only one natural unit for the ethnologist – the culture of all humanity at all periods in all places.[51]

It is difficult to attribute essentialism, reification, or organicism to these statements or to similar ones by Murdock or Sapir.[52] It rather seems that, at least on a general level, a good number of typical representatives of the "classic perspective" were no less aware of these dangers than are today's culture sceptics. Here I agree with Brightman that an "expendable 'straw culture' is … being retrospectively devised"[53] by the critics as a selective – and itself rather essentialist – construct that excludes those disciplinary traditions that are more in line with current theoretical concerns.

Where, then, are the unwelcome aspects associated with the culture concept presumed to have originated? Kuper identifies Boas as a main culprit, taking him to task for importing and bequeathing to his students a notion that was heavily influenced by Herder's idea of the *Volksgeist* – the spirit of a people presumed to be inherent in all of its material and mental creations.[54] Fox, however, emphasizes that Boas himself was not consistent and that his followers were divided about the coherence of cultures, some of them (including Kroeber, Benedict, and Mead) holding to a highly integrated notion while others (notably Lowie and Radin) spoke of "shreds and patches" or concentrated their research on diversity and individuals.[55] Overall, it appears to me that the former perspective gained weight with the "synchronic turn" in anthropology, the replacement of an earlier diachronic orientation (in evolutionism, diffusionism, historical particularism, or *Kulturkreislehre*) with a focus on the analysis of cultural systems at a fixed point in time (as in the culture-and-personality school, structural-functionalism, structuralism, and, later on, culture-as-text interpretivism). In the latter approaches there was certainly a strong inclination to see more cultural coherence than actually existed. This was further exacerbated in American anthropology by Parsons's influential segmentation of culture and society as separate fields of study, a theoretical decision that discouraged what interest there was in the social differentiation of culture and supported a mentalistic conception.[56]

Especially for exaggerated assumptions of boundedness and homogeneity, however, I believe that responsibility cannot be simply deflected onto particular theoretical approaches. Rather, a number of rarely discussed but powerful assumptions implicit in traditions of ethnographic writing, traditions that are much older than the discipline of anthropology, must also be accused. These assumptions include the existence of a mosaic of territorially bounded, discrete cultures of which the world supposedly consists; the irrelevance of intra- and interindividual variation; the timelessness of the cultures under study (which either have no history or have acquired one only by coming into contact with colonialism); and the superiority of precontact cultures as an object of investigation. In much classic ethnographic usage, a culture was simply understood as synonymous with what formerly had been called a people, and the units so designated were taken as the natural, internally undifferentiated, and unproblematic reference units for description just as they had been – and continued to be – in most pre- and nonanthropological ethnography. As a consequence, many portraits of "Japanese or Trobriand or Moroccan culture" are indeed marred by the shortcomings deplored by the critics. And when Malinowski meritoriously reminds his readers of "the natural, impulsive code of conduct, the evasions, the compromises and non-legal usages"[57] of the individual "savage"/Trobriander, he is somewhat like a statistician who gives the average, says that there is variance, but does not care to calculate the standard deviation. No doubt it would be mistaken to search for a full-fledged theory of praxis in the work of Malinowski, Lowie, or Radin.[58]

Yet still, at least in their more general and theoretical writings, there was a clear awareness of the constructed nature of the culture concept among a good number of representatives of the "classic tradition," and one of them even elevated "allowance for variation" to the status of a "central problem."[59] Hence, if a disciplinary precedent is needed, anyone seeking to retain a nonreified culture concept as an expedient abstraction (see below) can find it here. Definitions, as I have tried to show, have been open in this regard anyway, and therefore I propose to hold apart the historical usage of the concept – what it has been taken to mean by many in the past – and its optimal usage – what it could mean if used "to its best intents," so to speak. Sometimes a scientific concept can no longer be salvaged; for example, that of "race" has been proved to be empirically unfounded, has been abused enormously, and in subtle ways keeps getting in the way even of some physical anthropologists who use modern, non-racist methods to assess human biodiversity.[60] I am not convinced, however, that past and present misapplications of the culture concept are of a comparable degree and warrant similar avoidance.

Culture as an Abstraction

Discussing the culture concept, one has to distinguish between "culture" (or "Culture") in a general, and "culture/s" in a specific, sense.[61] The former meaning refers to the general potential of human individuals to share certain not genetically inherited routines of thinking, feeling, and acting with other individuals with whom they are in social contact and/or to the products of that potential. It is not very clear-cut and mentioned only in few definitions; besides, it seems to be derived from the second meaning, on which most of the definitions concentrate. Here a culture is the set of specific learned routines (and/or their material and immaterial products) that are characteristic of a delineated group of people; sometimes these people are tacitly or explicitly included. The existence of any such culture presupposes that of other sets of routines shared by other groups of people, thus constituting different cultures. The debate in fact focuses almost exclusively on this second meaning, and I will concentrate on it accordingly. It is the act of identifying *discrete* cultures that is held to be empirically unfounded, theoretically misleading, and morally objectionable by the concept's critics.[62]

Of course, cultures are always constructed, but they are so not only because of being "written"[63] within the confines of sociohistorically constituted tropes and discourses but also in a more profound sense. A culture – as the above quotation from Lowie reminds us – is not simply there in the unproblematic way that, for example, a cat or a bicycle is. Rather, the term refers to an abstract aggregate, namely, the prolonged copresence of a set of certain individual items, and thus is employed not too differently from other nouns such as "forest," "crowd," or "city." In identifying a culture, we have to abstract such a set of items from observed instances of thought and behaviour, selecting that which occurs repeatedly rather than that which is singular. This is a mental operation that is not in principle different from, say, identifying a style in individual works of art, and the same capabilities of memorizing previously perceived instances and ignoring minor differences for the sake of commonalities are required of anyone who undertakes it. Since in the empirical world no two things are completely identical, the result of any such operation is always contestable, and therefore one can no more prove the existence of Japanese culture than prove that of the Gothic style. Cultures can have no "natural" boundaries but only those that people (anthropologists as well as others) give them, and delimiting a certain set of elements as a culture can therefore be only more or less persuasive, never ultimately "true." Nonetheless, we may consider it expedient to go on using the concept in the same way that we go on speaking of art styles, forests, crowds, or cities; and we may do so in spite of the disagreement that often arises over whether these terms really apply to the specific body of artworks, concentration of trees, gathering of people, or settlement that is so designated or where precisely their boundaries are located in a given case.

The core of the problem of identifying cultures can be illustrated with the three diagrams in figure 1. In these, capital letters stand for individuals and numbers for identifiable ways of thinking, feeling, and acting.[64] In the top diagram, there is perfect sharing among individuals A through F regarding features 1 through 6 and among individuals G through L regarding features 7 through 12. Identifying cultures is not difficult here: features 1 through 6 represent one culture, features 7 through 12 another. Since there is perfect discreteness between the two groups of features as well as between the two groups of individuals carrying them, this partition represents the only possible way of distinguishing cultures. In contrast, features in the middle diagram are randomly distributed across individuals, and it is impossible to make out cultures in the same unproblematic way or perhaps in any convincing way.

The problems start with a situation such as that of the bottom diagram. This distribution is far from random, yet no discrete blocks can be discerned either. One possible partition would place features 1 through 6 in one culture and features 8 through 12 in a second. Each culture, however, would then contain features that are sometimes asso-

Figure 1 Three hypothetical distributions of features across individuals.

	1	2	3	4	5	6	7	8	9	10	11	12
A	x	x	x	x	x	x	.	.	.	.	.	.
B	x	x	x	x	x	x	.	.	.	.	.	.
C	x	x	x	x	x	x	.	.	.	.	.	.
D	x	x	x	x	x	x	.	.	.	.	.	.
E	x	x	x	x	x	x	.	.	.	.	.	.
F	x	x	x	x	x	x	.	.	.	.	.	.
G	.	.	.	.	.	.	x	x	X	x	x	x
H	.	.	.	.	.	.	x	x	X	x	x	x
I	.	.	.	.	.	.	x	x	X	x	x	x
J	.	.	.	.	.	.	x	x	X	x	x	x
K	.	.	.	.	.	.	x	x	X	x	x	x
L	.	.	.	.	.	.	x	x	X	x	x	x

	1	2	3	4	5	6	7	8	9	10	11	12
A	x	x	x	.	x	.	x	.	.	x	.	x
B	.	.	.	x	.	.	x	.	X	.	x	x
C	.	.	x	x	.	x	x	.	X	.	.	.
D	x	.	x	.	.	x	x	.	X	x	.	.
E	.	x	.	.	x	x	.	x	.	x	x	.
F	x	.	x	x	x	.	.	x	.	x	.	.
G	.	x	.	x	.	x	.	x	.	x	x	.
H	x	.	x	.	x	.	x	x	.	x	.	x
I	.	x	.	x	.	x	x	.	X	.	x	.
J	.	x	.	x	x	.	.	x	.	x	x	.
K	x	.	.	x	x	.	.	x	.	x	.	x
L	x	x	.	x	.	.	x	x	X	.	x	.

	1	2	3	4	5	6	7	8	9	10	11	12
A	x	x	x	x	x	x	.	.	.	.	.	.
B	.	x	x	x	x	x	.	.	.	.	.	.
C	x	.	x	.	x	x	.	.	.	.	.	.
D	x	x	x	x	x	x	.	x	.	.	.	x
E	x	x	x	x	.	x	x	.	.	.	.	.
F	x	x	x	x	x	.	x	.	.	.	.	.
G	.	.	.	.	.	.	x	x	.	x	x	x
H	.	.	.	.	.	.	x	x	X	x	x	x
I	.	.	.	.	.	x	.	.	X	x	x	x
J	.	.	.	.	.	.	.	x	X	x	x	x
K	.	.	.	.	x	.	.	.	X	x	.	x
L	x	.	.	.	.	.	.	.	.	x	x	x

ciated with features of the other. Moreover, feature 7 does not readily group with either of the two cultures, and individual *D* may be seen as participating in both.

Incomplete Sharing and the Identification of Cultures

No distribution of learned routines among real people will ever be much clearer than that in the bottom diagram, and consequently there will always be more than one way to cut out cultures from the fuzzy-edged clusters of habits that we observe. I suspect that most of the culture sceptics do not really want to imply that there are no such clusters of habits and that the distribution of cognitive, emotive, and behavioural routines among humans is as in the middle diagram. However, they seem to fear that by identifying cultures when confronted with a distribution like that of the bottom diagram anthropologists will invariably be misunderstood as implying a distribution like that of the top diagram. Ceasing to speak of cultures, however, also entails a cost, namely, being understood as saying that features are distributed randomly, as in the middle diagram. I doubt very much that this kind of misunderstanding is preferable, since it is not borne out by the results of anthropological research. Moreover, it flies in the face of the experience of the billions of amateur anthropologists who inhabit the world, who in their everyday lives continue to identify commonalities in the thought and behaviour of different individuals and attribute these to their belonging to the same family, kin group, gender, age-group, neighbourhood, class, profession, organization, ethnic group, region, nation, etc. Of course, they do so in an on-and-off, often semiconscious way that – true to its commonsensical nature – cares less about oversimplifications, contradictions, and incompleteness than anthropologists do and often explains difference incorrectly, for example in terms of genetic or quasi-genetic transmission. But many of these amateur anthropologists would be puzzled indeed if we tried to persuade them that what until recently we would have advised them to call a culture (instead of, for example, "the way we/they do it") does not really exist.

Just as there is no way of deciding whether a glass is half-full or half-empty, there is no ultimate solution to the dilemma of being misunderstood as implying either perfect boundedness and homogeneity (when speaking of cultures) or perfect randomness of distribution (when denying the existence of cultures). Confronted with this dilemma, I propose that we go on using the concept of culture, including the plural form, because of its practical advantages. We should do so in a responsible way, attentive to the specific audience and also to the problem of communicative economy.[65] There are many situations in which "Japanese culture" is a convenient shorthand for designating something like "that which many or most Japanese irrespective of gender, class, and other differences regularly think, feel, and do by virtue of having been in continuous social contact with other Japanese." And I am confident that at least among contemporary anthropologists the first phrase will very often be understood as equivalent to the second. After all, anthropology did not discover intrasocietal variation only yesterday. While many classic studies of small-scale, out-of-the way societies certainly do not show any awareness of it, peasant studies, explorations of great and little traditions and of centre-periphery relations, research on gender, and the ethnographic study of complex societies and cities have been with anthropology for quite some time now and have frequently occupied themselves explicitly with such variation or at least acknowledged its existence.[66] Consequently, the danger of being misunderstood by fellow anthropologists when speaking of a culture is, I think, much smaller than the critics claim.

Moreover, when there is enough time and space, nothing prohibits us from representing the arbitrariness and internal variation of such cultures as faithfully as possible or resorting to formal methods of analysis for delimiting cultures instead of trusting our intuition or – as is commonly done when delimiting ethnic cultures – the judgment of the people we investigate. One could also specify a minimal numerical level of consensus required for a culture and then search for maximal sets of features that fit this requirement (standard statistical procedures such as cluster analysis offer themselves for this task). When describing the two cultures in the bottom diagram, we may distinguish between core features that are shared universally (feature 3 for the first, features 10 and – arguably – 12 for the second) or close to universally by the carriers of the culture in question and others that are less widely and unequivocally distributed and may be seen as less central. Nothing prevents us from introducing temporal variation into the picture: searching for the same features in the same individuals at other points in time may produce different distributions which, however, could again be expressed in matrices and superimposed on the previous ones to introduce a third dimension. One may also think of replacing the simple dichotomy of presence/absence with quantitative values, since people will often act differently or with varied intensity in repeated instances of the same situation. All this increases complexity, but the distribution will very likely still be clustered, and we are still not necessarily thrown onto intuition as the only method for finding such clusters. Thus we are also left with the problem of naming them. It may be objected that the total matrix we are dealing with (Lowie's "only ... natural unit for the ethnologist") has six billion rows – one for each living individual in the world, not to mention corporate actors that could also be regarded as culture carriers and dead individuals – and that it has an almost infinite number of columns, there being hardly any limit to identifiable features. On top of that, the matrix changes at a tremendous pace. Nevertheless, from all we know and from what social psychologists have found out about human striving for conformity,[67] we can be sure that it will not show a random distribution but will be highly patterned. In an analogy with what I have said about historical and optimal usages, the fact that we are as yet not particularly well equipped to describe and explain this enormous matrix and the clusters therein does not mean that we never will be or that we are better off not even trying, and for this purpose, a word to designate the clusters will be useful.

Let me now turn to the way in which one culture sceptic arrives at the conclusion that positing "a culture" is something we should avoid. Borofsky, doing ethnographic fieldwork on Pukapuka, a small Polynesian atoll, learned that the islanders were all well acquainted with a certain "tale of Wutu," which according to most of them dealt with a man who cleverly escapes persecution by a couple of anthropophagous ghosts. However, individuals' renditions of the tale varied considerably, and even having it told repeatedly by the same person could produce different versions. These would deviate again from what the very same person presented when telling the tale in a group. Accordingly, there was no single content element of the plot that was included in every rendition of the tale, and even those elements that reached a 67 per cent consensus in any gender or age-group were few. Only focusing on the 67 per cent consensus of those individuals considered experts on the topic of tales by their fellow islanders would include enough elements to produce a version that approached the clarity and coherence which none of the individual renditions failed to display.[68]

Clearly, there is no universal sharing here. Having a number of other Cook Islanders – or readers of this article – render the tale, however, would result in versions that would show hardly any commonalities either with one another or with the Pukapuka renditions. Most people would very likely reject the task, saying that they did not know the story. But among the tales Pukapuka individuals told, a general family resemblance is difficult to deny. Some elements appeared with greater frequency than others, and one may see these as more cultural and the rarer ones as more idiosyncratic or introduce an arbitrary minimal frequency of occurrence above which a specific element is to be considered cultural (and mention that limit whenever speaking of such cultural elements). Alternatively, one may search for those persons showing the highest consensus with each other and take their average version as the "most cultural"[69] or – in a kind of analysis that Borofsky does not consider – search for elements that co-occur with a certain frequency or that even implicate one another's presence, making for larger building blocks that can be subjected to the above operations instead of the individual elements. In any case, sequence seems to be unproblematic, since Borofsky offers without comment an apparently standard succession of all content elements.[70] Whatever the approach, it is clear that all these content and sequential elements and aggregates which occur with significant frequency belong to a repertoire on which individuals may draw when telling the tale, constituting the material for their "guided improvisations."[71] No Pukapuka individual is unaware of this repertoire, while most outsiders certainly are.

In contrast to Borofsky, who would not venture beyond "the cultural," I do not consider it problematic to call this repertoire a part of Pukapuka culture. Moreover, a description of the tale's elements and their frequencies and likelinesses of co-occurrence or even – if such can be found – the identification of larger clusters that constitute alternative versions of the tale would in my eyes constitute a faithful ethnographic representation of that specific part of Pukapuka culture, without confusing anyone about the fact that individuals will disagree with each other and even with themselves in their ways of making use of that repertoire. Representational techniques such as bell curves of certain features' distributions or identifying centre and periphery within a cultural inventory – or domain, or schema, or semantic network – may help us here. This would perhaps come close to what Keesing seems to have had in mind when he expressed the hope that "'a culture' as a bounded unit would give way to more complex conceptions of interpenetration, superimposition, and pastiche"[72] and what Appadurai is looking for when he proposes "that we begin to think of the configuration of cultural forms in today's world as fundamentally fractal, that is, as possessing no Euclidean boundaries, structures, or regularities.... [W]e have to combine a fractal metaphor for the shape of cultures (in the plural) with a polythetic account of their overlaps and resemblances."[73]

The approach just outlined can easily be extended to other domains not only of knowledge but also of observed behaviour. Everywhere we find sets of certain learned features that are shared more extensively by people who interact with each other than between these people and others with whom they do not interact or among those others. And everywhere we will find that people are aware of this fact, while they are certainly not ignorant of individual variation even among those who have much in common. We should try to describe the unevenness of any such "differential distribution"[74] as well as we can, and it is clear that as yet the precise extent of interindividual conformity and variation within human groups has received insufficient attention, and therefore we do not have a clear theory, for instance, about how much social interaction gives rise to how much culture. We must also face the fact that once culture is found to be incompletely shared it will have that much less explanatory power for specific instances of individual thought and behaviour. But sometimes communicative economy may make it expedient to speak of "a culture" and identify the constituent units of such a cluster as "elements," "features," "parts," or "traits" of that culture. In doing so we at the very least avoid the impression that there is no such thing as the tale of Wutu on Pukapuka.

In my view, speaking of culture while making it clear that universal sharing is not implied does not automatically privilege coherence. Just as we may concentrate on explaining why a glass is half-full as well as why it is half-empty, sharing is as good a theme for anthropological research as nonsharing, and I wonder how we can avoid either when attempting to portray and explain people's ways of life realistically. And neither does such an approach preclude temporal variation or presuppose that the always arbitrary, abstract entity that we call a culture becomes a thing, an essence, or a living being. Moreover, defining anthropology as the science of culture does not mean that culture must be the sole focus of analysis: obviously, we do want to know what "events, acts, people, and processes"[75] do with culture and what they let culture do to them. Dropping "culture/s," however, will leave us without a word to name those clusters that, ill-shaped though they may be, are nonetheless out there and do play an important role; and it also makes it difficult to define the discipline in short and positive words, at least if we do not content ourselves with practising "the fieldwork science."

As pointed out, there is no ultimate logical reason to retain "culture/s" (or to abandon it), but there are pragmatic ones even beyond that of communicative economy. They have to do with the success of the concept, and it is to them that I will now turn.

Pragmatic Reasons for Retaining "Culture/s"

The concept of culture has undoubtedly exerted an influence beyond the borders of the discipline:

Suddenly people seem to agree with us anthropologists; culture is everywhere. Immigrants have it, business corporations have it, young people have it, women have it, even ordinary middle-aged men have it, all in their own versions.... We see advertising where products are extolled for "bed culture" and "ice cream culture," and something called "the cultural defense plea" is under debate in jurisprudence.[76]

It is concern for the nation's culture that makes the French government establish commissions to search for indigenous equivalents of unwanted loanwords, and it is again in the name of culture that the Chinese and Indonesian leaderships reject the claim to universal application of the Declaration of Human Rights, declaring it a product of Western culture unfit for exportation. "Everyday ways of contemporary talk have been heavily influenced by our anthropological concept of culture."[77] Thus, it is no longer certain that an "evaluative, elitist view of 'culture'"[78] prevails, and it cannot be taken for granted that laypeople will invariably associate the word with the original meaning, in which it was reserved for improvement and its results (first of gardens, then of individuals, and finally of societies).[79] Instead, they will often understand us fairly well, and this is quite remarkable, since the word in its anthropological meaning did not enter standard dictionaries of the English language before the late 1920s.[80] It is precisely this success that makes anthropology's brainchild difficult to control:

As many commentators have noticed, the first thing to realize is that anthropology no longer owns the concept of culture (if it ever did). Virtually all elements of society – across the political spectrum ... – have learned the language of culture.... American society has become culture-conscious, to the point of a "culture cult" in civic society.... Culture and difference have become the dominant paradigm of the day, and individuals are being encouraged, even driven, to conceive of themselves in these terms.[81]

Moreover, this trend is by no means restricted to postindustrial societies or those aspiring to such a position. On the contrary, Sahlins states that:

... the cultural self-consciousness developing among imperialism's erstwhile victims is one of the more remarkable phenomena of world history in the late twentieth century. "Culture" – the word itself, or some local equivalent – is on everyone's lips.... For centuries they may have hardly noticed it. But today, as the New Guinean said to the anthropologist, "If we didn't have *kastom*, we would be just like white men."[82]

Within the academy, the culture concept is also gaining popularity. At least in Germany, major feuilletons keep announcing the "cultural turn" in the humanities,[83] and the replacement of *Geisteswissenschaften* with *Kulturwissenschaften*, centering on a less highbrow notion of culture,[84] has its proponents. Cultural studies has fast established itself in many countries, and its adherents have moved into a more anthropological direction of conceiving culture,[85] with, for example, scholars of high literature descending onto the worldly levels of popular novels, comic strips, soap operas, and advertisements. And after the demise of the two-block paradigm in the field of international relations, the Harvard political scientist Samuel Huntington predicts a "clash of civilizations" in which cultural differences give rise to multiple new blocks that are no less incompatible than the old, ideological ones.[86] While far from controversial within his own discipline,[87] Huntington's writings have certainly had a greater influence on the general public than any contemporary anthropological study can claim, extending, for example, to the German president Roman Herzog, who found Huntington's work a useful companion when visiting China.[88]

Huntington is an extreme representative of a more general figure of thought that is identified as culturalism or "cultural fundamentalism."[89] It posits the existence of a finite number of distinct cultural heritages in the world, each tied to a specific place of origin. Since these are taken to be ultimately antagonistic and incommensurable, they and the individuals associated with them are considered best kept separate, ideally in their respective homelands or, if that fails, in ethnically defined quarters, as is currently being suggested by some urban planners in Germany.[90] Stolcke finds that in European reactionary political discourse the new rhetoric of culture has largely supplanted the older one of race. Culture is a more egalitarian notion, since everyone is supposed to have it (although, of course, in distinct variants). But this is still unlike racism, in which some people are believed to be genetically defective while others – usually of the ego's group – are not. Cultural fundamentalism, therefore, will not serve as ideological buttressing for new colonialisms, but for fueling xenophobic tendencies in the Euro-American immigration countries it is already being amply used.[91]

The notion of incommensurable cultures best kept distinct is not restricted to the political right wing, as Stolcke emphasizes.[92] It can be detected in recent papal encyclicals that introduce the concept of "inculturation," that is, synthesizing elements of two cultures while maintaining the integrity and identity of each,[93] on either side of the current multiculturalism debate over educational contents in the United States,[94] and among those Greek anthropologists who deny foreigners membership in their association because they consider them not really able to understand Greek culture.[95] It is also never far from most contemporary nationalist, ethnic, and fundamentalist movements. Here, at last, one finds culture being used in the way denounced by the culture sceptics, with, for instance, routine references to questionable megacultures such as "African culture" or "Western culture," reductionist conceptions that restrict culture to, for example, ritual, or vague *Volksgeist*-like ideas of a mystical substance or ethos that suffuses a given culture and the community of its carriers.[96] Whether anthropologists like it or not, it appears that people – and not only those with power – *want* culture, and they often want it in precisely the bounded, reified, essentialized, and timeless fashion that most of us now reject. Moreover, just like other concepts such as "tribe," culture has become a political and judicial reality, requiring any attempt to authorize more deconstructed notions to reckon with considerable institutional inertia.[97] In my view, however, this should not discourage us from deconstructing such understandings and developing our own truths (which does not necessarily mean "speaking for" others in any case). For this purpose, I think that three fundamental insights about culture require special emphasis.

First, the social reproduction of culture is always problematic and never guaranteed. Maintaining cultural consensus across time and individuals requires considerable effort. This point is almost always sidestepped by cultural fundamentalists, who seem to presuppose stability as the natural condition of cultures and speak unproblematically of, for example, the – usually old but unspecified – "age" of a given culture. Moreover, culture has often simply been adopted as a less controversial word by people who – consciously or unconsciously – still hold to racist ideas of pseudo-genetic transmission and its relatedness to phenotype (a point that is also made by several of the commentators on Stolcke's aforementioned article). Almost automatically, recognition of the problem of reproduction will lead to the role of power in achieving cultural consensus. Here it will be necessary to overcome the remnants of the "Parsonian divide" and re-sociologize anthropology – not simply by reciting the Foucault-inspired "discourse↔power" mantra and by routinely ascribing discourses, and culture in general, to very large and vague forces (such as "technoscience," "colonialism," or "the German imaginary")[98] but rather by tracing them as far as possible to the interests of specific individual and corporate agents, thus giving "authors"[99] to culture. I am fully aware that if there is one thing that Foucault wanted to discredit it was the idea of individual authorship, but what may be appropriate for the very large discursive formations he investigated need not be so for all of culture.

Secondly, there are limits to culture.[100] On the one hand, culture does not suffocate the idiosyncratic, and individuals can never be reduced to it. To conceive of culture as a toolkit that can be put to manifold uses but will never do anything of itself, however, is hardly controversial now for the numerous anthropologists who have taken up a concern with praxis and the relation between structure and agency. More neglected is the other limit of culture, between it and what is common to all of humankind. Anthropological research on human universals has not flourished recently, to the point that there are no entries or index entries on universals in two major new encyclopedias.[101] Cross-cultural studies leading to the identification of universals have not fared much better, if their share in major journals is any evidence. Moreover, research on the expanding level of "global culture" (wearing T-shirts, mourning Lady Diana, having heard about global warming, knowing how to use a thermometer, liking soccer, etc.) that is socially transmitted but no longer tied to any specific location or group is only just emerging[102] Yet it is precisely with reference to (genetically generated as well as acquired) universals that we can reject exaggerations of cultural difference and the notion of incommensurability, pointing also to fieldwork experiences in which anthropologists and their informants frequently develop common understandings and emotional affinity relatively quickly. And it is also – possibly only – from here that legitimation for universalist projects such as basic human rights can be drawn and their rejection as "merely Western culture" denounced. I do not agree that "anthropology is fundamentally about difference"[103] if this is intended to be a programmatic – instead of merely historical – statement.

Thirdly, culture is not always ethnic culture, and neither is it always tied to identity. Yet anthropological as well as lay expositions of culture are frequently premised on a presumed synonymy of the three, quite irrespective of any commitment to cultural fundamentalism. For example, the *Encyclopedia of World Cultures* lists ethnic cultures, and, although thought is being given to including national cultures in the Human Relations Area Files,[104] there is still no talk of including, say, academic culture, punk culture, or gay culture in their clearly trans-ethnic manifestations. Not that I would envy anyone who wanted to undertake such a difficult task, but I still think that we should be careful not to overethnicize anthropology and pay due attention not only to gender cultures but also to age,[105] regional, professional, and class cultures, as well as to the global cultural level mentioned above. We should also more closely analyze the interplay of ethnic cultures with these other cultures that often do not stop at ethnic or national boundaries. On the same account, I do not consider it a wise move to follow Appadurai in restricting the concept of culture (or "the cultural," as he prefers) "to those differences that either express, or set the groundwork for, the mobilization of group identities"[106] or to agree with Knauft that "culture is now best seen ... as a shifting and contested process of constructing collective identity."[107] To do so would prevent us from showing that not all culture is relevant to identity formation and that what collective cultural identity exists need not be ethnic. I believe that anthropology's critical potential with regard to ethnic and national-ist movements and to cultural fundamentalisms in general would be seriously hampered as a consequence. After all, it could be a healthy reminder that what people of a given nation really have in common is often trivial things such as familiarity with certain soap brands, commercial slogans, or TV stars and not an ever-present awareness of their common history and heritage. Anthropologists should remain capable of showing people that what they see as "their culture" is often a rather arbitrary selection.

These insights, of course, cannot be allowed to obscure that the reified notion of culture has become a social fact that itself deservedly receives anthropological attention. Nor will they rescue us from the dilemma that the demand for unproblematically reproduced, overlarge, and ethnicized cultures often comes from precisely those people we sympathize with and that this kind of culture is often deployed or commoditized more effectively than what we have to offer as an alternative. Moreover, any – anthropological or amateur – identification and description of one's own or another culture is potentially reactive, that is, capable of influencing that specific culture and the people carrying it when it becomes publicly accessible. Consequently, ethnographic innocence is a vain hope in an age in which mass media proliferation can very quickly turn any statement about cultural affairs into a political asset – or target.[108]

Still, there is no denying that many ordinary people have grasped at least part of anthropology's message: culture is there, it is learned, it permeates all of everyday life, it is important, and it is far more responsible for differences among human groups than genes. Therefore, I think that retaining the concept will put us in a better strategic position to transmit the other things we know than we would achieve by denying the existence of culture/s.[109] Choosing the former strategy, we can try to establish anthropology as the expert on – if no longer the owner of – culture, whereas opting for the latter places us in the difficult position of denying something about which we rightly claim to be more knowledgeable than others.

Staying with culture/s, we could object to Huntington that he is justified in paying attention to the role of culture but that the drive to power and wealth that underlies much of global politics is very likely universal and more often clothes itself in cultural differences than is caused by them. We could add that there are indeed anti-Western or anti-Islamic feelings in the world but that currently none of the pannational "civilizations" he identifies can count on a degree of internal solidarity that is in any way comparable to what frequently develops in smaller culturally defined groups such as nations or ethnic groups. We could alert him to the fact that almost any of the eight major "civilizations" he identifies conceals so much cultural diversity that their analytical value must be doubted and that global communication, migration, and cultural diffusion will certainly not make the picture any clearer in the future. We could point out that political salience seems to be more important than cultural diversity when categories as narrow as "Japanese civilization" and as broad as "African civilization" are considered to be of the same order. We could refer him to anthropological studies that try to identify wider cultural areas with less intuitive methods[110] and arrive at units far from congruent with the "civilizations" he proposes. We could sensitize him to the degree to which his separating a "Confucian civilization" from a "Japanese civilization" disregards important East Asian cultural commonalities (including precisely the influence of neo-Confucianism) and thereby falls prey to a myth of Japanese uniqueness that Japanese and foreigners alike have done much to maintain.[111]

Moreover, we could tell practitioners of cultural studies and other disciplines that they are indeed right to extend their study of culture to the more mundane and everyday, but we could go on to argue that an internal analysis of the products of popular culture alone[112] remains ungrounded if it is not complemented by ethnographic field research on recipients' engagement with these products and the resulting practices, discourses, and fantasies, referring them to, for example, anthropological research on television as a source of inspiration.[113]

Of course, if a sufficient number of anthropologists agree that the use of the term "culture" undermines such a strategy and contradicts all our scientific results, its meaning will eventually converge with this assessment and the term will have to be dropped.[114] But I am not convinced that this is inevitable, and I regard the resulting speechlessness as too high a price to pay. We might consider a move similar to that of the pop star Prince, who lately gained much attention by renaming himself "The Artist Formerly Known as Prince," or "TAFKAP" for short.[115] If only for the more difficult pronunciation, however, I doubt very much that "TCFKAC" would become a comparable success. Therefore, I propose that we retain "culture" the noun in its singular and plural form and clarify for those non-anthropologists who are willing to listen what the phenomenon so designated really is – which, as I have tried to emphasize, requires very clear and definite formulations about all the things it is *not*.

Conclusion

There is no immanent justification to be drawn from the empirical world either for using or for discarding the culture concept. Any set of persons who have specific routines of thinking, feeling, and acting in common will invariably be different with regard to other such routines, and therefore wherever we find sharing there is also nonsharing. If we agree, however, to "imagine the world in which people dwell as a continuous and unbounded landscape, endlessly varied in its features and contours, yet without seams or breaks,"[116] we will still need a vocabulary for describing its mountains, plains, rivers, oceans, and islands. The anthropological concept of culture offers itself for that task, all the more so since it has persuaded many people outside anthropology of its usefulness. There is no denying that it has often been applied wrongly and that it continues to be so, especially in the hands of cultural fundamentalists. But, weighing the successes and failures, I am not convinced that the concept really entails the criticized connotations, and I think that it can be dissociated from them and used "to its best intents." Staying with culture – while emphasizing its problematic reproduction, the limitations imposed on it by the individual and the universal, and its distinctness from ethnicity and identity – will enable us to retain the common ground it has created within anthropology and profit from the fact that the general public increasingly understands what we mean when we employ it. Denying the existence of culture and cultures will be difficult to transmit to the many that see them out there, and they will very likely turn to others who may then disseminate their questionable expertise without serious competitors. Any scientific concept is a simplifying construct and has its costs, but once the advantages have been found to outweigh these costs it should be employed with a clear conscience.

Notes

1   In writing this article, I have benefited from discussions of previous versions with Hartmut Lang, Thomas Widlok, and particularly Thomas Schweizer, from the remarks of participants in a presentation to Schweizer's research seminar, and from the valuable comments of the editor and two anonymous referees. I am grateful for all this advice, although responsibility for any shortcomings of my arguments – which did not find favour with all those mentioned – rests with me alone.

2   Marshall Sahlins, "Goodbye to Tristes Tropes: Ethnography in the Context of Modern World History," in *Assessing Cultural Anthropology*, ed. Robert Borofsky (New York: McGraw-Hill, 1994), 386.

3   Lila Abu-Lughod, "Writing against Culture," in *Recapturing Anthropology: Working in the Present*, ed. Richard G. Fox (Santa Fe: School of American Research Press, 1991), 137–62.

4   James W. Fernandez, "Culture and Transcendent Humanization: On the 'Dynamics of the Categorial.'" *Ethnos* 59 (1994): 161.

5   Arjun Appadurai, *Modernity at Large: Cultural Dimensions of Globalization* (Minneapolis: University of Minnesota Press, 1996), 12.

6   Renato Rosaldo, *Culture and Truth: The Remaking of Social Analysis* (London: Routledge, 1993), 27–28, 209.

7   James Clifford, *The Predicament of Culture: Twentieth-Century Ethnography, Literature, and Art* (Cambridge: Harvard University Press, 1988), 232–35.

8   Jonathan Friedman, *Cultural Identity and Global Process* (London: Sage, 1994), 207.

9   Robert Borofsky, ed., *Assessing Cultural Anthropology* (New York: McGraw-Hill, 1994), 245.

10 Roger M. Keesing, "Theories of Culture Revisited," in *Assessing Cultural Anthropology*, ed. Robert Borofsky (New York: McGraw-Hill, 1994), 301–2.

11 Appadurai, *Modernity at Large*, 12.

12 Friedman, *Cultural Identity and Global Process*, 206–7.

13 Clifford, *The Predicament of Culture*, 235.

14 Appadurai, *Modernity at Large*, 12.

15 Friedman, *Cultural Identity and Global Process*, 207.

16 Abu-Lughod, "Writing against Culture," 144.

17 Ibid., 137–38, 143, 146.

18 Tim Ingold, "The Art of Translation in a Continuous World," in *Beyond Boundaries: Understanding, Translation, and Anthropological Discourse*, ed. Gisli Pálsson (London: Berg, 1993), 212.

19 Friedman, *Cultural Identity and Global Process*, 208.

20 Keesing, "Theories of Culture Revisited," 303.

21 Ibid., 309.

22 Appadurai, *Modernity at Large*, 12.

23 Alan Barnard and Jonathan Spencer, "Culture," in *Encyclopedia of Social and Cultural Anthropology*, ed. Alan Barnard and Jonathan Spencer (London: Routledge, 1996), 142.

24 Robert Borofsky, "Rethinking the Cultural," in *Assessing Cultural Anthropology*, ed. Robert Borofsky (New York: McGraw-Hill, 1994), 245.

25 Friedman, *Cultural Identity and Global Process*, 206. The "verb" is not given.

26 Sally Falk Moore, "The Ethnography of the Present and the Analysis of Process," in *Assessing Cultural Anthropology*, ed. Robert Borofsky (New York: McGraw-Hill, 1994), 373.

27 Clifford, *The Predicament of Culture*, 274.

28 Jack Goody, "Culture and Its Boundaries: A European View," in *Assessing Cultural Anthropology*, ed. Robert Borofsky (New York: McGraw-Hill, 1994), 255.

29 Ingold, "The Art of Translation in a Continuous World," 230.

30 Fredrik Barth, "A Personal View of Present Tasks and Priorities in Cultural and Social Anthropology," in *Assessing Cultural Anthropology*, ed. Robert Borofsky (New York: McGraw-Hill, 1994), 358.

31 Abu-Lughod, "Writing against Culture," 147.

32 For a more sustained and systematic analysis of the presumed defects of the culture concept, see Robert Brightman, "Forget Culture: Replacement, Transcendence, Relexification," *Cultural Anthropology* 10 (1995): 509–46.

33 Marvin Harris, *Culture, People, Nature: An Introduction to General Anthropology*, 2nd ed. (New York: Thomas Y. Crowell, 1975), 144.

34 Roger M. Keesing, *Cultural Anthropology: A Contemporary Perspective*, 2nd ed. (Fort Worth: Holt, Rinehart and Winston, 1981), 68.

35 James Peoples and Garrick Bailey, *Humanity: An Introduction to Cultural Anthropology*, 3rd ed. (St. Paul, MN: West, 1994), 23.

36 Edward B. Tylor, *Primitive Culture* (London: John Murray, 1871), 1. A. L. Kroeber and Clyde Kluckhohn, *Culture: A Critical Review of Concepts and Definitions* (New York: Vintage Books, 1952), 81.

37 Franz Boaz, "Anthropology," in *Encyclopedia of the Social Sciences*, ed. Edwin R. A. Seligman (New York: Macmillan, 1930), 79. Kroeber and Kluckhohn, *Culture*, 82.

38 Ralph Linton, *The Study of Man: An Introduction* (New York: Appleton-Century, 1936), 288. Kroeber and Kluckhohn, *Culture*, 82.

39 Margaret Mead, *Cooperation and Competition among Primitive Peoples* (New York: McGraw-Hill, 1937), 17. Kroeber and Kluckhohn, *Culture*, 90.

40 Harris, *Culture, People, Nature: An Introduction to General Anthropology*, 144. Keesing, *Cultural Anthropology*, 68. Conrad Phillip Kottak, *Cultural Anthropology*, 3rd ed. (New York: Random House, 1982), 6. Peoples and Bailey, *Humanity: An Introduction to Cultural Anthropology*, 21.

41 Barnard and Spencer, "Culture," 137. Ward Goodenough, "Culture," in *Encyclopedia of Cultural Anthropology*, ed. David Levinson and Melvin Ember (New York: Henry Holt, 1996), 291. Charlotte Seymour-Smith, *Macmillan Dictionary of Anthropology* (London: Macmillan, 1986), 67.

42 *Pace* Brightman, "Forget Culture: Replacement, Transcendence, Relexification," 527.

43 Ralph Linton, *The Study of Man*, 288.

44 "Every individual is ... in a very real sense, a representative of at least one subculture which may be abstracted from the generalized culture of the group of which he is a member. Frequently, if not typically, he is a representative of more than one subculture, and the degree to which the socialized behavior of any given individual can be identified with or abstracted from the typical or generalized culture of a single group varies enormously from person to person." Edward Sapir, *Selected Writings in Language, Culture, and Personality*, ed. D. G. Mandelbaum (Berkeley: University of California Press, 1949), 515–16.

45 Kroeber and Kluckhohn, *Culture*, 165–66.

46 Richard Thurnwald, *Der Mensch geringer Naturbeherrschung: Sein Aufstieg zwischen Wahn und Vernunft* (Berlin: de Gruyter, 1950), 104. As translated in Kroeber and Kluckhohn, *Culture*, 84.

47 These speak of culture as a "stream" (Blumenthal, *The Best Definition of Culture*, 12; Ford, *Cultural Dating*, 38; Kroeber and Kluckhohn, *Culture*, 130, 132), an "embodiment" (LaPiere, *Sociology*, 68; Kroeber and Kluckhohn, *Culture*, 112), or a "self-generating ... pattern-creating order" (Panunzio, *Major Social Institutions*, 106; Kroeber and Kluckhohn, *Culture*, 106). Even here, however, I assume metaphorical intentions.

48 Leslie White, "Ethnological Theory," in *Philosophy for the Future*, ed. Roy Wood Sellars, V. J. Mcgill, and Marvin Farber (New York: Macmillan, 1949), 363. Kroeber and Kluckhohn, *Culture*, 137.

49 A. R. Radcliffe-Brown, "On Social Structure," *Journal of the Royal Anthropological Institute of Great Britain and Ireland* 70 (1940): 2.

50 Melville J. Herskovits, *Man and his Works* (New York: Knopf, 1948), 154.

51 Robert Lowie, as quoted in Kroeber and Kluckhohn, *Culture*, 165.

52 According to Murdock "culture is merely an abstraction from observed likeliness in the behavior of individuals organized in groups." George Peter Murdock, ed., *Studies in the Science of Society: Presented to Albert Galloway Keller* (Freeport, NY: Books for Libraries Press, 1937), xi. Sapir argues that "the true locus ... of ... processes which, when abstracted into a totality, constitute culture is not in a theoretical community of human beings known as society, for the term 'society' is itself a cultural construct which is employed by individuals who stand in significant relations to each other in order to help them in the interpretation of certain aspects of their behavior. The true locus of culture is in the interactions of specific individuals and, on the subjective side, in the world of meanings which each one of these individuals may unconsciously abstract for himself from his participation in these interactions.... It is impossible to think of any cultural pattern or set of cultural patterns which can, in the literal sense of the word, be referred to society as such.... The concept of culture, as it is handled by the cultural anthropologists, is necessarily something of a statistical fiction." Sapir, *Selected Writings in Language, Culture, and Personality*, 515–16.

53 Brightman, "Forget Culture: Replacement, Transcendence, Relexification," 528.

54 Adam Kuper, "Culture, Identity, and the Project of a Cosmopolitan Anthropology," *Man* 29 (1994): 539.

55 Richard G. Fox, "For a Nearly New Culture History," in *Recapturing Anthropology*, ed. Richard G. Fox (Santa Fe: School of American Research Press, 1991), 101–6. See also Brightman, "Forget Culture: Replacement, Transcendence, Relexification," 530–34.

56 Brightman, "Forget Culture: Replacement, Transcendence, Relexification," 512–13. Kuper, "Culture, Identity, and the Project of a Cosmopolitan Anthropology," 540–41. By contrast, leading proponents of British social anthropology such as Fortes, Nadel, and Firth continued to view society and culture as complementary "concepts of which the significant elements phase into one another" in such a way that they cannot be adequately studied in isolation. Raymond Firth, "Contemporary British Social Anthropology," *American Anthropologist* 53 (1951): 483. According to Murdock, however, British social anthropologists rather one-sidedly neglected the analysis of culture for that of society, so much so that he suggested repatriating his trans-Atlantic colleagues into sociology, where they would constitute a specialized subfield. George Peter Murdock, "British Social Anthropology," *American Anthropologist* 53 (1951): 471–72.

57 Bronislaw Malinowski, *Crime and Custom in Savage Society* (Totowa, NJ: Littlefield, Adams, 1976), 120.

58 See also Brightman, "Forget Culture: Replacement, Transcendence, Relexification," 540.

59 Firth, "Contemporary British Social Anthropology," 478.

60 S.O.Y. Keita and Rick A. Kittles, "The Persistence of Racial Thinking and the Myth of Racial Divergence," *American Anthropologist* 99 (1997): 534–44.

61 In the same way that Mead did; see above.

62 One might object that culture is more than just the sum total of certain features that co-occur with a certain frequency in a group of people. This latter, additive view will perhaps appear entirely mistaken to those who see culture as a process rather than as a static distribution of traits or who follow Bourdieu in his *Outline of a Theory of Practice* in assuming that the loose structures of habitus will guide people's everyday improvisations

but never determine them in a strict sense. Neither of these ideas, however, can manage without determining distributions of features across people as a methodological starting point. Otherwise, there would be no recognition of processes – defined as that which causes the presence of certain features at one point of time and their absence at another – in the first place and no way of discovering that some specific habitus is at work leading to creative variations on a *common* (i.e., temporally and interindividually stable) theme in actual behaviour. Wherever we locate culture and however dynamic we consider it, there will be no way around determining how given features are distributed over a given number of persons at a given time and how this compares with other times and/or other persons if we are to identify a culture, a cultural process, or a habitus guiding individuals' improvisations.

63 James Clifford and George Marcus, eds., *Writing Culture: The Poetics and Politics of Ethnography* (Berkeley: University of California Press, 1986).

64 For the sake of this argument and also for the criticisms raised, it does not matter if any of the latter are excluded or if institutions or artefacts are added. Moreover, any observable feature can be included in such a matrix, including emic categories, ideal as well as observed behaviour, norms and values, and people's cultural self-perception and self-categorization.

65 By the latter I mean that, with space and time always scarce, simplification is inevitable, and therefore it is wise to decide circumstantially rather than in principle how much of it is permissible without distorting one's argument.

66 Thus, there is perhaps less need than Keesing has argued to turn to cultural studies as a guide in this regard. Keesing, "Theories of Culture Revisited," 303; 307–8.

67 Hartmut Lang, "Kultur und Evolutionstheorie," *Zeitschrift für Ethnologie* 123 (1998): 5–20.

68 Robert Borofsky, "On the Knowledge and Knowing of Cultural Activities," in *Assessing Cultural Anthropology*, ed. Robert Borofsky (New York: McGraw-Hill, 1994), 331–34.

69 This is commonly done in consensus analysis and is based on the assumption that, when asked for their judgment on cultural questions, experts will agree more often than laypeople. The latter base their answers on chance or improvisation, not on knowledge, and are therefore less likely to come up with identical answers to a given cultural question. Consensus analysis is a statistical model for determining whether there is a common culture behind informants' responses and, if so, how to estimate the "culturally correct" answer to a given question from those responses. The answers of each informant are weighted in proportion to the informant's average agreement with the others, a method which privileges the experts, since they tend to agree with at least some people (other experts). It should be noted that fairly small samples suffice to produce highly reliable estimates. A. Kimball Romney, Susan C. Weller, and William H. Batchelder, "Culture as Consensus: A Theory of Culture and Informant Accuracy," *American Anthropologist* 88 (1986): 326–27. Romney, Batchelder, and Weller, "Recent Applications of Cultural Consensus Theory" *American Behavioral Scientist* 31 (1987): 163–77, and Romney in an annotated bibliography on his Internet home page give overviews on the now-numerous applications of this method.

70 Borofsky, "On the Knowledge and Knowing of Cultural Activities," 332.

71 Pierre Bourdieu, *Outline of a Theory of Practice* (Cambridge: Cambridge University Press, 1977).

72 Keesing, "Theories of Culture Revisited," 310.

73 Appadurai, *Modernity at Large*, 46.

74 Ulf Hannerz, *Cultural Complexity: Studies in the Social Organization of Meaning* (New York: Columbia University Press, 1992).

75 See Barth, "A Personal View," 349–60.

76 Ulf Hannerz, *Transnational Connections: Cultures, People, Places* (London: Routledge, 1996), 30.

77 Keesing, "Theories of Culture Revisited," 303.

78 Goody, "Culture and Its Boundaries: A European View," 254–55.

79 See Clifford, *The Predicament of Culture*, 337. See also Kroeber and Kluckhohn, *Culture*, 15; 44.

80 Kroeber and Kluckhohn, *Culture*, 63.

81 Jack David Eller, "Anti-Anti-Multiculturalism," *American Anthropologist* 99 (1997): 253, 251.

82 Sahlins, "Goodbye to Tristes Tropes: Ethnography in the Context of Modern World History," 378.

83 For example, Doris Bachmann-Melik, "Weltweite Vogelperspektive: Anthropologische und Postkoloniale Herausforderungen der Literaturwissenschaft," *Frankfurter Rundschau*, December 10, 1996.

84 Renate Schlesier, "Zauber der Unschärfe: Ein Plädoyer für einen Wandel der Fächer," *Die Zeit*, November 22, 1996.

85 Keesing, "Theories of Culture Revisited," 303.

86 There are whole passages in Huntington's article which read as if copied from anthropological textbooks. Consider the following: "Villages, regions, ethnic groups, nationalities, religious groups, all have distinct cultures at different levels of cultural heterogeneity. The culture of a village in southern Italy may be different from that of a village in northern Italy, but both will share in a common Italian culture that distinguishes them from German villages. European communities, in turn, will share cultural features that distinguish them from Arab or Chinese communities.... People have levels of identity: a resident of Rome may define himself with varying degrees of intensity as a Roman, an Italian, a Catholic, a Christian, a European, a Westerner.... People can and do redefine their identities, and, as a result, the composition and boundaries of civilizations change." Samuel P. Huntington, "The Clash of Civilizations?" *Foreign Affairs* 72, no. 3 (1993): 23–24. Especially the last sentence, however, is all but forgotten in the further course of Huntington's argument.

87 See Barrie Axford, *The Global System: Economics, Politics and Culture* (Oxford: Polity Press, 1995), 191–94.

88 Matthias Nass, "Unverkrampft im Reich der Mitte: Bundespräsident Herzog suchte eine neue Gesprächsbasis mit der aufsteigenden Weltmacht," *Die Zeit*, November 29, 1996.

89 Verena Stolcke, "Talking Culture: New Boundaries, New Rhetorics of Exclusion in Europe," *Current Anthropology* 36 (1995): 1–24.

90 *Die Tageszeitung*, November 26, 1997.

91 Stolcke, "Talking Culture" 4–8.

92 Ibid., 6.

93 Michael V. Angrosino, "The Culture Concept and the Mission of the Roman Catholic Church," *American Anthropologist* 96 (1994): 825.

94 Eller, "Anti-Anti-Multiculturalism," 252. Vered Amit-Talai, "Anthropology, Multiculturalism, and the Concept of Culture," *Folk* 37 (1995): 140.

95 Kuper, "Culture, Identity, and the Project of a Cosmopolitan Anthropology," 545–46.

96 Angrosino, "The Culture Concept and the Mission of the Roman Catholic Church," 827–28. Eller, "Anti-Anti-Multiculturalism," 252–53.

97 See the experience of the expert witnesses for the Mashpee Wampanoag claim to cultural continuity. Clifford, *The Predicament of Culture*, 277–346.

98 See Uli Linke, "Gendered Difference, Violent Imagination: Blood, Race, Nation," *American Anthropologist* 99 (1997): 564–61. This article demonstrates how even the deconstruction of racist ideas can sometimes border on cultural fundamentalism. Linke observes

an interesting obsession with blood imagery in "the German public imaginary." That the latter is homogeneously distributed and clearly bounded and has been handed down unproblematically from the Nazi period to the present seems, however, to be taken for granted throughout her analysis. This appears questionable, since the metaphors of "floods" of immigrants – which, representing another kind of liquid, are found to be related to blood – are hardly unique to Germany and since many of the extreme utterances of politicians that are quoted provoked public outcries showing that "German political fantasy" is, at the very least, divided. While I do not want to deny continuities in the history of German racism, I think that an analysis of public discourses which does nothing to gauge their distribution and influence over time must remain incomplete and suspect of arbitrariness.

99   Richard G. Fox, "Cultural Dis-Integration and the Invention of New Peace-Fares," in *Articulating Hidden Histories: Exploring the Influence of Eric R. Wolf*, ed. Jane Schneider and Rayna Rapp (Berkeley: University of California Press, 1995), 277–78.

100   On this point, Hannerz, borrowing from Redfield, has an insightful discussion. Hannerz, *Transnational Connections: Cultures, People, Places*, 30–43.

101   Alan Barnard and Jonathan Spencer, eds., *Encyclopedia of Social and Cultural Anthropology* (London: Routledge, 1996). Tim Ingold, ed., *Companion Encyclopedia of Anthropology: Humanity, Culture, and Social Life* (London: Routledge, 1994). But see Donald E. Brown, *Human Universals* (Philadelphia: Temple University Press, 1991).

102   Hannerz, *Transnational Connections: Cultures, People, Places*, 38. Christoph Brumann, "The Anthropological Study of Globalization: Towards an Agenda for the Second Phase," *Anthropos* 93 (1998): 495–506.

103   Eller, "Anti-Anti-Multiculturalism," 251.

104   Melvin Ember, "Evolution of the Human Relations Area Files," *Cross-Cultural Research* 31 (1997): 12.

105   Vered Amit-Talai and Helena Wulff, eds., *Youth Cultures: A Cross-Cultural Perspective* (London: Routledge, 1995).

106   Appadurai, *Modernity at Large*, 13.

107   Bruce M. Knauft, *Genealogies for the Present in Cultural Anthropology: A Critical Humanist Perspective* (London: Routledge, 1996), 44.

108   See, e.g., the public debate about Hanson, "The Making of the Maori," as documented in Hanson, "Reply," Linnekin, "Culture Invention," and Levine "Comment." See also the controversy about Karakasidou, *Fields of Wheat*. This is an ethnography about Greek Macedonia which in 1995 was rejected for publication by Cambridge University Press, not because of qualitative deficiencies but for fear of retaliation from Greek nationalist sources (see the Internet documentation of events, opinions, and protests under http://www.h-net.msu.edu/~sae/threads/CUP).

109   One anonymous reviewer considered the idea "to 'educate' the general public ... a strangely sanctimonious view of anthropology's role in the world." I agree that a scientific discipline as such is not obligated to anything, but those of its practitioners who are paid for teaching or for research, often out of public funds, should feel some responsibility for disseminating truth. I also sympathize with pleas "to integrate the discipline more centrally within academia, and in public policy debates." Annette B. Weiner, "Culture and Our Discontents," *American Anthropologist* 97 (1995): 14. As I see it, all this leads to one or another form of educating the general public.

110   Michael L. Burton et al., "Regions Based on Social Structure," *Current Anthropology* 37 (1996): 87–123.

111   Peter N. Dale, *The Myth of Japanese Uniqueness* (New York: St. Martin's Press, 1986); Roy A. Miller, *Japan's Modern Myth: The Language and Beyond* (New York: Weatherhill, 1983); Kosaku Yoshino, *Cultural Nationalism in Contemporary Japan* (London: Routledge,

1992). I restrict myself to the objections we can raise as experts of culture. There are other, equally serious flaws in Huntington's model which, however, need no anthropologist to denounce them, such as the claim that armed conflicts arise more often at the fault lines between his "civilizations" than within them – the inhabitants of Rwanda certainly did not need cultural differences of a "civilizational" order to slaughter each other, and the Europeans for centuries did not need them either – or the spectre of an "Islamic-Confucian" alliance forming against "Western civilization," which, to my mind, is simply unfounded.

112 As, for example, in most contributions to Cathy Schwichtenberg, ed., *The Madonna Connection: Representational Politics, Subcultural Identities, and Cultural Theory* (Boulder, CO: Westview Press, 1993).

113 Conrad Phillip Kottak, *Prime-Time Society: An Anthropological Analysis of Television and Culture* (Belmont, CA: Wadsworth, 1990); Andrew P. Lyons, "The Television and the Shrine: Towards a Theoretical Model for the Study of Mass Communications in Nigeria," *Visual Anthropology* 3 (1990): 429–56; Harriet D. Lyons, "Television in Contemporary Urban Life: Benin City, Nigeria," *Visual Anthropology* 3 (1990): 411–28; Purnima Mankekar, "National Texts and Gendered Lives," *American Ethnologist* 20 (1993): 543–63; Richard Pace, "First-Time Televiewing in Amazônia: Television Acculturation in Gurupá, Brazil," *Ethnology* 32 (1993): 187–206; Richard R. Wilk, "'It's Destroying a Whole Generation': Capitalism and Moral Discourse in Belize," *Visual Anthropology* 5 (1993): 229–44.

114 Brightman, "Forget Culture: Replacement, Transcendence, Relexification," 541.

115 An interim as "symbol" – graphically expressed by a symbol and never written out – attests to this artist's versatility in the field of applied semiotics.

116 Ingold, "The Art of Translation in a Continuous World," 226.

2 Geoffrey Hartman begins his wide-ranging and erudite contribution to this volume by identifying in himself what he describes as an "acute sense of phantomization," the ghostly feeling of not fitting-in or belonging which culminates in his strong desire to share the feelings of others in some immanent and real way. "Culture," Hartman notes, is often held to be the space within which such sharing typically occurs – within which it becomes possible to participate in the processes of "constantly reinforced self-inclusion" the most important consequence of which for him is our embodiment. By "embodiment" Hartman means something like our assumption of an identity, the settling upon a particular social subjectivity responsible for letting us and others know exactly who and what we are. Complicating our embodiment, however, is the ghostliness of "culture," its phantom vagabondage resulting from its (negative) dialectical suspension in between such antithetical operational registers as the functional ("the culture of ideas") and the formal ("kulcha"), the active ("cultivation") and the passive ("acculturation"), the universal ("culture") and the particular ("a culture"). "Culture," in other words, pulls us in two very different directions: towards opportunities for local solidarity and attachment attractive to us in virtue of our sense of our own distance from the terms of reference around which the general culture is organized; and towards the general culture in the name of the freedoms and privileges its membership entails. The former is a movement towards embodiment; the latter moves us towards abstraction. The former gives rise to more and less problematic parochial or sectarian groupings, while the latter champions a kind of universalism. For on the latter view one is either cultured or not and, if cultured (a condition typically requiring a measure, or at least an appearance, of affluence), one is so to the same degree, and in exactly the same way, as everyone else.

There are thus for Hartman two major senses of "culture": one referring to a "specific form of embodiment or solidarity," the other more generally referring to a shared human heritage. And yet it is impossible to distinguish these two senses completely, for what is required for one kind of embodiment must be protected from the demands of others to whom embodiment looks very different, perhaps even incommensurably so. There remains a need, in other words, for what Hartman terms "a larger and transpolitical perspective, a universal culture," capable of resolving disputes between competing cultures in the name of a common humanity. But as he also makes clear, the responsibility for delineating this universal outlook, for mapping culture's contours, devolves onto members of small elite groups such as university professors and special members of the art world. Universalism is thus underwritten by a highly self-selective intellectual (and social) particularism which finds expression in an extremely specialized discourse undermining the very qualities of "accessibility" and "participatory momentum" that "culture" is meant to affirm. While Hartman defends the rarefied language of academic criticism on the grounds of its imaginative appeal, he nonetheless argues that it functions best oppositionally. How long, he asks, must critical discourse remain critical? "Can an affirmation emerge from all this splendid – cerebral, demystifying, deconstructive – 'labour of the negative'?"

Whatever the answer, and one is provided by Imre Szeman later in this volume, Hartman notes the many risks to moving quickly towards an accessible and affirmative culture criticism, chief among which remains the possibility of cooptation. Deprived of an oppositional language *qua* linguistic practice, critique far too easily slips into affirmation of the status quo. Words' effectiveness, argues Hartman, have come to assume an inverse relation to their truth. But if "the culture of words cannot contribute adequately to truth," he asks in closing, "what can?"

CULTURE AND THE ABSTRACT LIFE*

GEOFFREY HARTMAN

"This is not a real world. This life is not the real life." "But you're really suffering, I said." "Yes," Tang said, "It's a problem, this real suffering in a not-real world." – Philip Gourevitch, *The Boat People*

I begin with a feeling; then I throw some history after that feeling, hoping it will stick, spark, or make the feeling and its consequences (rather than its causes) more visible.

The feeling is that of being an outsider to life. Not just to social life or a particular group that I aspire to join, although this wish may play a part, but to participation (perhaps always mystical) in life itself. I want to be a part of all I perceive; I want to know myself, not only my processes of knowing. I want to share, be part of, the feelings of others and not simply feel for them, sympathize in an abstract way. The sense, moreover, that someone else (even more uncannily, something else) may be living my life can become psychologically unsettling. The search for identity, which never seems to cease, plays its role in this

* This article was originally published as a chapter in Geoffrey Hartman's *The Fateful Question of Culture*. It appears here with permission, and unchanged.

strong and potentially pathological fantasy that others live my life, a life I want to live – fully – myself.

It is also at the level of *ideological explanation* that I want to intervene, in order to explore how attributions of causes and prescriptions of remedies may have consequences that are destructive rather than creative. But I should first describe this feeling that it is not exaggerated to call a phantomization, one that makes a ghost of us, even a vengeful ghost, while we are still alive, patently flesh and blood. That it can be trivialized, and is found in most popular literature as a belief in ghosts or spirits, that it is *permitted* in this form or gleefully *exploited*, merely shows its inveterate hold. For the purpose of description, however, I turn to examples from canonical poetry and fiction.

Shelley's atheistic mysticism seems to come from an overwhelming sense of powers residing in nature or the cosmos. Intuiting those powers suggests that life on earth is the mere shadow of another world to which fuller access comes with death. Shelley is quite aware of the seduction of this thought, and he cannot always decide whether to follow or to resist it. Despite the Enlightenment he remains unawakened, wrapped in spiritual and ghostly feelings that fail to bring revelation:

> I look on high;
> Has some unknown omnipotence unfurled
> The veil of life and death? Or do I lie
> In dream, and does the mightier world of sleep
> Spread far around and inaccessibly
> Its circles?[1]

In "Adonais," prompted by the death of fellow poet John Keats, this dreamy uncertainty about the intersection of life and eternity – his phrase "the veil of life and death" evokes a mixed or occulted condition – leads him into the overpowering temptation to conjure up, if only in dream vision, what is behind the veil and to merge with it, even if it proves to be the power of blackness:

> The breath whose might I have invoked in song
> Descends on me; my spirit's bark is driven,

Far from the shore, far from the trembling throng
Whose sails were never to the tempest given;
The massy earth and sphered skies are riven!
I am borne darkly, fearfully, afar.[2]

Shelly becomes his own Charon in a movement that rejects Wordsworth's trivial "sky-canoe" (in *Peter Bell*), anticipates Rimbaud's
"drunken boat," and depicts an impulse deriving from inspiration
rather than impotence but therefore all the more persuasive and
suicidal.

My second example is the plot of one of the most uncanny short
stories ever composed. An exemplary Gothic fantasy, its influence
reached Dostoyevsky. Friedrich Schiller's *Der Geisterseher* (*The Visionary*) recounts how the prince of a small German state who is visiting
Venice begins to experience strange phenomena that rouse his self-
awareness. They seem to be accidental or unplanned and therefore
impinge on him as omens. Behind their exotic trappings, is there more
than a psychological truth, such as our propensity to succumb to what
psychoanalysts have called "ideas of reference"?

A troupe of young girls and boys, all in theatrical dress, welcomed us with a
dance that was a pantomime. It was inventive; lightness and grace inspired
every gesture. Before it was completely finished, the leading dancer, who
played a queen, seemed suddenly arrested by an invisible hand. Lifeless she
stood, as did everyone around her. The music stopped. In the whole assembly you could not hear a breath, and she stood there, her eyes fixed on the
ground, withdrawn, paralysed. Then, suddenly, with the fury of inspiration,
she startled, looked around her wildly – "A King is among us," she cried, tore
the crown from her head and ... laid it at the feet of the Prince. Everyone there
now turned to look at him.

Such incidents, which single out the prince as if he were chosen to
embody a mysterious destiny, are expertly Gothic, indebted to a late
eighteenth-century formula in which preternatural episodes intrigue
the reader as well and induce a state of wonderment or suspension of
judgment. Is it still possible, given an enlightened age, to believe in the

supernatural: in marvellous, extraterrestrial influences? Eventually, of course, the reader's "hesitation," as Todorov calls it in his fine book *The Fantastic*, is resolved. After the permitted shudder, which Schiller extends to paranoid detail and length, strengthening a genre that continues to exert its formulaic charm on Thomas Mann's *Death in Venice* (remember the strange incidents that befall Aschenbach and entice him toward his fate?), the Gothic tales miraculous parts are then exposed as machinery, not yet that of the artist, but the machination of a mortal and devilish conspiracy. This pattern of the *surnaturel expliqué* still dominates, suitably adjusted, modern detective fiction, where the corpse is "explained," laid to rest, as it were, by the plot's ingenious if temporary challenge to the reasoning reason.

In Schiller's mystery story it turns out that the Catholic Church is behind it all: it wished to have this Protestant prince convert to Catholicism, to make him a vassal of Rome and to that end decided that his capacity for wonder had to be renewed as a first step. But the reader easily exits this polemical frame. We know that what is at stake is poetry, or the faculty of wonder itself: the romantics' fear, and ours, that a progressive disenchantment of the world, associated with the Age of Reason, will make outsiders of us all. Indeed, Schiller's paradigmatic story leaves us in limbo, in suspense between two coldnesses, that of a world without its animating supernatural, without gods or ghosts, genii or genial surprises, and a world created by those who engineer spiritual revolutions, who exploit and instrumentalize our obstinate hunger for the wonderful, which remains a dream always ready to enter the waking life. Therefore the Gothic persists in Brockden Brown, Hawthorne, and Melville, in cultic horror movies or science fiction, in Bergman's *The Magician*, Yeats's *A Vision*, or Buñuel's experiments with surrealism.

My third example comprises evocative lines from Wallace Stevens's "The Rock" that point to the passage of time as the abstracting or ghosting principle yet hardly explain why mutability should have this effect:

> It is an illusion that we were ever alive,
> Lived in the houses of mothers, arranged ourselves
> By our own motions in a freedom of air.

It is just this fading or fugacity, moreover, that challenges the poet "as if nothingness contained a métier." From the void of memory or desire or from an absence he calls "the remotest cleanliness of heaven," from this unreal a simulacrum springs, a fiction of the real. It challenges the fallacious, anthropomorphic imagination. "Less and less human, O savage spirit." Whatever the ultimate source of such "Phantomerei," Stevens orchestrates it, draws from it an extraordinary decorum.

Postmodernists will say at this point that Stevens has it the wrong way around: the unreal springs from our accelerating capacity to fashion simulacra. Indeed, Jean Baudrillard challenges the notion of "taking place." Everything tends toward a condition of *non-lieu*, even as our desire for authentic or auratic objects (in Walter Benjamin's sense) is artificially stimulated.[3] But I have said I do not want to speculate on the causes of, or historicize, this acute sense of phantomization. Instead of multiplying instances of it – dramatic exhibits would be Mallarmé's well-publicized struggle with the *Néant* or Virginia Woolf's portrait of Rhoda in *The Waves* – let me quote a deeply moving and ironic passage from Emily Dickinson, in which the desire to live frustrates itself, creates an overestimation, a sense of panic that distances passion from fulfillment in the same way that the Parousia of divine presence is deferred in Christianity:

> I cannot live with You –
> It would be Life –
> And Life is over there –
> Behind the Shelf
> The Sexton keeps the Key to –[4]

Yet pride of place in my symptomatic anthology must go to Hegel's *Phenomenology of Mind*. Hegel accompanies a description of this dissociated or abstracted state, this feeling that life is a phantom, or elsewhere, or haunted by something other than what we see, with an acknowledgment that only an odyssey, as he says, a close to interminable historical and dialectical process, can fill the void. Hegel's epic history of humanity will (1) make us aware of all "the forms of unreal consciousness," (2) show that "the exposition of untrue consciousness in its untruth is not a merely negative progress" (this should inhibit the charge of negativism or nihilism), (3) disclose that it is in the character of conscious life, as distinguished from "a life of nature," to suffer a "violence at its own hands in progressing beyond the determinate," to *alienate* itself in order to go forward and be fulfilled. Even the Here and the Now are too abstract in their immediacy: when we try to hold them fast in writing, they are unmasked as empty or labile impressions. Our wishful endowment of objects of sense with being, and our disappointment in them as they become, inevitably, mere symbols, as they betray their self-insufficiency, is a lesson that even the animals can teach us. They know instinctively the religious scepticism taught by the Eleusinian mysteries, as Hegel tells us in a passage that is itself quite wonderful: "[Animals] do not stand stock still before things of sense as if these were things *per se*, with being in themselves: they despair of this reality altogether, and in complete assurance of the nothingness of things they fall-to without more ado and eat them up. And all nature proclaims, as animals do, these open secrets, these mysteries revealed to all, which teach what the truth of things of sense is." [5]

My announced subject is culture, not a primordial feeling. But I have a good if daunting precedent in Freud, whose *Civilization and its Discontents* (*Das Unbehagen in der Kultur*)[6] also begins by speculating on a feeling, although one that is eudaemonic rather than daemonic and so perhaps the obverse of what I have described. I would prefer, of course, to keep some suspense as to how I will get from ghostliness to culture, but since there will be enough shoals and indirections to negotiate, let me state my argument at this point. "Culture" at present – I mean the ring and function of the word, its emotional and conceptual resonance – even when it is abusively applied, keeps hope in *embodiment* alive. Consciousness, as ghostly as ever, cannot renounce that hope in a living and fulfilling milieu. "We live in a place that is not our own," Stevens writes; such honesty, however, is a torment. He continues, therefore: "And hard it is in spite of blazoned days." [7]

I need not emphasize that the strongest imaginative needs are also those most likely to be trivialized, even deliberately "wasted." Whenever a novel, biography, news story or new historical essay begins in the manner of "It was a cold and foggy evening … ,"[8] this is a repetition of a venerable technique, called "composition of place," that continues to stir us deeply and tritely. It is also a fact that with the advent of television a new kind of communal memory is created, promoting false embodiments, charged images that are the equivalent of fixed ideas. Artists must work with these as well as against them. Yet historically each superrealism proves to be a phantom. Ideologies of culture, which are as dangerous and effective as the art they inspire, also exploit our reality hunger by proposing "a cure of the ground" (Stevens, "The Rock").[9]

That phrase, "a cure of the ground," remembers culture as cultivation. But in Stevens it is also a euphemism for death. Nothing, he implies, can relieve us of imagination except imagination itself, even as that faculty conceives, ironically, its own demise and so approaches both the "plain sense of things" and an absence of the imagining self close to death. I take that to be the meaning of "a cure of ourselves, that is equal to a cure / Of the ground, a cure beyond forgetfulness." The rock – from which Stevens's poem derives its title – exists, but not as a foundation; it is, necessarily, the motive for metaphor. A restless imagination localizes itself by a pseudospecification that is not unlike love's fantasia. This rock, or "the gray particular of man's life," is transformed, humanized; its barrenness becomes, through poetry, "a thousand things." The spirit seeks, that is, the local, not the literal: indeed, to advocate that cure of the ground as a literal "blood and soil" doctrine would curse the ground.

Yet we should not ignore the political backdrop of this distinction between local and literal. The cosmopolitan ideal of "civilization" – the Enlightenment picture of the world citizen – has proved to be too vague, has not engaged our full imaginative and symbolic powers. "If we are dreaming of a 'national culture' today," Van Wyck Brooks writes in 1918, "it is because our inherited culture has so utterly failed to meet the exigencies of our life, to seize and fertilize its roots." And, he adds sarcastically, "that is why we are so terribly at ease in the Zion of world culture."[10] Indeed, intellectual history teaches us that "culture" achieves its pathos as a counterconcept to "civilization," especially in Germany. Consider Max Weber's famous definition: "Culture is something finite, excerpted by human thought from a senseless and boundless world history, and invested with sense and meaning." [11]

In such definitions the feeling of nonpresence I have described seeps back and infects the very ideas intended to exorcise it. We continue to sense an incipient nihilism. This nihilism can turn against culture as well as nature, renounce all hope in secular incarnation, and become near-apocalyptic. [12] Theology and metaphysics have always engaged with a desire that is distinct from mere need in that it cannot be assuaged. The relation between idealism and scepticism, as in Plato, or of spiritualism and the anxiety of being perpetually excluded from true knowledge, as perhaps in Descartes, also points to a phantomization that lies just beneath the proud architectonics of philosophy, religion, and art and leads to the Pandemonium of political theologies. [13] Moreover, sociology has recently suggested that the dominant class creates and sustains itself by a principle of "aesthetic" distinction that limits both use and exchange value, a principle I interpret as a way of pursuing embodiment through a continually reinforced self-inclusion. [14] By a systematic, continuous and institutionalized closure, we remain insiders. No wonder Bourdieu writes: "There is no way out of the game of culture."

So, after documenting the modern explosion of "culture" as word and idea, I want to ask: are not images of embodiment that haunt us and feelings of abstractness or nonembodiment that tell us we are not real enough, or that we inhabit the wrong body, the post-religious source of ideologies whose explanatory and remedial strictures increase rather than lessen abstraction and too often incite a cannibalistic violence far greater than that of Hegel's animals?

It is here, also, with this kind of question, that one encounters Marx's strength as an imaginative and consequent thinker. He would claim that I have described the "ghostly objectivity" of reified life, "Monsieur Le Capital and Madame La Terre ghost-walking," but divorced it from its foundation in the socioeconomic realities of capitalism by depicting the ghost feeling as independent and permanent, "as the timeless model of human relations in general." [15] Like Hegel, I have stood matters on their head and not understood that my suspicion of postreligious ideologies is itself deeply ideological. Marx's vivid sense of alienated labour and damaged life brings a specific formula for reform and so for hope; unfortunately, all attempts to embody that reform by revolutionary change, to remove the false mystique of reified gods or human goods, have so far not exorcised the ghost feeling but continue to water it with blood.

Culture speech is an aspect of our culture: everything now tends to be seen in culture terms. "Culture" has become our most prevalent "complex word," to use Empson's striking phrase.[16] There is no mystery about its linguistic development, starting with Cicero's metaphor "cultura animi": culture of the soul, rather than of earth or deities associated with agriculture. (The transferred meaning, as Hannah Arendt points out, fortifies the intuition that the soul needs a human habitation, a dwelling place that does not simply subject nature to man.[17]) The well-known ambiguity of the genitive allows the construction "the culture of" to go in two semantic directions. One is the dynamic or functional meaning, as when we construe Rémy de Gourmont's "culture of ideas" to mean "cultivating the ideas," developing, understanding them better; the dynamic is also aptly caught by John Stuart Mill, when he praises the "culture of the feelings" transmitted by Wordsworth's poetry. The other direction of the genitive focuses on the formal product, the "culture" produced by this activity. When a police department claims that it is "the culture of the agency" to undertake certain procedures, the second kind of meaning has taken over, though the first persists.[18]

A world in which a Paris street still bears the name "La culture de Sainte Cathérine" and that advertises a book *Beyond Beef: The Rise and Fall of the Cattle Culture* remains unified in the sense that we catch the connection between cult and agriculture;[19] at the same time the gap between provincial and global, between the church as a toponymic institution (however universal its hopes) and mass technology, can jar us into a sense of nostalgia about local attachments. The same is true when writers try to suggest a link between place and spirit, as if "culture" were continuous with soil and climate: "the peculiar flavor," we read, "of that old New England culture, so dry, so crisp, so dogmatic, so irritating."[20] Even if such expressions as "mass culture," "popular culture," "working-class culture," and "inmate culture" (Erving Goffman) make a certain sense – because they point to a sizable group, a quantitative spread, and because they are often applied in a provocative or questioning way (is *this* what or where culture is today?) – surely the quantitative factor is not defining, except as an undertone of anxiety, in such offshoots as camera culture, gun culture, service culture, museum culture, deaf culture, football culture, bruising culture (boxing, and all who follow the sport), the "insistently oral culture of Washington" (i.e., gossip and slander), the culture of dependency, the culture of pain, the culture of amnesia, etc.[21] Why has this word taken over, like a linguistic weed? Let me add some examples of its proliferation.

An average day. In the *New York Times*, after the Jefferson High School killings, there is mention of a "culture of hidden weaponry." My *London Review of Books*, just out, describes a new theory speculating that the origin of culture was in a "sex strike," during which the females, in order to defeat the "alpha male," a macho type capable of inseminating many of them one after the other, devised a way of hiding their ovulation. This so-called strike gave the averagely sexed male a chance and increased female control of the entire matter. Here culture does not mean lifestyle but the control of nature.

But what does "Adjusting to Japan's Car Culture" mean, a headline on the first page of the next day's business section? Does, it refer to the role cars play in the life of the Japanese, with a suggestion that cars run them (an inversion of culture managing nature)? The article actually describes the "corporate culture" of Japanese industry and the difficulty American executives have fitting in. (Headlines are the one place in a newspaper where condensation permits striking and even malicious ambiguities. Perhaps we should talk of a "headline culture.") "Culture," in the cases just cited, generally takes on the meaning of a habitual way of doing things that claims to express a basic national or group trait, as if it were "the nonhereditary memory of the community."[22] But principally the word serves as a means to age a modern practice instantly, to give a product – obviously of our making – traditional status.

This is problematic of course. The anthropological meaning of "culture" as a traditional way of life[23] is now extended to cover what is merely a lifestyle, whose legitimacy does not derive from tradition but precisely from what challenges tradition: modern technology. It is ironic that a word that Nietzsche had defined as "a unity of artistic style manifest in all the vital activities [*Lebensäusserungen*] of a people"[24] and that for the greater part of its semantic career in English denotes "harmonious development of the whole person" (Raymond Williams), a development compensating for scientific and industrial specialization, now presents that specialization itself as the basis of a way of life.[25]

While one is tempted to see this antithetical extension of meaning as parody rather than paradox, it could not have prevailed without something attractive in the very notion of cultural history. What is suggested, beginning with Vico, is a view of history (he says "civil society" and "the world of nations") as human creation, a history, therefore, that we can understand, reinvent, and even control. The diversity of historical event, as well as the creative energy of a historical writing that changes nature from indifferent background to cultural milieu, raises the hope that Stevens will be proved wrong in his rearguard action on behalf of the universe: "It is the human that is the alien, / The human that has no cousin in the moon." Yet has our knowledge of history and nature as it leads to power over them worked to our benefit? This is the great post-Enlightenment issue, which confronts us daily.[26]

For this entrepreneurial vision of human development could be an illusion fostered by advanced capitalism; it is not, moreover, entirely absent from Marxism.[27] Whereas "culture" used to point to the way we organized our leisure time (the culture page of the newspaper, which sees no difference between culture and entertainment, reflects and abets that meaning), a not-so-subtle reversal has recently taken place. It makes "changing the culture" short hand for an alteration in habits of work rather than of leisure, an alteration, for example, that might benefit the national economy or industrial policy.[28] Thus it includes the recognition that we now have greater powers to shape the environment but also that habits of the workplace carry over into our free or leisure time. As a result, the concept of leisure as the realm of freedom (freedom from governmental or social interference as well as from toil) weakens, even though our power to alter nature or society has significantly increased. Culture, I read, "is imagined as a plastic medium which politically powerful social elites may rework and remould at will"; indeed, when such "reworking" is shorn of its exclusively economic goal, such as improvement of productivity in the workplace, then "culture" moves very close to the sense it has in contemporary culture studies.

Culture is thought of as directly bound up with work and its organization; with the relations of power and gender in the workplace and the home; with the pleasures and the pressures of consumption; with the complex relations of class and kith and kin through which a sense of self is formed; and with the fantasies and desires through which social relations are carried and actively shaped.... It is not a detached domain for playing games of social distinction and "good" taste. It is a network of representations – texts, images, talk, codes of behaviour, and the narrative structures organizing these – which shapes every aspect of social life.[29]

That same day, entering Phelps Gateway at Yale, I see a metal coat hanger with the inscription: "This is not a medical instrument." I think: to understand a symbol like this requires some knowledge of a specific cultural context. Damn it, culture again, in the cultural studies aspect of a "network of representations" that shapes social life. What has to be recalled is, first, the abortion debates of fin-de siècle America. Then, to savour the exhibit fully, Magritte's well-known picture of a pipe with the motto: "This is not a pipe." For something like the metal hanger is, alas, too often used as a medical instrument. The hanger is not a clever symbol drawing attention to the difference between art and reality but an object highlighting an underground practice that society denies or refuses to take responsibility for. The negative ("This is not ...") serves to affirm the existence of the practice.

Here "cultural context" points not only to a specific social situation but also to a scandalous mode of representation that made toilets into works of art and generally disrespected boundaries, especially those between private and public, popular and sophisticated, marginal and established. (Picasso's *Venus du Gaz*, a burner framed as a fetish, mocks our own art fetishism.) But this mode – related to Murray Krieger's "fall of the elite object"[30] – cannot entirely control the meaning of the symbols it creates: their transgressive character transcends any assigned, stable significance, so that the cheap wire hook that stands for the endangering and demeaning of women forced into back-alley abortions may also evoke a violence intrinsic to all acts of abortion, whatever the instrument. The pro-choice symbol becomes ominous when it links up with an unlimited claim to control nature, with the idea that culture reinvents nature and could desanctify or instrumentalize life.

Now science enters, as Bacon's improvement of nature, implicit even in such common phrases as "cell culture,"[31] but also as it tends to challenge, by alternatives, long-established social patterns. A pro-choice fantasy, a feminist tract as visionary as Erasmus Darwin's *Love of the Plants*, is entitled *Simians, Cyborgs, and Women: The Reinvention of Nature*.[32] It describes a potential liberation of the body more radical than N. O. Brown's *Life against Death* or *Love's Body* by treating physical intercourse as an evolutionary stage, with the present state of affairs as stodgy as the nuclear family. For literary readers Donna Haraway writes a form of science fiction based, like Ferenczi's *Thalassa*, on biological (now sociobiological) data. But where Ferenczi was interested in the genealogy of sexual feelings and drives, in how our evolutionary past has influenced present comminglings, Haraway is resolutely future-oriented and therefore ends with the conviction: "Science is culture." Not a culture, mind you, as in C. P. Snow's *The Two Cultures*, which deplored that the specialization endemic to modern society had divorced scientists and humanists.[33]

Of course, not all uses of "culture" converge. But whatever the word touches receives at present a sort of credibility. One hears of a smokers' culture, of [Australia's] beach culture: do such things really exist? The point is that the term bestows, like rights language run amok, a certain dignity, one that is based not so much on numbers as on a sense that *a meaningful nucleus of life, a form of social existence, has emerged or is emerging.* And we pay attention to it, I suggest, because social fragmentation means two things that together amount to a disabling paradox: the general culture seems too distant or alien, while the hope for some unity of being – which I call embodiment – can migrate to groupings often held together by parochial, sectarian, self-serving, and even anti-social interests.[34]

These interests range from the folklore of indigenous or immigrant cultures, or the practices of a religious cult that has broken with a mainstream denomination, to the lifestyle of gay people or the agenda of political, commercial, and even criminal organizations (a TV report on the Bank of Credit and Commerce International talked as easily of "BCCI's criminal culture" as of a "Washington culture"). So abusive is the extension of the word, so strong and vulgar its pathos, that I begin to understand an Africanist claim about the West. It is alleged that an ingrained Cartesianism has *ghosted* the colonizers, abstracted them from life, so that "culture" becomes a dream for what is missing, a phantom or proxy comforting the "white-man-who-has-problems-believing-in-his-own-existence."[35]

Yet, to repeat, not all uses of "culture" converge. In fact, the proliferation of the word in the sense I have singled out is only part of the picture, if a part that seems to have taken over. The *other* major sense of the word, as in "high culture" or "a cultured person" or Arnold's *Culture and Anarchy*, has almost an antithetical resonance. Often an elegiac aura surrounds it. "To say, 'Here we no longer use citation' means the end of our culture, in the West, as we have known it, more or less, since the PreSocratic thinkers."[36] This threatened "culture" is, so to say, less culture-bound; a distinct cosmopolitan perspective enters. *Bildung* (liberal education leading to self-development) rather than *Erziehung* (systematic or specialized training) is emphasized, while an aesthetic element or prestigious "je ne sais quoi" is tolerated. So a French philosopher writing for a general audience, fudges elegantly when he says that his book presupposes "une certaine culture, un certain acquis philosophique." You acquire this culture actively, as a modification of some natural traits; at the same time, you make it seem natural, as if breeding and background had predisposed you to receive it. Sainte-Beuve claims that it pervades, because of the classical tradition, French literary life, which "consists in a certain principle of reason and culture [*un certain principe de raison et culture*] that has over time penetrated, and modified, the very character of this gallic nation."[37] The word still suggests an integrated way of life, although what is integrated is understood to be artificial, even consciously highbrow ("kulcha").[38]

Culture in this older sense goes together with affluence or social climbing, for it is freedom from ordinary conditions of a material, parochial ideologically exigent kind that invests the word with promise.[39] The relation between being cultured and being free is one of the great commonplaces of humanistic (or "liberal") education. (Kant, in an especially subtle move, claims that the real end of culture is freedom rather than happiness and that it promotes the former by instilling an affection for thoughtfulness.)[40] Yet despite culture's "free play of ideas," a respect for embodiment continues to prevail, and nation or religion or ethnic identity is often viewed as a necessary form of local attachment. Toward the end of his life Coleridge wrote in his notebook that "the self is in and by itself a Phantom"; nonetheless, it was "capable of receiving true entity by *reflection* from the *Nation*." Both the self and mankind were, as graspable, psychological notions, too abstract. The nation, however, was "something real to the imagination of the citizen" and became distinct "in relation to the personalities of other nations."[41] The *other* idea of culture, then, while stressing the play of ideas and its effectiveness in modifying or even (as Matthew Arnold hoped) gradually doing away with the class structure, was not free of a tension between culture and nation, or culture and society (which gives Raymond Williams's crucial study of the word its title).[42]

The creation of a cultural sphere within society or nation-state, a sort of free zone for the market of ideas, can be traced back to the *honnête homme* concept, promoted by the salons of Parisian society in the eighteenth century. They were themselves a development of courtesy ideals that emanated, as the word suggests, from the court. In the seventeenth century, culture moves closer to urbanity, the culture of cities. The new decorum joins courtiers and significant personalities from the bourgeoisie to create an ideal public of court and town ("la cour et la ville").[43] Within that charmed circle of sociability, and within it alone, people of different ranks and professions mingled and talked freely, affirming values characterized as "honnête," that is, *unaffected*, in the twofold sense of unpretentious and independent of vested interests. A premium was placed on an intelligence that could see mailers from a broad perspective and did not specialize itself in turn: that remained conversational and not excessively ostentatious.

That this ideal degenerated into a new "culture of wit" was inevitable; and Rousseau's attack on its far-from-simple "honesty" as another form of hypocrisy revealed the problem. Still, in this ideal of the *honnête homme*, which Erich Auerbach already associates with Montaigne the self-reflective essayist, who is more interested in being a writer than a gentleman – an ideal infiltrating the citified and robuster café society of *The Tatler, The Spectator*, and the beginnings of English literary journalism – we catch a glimpse of Matthew Arnold's understanding of how culture promotes a wholeness of being that might overcome the divisiveness and parochialism of the class structure. Also adumbrated is Karl Mannheim's definition of intellectuals as an interclass stratum. Though from a socially stratified and class-conscious point of view intellectuals appear to be deracinated airheads (*Luftmenschen*), they alone may be in a position to demystify the conversion of special interests into universals.

To define these two major senses of culture – the one denoting *a* culture, that is, a specific form of embodiment or solidarity;[44] the other pointing to a general ideal, held despite class, profession, or broader allegiance (religion, race, collectivity, nation) and positing a shared human heritage, a second or accrued nature[45] – is to differentiate contrasting and perhaps contradictory concepts. We can spot this contrast as early as Moses Mendelssohn's "On the Question: What Does Enlightenment Mean?" (1784),[46] written at a time when "culture," as well as "enlightenment" and "formation" (*Bildung*) – three words Mendelssohn tries to clarify by a veritable intellectual minuet – are so new that he calls them bookish and barely intelligible to the common reader.

Compared to "enlightenment," Mendelssohn says, "culture" is a practical and sociable virtue, an embodied quality, "just as a piece of land [*Grundstück*]" – falling back on the agricultural analogy – "is said to be cultured and developed the more it is made capable of producing things useful to mankind by human industriousness."[47] In what is a most interesting distinction for our purpose he also claims that as human beings we need enlightenment more than culture, which suggests that "culture" is indeed a word emphasizing practical over universal. Our way of life as citizens (*Bürger*) rather than human beings (*Menschen*) is determined by class and profession, and the impression given by the philosopher's phrasing is that he advocates qualities of culture and polish for each differentiated segment of society while hoping that this will affect the entire nation. "The more the latter [*Kultur und Politur*] harmonize [*übereinstimmen*] throughout the classes and their professions, that is, [harmonize] with the latters' respective destiny [*Bestimmung*] as members of society [literally *Glie-*

der, body parts], the more a nation has culture." Mendelssohn, then, describes both a "culture" that permeates the entire nation and "a culture" appropriate to each class and profession in a society that will soon become even more specialized and segmented because of industrialization. This tension between national (general) culture and class-bound culture anticipates a later debate, reaching its height in the 1930s, as to whether there can be a proletarian culture; that is, whether a single class in a divided society can produce a more authentic, less "abstract" mode of life than the despised bourgeoisie.[48] Mendelssohn seems to suggest that a national culture can be built, not on the repression of the productive power of the working (or any other) class, but on the corporate integration of all *Glieder*.

My purpose in examining the resonances of "culture" is critical as well as historical. There are, no doubt, other sexy words around – "community" or "identity" – that exude a similar promise.[49] But the historical semantics of "culture" clarify what we are experiencing in literary studies at this time. The conversion of literary into cultural studies arises, certainly, from an urgent and growing concern with social justice and what may be called *species thinking* (now that we know so much of our history, what does it tell us about the human species?). Yet it also arises from an imaginative need that operates at all levels of life, private as well as public. Our hope that culture can provide an embodiment to satisfy a ghostly hunger, as devouring as a vampire, persists despite an impasse. The intimacy of the small or homogeneous group, of an extended family that promises to transmit and foster a tradition, runs up against other such formations and requires, in order to prevent a perpetual war between communities, a larger and transpolitical perspective, a universal culture. This other "culture" has the mission to make what seems intransitive transitive again. The very effort, however, leads to a further contradiction, perhaps because it takes place primarily in another relatively small group, an international elite of universities that are never the communiversity we hope for. As we debate the issues, a highly specialized discourse is produced, a *Fach* that sins by its technical diction and aggressive bearing against the very qualities that "culture" as a historical and progressive movement is meant to achieve: qualities of accessibility and participatory momentum.[50]

The critical yield of these reflections affects two areas. The first is our understanding of the relation, or rather contest, among art, religion, and politics. The ghostly feeling I have evoked has been traditionally honoured and regulated by an established church. But poetry often strikes us as a wild religion – indeed, as a city of refuge for suppressed or exiled spirits (the "parting Genius" of Milton's *Nativity Ode*, the nymphs and satyrs displaced by "faery broods," exorcised in turn by the vacuum of a stricter doctrine). These spirits are not as innocent as they appear to be. They always represent a defeated religion or world-view, some archaic power, often more explosive because of time spent underground. John Edgar Wideman's story "Damballah," about the survival of a voodoo god who brings death to a slave, is an example. The imagination refuses to be emptied out: it strikes back by aggressively developing its prior inheritance, one that seems indissociable from a visionary or figurative language indebted to either Christian or hetero-dox sources. Smart, Blake, Shelley, and Yeats are obvious instances of modern poetry becoming more rather than less ghostly. The imagina-tion is seen as religion's birth mother and in that role rescues the reli-gious sensibility from religion.

T.S. Eliot, after the Second World War, in an address entitled "The Unity of European Culture" (which he eventually appended to his *Notes Towards the Definition of Culture*), asserts that he cannot conceive of culture without a religious foundation. I would agree that, despite upheavals in church history, the ghostly feeling has been at once delimited and preserved by traditionary ceremonies and symbols that form a national way of life, whatever the degree of religious conviction. Spectral speech, the detritus of past beliefs, haunts cultural memory: in Eliot's *The Waste Land* it figures as an incurable wound. Yet Eliot neglects the fact that culture often turns into culture politics because the pressure for a particular form of embodiment is felt to be salva-tional. It is possible to revise his insight about "the common tradition of Christianity which has made Europe what it is" and suggest that the only religions that count are political religions.[51]

But these will try to suppress, or at the very least regulate, the "wild" symbolism of art, and indeed all unlicensed images. Eliot's statement, in the same essay, that "our common responsibility is to preserve our common culture uncontaminated by political influences" is laudable.[52] However, his divorce of Christianity from the political sphere and his failure to acknowledge the drive for embodiment that the pathos of the titular word "unity" and his pleonastic repetition of "common" still convey make an otherwise sane and sophisticated essay as evasive a gesture after the Second World War as "Tradition and the Individual Talent" was after the first.

The conflict between art and religion (almost always a state religion, or the state as a religion) opens a breach between the notion of "a culture" as a distinctive and unified whole and "culture" as an ethos that guarantees the free play of ideas and the individual exercise of imagination in the context of tradition. Indeed, a turning point is reached early in formal cultural historiography when Jacob Burckhardt gives up the belief that "a culture" is a synchronic entity, unified by the zeitgeist and so embracing all aspects of society. That basically Hegelian conception (though less dialectical) had inspired Burkhardt's famous *Civilization [Kultur] of the Renaissance in Italy.* Only a decade later, in "The Study of History" and as he is planning lectures on Greek culture, Burckhardt's concern with decadence leads him to a more nuanced view of the great but fragile civilization of Greece. He now stresses, perhaps under Nietzsche's influence, the agonistic relation among culture, religion, and politics. I quote Felix Gilbert's summary of Burckhardt's point of view:

Whereas state and religion claim universal validity and feel justified to enforce their claim by coercion, the existence of culture depends on the possibility of individuals' moving freely in different directions, of spontaneity.... The particular character of a culture is determined by the extent to which state and religion allow or restrict a free development. The Greek culture and the modern world exemplify that, at least for a time, culture can escape the embrace of state and religion and develop freely.[53]

Religions must be taken seriously, then, though I feel foolish making so obvious a statement. Religions (including the state presenting itself as a religion) are political in urging as total an embodiment as possible; they are not just the source of a cultural sedimentation that provides continuity and an option. In countries where a de facto or a constitutional separation of church and state has occurred, religions cannot enforce their totalizing way of life. But they continue to flourish there and will do so until every ghost is laid, until, in Blake's words, "All Human Forms [are] Identified" by a political revolution or apocalyptic reincarnation. A society, therefore, that claims to be secular or even antireligious will continue to foster pledges of allegiance and what has been called "civil religion."[54] Even if diversity is nominally cultivated by this society, the religions it has exorcised, or any residual, unbound spirituality, is feared; consequently, it too may seek a total commitment and insist on political correctness, even in art.

Today there are those who see the "general culture" as hegemonic. If we acknowledge, however, the antinomy between "a culture" and "culture," then the right conclusion would be that it is "a culture" that tends toward hegemony, while "culture," understood as the development of a public sphere, a "republic of letters" in which ideas can be freely exchanged, is what is fragile.[55] In this area, things are very complex. On the one hand, the general culture can deceptively claim to be on the side of breadth and generosity, while it is actually imperious or imperialistic. On the other hand, "a culture" can be deeply conformist and seek to limit individual rights, which it may even denounce as a *culte du moi*, as excessive individualism. So Maurice Barrès plays on the organicist and agricultural analogy to express his belief in the necessity of a culture grounded in French soil: "J'ai besoin qu'n garde á mon arbres la culture qui lui permet de me porter si haut, moi faible petite feuille" (I need culture to conserve my tree and to allow it to carry me, a feeble, small leaf, upward).[56]

With Burckhardt and Nietzsche the historical image of Greece begins to change, and "culture" is now seen as a precarious, even heroic, achievement against great odds, a sort of tragic *agon* always threatened by decadence. It does not solve anything, therefore, to denounce "culture" as "high culture," that is, as elitist and obsolete. Herbert Marcuse called this move a "repressive desublimation," and he insisted on the importance of "aesthetic incompatibility." Although the main target of his attack was mass culture, his words on the "flattening out of the antagonism between culture and social reality through the obliteration of the oppositional, alien, and transcendent elements in the higher culture" remain cogent.[57]

Perhaps Václav Havel is a better guide here than either Marcuse or T.S. Eliot. Coming from the republic of letters to politics, he insists that "civility," or what he renames "the culture of everything," must penetrate the political sphere as well. The notion of a high or autonomous sphere of culture is neither conceptually protected nor attacked by him: his argument is that manners must become *moeurs*, a second nature or tradition, if everyday life in post-Marxist society is not to be ravaged once more by regressive nationalisms or an all-usurping economic imperative.[58]

The question that remains, however, is whether Havel's ideal can accrue enough imaginative force to displace the appeal of political religions and their uncompromising, spiritualistic demand for total devotion, sacrifice, embodiment. Civility, as Havel uses it, comes close to what Hannah Arendt called "classic virtues of civic behavior" that distinguish "a responsible member of society, interested in all public affairs" from a bourgeois, "concerned only with his private existence" and who becomes too easily a "functionary" of the state.[59] Nationalism, in Arendt's view, is not genuine patriotism at all but eliminates open public discussion in favour of a propagandized mass ideology. My provisional conclusion about Havel's civic ideal is pessimistic. Once the nation-state or a faith community has appropriated what might be called the superego ideal of culture by promising embodiment and exacting collective obedience, civility is often viewed as a minor virtue to be sacrificed on the altar of a higher destiny.

The antinomy between "a culture" and "culture" leads to a second critical observation. I have mentioned my concern that ideological strictures, intended as social remedies, may increase rather than lessen abstraction; certainly, the exponential growth of cultural studies has produced a highly specialized and sometimes cultic discourse. What Henry James called, at the beginning of [the twentieth] century, when immigration was making its impact, "The Question of Our Speech," must now be posed in every generation of *professionals*. One form this question takes at present is whether the culture speech of the last fifty years has achieved anything more than that of the last two hundred.

I am not concerned, as in *Minor Prophecies*, at least not primarily, with the culture wars that pit the public intellectual against professors and their jargon. Yes, cultural critique can be countercultural in diction and spirit; it is still fighting gentility, civility, middle-class hypocrisy, etc. But there is nothing intrinsically wrong with a technical vocabulary that is inventive, that renews tired analytic terms by an energetic mixture of the vernacular or the exotic (*vide* Frye, Burke, Bloom, all of them *bricoleurs*, as well as Barthes, at his essayistic rather than schematic best). The question of our speech, the contemporary question, asks how long critical discourse must remain critical: that is, questioning; that is, in a negative mode. Can an affirmation emerge from all this splendid – cerebral, demystifying, deconstructive – "labour of the negative"?

Sometimes, in the midst of reading our strongest readers – Derrida, for example – I begin to think we have simply expanded the linguistic sway of periphrasis and praeteritio. How not to speak ("Comment ne pas parler"), when our humanity is deeply offended, our social agony aroused daily, our profession in disarray; yet also how to speak in a scrupulously negative way ("Comment ne pas parler"), avoiding ideas of reference, the seductive promissory melody in every gesture of voice and the tricks and errors of cultural prophesy with its "present futur"?[60] Are we caught between two extremes: on the one hand, artful structures of avoidance that turn us into philosophical *précieuses ridicules*; on the other, a diction with more pathos than ever, as embodiment, empowerment, fulfillment, identity rise from undersong to theme song?

This question of our speech is also the question of "our" speech. Two related kinds of integrity are involved: that of language under modern conditions, and that of the critic's – the language bearer's – relation to a particular community, to "a culture" as well as to "culture." These are difficult issues to raise in conclusion. On the critic's relation to a community, let me recall Trilling's preface to *Beyond Culture* (1965), where he sticks up for his right to say "we" though he admits to representing a rather narrow class, that of New York intellectuals. In short, his concern in 1965 is more with the "we" than the "me" generation, because of the "tendency toward homogeneity in modern culture." Despite claims of difference, he argues, despite contemporary attempts to liberate us from the tyranny of middle-class values ("the free creative spirit at war with the bourgeoisie"), despite the advocacy of new experience and new knowledges, even the "adversary culture" is forming a class:

> There has formed what I have called a class. If I am right in identifying it in this way, then we can say of it, as we say of any other class, that it has developed characteristic habitual responses to the stimuli of its environment. It is not without power, and we can say of it, as we can say of any other class with a degree of power, that it seeks to aggrandize and perpetuate itself. And, as with any other class, the relation it has to the autonomy of its members makes a relevant question…. There is reason to believe that the relation is ambiguous.[61]

Here the definition of "class" is almost as broad as "culture" is coming to be and understates the social struggle. Indeed, Trilling uses this convergence of terms to emphasize a well-known mechanism of progress: "How else are civilizations ever formed," he asks, "save by syntheses that can be read as paradoxes?" Yet if that is so, if syntheses can be read as paradoxes (or vice versa), language does not have integrity in the sense that we ascribe it to *character.*

The vista opened by Trilling's urbane question is disconcerting. Language is either very manipulable, or contemporary language has become so. Among the most relentless and influential statements concerning our language condition are those of Adorno and Horkheimer, and – more specifically focused on the weakening of social bonds – of Henri Lefebvre.

The founders of Critical Theory see a collapse of bourgeois civilization, a movement toward uniformity and pseudoclarity that they describe as an Enlightenment ethos bound for self-destruction. As the public sphere and modern economic forces take over, thought is commodified and speech pervaded by promotional purposes. This tendency has gone so far that we glimpse an impasse: social critique, even their own, becomes impossible because its words are involuntarily co-opted by the forces of rationalization. Deprived of an effective oppositional language, critique turns into affirmation. In this incurable condition, "the most honest reformer, who urges renewal in current terms of speech, because he adopts a smooth, adaptable category machine and with it the supporting structure of a bad philosophy, reinforces the established power he seeks to demolish."[62]

Sadly, the effectiveness of words may now stand in inverse relation to their truth. Lefebvre takes up the other side of this false yet coercive "we" denounced by Critical Theory: its shallow, even hypocritical nature. He argues that today every "we" is weak and has to be reinforced by a special rhetoric "packed with allusions, stuffed with icons ... with images and chants that celebrate an ill-defined cohesion and tries to consolidate it." The object of Lefebvre's critique is not, or not primarily, the pseudocommunitarian bias of post-Marxist rhetoric, as that becomes an aggressive, even counter-cultural means of identity formation. He does not target a shocking outcome of the Enlightenment but focuses on the deterioration of language as it adjusts to the technological networks of postindustrial society and dissipates a referentiality that, according to him, had preferred clarity and closure over a polysemic float in the linking of signified and signifier.[63]

One does not have to accept this account of the decline and fall of referentials to appreciate Lefebvre's analysis of the increasing slippage of keywords.[64] Nor does one have to accept Adorno and Horkheimer's view of the consequences of the Enlightenment to be concerned with the question of our speech, and in particular with how to maintain a critical language that is not co-opted by the very fact of communicating successfully. For in literary studies the relation of paradox to synthesis or of ambiguity to the creation of meaning has been the single most important topic of poetics since Richards and Empson. The recurrent concept of a second fall of language, in modern or postmodern times, leads by reaction to new efforts that would limit language doubt, our scepticism about the truth of words. These efforts are many and intriguing; they make up the bulk of what we call literary theory, which has allied itself to an intense and ongoing scrutiny of language and its communicative powers. If the culture of words cannot contribute adequately to truth, what can?

A decorum is often suggested that seems distinctively though not dogmatically moral. Both Trilling's "authenticity" and Heidegger's

"*Eigentlichkeit*" not only revise previous criteria of sincerity or *honnêteté* but endow speech with a tacit dimension, a quality that, though fully verbal, cannot be reduced to either intentionality or phenomenality and so approaches silence. This intelligible silence, more primordial than speech, is "embodied" as writing. The impotence of words, and of culture generally, both before and after such disasters as two world wars and the Holocaust, intensifies the dilemma. "To keep the silence, that is what unknowingly we all wish for, as we write," observed Maurice Blanchot in *Disaster Writing*.[65] We are back to "Comment ne pas parler."

Notes

1 "Mont Blanc," ll. 52–57.

2 "Adonais," LV.

3 See, e.g., Jean Baudrillard, *La Guerre du golfe n'a pas eu lieu* (Paris: Galilee, 1991). Andreas Huyssen, *Twilight Memories: Marking Time in a Culture of Amnesia* (New York: Routledge, 1995) explores the impact of postmodern derealization on our principal cultural institutions.

4 Thomas H. Johnson, ed., *The Complete Poems of Emily Dickinson* (Boston: Little, Brown, 1960), poem 640.

5 G.W.F. Hegel, *The Phenomenology of Mind*, trans. J. B. Baillie (New York: Harper and Row, 1967), 159. "Open secrets" adapts Goethe's view of nature, which is itself based on an earlier commonplace describing nature as the open book of God.

6 Sigmund Freud, *Civilization and its Discontents*, ed. and trans. James Strachey (New York: Norton, 1962).

7 Wallace Stevens, *Notes toward a Supreme Fiction* (Cummington, MA: Cummington Press, 1942). Another side of the organic feeling of harmony, "of an indissoluble bond, of being one with the external world as a whole" (Freud, *Civilization and its Discontents*, 12), linked by Freud to the experience of the child in the maternal body, is developed by and at once delights Julia Kristeva and others who seek to understand the role of a pre-Oedipal stage in human development. The oceanic feeling may explain a basic anxiety in the grown child, insofar as it continues to sense a lack of ego boundaries and fears to be engulfed by the "ocean."

8 "One evening in 1919, a short, shy fellow named Irving Caesar [to become Irving Berlin], who was just short of his 25th birthday, sat close to the stage of one of the cavernous theaters on Times Square and took in a performance of the song 'Swanee'" (*New York Times Book Review*, 3 May 1992, 22). "It was a fine autumn evening in 1922. I was a notary's clerk in Maromnies" (J.-P. Sartre, on narratable "reality," in his novel *Nausea* [1938]). Even putting the date after the title of a novel reveals a certain nervousness of the same kind, a minimal gesture of emplacement.

9   Embodiment should be, strictly speaking, a "cure of the body," as the erotic imagination always demands, or as the poetic imagination strives for, giving voice a body or not being satisfied with imperfect words. This aspect, neglected here, points to Ovid and the Ovidian tradition in the West. Cf. Lynn Enterline, *Pursuing Daphne: Body and Voice in Ovid and Renaissance Ovidian Poetry* (Stanford: Stanford University Press, 1997). The complex task of sexualizing and gendering embodiment is taken up by Sandor Ferenczi, *Thalassa: A Theory of Genitality*, and Erich Neumann, *Apuleius: Amor and Psyche, the Labors of the Feminine* (New York: Pantheon, 1965).

10 Van Wyck Brooks, *Letters and Leadership* (New York: B.W. Huebsch, 1918).

11 "Kultur ist ein vom Standpunkt des Menschen aus mit Sinn und Bedeutung bedachter endlicher Ausschnitt aus der sinnlosen Unendlichkeit des Weltgeschehens" (*Gesammelte Werke zur Wissenschaftslehre*, quoted in Aleida Assmann and Jan Assmann, "Kultur und Konflikt: Aspekte einer Theorie des unkommunikativen Handelns," in *Kultur und Konflikt*, ed. Jan Assmann and Dietrich Harth (Frankfurt-am-Main: Suhrkamp, 1990), 35. My translation.

12 Harold Bloom, after a life of studies centring on Shelley, Blake, Yeats, and Stevens, has recently revised his earlier critique (inspired by them) of "Natural Religion." He has identified the primordial feeling of ghostliness, as it becomes a conviction and a religion, with the ancient gnostic heresy that the Nature we know is the work of another power than God, that the Creation is already a Fall, and that we have a spiritual existence apart from any such embodiment, apart from the secular world. See Harold Bloom, *The American Religion: The Emergence of the Post-Christian Nation* (New York: Simon and Schuster, 1992).

13 Stanley Cavell has linked philosophy to literature (especially through his readings of Shakespearean tragedy) by disclosing in both an alive and pervasive scepticism as the provocative workings of a ghost feeling surely similar to the one I have described. Descartes's philosophical and Shakespeare's tragical method at once acknowledge and avoid a dispossession: the unavailability of our own private world (a scepticism from the fact that we cannot know ourselves intimately enough) and of public reality (a scepticism from the fact that the minds of others, or of whoever orders the world, also may be closed to us). Yet writers like these continue to dare to know. I sin against Cavell's patient elaborations with this instant summary and send the reader to, above all, Stanley Cavell, *The Claim of Reason: Wittgenstein, Skepticism, Morality, and Tragedy* (New York: Oxford University Press, 1979).

14 Pierre Bourdieu, *La Distinction: Critique sociale du jugement* (Paris: Editions de Minuit, 1979).

15 See Georg Lukács, *History and Class Consciousness: Studies in Marxist Dialectics*, trans. Rodney Livingstone (Cambridge, MA: MIT Press, 1971), 95. Lukács supports Marx's attempt to disenchant the "mysticism of commodification." Derrida traces Marx's pervasive recourse to spectral metaphors in the *Specters of Marx*. Lucien Goldmann suggests that Heidegger's concept of Dasein responds to Luk Verdinglichung (reification), itself developed from Marx's basic intuition about the historical rather than permanent status of a world of things, of objects standing against the subjectivity of the worker with a spuriously independent life.

16 Cf. Raymond Williams, *Keywords: A Vocabulary of Culture and Society* (New York: Oxford University Press, 1976), 76: "Culture is one of the two or three most complicated words in the English language."

17 See the suggestive survey of the word in Hannah Arendt, "The Crisis in Culture," in *Between Past and Future* (New York: Viking, 1961), 197–226.

18 An early analysis of the historical semantics of the word, with some remarks on its grammatical development, is in Joseph Niedermann, *Kultur: Werden und Wandlungen*

des Begriffs und seiner Ersatz-Begriffe von Cicero bis Herder (Florence: Libreria Editrice, 1941). It provides an indispensable survey but does not touch sources beyond Herder. For later uses of the word, see A.L. Kroeber and Clyde Kluckhohn, *Culture: A Critical Review of Concepts and Definitions* (New York: Vintage, 1963). A further, but contemporary, linguistic factor favouring the spread of the word promotes all subcultures to cultures by dropping the prefix sub-, as if it were infra dig, or a carryover from "subversive." in the culture/civilization antithesis as it coincides with national self-imagining in Germany and France, see Norbert Elias, *The Civilizing Process* (Cambridge: Blackwell, 1994).

19   Cf. Jack Goody, *The Culture of Flowers* (Cambridge University Press: New York, 1993), which examines, according to the advertisement, "the secular and religious uses of flowers across a wide range of cultures, from ancient Egypt to modern China."

20   Van Wyck Brooks, *America's Coming-of-Age* (New York: B.W. Huebsch, 1915).

21   Cf. Assmann and Assmann, "Kultur und Konflikt: Aspekte einer Theorie des unkommunikativen Handelns," 35.

22   Y.M. Lotman and B.A. Uspensky, "On the Semiotic Mechanism of Culture," *New Literary History* 9, no. 2 (1978): 211–32.

23   "By 'culture,' then, I mean first of all what the anthropologists mean: the way of life of a particular people living together in one place. That culture is made visible in their arts, in their social system, in their habits and customs, in their religion," T. S. Eliot, *Notes towards the Definition of Culture* (London: Faber and Faber, 1948), 122. We see here how infectious the anthropological meaning is: we have slipped from "tradition" (as in his well-known essay "Tradition and the Individual Talent") to "traditional way of life" to "culture." Eliot does not specifically argue that culture, in this sense, is the only way of conferring identity; that stage, with its "determination to respect art only within the ground rules of culture" and stemming "from a prior definition of culture that ties it to the social or anthropological group, rather than individual taste or judgment" is attacked by a recent critic as "cultural idolatry." See David Bromwich, *Politics by Other Means: Higher Education and Group Thinking* (New Haven: Yale University Press, 1992), 12ff.

24   See the first of his "Untimely Observations" of 1873.

25   While in the modern era complaints about the "machinery" of living increase (see n. 250 below), there is evidence that specialization can also simplify the multicultural demands of traditional societies. As Ganash N. Devi has pointed out, "The English term 'culture' is not sufficiently large to cover the semantic scope" of India's cultural situation, where people live "within a bilingual and even multilingual cultural idiom" and have to switch their culture codes according to the needs of their social situations (in Ganash N. Devi, "The Multicultural Context of Indian Literature in English," in *Crisis and Creativity in the New Literatures in English*, ed. Geoffrey Davis and Hena Maes-Jelinek [Amsterdam: Rodopi, 1990], 345–53). Multiculturalism, which represents subcultures as cultures, tries to restore a complexity that was removed by modern political and scientific streamlining. For how these complexities turn into perplexities when a modern national culture tries to control a traditional multicultural situation, see Clifford Geertz, "Thick Description: Towards an Interpretive Theory of Culture," in *The Interpretation of Cultures* (New York: Basic Books, 1973), 3–30.

26   Both Michel Foucault and Michel de Certeau are of importance here. See, especially, Certeau's remarks on "l'articulation nature-culture" in *L'Écriture de l'histoire* (Paris: Gallimard, 1975), 82ff. Certeau emphasizes how history, as a discipline, actively moves "natural" elements into the "cultural" domain, making them more available, for instance, for a literary transformation into symbols: "Of waste materials, of papers, of vegetables, even glaciers and 'eternal snows,' the historian makes *something else*: he makes history out of them. He participates in the work which changes nature into environment and modifies in this way man's nature." Ernst Cassirer, in his *Logic of the Humanities [Kultur-*

wissenschaften], trans. C.S. Howe (New Haven: Yale University Press, 1961), credits Vico (followed by Herder) with a "logic" that "dared to break through the circle of objective knowledge, the circle of mathematics and natural science, and dared instead to constitute itself as the logic of the humanities – as the logic of language, poetry, and history" (54).

27 If we adduce Althusser's concept of "Ideological State Apparatuses," or the way the dominant class reproduces through superstructural organizations such as schools and churches, opinions favourable to its control of the modes of production, then such proliferating talk about "corporate culture," the "culture of the agency," etc., could be seen as spreading a deceptive idea of human creativity yet favouring the actual "State Apparatus": business, police, and so forth. (Marxism has its own, competitive understanding of how human creativity, as a means to mastery over nature, is to be developed.) In *L'État culturel: Essai sur une religion moderne* (Paris: Fallois, 1991), Marc Fumaroli describes a similar technique of control. He documents the "elephantine" growth and spread of the word "culture" in contemporary France and charges that it has become the name of a state religion, permitting "the flattering illusion that administrative and political activity applied to the arts is in itself of artistic and genial quality." The "creative" *dirigisme* of the state in cultural matters reduces culture to client status: it is the extension, the Frankfurt School might say, of administrative reason and celebrates a state apparatus rather than the liberal arts. "Abstract and sterile, the culture of cultural politics is the insinuating mask of power, and the mirror in which it wishes to take pleasure [*jouir*] in itself" (my translation). See ch. 3, "La Culture: Met valise, mot-écran."

28 During the pope's visit to the United States in October 1995, I heard in the media that his speeches aimed at "changing the culture," which now meant the moral culture, worldwide. And consider the following, from Meaghan Morris's *Ecstasy and Economics: American Essays for John Forbes* (Sydney: emPress, 1992): "During the 1980s, the word 'culture' began to be used in a rather peculiar sense. In 1990, a week after the worst company crashes in Australian history had ended a decade of financial mismanagement and 'de-regulated' corporate crime, a grovelling TV current affairs show host asked Rupert Murdoch (back home to shut down a couple of newspapers) what 'we' could do to save 'our' economy. The mighty multinationalist replied, 'Oh you know – change the culture.'… What Murdoch 'meant' was a cliché: a 1980s media commonplace that Australia's biggest problem is the lazy, hedonist, uncompetitive, beach-bound, lotus-eating ethos of the ordinary people" (124). Morris's entire essay "On the Beach" should be of great interest to cultural studies.

29 From the introduction to John Frow and Meaghan Morris, eds., *Australian Culture Studies* (St. Leonards, NSW: Allen and Unwin, 1993). Cf. Morris's *Ecstasy and Economics*, 124ff. A *New Yorker* portrait of Colin Powell, which contrasts him with Jesse Jackson, shows both leaders using the "culture" word in a similar way. Powell, Jackson says, is "flowing with the culture…. He's created a comfort zone among the guardians of the culture." Powell is reported to say that "As a culture, the Airforce …" Jackson, though oppositional, "countercultural" to "the dominant culture," must still express himself in culture terms. See Henry Louis Gates Jr., "Powell and the Black Elite," *New Yorker* 7 (September 25, 1995): 64–80.

30 Murray Krieger, *Arts on the Level: The Fall of the Elite Object* (Knoxville: University of Tennessee Press, 1981).

31 A December 1992 article in the *New York Times* on the popularity of vampire movies is headlined "Blood Culture" (Frank Rich, "The New Blood Culture," *New York Times*, 6 December 1992, sec. 9, 1). This brings together the scientific connotation with the ordinary sense of art-as-culture but also, wittily and ominously, with the claim that, because of AIDS, an entire subculture is being created of people united by their concern with that disease.

32 Donna J. Haraway (London: Free Association Books, 1991).

33 Further signs of the times: I receive a reader's catalog from the University of Chicago Press. It lists the following titles or subtitles: *Cultural Misunderstandings; Cultural Aesthetics; Culture and Anomie; Re- envisioning Past Musical Cultures; Women's Culture, Occultism, Witchcraft, and Cultural Fashions; Symbolic Action and Cultural Studies; The Culture of Politics and the Politics of Culture in American Life; The Cultural Politics of Race and Nation; Science as Practice and Culture; Women, Achievement, and College Culture; Culture Wars.* Or consider this, from a 6 July 1994 *New York Times* op-ed piece on a city kid by Barbara Nevins Taylor: "He didn't bother with his homework and fell behind. The culture of the housing projects and the hormones of adolescence collided with the culture of the school" (21).

34 A theory recently put forward is that we have become a *Kultur-gesellschaft*, the German word demonstrating the symptom that it seeks to describe. It defines "a society in which cultural activity functions increasingly as a socializing agency comparable to and even often against the grain of nation, family profession, state" (quoted in Huyssen, *Twilight Memories*, 31ff).

35 Wole Soyinka, *Myth, Literature and the African World* (Cambridge: Cambridge University Press, 1976), 138–39. Yet "culture" appeals just as strongly to Africanists; it stands for an original cohesion, an organic community, that the colonizers are said to have destroyed. A fuller discussion would begin with Frantz Fanon's "On National Culture" in *Les Damnés de la terre* (Paris: François Maspero, 1961; published in English as *The Wretched of the Earth*, trans. Constance Farrington [London: MacGibbon and Kee, 1965]), which delineates in compelling detail the situation of the "colonized intellectual" who participates in the project of decolonization. Here I wish only to note the abundance of body or embodiment metaphors in Fanon's essay. Commenting, for instance, on the style of the conflicted intellectual who is freeing himself from the colonial culture but has not integrated with ("faire corps, c'est à dire, à changer de corps, avec") European civilization, Fanon writes: "Style nerveux animé de rhythmes, de part en part habité par une vie éruptive.... Ce style, qui a en son temps étonné les occidentaux, n'est point comme on a bien voulu le dire un caractère racial mais traduit avant tout un corps à corps, révèle la nécessité dans laquelle s'est trouvé cet homme de se faire mal, de saigner réellement de sang rouge, de se libérer d'une partie de son être qui déjà renfermait des germes de pourriture. Combat douloureux, rapide où immanquablement le muscle devait se substituer au concept."

36 George Steiner, in Pierre Boutang and George Steiner, *Dialogues: Sur le mythe d'Antigone/ sur le sacrifice d'Abraham* (Paris: Lattès, 1994), 154. My translation.

37 "De la tradition en littérature, et dans quel sens il la faut entendre," *Causeries du Lundi*, vol. 15 (Paris: Gamier Frères, 1857–62). My translation.

38 In "The Crisis of Culture," Hannah Arendt adopts Herbert Marcuse's famous attack on the "affirmative culture" of a bourgeoisie that reduced Schiller's "aesthetic education" to climbing out of the lower regions into "the higher, non-real regions, where beauty and the spirit supposedly were at home." See Arendt, *Between Past and Future* (New York: Viking, 1961), esp. 201–5. See also Herbert Marcuse, "The Affirmative Character of Culture" (1938), in *Negations: Essays in Critical Theory* (Boston: Beacon, 1968).

39 There is a third meaning of "culture" that lies uneasily between the two I have mentioned. Perry Anderson, in a well-known critique of "National Culture" in 1968, draws up a devastating inventory of what culture amounts to in England at that date. He exempts the hard sciences and the arts from this inventory, which – as he admits in a later statement – belies the "national" in his title or confuses culture with what happens in the academy or gets absorbed through that conduit. Yet Anderson did make the point that the British university had become an inertial system in which innovation came largely from Central European refugees and that even these innovations had been only selectively successful, the

criterion of success being whether they could be accommodated to an inertial "English-ness." The inventory meaning of "culture" thus cannot avoid a critical edge: Anderson, like Marcuse, uses non-national cultural achievements to challenge the national status quo, to rouse the national consciousness to equal achievements. Moreover, Anderson's emphasis on *academic* culture as an inertial system promoting "national" values paral-lels the more scientific and elaborated analyses by Pierre Bourdieu, which show how the French educational establishment reduces culture to style rather than substance, to a "relation to culture" that perpetuates the *honnête homme* ideal of the seventeenth century and reproduces a pattern of social distinction paradoxically based on the attempt of the upper class (the "dominant culture") to make its imposed values seem natural or invis-ible ("une certaine culture"). See Perry Anderson, "Components of the National Culture," *New Left Review* 50 (July–August 1968): 3–58; and Pierre Bourdieu, "Literate Tradition and Social Conservation" (written with Jean-Claude Passeron), in *Reproduction in Education, Society and Culture* (London: Sage, 1990; original French ed.: Pierre Bourdieu and Jean-Claude Passeron, *La Reproduction: Eléments pour une théorie du système d'enseignement* [Paris: Minuit, 1970]).

40 For the ramifications of this, see Cassirer, *Logic of the Humanities*, ch. 5, "The 'Tragedy of Culture,'" and cf. Arendt, "Crisis in Culture," where she brings Cicero and Kant together: "The humanist, because he is not a specialist, exerts a faculty of judgment and taste which is beyond the coercion which each specialty imposes upon us" (225).

41 David P. Calleo, *Coleridge and the Idea of the Modem State* (New Haven, CT: Yale Univer-sity Press, 1966), ch. 5, "The Psychological Basis of the State."

42 *Culture and Society: 1780–1950* (London: Chatto and Windus, 1958). Leonard Woolf, continuing his autobiography under the title *Principia Politica: A Study of Communal Psychology* (London: Hogarth, 1953), suggests that politics, by which he means "construct-ing the framework or manipulating time machinery of government or society," became more inevitable and preoccupying during his lifetime. "There is something strange in the fact that so much of [my life] has been occupied, not with living, but with the machin-ery of living. But the strangeness does not end there; it is not limited to my particular experience, for it is part of a general strangeness, a new and fantastic pattern, which has appeared in human life during the last 50 or 100 years. This pattern has been determined by the encroachment of the machinery of life upon living and the art of living" (9–10). The values implied by "culture" seem to offer an antidote to this fact. But Woolf himself, interested in the relation of communal psychology to sociopolitical action, rehabilitates the word "civilization": "What determines whether a society is civilized is its material standard of life, its intellectual and spiritual standards of life, and its contributions to art, science, learning, philosophy, or religion" (53). He refuses to value "culture" (as the fine arts) and its products higher than the other civilized standards.

43 My account is primarily indebted to Erich Auerbach, "La cour et la ville," now in *Scenes from the Drama of European Literature* (Minneapolis: University of Minnesota Press, 1984), 133–82. See also Elias, *The Civilizing Process*, 32: "The *homme civilisé* was nothing other than a somewhat extended version of that human type which represented the true ideal of court society, time *honnête homme*." Hannah Arendt concurs in interesting and sardonic remarks on the origin of "good society": *Between Past and Future*, 199–200. Rémy de Gourmont is characterized as an *encyclopédiste honnête homme* in the introduc-tion to essays translated from his *La Culture des idées*: see *Decadence and Other Essays on the Culture of Ideas* (New York: Harcourt, Brace, 1921).

44 "Solidarity" is the word Raymond Williams uses as a near equivalent of what I call "embodiment": I introduce it deliberately here. See, e.g., *Culture and Society*, 332: "The feeling of solidarity is, although necessary, a primitive feeling."

45 While I cannot accept Arendt's sharp dichotomizing – assigning culture to objects and the world and separating it from entertainment that relates to people and consumable life – she makes a charge that still needs answering: "Culture is being threatened when all worldly objects and things, produced by the present and the past, are treated as mere functions for the life process of society, as though they are there only to fulfill some need" (*Between Past and Future*, 208). Her intuition that cultural objects have a "thingness" and can only be evaluated by their permanence (to which she says life is indifferent), while it saves culture from the philistine or from consumer society generally, points once more to the desire for embodiment, one that is associated with durability rather than reification. What the "function" of this desire may be or that of art objects "which every civilization leaves behind as the quintessence and lasting testimony of the spirit which animated it" (201), is not clarified by her.

46 My translation. My text for Mendelssohn's *Über die Frage: Was heisβt Aufklären?* is taken from Immanuel Kant, *Was ist Aufklärung? Aufsätze zur Geschichte und Philosophie*, ed. Jürgen Zehbe (Göttingen: Vandenhoeck and Ruprecht, 1967), 129–33. Kant's essay also appeared in 1784.

47 There exists an external form of culture he names polish (*Politur*), but it is said to be, ideally, the outer splendor of culture and enlightenment working from within. Whereas speech achieves enlightenment through scientific knowledge, it achieves culture through sociability, poetry, and rhetoric. Together these fashion a well-formed (*gebildete*) language. Mendelssohn translated Rousseau's Second Discourse and perhaps used *Politur* on the analogy of that author's *politesse* – a synonym for *civilisé* – which is not used.

48 See, e.g., Marcel Martinet, *Culture prolétarienne* (Paris: Librairie du Travail, 1935). Martinet complains at the very threshold of his book about the word "culture," "which I am forced to repeat so often [and which] is so displeasing. It is abstract, obscure, pretentious and has a pronounced aftertaste of conformism, self-satisfaction and treachery." But, he goes on, "The question is to learn if this disagreeable word points all the same to a reality, if the working class can renounce the intellectual life and possession of this reality without abandoning itself."

49 For "identity" as a "plastic word," see Lutz Niethammer, "Konjunkturen und Konkurrenzen kollektiver Identität. Ideologie, Infrastruktur und Gedächtnis in der Zeitgeschichte," *PROKLA: Zeitschrift für kritische Sozialwissenschaft* 96 (1994): 377–99.

50 Not only the study of culture but culture itself as a separate and quasi-autonomous sphere is subject to this paradox pointedly expressed by Guy Debord in *La Société du spectacle* (Paris: Bucliet/Chastel, 1967): "La culture est le lieu de la recherche de l'unité perdue. Dans cette recherche de l'unité, la culture comme sphère séparée est obligée de se nier elle-même" (149). See also ch. 1, above.

51 Eliot, *Notes towards the Definition of Culture*, 122.

52 Ibid., 123.

53 *History: Politics or Culture? Reflections on Ranke and Burckhardt* (Princeton: Princeton University Press, 1990), 71.

54 For the concept, see Robert N. Bellah, *The Broken Covenant: American Civil Religion in a Time of Trial* (Chicago: Chicago University Press, 1992).

55 A good historical treatment of the concept of a "republic of letters" is found in Michael Warner, *The Letters of the Republic: Publication and the Public Sphere in Eighteenth-Century America* (Cambridge: Harvard University Press, 1990). For contemporary thought, the strongest development of the idea is Hannah Arendt's notion of "world" as a public sphere in which political action can be freely debated and a communal sense (Kant's *Gemeinsinn*) is made manifest, "a faculty of judgment which, in its reflection, takes account ... of the mode of representation of all others" (*Critique of Judgment*, trans. Werner S. Pluhar [Indianapolis: Hackett, 1987], 294; translation modified). See Kant, *Critique of Judgment*,

paragraph 40. I comment on Arendt's "republic of letters" in "Art and Consensus in the Era of Progressive Politics," *Yale Review* 80 (1992): 50–61. Habermas's magisterial treatise on *Öffentlichkeit* is well known.

56 Cited by Alain Finkielkraut, *La Défaite de la pensée* (Paris: Gallimard, 1987), 61. My translation.

57 Herbert Marcuse, *One-Dimensional Man: Studies in the Ideology of Advanced Industrial Society* (Boston: Beacon, 1964), ch. 3. Cf. Fredric Jameson's *Postmodernism; Or, The Cultural Logic of Late Capitalism* (Durham, NC: Duke University Press, 1991), which expresses Marcuse's complaint in terms of a new and disorienting cultural space that requires our mapping. After noting what he calls the dissolution of an autonomous sphere of culture in the form of an "explosion," that is, a "prodigious expansion of culture throughout the social realm, to the point at which everything in our social life – from economic value and stare power to practices and the very structure of the psyche itself – can be said to have become 'cultural,'" he admits that no leftist theory of cultural politics has been able to do without "a certain minimal aesthetic distance, of the possibility of the positioning of the cultural act outside the massive Being of capital." But he then goes beyond these theories (and beyond Adorno) in asserting that "distance in general (including 'critical distance') has very precisely been abolished in the new space of postmodernism" and that the task of theory is to find out the historical reality of that new global space. Jameson seems to position himself at once as a scientist observing an objective phenomenon and an explorer charting unknown seas of thought – for purposes of *disalienation*, or "the practical reconquest of a sense of place" (47–51).

58 "'The Culture of Everything,'" *New York Review of Books* 34, no. 10 (28 May 1992): 30.

59 Arendt's distinction is already put into play in "Organized Guilt and Universal Responsibility," a discussion of "real political conditions which underlie the charge of collective guilt of the German people," published in 1945. See Hannah Arendt, *Essays in Understanding, 1930–1945*, ed. Jerome Kohn (New York: Harcourt Brace, 1994), especially 128–32.

60 I am referring mainly, of course, to Derrida's essay in *Psyché: Inventions de l'autre* (Paris: Galilée, 1987), translated as "How to Avoid Speaking: Denials," in *Languages of the Unsayable*, ed. Sanford Budik and Wolfgang Iser (New York: Columbia University Press, 1989), 3–69.

61 Lionel Trilling, *Beyond Culture: Essays on Literature and Learning* (New York: Viking, 1965), xv–xvi.

62 Max Horkheimer and Theodor W. Adorno, Preface, *Dialektik der Aufklärung: Philosophische Fragmente* (Amsterdam: Querido, 1947). My translation.

63 Henri Lefebvre, *Le Langage et la société* (Paris: Gallimard, 1966). This question of the "we" has been raised by Jacques Derrida and linked to the issue of "culture" in its identitarian and nonidentitarian aspects. See Jacques Derrida, "The Other Heading: Memories, Responses, and Responsibilities," *PMLA* 108, no. 1 (1993): 89–93. But compare, already, the (more) Hegelian "nous" in the opening line of Jacques Derrida, *Glas* (Paris: Galilée, 1974).

64 Raymond Williams chronicles a similar experience, after the Second World War, in the introduction to *Keywords* (New York: Oxford University Press, 1976), and Paul Fussell suggests over and over again, both in his important *The Great War and Modern Memory* (New York: Oxford University Press, 1976) and *Wartime: Understanding and Behavior in the Second World War* (New York: Oxford University Press, 1989), that the euphemistic and propagandistic use of words left a mark on writers that contributed to the irony of modernism and language skepticism generally.

65 Maurice Blanchot, *L'Écriture du désastre* (Paris: Gallimard, 1980).

In this sharply critical essay, Jacques Barzun bemoans the fact that there is no longer any such thing as "popular" culture and begins to isolate the various symptoms and causes of its disappearance. First among these is the absence in the contemporary cultural sphere of art truly by and of the people. Not even film, argues Barzun, can claim a broad enough viewership to count as genuinely "popular" entertainment, since even its most general themes, rooted as they are in often graphic depictions of sex and violence, fail to address broad segments of the population – children, social and religious conservatives, and others alienated by such depictions – in anything resembling an effectively inclusive way.

It is worth noting insofar as this rather controversial (indeed quite intellectually and aesthetically conservative) point is concerned, that for Barzun "popularity" means the public's recognition of "their life and soul in their art." Art which divides, or otherwise presumes the fragmentation of its audience (into, for example, clusters of individuals possessing, respectively, "highbrow," "lowbrow," or "middlebrow" tastes) and packages itself accordingly, cannot therefore be understood as truly popular. This fragmentation for Barzun mirrors the larger dissolution of the social lifeworld, which accelerated following the birth of modern industrialization in a process mapped cogently by Émile Durkheim and Axel Honneth, among many others. Industrialism, and particularly its technologies, has dynamically enlarged our sense of our own humanity by multiplying the number and rate of our exchanges with others both alike and tremendously different from us, even as it has simultaneously commodified, standardized and reduced (to the lowest common level, claims Barzun) all matters of aesthetic preference, or taste. Far from reflecting a public's "life and soul," then, mass entertainments instead exist solely to mine the resources of carefully cultivated consumers whose self-understanding and sense of belonging – "life" and "soul" on at least one reading of those terms – resists "culture," broadly construed, by remaining to some degree inseparable from the segregated niche markets to which Adorno's "culture industry" confines them.

Note that Barzun echoes Arnold in assuming that, whatever a culture is, it necessarily depends for its existence on its ability to organize around a relatively stable, commonly held and valuable set of core beliefs and feelings, and presumably therefore also some constellation of artworks consistently capable of generating them. The implication here of course is that what matters centrally to those who can, pending some satisfactory definition of the term, adequately be labelled "highbrow" must also matter in the same way to those who are "lowbrow" or "middlebrow" – must, that is, if members of all three groups are to be understood as cohabitants of the same larger culture. This is why education matters so crucially for Barzun. In the same vein as critics of U.S. education like E.D. Hirsch, whose *Cultural Literacy* caused an outcry amongst progressive educators in the late 1980s following Hirsch's insistence that all American students be required to know and understand the same specific set of terms and concepts, Barzun seems to view public education as a process whereby young people come to understand themselves as broadly social beings: mutually intelligible and further linked by a shared and abiding respect for the deeply civic character of American democracy. Thus Barzun's nostalgia for the kind of education capable of giving rise to a Clifton Fadiman, and his contempt for those of the clubby and anti-demotic intellectual establishment (i.e., "highbrows") who condescendingly labelled Fadiman's many cultural achievements insubstantially, liminally, "middlebrow."

THE TENTH MUSE*

JACQUES BARZUN

Who is Demotica, what is she?

She is the muse of popular culture, the tenth muse, the muse who inspires the poems and tales and tunes that express the hearts and minds of the people. Reliable reports say that she has disappeared, and this worries a good many observers. Their concerns point in various directions, but together they confirm the impression that in the modern world there is no popular culture. Listen to some of these complaints. *The New York Times* says that the whole country argues about taste and concludes that "when it comes to enforcing it, it's best to tread lightly, if at all."[1] A book by Thomas S. Hibbs entitled *Shows about Nothing* has the subtitle: "Nihilism in Popular Culture from The Exorcist to Seinfeld." Another, *Crowd Culture*, by Bernard I. Bell, points out that although the culture that offers "escape ... into a dream world of carnality and brutality"[2] is conspicuous, it is far from being acceptable as culture at all. The columnist Leonard Pitts deplores the "insidious" message that gangsta rap sends to the young. "You struggle

* This article originally appeared in *Harper's Magazine* in September 2001. It appears here, unaltered, with the permission of the author and the magazine.

to make [black youth] hear you over the beat of a song"[3] that rewards death by drugs and gunshot, but it is difficult. On a broader plane, Joseph P. Lawrence asks "What Is Culture?" in order to discuss whether popular culture is the contradiction of high culture or its foundation.[4] To decide, one must first make sure which of innumerable things that flourish under the name is *the* popular culture of the times.

The issue is not confined to the United States. In England the director of the Barbican Arts Centre in London sees a dangerous conflict: "Populism versus Elitism in the Arts," which is something new and alarming because of its effect on where the money for art goes. To save themselves, the high arts must engage in "outreach" and "educating" the public. Meanwhile, the warden of Goldsmiths College wonders "Should the Arts Be Popular?" He means, Should the distinction be erased by a merger of styles and genres?

In France the same topic has received attention, but the only extended treatment, in Mona Ozouf's book *La Muse démocratique*, treats the popular with disdain and invokes the works of Henry James as a shield against "the gray, dull, and vulgar world."[5] His novels serve this purpose because they show up and condemn vulgarity while steadfastly upholding the true democratic ideal.

Ozouf's sheer avoidance could be labelled sheer elitism, but it also suggests the absence in the popular genres of those qualities that in the past "elitist" minds enjoyed and respected. If, to return to this country, one goes to the *Journal of Popular Culture*, one is likewise disappointed to find it silent on its declared subject. It deals with such topics as "Fairy Tale Elements in *Jane Eyre*," H.L. Mencken and Methodism, and Sir Thomas Browne's *Pseudodoxia Epidemica*. That Georges Simenon's Maigret novels and Maurice Sendak's books for children are also discussed does not conceal the remoteness of all such considerations from the reality on the streets.

Let us take a quick look at the popular. In music, it includes cowboy and country, rock and rap, and other offshoots of early-twentieth-century ragtime and jazz. These have subdivided endlessly, each with a special name, fine-drawn characteristics, and clannish devotees. In storytelling, the popular ranges from tough crime to pornography; in graphics, from the comic strip to pop art; and in magazines, from the supermarket level to the group-interest form that rises out of body-building and house-keeping to the dizzy literary heights of *The New Yorker* and *The Paris Review*. The television screen features soap operas, legal or other dramatic episodes, and moneyed competitions, while the Internet offers games and pseudo culture – a congeries of pastimes that, with some overlapping, cater to diverse publics. The newspapers record the diversity in review articles by different experts.

Can it be said that any of these entertainments expresses the hearts and minds of the people? Some think that rap lyrics echo a prevailing disgust with life and society at the end of an era. Sentimental balladry under various names depicts the world that simple souls desire but nobody believes in. And even these two extremes of feeling might qualify as popular culture if they sounded more spontaneous, less like standardized products modified only to compete within an industry.

Clearly, in the modern demotic society there is no art of and by the people. True, the many new immigrant groups in Western nations cling to their folk songs and dances, but one cannot expect original departures or any spread of innovations from one ethnic enclave to another.

That a popular culture can express the people as a whole is not a fanciful idea; it has been done. The Athenian population, brought up on Homer, flocked to the Greek drama. The illiterate medievals listened to the tale of Beowulf (recently resuscitated by an Irish poet), to the *Nibelungenlied*, to the stories of Tristan and Parsifal and the Nordic sagas, while they could also "read" the Bible in the stained glass and sculpture of their churches. Next, the Renaissance created the superb Spanish ballads that inspired Spanish poets down to Lorca, the English and Scottish border ballads, and a vast collection of folk songs and tales. It developed the modern form of the play, and a mixed crowd filled Shakespeare's Globe Theatre. Rabelais and Cervantes wrote bestsellers. The age cultivated domestic music and made abundant use in church and at home of the new art of painting in perspective. From far back, then, popularity meant the people's recognition of their life and soul in their art.

But have I not omitted the modern equivalent, the movies? I kept them out of the list with the thought that they might prove the one genre of ecumenical appeal. Hollywood films reach all parts of the country, indeed travel to the ends of the earth, and thus seem to express all humankind. But that is an illusion. A large part of the output expresses chiefly the "carnality and brutality" that many object to; the ratings system to protect the young makes it plain that "the people" do not see their hopes and fears mirrored on the screen. A segment of the public avoids the lust and mayhem and looks for the sophisticated work of the artist-producer, native or foreign. Since, we are told, a commercial film must aim at the mind of the thirteen-year-old, the failure to produce films for adults endowed with common sense about what matters to them is *anti*-populism. They patronize the movies and tolerate, often with disgust, the routine offering, but they are in fact undernourished by it, and their best selves remain unexpressed.

What takes some explaining is why the ordinary people of Athens could appreciate Sophocles' *Antigone*, medieval peasants the tale of Tannhäuser, and sixteenth-century Londoners the pointedly named *As You Like It*, when these works and their like are now deemed too difficult to appeal to the common taste. The cause is not the language alone, which can be glossed or modernized. It is the lack of certain mental and emotional habits. Not only has a verbal and oral tradition been broken but a mental power has been lost: the capacity, developed from infancy by myths and other domestic lore, to enjoy things that are beyond the fully understood. In Athens not everybody could gauge the sublime in the tragedies, but all found something to be moved by and to remember. This possessive curiosity seems nowadays in abeyance. Culture, in the sense of all things of the mind, has been split, first in half, and then the lower half into bits and pieces at once obvious and obsessive.

The first writer to deal seriously with this division used the then recently coined terms "lowbrow" and "highbrow." In *America's Coming-of-Age*, published in 1915, the critic of New England literature Van Wyck Brooks ascribed the split to the Puritan dogma that the Deity directs with equal concern the moral and the practical successes of mankind. This belief, according to Brooks, gives equal value to cultural effort and to selfish opportunism – the low cunning of business, the identification of worth with money. Shrinking back from this materialism, said Brooks, the first American geniuses in art and thought – Emerson and his peers – made culture "fastidious, refined, and aloof." Hence the division into high and low.

The fact is clear but the explanation hard to accept. No Puritan tradition swayed continental Europe, yet the same separation came about there. Nor can one see how the Almighty could do other than oversee all the doings of humanity, moral and material. Brooks's view was but one form of the anti-bourgeois, anti-Puritan animus current early in the century.

A more tenable origin of the unequal brows is the physical uprooting that occurred in late-eighteenth-century society – first, of those who came to people this country and who faced the task of building it from the ground up. This effort and its continual westward movement interfered with the handing down of old traditions, which did not fit the immigrants' new experience. The generations born here intermarried, wanted to be Americans, and spoke English, not the language of their folktales. For a popular culture to thrive, it must be part of a continuous fabric of ideas and feelings from low to high, each level inspiring and borrowing from the next. The continuity enables the uneducated to find ports of entry into high art and encourages the geniuses to make use of popular creations in their masterpieces.

A different uprooting "brainwashed" the Europeans who stayed home. Its cause: the Industrial Revolution and the cities it produced. Factory and slum put an end to the rural pleasures of the people. The tumult of the city, of many cities with shifting populations, destroyed reflection in idle hours and bred barbarians. It is significant that jazz, the one wholly American form of music, came out of a segregated group in New Orleans, a town free of industry. Later, it was again the South that produced poets and novelists who for their materials and outlook drew on the rustic past and called themselves Agrarians. The rest of the country responded to the insights of varying depth embodied in the world of Faulkner or in *Gone with the Wind.*

If the question were put abruptly, Does the machine lower the mind? one would have to answer yes and no. In direct contact, it stretches the senses, sharpens the wits, and by multiplying human relations it has a civilizing effect that we call sophistication. But a contrary effect accompanies the broadened outlook. The machine's multiplying power turns out goods in huge quantities and demands masses of consumers. To please them all, products must satisfy the most elementary taste – or so those who make them believe, rightly or wrongly. The net result is the lowering required: when a television show pleases 12 million viewers, one that pleases only 6 million is a failure. It brings the curtain down, and the upshot: 6 million deprived and their taste debased. The tinny flavour of mass-produced entertainment is the outcome of this numerical compulsion.

For a true culture to arise and survive, a common core of ideas and feelings must exist. The gifted among the people then produce works that on their merits turn out to please beyond the immediate audience. Hence the quality of past popular culture: the ballad of Chevy Chase shows a finer sense of words and rhythm than gangsta rap, and its pathos trains the emotions to a finer sensibility.

Seeing the political danger from industrial barbarism, thinkers and lawgivers in the mid-nineteenth century decreed free education for all – to create political responsibility and also to extend economic opportunity. In this effort the United States took the lead. It established primary schools that assimilated the great tide of immigrants, and, what is most remarkable, by 1900 the American free public high school, compulsory for all, was providing a secondary education that embraced the cultural heritage. As late as the 1920s and '30s, a high school senior had had three years of Latin and was parsing Virgil, had read some Dickens, Scott, Hawthorne, and George Eliot, and was being taken through Milton's shorter poems by a teacher who knew how to make them clear and moving. In the Oak Park High School that Ernest Hemingway attended, there was a Latin Club with a room specially assigned to it, where the students talked to one another in Latin.

I cite this as indicative of the lengths to which it was once possible to go. So cruel a discipline today would cause an outcry, and it is not needed for a popular culture. But something like it is called for. The early and mid-twentieth century devised various means to supply it. Night schools for adults, and the Carnegie and other educational foundations, special periodicals, book clubs, libraries, innumerable series of classics in cheap but good hardcover editions – these, together with the new nationwide radio, seconded the work of the high school. As for the colleges and universities, they uniformly maintained a curriculum with liberal-arts requirements. The academic and intellectual elites were bent on giving everybody a chance to reconnect with the heritage.

Among the persons engaged in this crusade, the great hero was the late Clifton Fadiman. Every aspect of his career and achievement illustrates the vicissitudes of the endeavour first proposed by Matthew Arnold under the heading *Culture and Anarchy*. Arnold's aim was to civilize the philistines and barbarians of England by making "the best that has been thought and known in the world current everywhere," affording not only enjoyment but also an upward mobility in taste.

Fadiman's dedication to this task was not an inspiration of youth but a mature second choice. As a senior at Columbia College in 1925, Clifton ("Kip" to his classmates) was the acknowledged intellectual leader of his class, the model scholar and writer. Every issue of the literary magazine *Morningside* contained one or more of his poems – often a sonnet – or an essay, a fragment of philosophy translated from the French, or an imaginary scene between figures in a tragedy by Sophocles. The poetry was Georgian in style and sometimes down to earth like Edgar Lee Masters' narratives. Nobody could doubt that Fadiman would soon become a name in contemporary letters. The expectation was confirmed when the Modern Library commissioned him to translate and introduce a volume of works by Nietzsche.

With an academic record that matched this extracurricular performance, he had good reason to expect what he most desired: an academic career. His college instructors had encouraged this ambition, notably John Erskine, then famed as a scholar and novelist and the father of the Great Books program. But when in graduate school Fadiman was interviewed by the head of the English department, he was told with blunt kindness that he could not hope for a post at Columbia: he was Jewish. This exclusionary custom was not limited to that department. All but two or three observed a tacit rule that was broken only in the late thirties when President Nicholas Murray Butler forced the tenure appointment of Lionel Trilling.

Facing a blank wall, Fadiman turned to literary journalism. He became a reviewer for *The Nation*, like Mark Van Doren, who, though newly made assistant professor, was a little suspect as a scholar because of this venture into the marketplace. Fadiman reviewed books for *The Nation* for seven years, and so acutely and attractively that *The New Yorker* recruited him as its chief critic. He occupied the post for a decade before Edmund Wilson. Concurrently, Fadiman was acting as reader – and soon as editor in chief – for Simon & Schuster, thus serving literature like George Meredith and T.S. Eliot while contributing to it.

As a seasoned judge of books, Fadiman was next taken on by the Book-of-the-Month Club. Its mission was to distribute new books of high merit to a wider public than was reached by the antique methods of trade publishers. The new club meant to offer more solid works than those supplied by the Literary Guild. It is at this point – the year was 1944 – that Clifton Fadiman began to be condescended to by academics and the literati. He was deemed to have gone down one level in the cultural hierarchy measured by height of brow.

This notion of brow levels requires explanation. Paradoxically, it was ushered in by the success of free public schooling. Enlarged literacy fostered the mass newspaper. Artists and intellectuals were appalled at its tone and contents and united to condemn the type of mind it created, again by lowest appeal. Baudelaire called it Satanic. Contempt followed hatred until a radical difference in human minds was accepted as a fact of nature; the code words "lowbrow" and "highbrow" have been traced as far back as 1906. One's choices in books and pictures, hobbies and employment, showed to which division of mankind one belonged. Anything popular meant low; popular culture was deemed a contradiction in terms. As time went on, the distance between the poles kept increasing until art and "journalism" were worlds apart.

The caste system held in spite of disputes about particulars (Dickens was a great genius – No! he was "a writer for chamber maids," etc.). Arguing about such double-tongued classics suggested that perhaps the chasm between the high and the low was inhabited; a large contingent thrived there unabashed: the middle brow. The astute observer Russell Lynes mapped the three zones of mind in an entertaining essay published in *Harper's Magazine* in 1949. By Lynes's reckoning, Clifton Fadiman, the respected critic and once certified highbrow, was déclassé. While he pursued his chosen task, a writer for *Partisan Review*, whose name is now obscure and who has left no work of any moment, wrote an essay entitled "Masscult and Midcult" and branded Fadiman "the standard bearer of middle-brow culture."

The inferior status assigned to Fadiman in mid-career sank even further when he became the host of *Information, Please*. This was a radio quiz program of the simple kind, without money prizes, which sparked a conversation among half a dozen notables who indulged in witty digressions. Like the later *Conversation*, which discussed current books and in which Fadiman also took part, this program entertained, obscuring the fact that it was manned by highbrows and widely enjoyed by that same breed. But popularity was the fatal stain.

Popularity, though, is a relative term. A little after *Information, Please* came *Invitation to Learning*, of which I was the moderator for two years. It brought together knowledgeable people as different from one another as Rex Stout and Bertrand Russell, who debated the message of a work by Tocqueville or Walt Whitman or some other classic author. The program was protected by William Paley, head of CBS, who kept it alive in spite of its reaching only 2 million listeners when "success" called for 10.

These not-at-all-learned broadcasts somehow escaped censure by the friends of intellectual purity, but other, comparable ventures aimed at large audiences were finally outlawed, at least in words. When, for example, Time-Life Records in the 1960s offered a series of LP albums anthologizing Western music since the sixteenth century accompanied by well-written commentary (which I was given the task of editing), various academics condemned the set because all the discs were from one company and thus not the best recorded performance of each work – as if these carpers would ever have agreed on the best.

The highbrow guardians failed to understand how the things they cherished depend on stirrings down below. A chance encounter with a novel, a symphony, a painting, will impel a young mind to go on – and up. Highbrows are self-made, and even before reaching that glorious state, one possessed by cultural passion may produce original work. The creative geniuses are not invariably cultivated minds. But they must at some point have felt the power of the real thing, no matter how simple. All Burns and Lorca needed were the popular ballads of their country. Others, more fully self-educated, become the appreciative listeners they need.

Here again, Clifton Fadiman's odyssey is relevant. He was the son of unpretentious people who lived modestly – at times precariously – in Brooklyn. Both Kip and his older brother, Edwin, early showed a lust for learning that the local Boys' High School nourished by the kind of curriculum described above. Edwin, the first to attend Columbia College, did well there and shared what he acquired. He would "assign" his course readings to Kip, so that when the younger brother entered the college as a freshman aged sixteen he already had a command of English and American literature and a reading knowledge of French and German. No wonder that when I met him two years later, he impressed me and others of us as the bearer of all Western culture since the Greeks.

Being so young, he often felt scared (as he later confided), but most of the time he was buoyant, full of humour, fond of puns – anything but pedantic or solemnly learned, though he could be impatient and abrupt with the slow-witted when they were stubborn. He rejoiced in how vast the universe of learning was; he read with the speed of light and retained all that he ever set eyes on or heard. Such is the typical tale in the social history of civilization. The makers and carriers of art and thought come from nowhere in particular; they are suddenly there. No social class, no "method," turns them out like marketable goods; but a fund of culture, plain or subtle, simple or complex, must exist, alive in human beings, to attract and impel other individuals.

While Fadiman was giving some of his time to radio programs, he was also pursuing his Arnoldian mission, writing essays about books and ideas that now fill half a dozen volumes. His introductions to classic and contemporary works number nearly fifty, some of which, like the one to *Pickwick Papers*, are small masterpieces. The anthologies he compiled number fifteen and range from the stories of O. Henry to those of Henry James. One other, *An American Treasury*, which brings together utterances of every kind about America from colonial times to the present, is a highly original sourcebook. Fadiman also kept the very young in mind. He selected a dozen or more readings with comments for the use of children, his expertise confirmed by his masterly monograph on the history of children's literature in the fourteenth edition of the *Encyclopaedia Britannica*. And for readers with a mathematical turn of mind, he gathered two collections of articles, short stories, and poems that display the curiosities of numbers.

What is sad to look back on is that Kip adopted for himself the judgment passed on him by the highbrows. It was not explicit but atmospheric. In conversation with close friends, literary or academic, who esteemed him highly, his one irritating trait was the recurrent depreciation of his work and his mind: "Of course I am not quali-fied like you to speak on the subject," or, "I am only a rank amateur in these things," when in fact he knew more on the topic than any of his listeners. He was not ashamed but thought that he ought to be. It is not far-fetched to say that feeling obliged to disavow *height* is now a national habit. For example, *Time* magazine assures us that "high style isn't highbrow. In fact, it's everywhere, for everyone, in everything from can openers to CD racks to cars" (March 20, 2000). In vain did Arnold point out that "the social idea and the men of culture are the true apostles of equality."

The printed word did not monopolize Fadiman's multiform ener-gies. He lectured on humanistic topics at colleges and universities, was roving reporter for the Metropolitan Opera and intermission speaker for the Boston Symphony. As consultant on the humanities for the Ford Foundation's Fund for the Advancement of Education and a trustee of the Council for Basic Education, Fadiman contributed to the "Back to Basics" reform of the schools. Robert Maynard Hutchins, when presi-dent of the University of Chicago, recognized the calibre and experi-ence of the man when he appointed him to the editorial board of the *Encyclopaedia Britannica*. Fadiman served it as writer and editor for twenty years. His devotion to the life of the mind persisted until his death at ninety-five. Although blind toward the end, he continued to "read" by audiotape six books a month for the Book-of-the-Month Club, while he co-edited a massive anthology of world poetry in Eng-lish translation.

It is clear that if the hundredth part of this noble work had been done from some campus or other, Clifton Fadiman would have been regarded as a scholar and a teacher of the highest attainable brow. Put together, his lectures amounted to courses and his essays to scholarly criticism. The labour of it all was not entirely overlooked. He received several prizes, culminating in the 1993 National Book Award for Distinguished Contribution to American Letters. His obituaries were full of respect, but their tenor was that of one of the headlines: "An Erudite Guide to the Wisdom of Others." The judgment not only ignores the wisdom needed for unerring guidance; it perpetuates a false view of culture and how it is kept alive.

Right now, working to that end is out of the question. Those who still think that *something* ought to be imparted to the next generation are struggling to rescue the public schools. It is a national goal, a presidential priority, but achieving it is hindered by many things, of which one is the absence of a popular culture. For such a culture by definition lives both in the world and in the home, where it provides the young with a springboard into what is taught in school. Today, all agree that for a majority of children the gap between the domestic and the school mind is unbridgeable.

If the efforts to restore the effectiveness of the public school succeed, the battle will then be joined with the ruling caste in higher education, which is busy destroying the heritage of the Western world by teaching the young to find ugly motives behind its creation.

Meantime, a miscellaneous public rejoices in the thought that the Internet "puts the whole world of knowledge at your fingertips." A fair number of fingertips itch for that wealth and are gratified with information at low cost, even with misinformation. But the lust for knowing creates less demand in the digital bazaar than games and porn, while the available "art shows" arouse less envy than the noted dilettante's collection of bottle tops from 159 countries. In any case, "the world of knowledge" is not something in a warehouse. Knowledge lives by being known, not stored. Like religion, like a popular culture, it is a possession held in common as widely as possible. No layer of culture exists on that scale today and nobody is preaching a revival of the mid-century crusade. As things stand, this is as it should be: first things first. We shall be fortunate if all the earnest agitation brings back to the people a common possession of the three Rs.

Notes

1 Virginia Postrel, "When It Comes to Enforcing Taste, It's Best to Tread Lightly," *New York Times*, July 13, 2000.

2 Bernard Iddings Bell and Cicero Bruce, *Crowd Culture: An Examination of the American Way of Life*, 4th ed. (Wilmington, DE: ISI Books, 2001).

3 Leonard Pitts, "Gangsta Rap Represents Destruction," *Milwaukee Journal Sentinel*, November 11, 1999.

4 Joseph P. Lawrence, "What Is Culture?" *Future: The Hoechst Magazine* 1 (1997): 10–17.

5 Mona Ozouf, *La Muse démocratique: Henry James ou les pouvoirs du roman* (Paris: Calmann-Lévy, 1998).

4 In a paper directly related to concerns voiced in a number of contributions to this anthology, Mette Hjort considers culture in the context of an analysis of the effects on educa-tion of multiculturalism and multiculturalist theory. Hjort is particularly concerned with the university's emergence over the last two decades as one of the main battlegrounds in the American Culture Wars, whose disputes cluster around multiculturalist challenges to what is perceived as the homogeneity of American culture, its refusal to celebrate and respect the beliefs, desires, needs, and priorities of members of minority groups. This complex set of problems, discussed more broadly by Christoph Brumann in terms of unity and diversity and by Hart-man in terms of universalism and particularism, is neatly summarized by E.D. Hirsch in his *Cultural Literacy*, a text Hjort strongly, perhaps too strongly, criticizes. For Hirsch the multicultural problematic reduces to an interpretive dispute metaphorically centring on the Latin motto proposed for the first Great Seal of the United States and now found on American coins: E Pluri-bus Unum ("Out of Many, One"). What multiculturalists and their opponents contest, Hirsch suggests, is how best, in the interest of justice, to reconcile the "many" with the "one."

Unfortunately, the university's ability to oversee a negotiated settlement of this dispute is significantly undermined by its own deep implication in the conflict, a situation no doubt arising from the university's manifestly cultural character, its dual role as culture's conservator (via canonization and the production of "distinction") and critic (especially within such sub-disciplinary formations as Globalization and Cultural Studies, Women's Stud-ies, Labour Studies, Queer Studies, and Black Studies). While Imre Szeman argues that globalization renders this institutional duality ruinous, particu-larly for the humanities, and so recommends abandoning conservation for more vigorous modes of criticism, Hjort demurs. On her more optimistic view, it is possible to find in contemporary multiculturalist criticism, as well as in the kinds of conflicts for and to which it speaks, a calculated neglect of what disputants share, indeed what they must share in order even to have their disagreements register with one another as such. She argues that by clarifying the university's role in the modern state, as well as the state's rela-tionship to "culture" (and to the various conflicting demands made in its name), it becomes possible to reimagine the university as a space within which consensus is possible at the same time that "difference" is taken seriously.

Understanding the university as an institution capable of this degree of subtle attentiveness, however, requires us to qualify but not reject the dependence of modern democratic societies on the existence of the sort of "common culture" whose deterioration Jacques Barzun bemoans earlier in this collection. Drawing on Ernest Gellner's work on nationalism, Hjort contradicts those like Stanley Fish who see nothing but differences "all the way down" society, and defends the necessity of the state's investment in a common culture shaped partly by a centralized system of education. Note that Hjort's defence of this common culture and the university's place within it is, like Brumann's defence of the culture concept, pragmatic. Industrial societies, she believes, depend for their long-term economic prosperity on people possessing the sort of general competence necessary for them to adapt quickly to all manner of changes in circumstance (new technologies, natural disasters, wars, revolutions, and so on), and for their democratic political vitality on what Habermas terms their "shared political culture." But, Hjort points out, the necessity of sharing a "political culture" by no means requires the sharing of a single cultural tradition. Accordingly, it becomes possible to see how we might come to treat multiculturalists' demands for diversification seriously without at the same time undermining what it remains important for us to hold, and to recognize as held, in common.

BETWEEN CONFLICT AND
CONSENSUS: REDUX*

METTE HJORT

An earlier version of this paper[1] was written in 1994 in response to an invitation from the Mcgill sociologist and now Dean of Arts, John Hall, who was responsible for organizing a mini-conference designed to mark the installation of the then new Principal and Vice-Chancellor of Mcgill, Bernard Shapiro. Entitled "An Ideal in Danger? Liberal Education at the End of the Millennium," the Faculty of Arts conference aimed to celebrate the principal's installation through vigorous intellectual debate rather than somewhat vacuous ceremonialism. Much has happened since 1994, or since 1999, for that matter, when this essay was first published in the electronic journal Æ. Were I to develop the piece today, I would wish, for example, to engage with the realist approach to cultural identity that has been so fruitfully developed by Satya P. Mohanty and Paula M.L. Moya, as well as with Smaro Kamboureli's work on Canadian multiculturalism.[2] Thinking about publicity and counter-publicity has evolved considerably, especially

* An earlier version of this essay was published electronically in 1999 in Æ: The Canadian Aesthetics Journal with the title "Between Conflict and Consensus: Multiculturalism and the Liberal Arts." It has been revised by the author and updated for inclusion in this collection.

as a result of Michael Warner's masterful recent book on the topic.[3] It would also, no doubt, be relevant to consider various types of globalization and some of the Jihads or ethnic nationalisms that they provoke. The argument is, however, reprinted below as it was first developed, my view being that its main points still speak to issues that warrant serious attention. Multiculturalism may at this point be a largely accepted ideal in Canada, but it is by no means an ideal beyond danger in other parts of the world. In my native Denmark, for example, the ethnic nationalist Danish People's Party played a key role in the election campaign that brought Anders Fogh Rasmussen's rightist party, Venstre, to power in 2001. This campaign focused on one issue and one issue only: the threat of multiculturalism as a corrosive force capable of undermining the cultural identity of people belonging to the Danish ethnie. The strategies and rhetoric deployed in this 2001 election were such that Amnesty International and other human rights organizations felt compelled to publish critical commentaries and warnings, warnings that have been reiterated in more recent times in connection with the coalition government's immigration laws, which are widely viewed as xenophobic and, more important, as basically at odds with the European Charter of Human Rights. In contemporary Denmark the displacements and transnational communicative networks effected by various globalizations ultimately amount to a multicultural reality that is believed by many to destroy a preferred common culture based on deep ancestral belonging.

The aim in "Between Conflict and Consensus" was not merely to defend a concept of multiculturalism, but to argue for a type of multicultural practice that eschews self-interested strategic action in favour of other modes of rationality. Indeed, the point was to show that the university has a particularly important role to play in fostering alternatives to strategic reasoning. On this score too the issues raised in "Between Conflict and Consensus" seem urgent, rather than settled or no longer relevant. When Bill Readings first started presenting what would become *The University in Ruins* in 1996, there were those who found his account of the corporate university, with its rhetoric of excellence, accountability, league tables, and performance indicators, somewhat hyperbolic, even paranoid. Yet, the corporatization of university life is now a fact in many parts of the world, and most certainly in Hong Kong, where I have lived and worked for the past five years. In the Hong Kong university context that is associated with prestige and regional pre-eminence in the minds of its members, the corporate model of the university clearly gives pride of place to zero-sum rationality and the kind of divisive and narrowly self-interested strategic reasoning that corrodes the social bond and destabilizes a community in the long run, to the point where energy is channelled mostly toward the second-order task of crisis management at all levels, rather than the primary goals of teaching and research. And while there are vibrant counterforces to the corporate model (most notably at the Liberal Arts university, Lingnan, where political activism oriented toward community building both locally and transnationally figures centrally in the self-understandings of many researchers, teachers, and students), there can be little doubt that the threat involved in conceiving universities on a business model is serious, and not only in Hong Kong. More than ever before, perhaps, there is a case to be made for the university as a site devoted to fair-minded debates about differences and commonalities that genuinely matter, as a site resistant to the temptations of lucre and power, at least normatively if not always in reality. The problems to which "Between Conflict and Consensus" proposed the beginnings of a solution in 1994 are, if anything, more acute more than a decade later. The geography may be different as ethnic nationalism, the war about culture, and the idea of culture as war find new and more fertile terrain, but many of the issues are, sadly enough, essentially unchanged.

. . . . .

If the titles of some recent books and articles are any indication, culture has become a matter of warfare.[4] "Culture wars" is by now a prevalent expression used in critiques of attempts to reform university curricula along multicultural lines. The culture wars are about culture, as much of the hostility being expressed is fuelled by a deep commitment to a certain conception of culture, as well as to a view of the scholar as responsible for preserving and transmitting a national heritage. Yet "culture wars" does not simply refer to ongoing disputes between proponents of rival conceptions of culture, for it polemically identifies a particular view of culture as war. Examples of this conception of culture abound in scholarly and popular writings alike. I am thinking, for instance, of a work by the journalist Kenneth McGoogan, which comprises a series of commentaries on cultural events of political relevance to Canada. Reflecting on his career as a book review editor and literary columnist, McGoogan reaches the following conclusion:

I [...] discovered that for 10 years, without realizing it, I'd been covering an undeclared war. That war is raging in the minds and hearts of Canadians and on many fronts: French-English, Canadian-American, native-white, East-West. The theatre of operations includes the whole world of books.[5]

What is described here is a view of culture, not as the expression of shared values and meanings, but as a site of strategic calculations motivated by various forms of more or less narrow self-interest. Referring indirectly to Clausewitz's famous dictum, Henry Louis Gates Jr. accurately identifies the extent to which the work of intellectuals is identified with war in certain contexts: "These days, literary criticism likes to think of itself as 'war by other means.'"[6]

It seems to me that many of the debates over the relative merits of a traditional as opposed to multicultural education hinge on attitudes concerning the place of consensus or conflict within our pedagogical imaginaries. In the course of my discussion I would like to suggest that there may well be a tendency within multiculturalist thinking to focus excessively on the virtues of conflict and irreducible difference at the expense of other possibilities. It is important, then, to try to articulate at least some of the ways in which multiculturalism within the academy relies on, and helps to create, forms of sharing that are largely overlooked in discourses rejecting dubious notions of consensus.

I should admit from the outset that I am by no means a neutral observer of the "culture wars," for I believe that multiculturalism is an ideal worth defending and that many of the changes currently being envisaged and implemented in fact are positive developments. I would like to begin, then, by identifying what I take to be some of the central tenets of multiculturalist discourses. At the same time I hope to inflect these discourses in a comparativist, transnational direction.

"Multiculturalism," it should be noted, can mean many things. For example, "multiculturalism," as it is used in the *Canadian Multiculturalism Act*, has a more restricted sense than participants in the "culture wars" would wish to allow. This Act takes as its premise the "diversity of Canadians as regards race, national or ethnic origin, colour and religion" (C-18.7), and goes on officially to acknowledge that Canadian citizens have the right to "preserve, enhance and share their cultural heritage" (C-18.7.3). The document recognizes the extent to which exercising the right in question involves government intervention, for it enjoins the relevant minister to undertake a number of measures. More specifically the minister is to "assist individuals, organizations and institutions to project the multicultural reality of Canada." He or she is "to assist the business community, labour organizations, voluntary and other private organizations, as well as public institutions, in ensuring full participation in Canadian society, [...] of individuals of all origins." The minister is also expected to "facilitate the acquisition, retention, and use of all languages that contribute to the multicultural heritage of Canada" (C-18.7.5). This Act focuses on respecting the dignity of Canadians by recognizing the value of diverse forms of cultural expression linked to ethnicity and religion. To move from the context of Canadian policy documents to that of writing in an academic vein is, as we shall see, to witness a shift in emphasis: the concept of ethnicity is retained, but is joined by others, such as class, gender, and sexual orientation. Religion, on the other hand, recedes into the background.

By the admission of both its proponents and its critics, multiculturalism in its utopian incarnation finds its origins in the civil rights movements of the 1960s. Multiculturalism has been understood as a form of identity politics rooted in the experiences of gays, blacks, women, and other marginalized groups. Indeed, multiculturalist discourses have been largely structured, perhaps excessively so, by concepts of victimization, race, class, gender, and sexual orientation. Although it is important to acknowledge multiculturalism's debt to the sixties, it is equally important to grasp the ways in which multiculturalist thinking is shaped by moral sources that pertain, not only to oppressed groups and visible minorities, but to modernity itself.

Charles Taylor argues persuasively that identity politics is motivated by a deep human need for recognition, just as it is informed by an understanding of the injurious effects of various forms of misrecognition. And recognition, claims Taylor, only becomes an issue with the transition from the pre-modern to the modern period, for in contexts where identities are "socially derived," fixed, and stable, recognition is largely automatic. When hierarchies of being collapse, allowing for an "inwardly" generated identity, the conditions arise "in which the attempt to be recognized can fail."[7] On this view, then, the problematic nature of recognition flows directly from aspects of modernity.

The strength of Taylor's analysis stems partly from his convincing account of how multiculturalism or identity politics combines elements from two strands of modern thought. A discourse of authenticity, traceable to the Romantics, supports the idea that it is the value of an inwardly generated, authentic self that must be acknowledged. If we owe the idea of authenticity to the Romantics, we are indebted to Enlightenment thinkers, such as Kant, for our modern notions of equality and dignity. These are the notions informing discourses of human rights, which are bent on an equalization of rights and entitlements. When these two strands of thought combine, as they do in a politics of recognition, an agent is assumed to have a basic human right to demand that his or her particular mode of authentic self-expression be recognized as having the same value as other forms of self-expression. The criterion of universalizability governing a politics of equal rights is thus held also to pertain to the area of authentic self-expression.

Taylor argues that the demand for recognition, as it is currently articulated by certain proponents of multiculturalism, is deeply problematic. Their claim, more specifically, is not simply that room must be made for various forms of self-expression, but that these different kinds of identity formation must be recognized in advance and in principle as having equal value or worth. It is in caricatural versions of this claim that the likes of Dinesh D'Souza find their ammunition, and one of his books is in many ways a litany of complaints directed against the idea that race alone provides a sufficient justification for teaching certain works by African-Americans.[8] Agents, claims Taylor, cannot as a right demand that all cultural expressions be recognized as having equal value. What they can reasonably demand is a stance that expresses a "presumption" of "value."[9] Whether different modes of self-expression are to be considered equally valuable is to be determined, not in advance, but through a process involving dialogue, the elaboration of shared vocabularies, and careful analysis. Although this part of Taylor's account is left undeveloped and thus remains vulnerable to rejoinders emphasizing the asymmetrical nature of any communicative exchange, his suggestions do help to bring into focus some of the goals of a multicultural education.

A useful distinction has been made by members of the Chicago Cultural Studies Group between "critical" multiculturalism and "corporate" multiculturalism.[10] And insofar as corporate multiculturalism tends to be viewed as a travesty of multiculturalist ideals, a consideration of its defining features helps to clarify the central tenets of the "critical" multiculturalism that is rightly associated with the academy and certain counterpublics.[11] In brief, corporate multiculturalism is motivated, not by notions of dignity or worth, but by a set of economic concerns. A certain form of multicultural literacy – the ability to speak a foreign tongue and to grasp the self-understandings of members of certain groups – may be sought for purely self-interested reasons. Insofar as the world of commercial exchange is governed by largely strategic calculations, its inherent tendency is to uphold patterns of domination, exploitation, and control.

Corporate multiculturalism does not, then, in any direct way further the project of what Taylor calls "a reciprocal recognition among equals."[12] A rejection of corporate multiculturalism on ideological grounds highlights the place of critical multiculturalism within an emancipatory, utopian project that seeks to redress various forms of victimization. What is more, the critique of corporate multiculturalism calls attention to the ways in which university curricula may be revised to include greater coverage of foreign cultures and languages without becoming any more multicultural in the desired sense of the term.

The distinction between corporate and critical multiculturalism does not rest on some naive assumption that modern societies can or should dispense with corporations. The aim, rather, is to ensure that curricular reform goes further than narrow self-interest requires. At the same time, however, members of the Chicago Cultural Studies

Group fail to consider the idea that intercultural understanding based on dignity and equality might benefit indirectly from the workings of corporate multiculturalism. Curricular changes motivated by a desire to prepare students to trade more effectively with citizens of countries situated on the Pacific Rim may not in themselves be sufficient, but they do have a legitimate place within a more general program of multicultural reform.

One feature of multicultural literacy is an ability to approach other cultures, be they subcultures, minority cultures, or foreign national cultures, with a presumption of worth. In an important article, Greg Urban argues that "a crucial aspect of culture is not only that it can be learned, but also that it can be unlearned."[13] To assume that a multicultural education is simply a matter of learning about marginal cultures is to overlook the ways in which processes of "unlearning" help to create the conditions of intercultural understanding. By allowing the prejudices of certain cultural contexts to be subjected to rational scrutiny, a multicultural education helps to remove some of the obstacles to symmetrical intercultural communication. A multicultural education brings about alienation in the Brechtian sense, for it underscores the conventional and largely arbitrary nature of what once seemed inevitable and wholly natural. A multicultural education is just as much about taking a certain distance from ourselves as it is about an enhanced understanding of others.

Critical multiculturalism, I have been suggesting, is intensely attuned to certain forms of exclusion and victimization and seeks to redress various injustices by making room for marginal voices and cultures. Yet, as Ben Lee and others have argued, multiculturalism remains largely a North American discourse to some extent blinded by its own cultural specificities. And the absence of a properly comparative and international perspective generates an inability fully to grasp the complexities of minority culture, which are not necessarily or invariably linked to violent forms of victimization.

North American multiculturalist discourses focus intensely on the value of culture produced by groups lacking economic and political power, and the demand for recognition is thus explicitly linked to a project of political empowerment. Interestingly, this focus on the link between cultural and political power makes it difficult for North American discourses to grasp the need for a politics of recognition in contexts where economic and political power are distributed more equitably among citizens. More specifically, there is a failure to understand the way in which problems of inclusion and exclusion are reconfigured at the international level.

The monologic nature of certain international publics dominated by a small number of major cultures and/or nations makes it particularly difficult for members of small nations to express themselves in anything resembling an authentic voice.[14] International publics are frequently intensely monolingual, with participation hinging on fluency in the tongue favoured by the dominant culture. Whereas members of minor cultures must be multilingual if they are to be part of an international public, members of major cultures need rely only on their mother tongues. In certain contexts all traces of national specificity appear only as so many uncanny and displeasing departures from what is dominant and seemingly natural. The lack of reciprocity in question here is not merely linguistic. Whereas citizens of small nations find themselves inundated with the cultural products of larger nations, certain factors conspire to ensure that the minority culture's context of production coincides largely with its context of reception. A particularly telling example of this asymmetrical process is the history of Hollywood's role in the smaller European countries after the Second World War.

What contemporary theories overlook, then, are the ways in which relations between major and minor cultures require a politics of recognition aimed at international publics. To suggest that current multiculturalist thinking stands to benefit from the elaboration of a properly comparative dimension is by no means to trivialize the histories of genuine victimization underwriting certain attempts at curricular reform. It is a matter, rather, of recognizing that exclusion takes many forms and that in some instances countries and cultures wrongly included within a monolithic European camp are themselves marked by histories of asymmetrical exchange.

Insofar as a comparative perspective undermines a set of reified oppositions, it makes possible a more nuanced approach to differences between various rhetorics and strategies of recognition. For example, a comparative analysis can show that an explicit emphasis on cultural difference is viable only when the difference in question is linked, as a matter of common knowledge, to political and economic injustices that a given society is committed, in theory or practice, to effacing. Given the impossibility of legitimately claiming victim status, citizens of small, but privileged nations necessarily pursue recognition by far more indirect means. More specifically, there is a tendency to yoke defining features of a national culture or identity to international elements that are deemed capable of winning the attention of larger publics.

Having highlighted some of the central features of various forms of multicultural thinking, I would like now to focus on a specific point of contention between proponents of multicultural and traditional curricula. On the whole, opponents of a diversified curriculum seem to agree that curricular reform along multicultural lines is undesirable, even dangerous, because it threatens to undermine a shared or common culture. Inasmuch as the shared culture in question is understood also to be a national culture, multiculturalism is considered a corrosive force capable of destroying the nation's social fabric. Multiculturalists, it is wrongly assumed, have largely ceased to teach and preserve the venerable touchstones of a shared tradition, having devoted themselves instead to an irresponsible glorification (among other things) of the ephemera of contemporary culture. Thus, Rambo is believed to have displaced Rimbaud, just as Shakespeare now must compete with "the collected works of Bugs Bunny."[15]

The charge just evoked has, I believe, been met with a number of fairly cogent responses. One compelling argument foregrounds the extent to which nostalgic notions of loss hinge on assumptions about the enduring and unchanging nature of a common culture. When considered in the light of historical evidence, the dubious nature of such assumptions becomes clear. Virulent debates, such as those between the *anciens* and the *modernes* in seventeenth century France, create instabilities that do not leave core curricula untouched. The point is that a commonly held culture is the product of strife and is subject to change. Change, in other words, does not in and of itself rule out important forms of sharing, provided that the newly included elements are properly disseminated.

A second and equally compelling rejoinder focuses on the highly selective nature of the cultural forms being upheld as common by those who resist change. Although it is the putative universality of such forms that makes them worthy of preservation, many of them are in fact firmly linked to particular histories, geographies, and modes of social organization. The common culture allegedly requiring preservation presents itself to its proponents as a form of zero-degree or unmarked culture, the main characteristic of which is an ability to transcend local differences of region, dialect, gender, class, and so on.[16] Yet, from the perspective generated by alternative histories and trajectories, the common culture in question appears as culture marked by a series of differentiating factors. To require the preservation of this common culture in the name of universality is to embark on a course of self-deception, bad faith, or ideological delusion. What is disputed is not so much whether the cultural forms in question can be imposed on diverse groups, but whether such an imposition is in any way desirable. Nor, as the following quote illustrates, does the attempt to pinpoint a process of false universalization entail a rejection of the notion of a common culture.

Ours is a late twentieth-century world profoundly fissured by nationality, ethnicity, race, class, and gender. And the only way to transcend those divisions – to forge, for once, a civic culture that respects both differences and commonalities – is through education that seeks to comprehend the diversity of human culture.[17]

It is true, as we shall see, that not all multiculturalists are moved equally by this vision of a common culture. What is equally true, however, is that it is a questionable gesture at best to equate multicultural critiques of a particular view of common culture with rejections of common culture *tout court*.

Critics of a diversified curriculum systematically overlook the extent to which multicultural perspectives have helped either to create or to strengthen certain traditions. I am thinking, for example, of the emergence in recent times of a series of countercanons centred around writings by women or African Americans. Gates' remarks concerning the importance of the *Norton Anthology of African American Literature* underscore the extent to which increased access to certain institutions can support a common culture: "a well-marketed anthology – particularly a Norton Anthology – functions in the academy to create a tradition, as well as to define and preserve it."[18] Indeed, according to one view, the effect of the emerging canons has been not so much to displace the traditional canon held to be central to a common culture, but to mark it as "a particular canon, a canon of mastery."[19] It is important, however, to note that ongoing processes of canon formation do more than consolidate modes of expression favoured by particular groups or counterpublics. There is a tendency to assume that since countercanons are the work of counterpublics, such canons necessarily promote a radical proliferation of mutually isolated cultural traditions. Yet, this fear is itself based on an erroneous conception of counterpublics, which, as Nancy Fraser notes, are not "by definition" "enclaves" although they frequently are "enclaved." Fraser's important point is that:

... the concept of a counterpublic militates in the long run against separatism because it assumes a publicist orientation.... After all, to interact discursively as a member of [a] public, subaltern or otherwise, is to aspire to disseminate one's discourse to ever widening arenas.[20]

On this view, countercanons are themselves interventions within a larger public sphere, and as such they help to identify some of the components of a properly inclusive common culture.

Although the above arguments pinpoint weaknesses in ongoing celebrations of a common culture, they barely begin to shed light on a far deeper question separating camps embroiled in the culture wars. The thorny issue, it seems to me, concerns the extent to which well-functioning, modern, democratic societies depend on the existence of something called "common culture." If the existence of such societies does in fact require certain forms of shared culture, then what is the nature of the sharing involved? How much sharing is needed? What exactly must citizens have in common? And, finally, to what extent is it the task of a liberal education to ensure that the appropriate levels and forms of sharing occur?

Not surprisingly, an analysis of the public discourses about education and the liberal arts reveals radically different answers to these difficult and to some extent imponderable questions. What is striking, however, is the fact that the divergences in question do not in any straightforward way reflect a stable opposition between traditionalists and multiculturalists. Some multiculturalists, as we have seen, share the traditionalists' view of the importance of a common culture, even as they dispute the precise nature of the required beliefs and attitudes. The voices of multiculturalism are diverse, and some of the more influential ones deny entirely the need for common culture. The extent to which multiculturalists disagree about the issue of common culture is largely overlooked in ongoing debates, which thrive on a rather caricatural view of multiculturalist perspectives. The failure to take note of a range of views is unfortunate, for it supports reified oppositions between traditionalists and multiculturalists and has the effect of foreclosing genuine debate about the substantive issues.

In thinking about the place of a common culture within modern democracies and their educational systems it is helpful to focus on a number of views. Ernest Gellner's influential work on the modernity of nationalism provides a compelling account of the extent to which industrial societies depend on the existence of a common culture.[21] As is well-known, Gellner's analysis hinges on a contrast between agrarian and industrial societies and focuses on key differences in their modes of social reproduction. Social reproduction in an agrarian society takes place within local communities, proceeds on a one-to-one basis, and aims at the vertical transmission across generations of roles, practices, and beliefs.[22] In industrial societies, on the other hand, forms of "intra-community training" are "significantly complemented (or in extreme cases, wholly replaced)" by a highly centralized educational system supported largely, if not entirely, by the state.[23] Industrial society, claims Gellner, is

... based on a high-powered technology and the expectancy of sustained growth, which requires both a mobile division of labour, and sustained, frequent and precise communication between strangers involving a sharing of explicit meaning, transmitted in a standard idiom and in writing when required.[24]

Industrial societies rely on citizens who are largely interchangeable and mobile by virtue of a shared, standardized education involving qualifications such as the following: "literacy, numeracy, basic work habits and social skills, familiarity with basic technical and social skills."[25] According to Gellner the requisite degrees of cultural homogeneity can only be guaranteed by the state, and it is for this reason that he considers a "monopoly of legitimate education" more central to a definition of the modern state than the "monopoly of legitimate violence" foregrounded by Max Weber.[26] Only the state, claims Gellner, has the resources needed to establish and sustain an educational system predicated on a generalized access to standardized knowledge.

Gellner's account is important in the present context for at least two reasons. It underscores the extent to which a reform of the educational system along multicultural lines must be compatible with the cultural conditions of industrial societies, unless, of course, the goal is to replace these societies with an entirely different mode of social organization. In the absence of a fully blown revolutionary intent, however, the forms of nation-state culture that are so reviled in certain circles prove inevitable. What seems equally inescapable is the role assigned to a national, or provincial, educational system in the production and reproduction of nation-state culture.

A further contribution is made by Gellner's decision to situate the need for a common culture within a properly socio-historical framework that involves none of the processes of false universalization characteristic of the views of Bloom, D'Souza, Bernstein, and others. What Gellner establishes is the necessity of citizens' sharing a range of skills, knowledges, practices, and attitudes, not the necessity of a monologic elimination of diversity through the imposition of a single cultural tradition. Literacy, for example, can be acquired by means of a wide range of readings from diverse cultural contexts. The social skills needed within a given industrial society depend in part on the nature of that society's work force. If, for example, the latter includes women and visible minorities, as well as males from dominant ethnic groups, then multicultural literacy will be one of the skills requiring widespread dissemination through a centralized educational system. What is more, inasmuch as industrial societies are part of a larger, overarching economic system, at least some of the skills in question will be transnational in nature. A desire to ensure that the cultural conditions of industrial societies are met does not, then, entail a commitment to a shared culture that is monologically generated.

What emerges clearly from Gellner's account is the need for a common culture and the importance of the state in ensuring that culture's existence. Yet, an attempt to mobilize his insights within the context of debates about curricular reform quickly reveals that the boundary between common and other forms of culture remains hard to determine. At the same time, it is necessary to have at least some sense of where this boundary can or should be inscribed, for the culture wars are to a large extent generated by diverging intuitions about this very issue.

Gellner, it seems to me, gives priority to a sharing of basic skills over common knowledge of particular texts and authors. Although a particular body of knowledge must to some extent be shared by students of a given discipline, students aiming at positions within a highly mobile work force may find basic skills, as opposed to specific academic content, more useful in the long run. This is not to deny that in certain cases competence or skill may be inseparable from certain forms of scholarly knowledge, as Jürgen Habermas's discussion of the boundary question makes clear. Habermas's aim in considering this issue is to arrive at an understanding of the basic conditions of democratic citizenship, and the context for his reflections is provided by a changing European landscape. Habermas argues convincingly that "democratic citizenship need not be rooted in the national identity of a people," and goes on to establish that what citizens of a modern, multicultural, and democratic society must share is "a common political culture."[27] "Political culture" is said to be different from a "cultural form of life," and whereas diversity can be tolerated when it is a matter of life forms, active citizen participation depends on attitudes and practices based on forms of common knowledge. What can be demanded, then, of citizens is a basic knowledge of and commitment to the political principles of a democratic society, what Habermas calls "constitutional patriotism." Ensuring that the requisite levels of common knowledge and commitment obtain would thus be one of the tasks of a national educational system.

A very different sense of where the boundary should be inscribed seems to preoccupy figures such as William Bennett, Lynne Cheney, Chester Finn, Hirsch, Bloom, Kimball, and members of the public who agree that "the foremost job of formal education is to teach our children – all of them – about those things we have in common."[28] Opponents of multicultural reform seek not only to link common culture to a particular group, but to establish a level of commonality that by far exceeds the requirements of industrial societies and democratic citizenship. What is deemed desirable is a kind of cultural homogeneity that effectively would negate what Edward Said calls "other varieties of the human adventure."[29] For example, a common taste culture, or at least a stable hierarchy of taste cultures, is considered preferable to the existence of multiple contexts and modes of aesthetic appreciation. And if taste is to be contained within a single framework, then so arguably is erotic desire, for the common culture is to be saturated with the various forms of cultural expression to which a single, heterosexual orientation gives rise.

The demand for consensus on multiple fronts is linked to a meta-cultural phenomenon that is worth considering briefly. One feature of a genuine consensus is that agents not only share certain beliefs but know that their beliefs are shared.[30] Inasmuch as the mutual beliefs that support a genuine consensus are linked to a sense of the collectivity, it is not surprising to discover that meta-cultural expressions of the group are particularly prized by traditionalists. Meta-culture may take many forms, including a honking of horns in support of a nurse's strike or of a nation's troops abroad. In its most familiar incarnation, meta-culture involves the deployment of a traditional arsenal of symbols of national pride. And one of the demands being made by opponents of multicultural reform is precisely that certain cultural artefacts rooted in a particular tradition be preserved, taught, and transmitted as icons of national belonging.

The consensus desired by traditionalists foregrounds, in what is at times a fetishistic and nationalistic manner, the importance of particular texts, names, and discrete items of learning. A caricatural expression of this focus may be found in E.D. Hirsch's well-known *Cultural Literacy: What Every American Needs to Know*, where "Teddy Roosevelt," "Hamlet," "DNA," and "consumer price index" figure in a list of terms and names that all informed citizens should know.[31] Hirsch's list privileges familiarity with a series of discrete items over access to a set of basic skills and attitudes. And it is in part this kind of preference that engenders resistance to multicultural reform, for whereas basic skills and attitudes can be acquired by diverse means, familiarity with a list of discrete items requires the existence of a rigid and unchanging canon. What is operative here is a strong desire for closure, as well as a commitment to the idea that the canon, however selective it may ultimately be, in fact finds a basis in an adequate and fair-minded survey of diverse cultural forms.

The views on common culture discussed so far contrast strikingly with the conception endorsed by a significant number of multiculturalist thinkers. Stanley Fish, for example, claims that "it is difference all the way down; difference cannot be managed by measuring it against the common because the shape of the common is itself differential."[32] The dual assumption that difference is irreducible and that a common culture is both unnecessary and illusory is equally apparent in the following extraordinary passage from Barbara Herrnstein Smith's commentary on Hirsch's *Cultural Literacy*:

... it is a "universal fact" that people can communicate without a "shared culture" and that they do it all the time. Japanese suppliers, for example [...], communicate with European and African buyers without sharing the latter's cultures in the anthropological sense; and, just to speak of other Americans, I communicate quite effectively with my eighty-five-year-old ex-mother-in-law from Altoona, Pennsylvania, my twenty-five-year-old hairdresser from

Hillsborough, North Carolina, my five-year-old grandson from Brooklyn, New York, and my cat, without sharing much, if anything, of what Hirsch calls "the shared national culture" with any of them. The reason I can do so is that all the activities that Hirsch classifies as "communication" and sees as duplicative transmissions that presuppose sameness – "common" knowledge, "shared" culture, "standardized" associations – are, in fact, always ad hoc, context-specific, pragmatically adjusted negotiations of (and through) difference. We never have sameness; we cannot produce sameness; we do not need sameness.[33]

This passage is truly idiotic in at least some of the etymological senses of the word, for the ancient Greek "idiots" refers to a private person, to someone who is ill-informed, as well as to what is commonplace. Herrnstein Smith's claim that agents marked by a series of purely private differences can communicate without any form of sharing, without even a basic orientation toward understanding, is nothing short of ill-informed. Herrnstein Smith does not simply reject the suggestion that communication between herself and her five-year-old grandson could require mutual knowledge of the meaning of "DNA," "Teddy Roosevelt," "Hamlet," and so on. In a dramatic crescendo she denies the need for any form of sharing whatsoever, be it of norms, practices, skills, or even interests. Herrnstein Smith seeks support for this extreme view in an example that serves only to highlight some of the shared bases of communication. Grandsons and former mothers-in-law are precisely individuals with whom one in fact shares a very great deal, including, for example, a set of non-defeasible relations in the first case and a history of familial disputes in the second. To assume that ineradicable differences based on age or profession provide the most basic context for a series of successful communicative exchanges is willfully to overlook the role played by shared norms, attitudes, and practices in bringing about understanding. Herrnstein Smith's alternative to ill-conceived notions of a common culture is to invite us to embrace its polar opposite – difference – as fundamental and ineliminable.

Herrnstein Smith's focus on difference at the expense of a range of shared phenomena is by no means uncharacteristic of certain forms of multiculturalist thinking. A more nuanced and interesting example of this tendency is Gerald Graff's insistence that the role of a multicultural curriculum is both to undermine an existing consensus and to "teach the conflicts" that emerge as a result.[34] According to Graff:

... a past consensus was made possible only by the narrow and exclusive social base from which educators and educated then were drawn. It is not too hard to get a consensus if you start by excluding most Jews, blacks, immigrants, women, and others who figure to make trouble.[35]

Graff points out that a multicultural university includes groups drawn from a much wider social base, just as it provides a hospitable environment for ideas generated within diverse contexts and life worlds. And this expanded social base, concludes Graff, makes impossible any form of consensus: "we should recognize that such conflicts are here to stay and start looking for ways to make them educationally productive."[36] According to Graff these conflicts must themselves become the topic of debate, and this involves taking issue with a well-established means of organizing knowledge, the "field-coverage model."

Underwriting the field-coverage model is the dual assumption that departments need specialists capable of covering a number of fundamental areas of knowledge, and that students should be required to cover a number of the areas in question.[37] One of the advantages of this model, claims Graff, is its flexibility. Thus, for example, the dissenting voices of newly included groups can be readily accommodated by simply adding a new area of specialized knowledge to the core curriculum. Yet, the model also has important drawbacks, the most important of which is that it ignores, even hides, the very conflicts that in Graff's mind are lasting features of a multicultural curriculum and university environment. The model discourages genuine debate about the curriculum, for the "grid of periods, genres, and other catalog rubrics" seems to embody "a clear and seemingly uncontroversial conceptualization of what the department [is ...] about."[38]

Graff does not so much propose to eliminate the grid in question as to bring into public the conflicts that it conceals. His intuition is that an institutional denial of conflict engenders, not harmony or consensus, but various forms of systematically distorted communication.

What is needed, then, is an ongoing debate between proponents of profoundly conflicting views. Students should not simply experience the ineliminable conflicts of a multicultural curriculum as they try to make sense of a series of mutually negating courses of Marxist, new critical, psychoanalytic, or analytic inspiration, but should instead be allowed to witness a public debate about the conflicts in question. Thus, suggests Graff, "the course on Rimbaud and modern French poetry and the course on Rambo and current popular film" might "meet for a joint conference" in order to explore conflictual relations between highbrow and lowbrow traditions.[39]

What Graff has in common with Herrnstein Smith is a stubborn interest in difference, for he fails to discuss the basic norms or frameworks that would make possible a productive, although conflictual, debate about culture. Nor does Graff acknowledge the extent to which individual professors must be committed to the norms in question. If, for example, the debate is to be more than a dogmatic confrontation of views, participants must be willing to respect certain modes of argumentation. The modern, secular university is part of civil society and provides an important context for rational discussion or what Habermas calls "discursive will formation." And inasmuch as Graff neglects to account adequately for the norms underwriting such processes, an important form of common culture is overlooked.

It would be unfair to accuse Graff of valorizing conflict for its own sake, for he explicitly states that we should not "spurn consensus when it proves possible to get it."[40] At the same time, it is important to note that Graff's focus on conflict at the expense of other realities supports the widespread view referred to above that sees culture and discourses about culture as "war by other means." Following in the wake of post-structuralism, identity politics and multiculturalism have set ajar the door to a renewed discourse of agency. And although it is still difficult to discern the features of the agents hovering behind this door, it is already clear that they differ markedly from the subjects populating the world of the traditional humanists who oppose multicultural reform. More specifically, the agents populating recent social imaginaries are deeply strategic, for they are convinced of the ineliminably conflictual nature of human interaction, just as they are motivated by self-interest and willing to mock the norms supporting communicative action oriented toward mutual understanding.

As I have argued elsewhere, this conception of agency and knowledge as fundamentally strategic rests on a number of dubious assumptions.[41] What needs to be emphasized here is the extent to which strategic behaviour is appropriate only in certain contexts. To assume that multiculturalism necessarily involves a foregrounding of strategic rationality within the university is not only to overlook the possibility of dialogue and mutual understanding, but to fail to recognize the emancipatory potential embodied in a culture of genuinely rational argumentation.

Compared to clerical universities, the modern, secular university enjoys a considerable degree of autonomy, and this is so even in those cases in which funding comes largely, or even entirely, from the state. The ideal of academic freedom embodied in secular universities does not, of course, provide a warrant for any and all forms of thinking, but establishes a right to scrutinize received truths, traditions, and conventions in a process of rational, public debate governed by basic norms. Conflicts, in universities, are to be settled discursively, rather than by means of brute force or intimidation, and this preference for discursive will formation is precisely a feature of civil society or what Habermas calls the "bourgeois public sphere."[42] Through their commitment to certain basic norms, universities help to create the conditions under which communicative action and research can unfold. For example, universities provide environments in which it is appropriate to require evidence for a particular point of view, and in which it is inappropriate knowingly to deceive interlocutors or to withhold information pertaining directly to an issue under discussion. To point in this manner to some of the norms underwriting communicative exchanges within the university is by no means to claim that the ideal is always realized. However, the very fact that the norms in question can be evoked to unmask forms of authority based illegitimately on notions of age, rank, or gender, merely underscores their hold on us.

It is by respecting the norms of rational debate that universities will be able to deal adequately with the challenges of an increasingly multicultural future. Multiculturalists have at times expressed scepticism about the norms in question, and we know that traditional-ists have been quick to see in multiculturalism nothing more than a radical curtailing of academic liberties. Yet, the creation of a properly inclusive common culture is best achieved, not by means of various forms of strategic action or separatist processes of regroupment, but by means of critical debate about the university's tasks and goals. What is more, it would be a mistake to assume that multiculturalism necessar-ily is accompanied by the demise of reason. Inasmuch as multicultur-alism foregrounds the untenable and contradictory nature of habitual modes of thinking, it encourages a spirit of critique. This critique is ultimately ethical as well as rational, for it is in some ineliminable way motivated by the idea that notions of dignity and fairness should play a role in our thinking about what citizens of a modern democratic soci-ety should know.

Notes

1   This paper draws on discussions with Sue Laver, Adam Muller, Trevor Ponech, Paisley Livingston, and Charles Taylor. Special thanks are due to Ben Lee, Greg Urban, and Dilip Gaonkar, who in various ways encouraged me to think through the issues in question. John Hall helped with the material on nationalism.

2   See Satya P. Mohanty, *Literary Theory and the Claims of History: Postmodernism, Objec-tivity, Multicultural Politics* (Ithaca, NY: Cornell University Press, 1997); Paula M.L. Moya and Michael R. Hames-García, eds., *Reclaiming Identity: Realist Theory and the Predica-ment of Postmodernism* (Berkeley: University of California Press, 2000), and Smaro Kamboureli, *Scandalous Bodies: Diasporic Literature in English Canada* (Oxford: Oxford University Press, 1999).

3   Michael Warner, *Publics and Counterpublics* (New York: Zone Books, 2002).

4   See, for example, Louis Menand, "The Culture Wars," *New York Review of Books* (1994): 16–21, a review of Richard Bernstein's *Dictatorship of Virtue: Multiculturalism and the Battle for America's Future*.

5   Kenneth McGoogan, *Canada's Undeclared War* (Calgary: Detselig Enterprises, 1991), 2.

6   Henry Louis Gates Jr., "The Master's Pieces: On Canon Formation and the African-American Tradition," in *The Politics of Liberal Education*, ed. Darryl J. Gless and Barbara Herrnstein Smith (Durham, NC: Duke University Press, 1992), 96.

7   Charles Taylor, "The Politics of Recognition," in *Multiculturalism and the Politics of Recognition*, ed. Amy Gutmann (Princeton, NJ: Princeton University Press, 1992), 35.

8   Dinesh D'Souza, *Illiberal Education* (New York: Free Press, 1991).

9   Taylor, "The Politics of Recognition," 68–69.

10   Chicago Cultural Studies Group, "Critical Multiculturalism," *Critical Inquiry* 18 (1992): 530–55.

11 I have in mind Nancy Fraser's definition of counterpublics as "parallel discursive arenas where members of subordinated social groups invent and circulate counterdiscourses to formulate oppositional interpretations of their identities, interests, and needs." See Nancy Fraser, "Rethinking the Public Sphere," in *Habermas and the Public Sphere*, ed. Craig Calhoun (Cambridge, MA: MIT Press, 1992), 123.

12 Taylor, "The Politics of Recognition," 50.

13 Greg Urban, "The Two Faces of Culture," *Working Papers and Proceedings of the Center for Psychosocial Studies* 49 (1992): 5.

14 For an influential discussion of the concept of a small nation, see Miroslav Hroch, *The Social Preconditions of National Revival in Europe: A Comparative Analysis of the Social Composition of Patriotic Groups among the Smaller European Nations* (Cambridge: Cambridge University Press, 1985). Hroch chooses to limit the term 'small nation' to "those [nations] which were in subjection to a ruling nation for such a long period that the relation of subjection took on a structural character for both parties" (9). This definition is, in my mind, overly restrictive since it effaces the important role played by the sheer size of a country and its population, as well as by the reach of its language.

15 The Rambo/Rimbaud substitution is evoked by Graff in the context of an analysis of objections to multicultural reform. See Gerald Graff, "Teach the Conflicts," in *The Politics of Liberal Education*, 68. The Bugs Bunny and Shakespeare example is from Roger Kimball, *Tenured Radicals: How Politics Has Corrupted Our Higher Education* (New York: Harper & Row, 1990), xii.

16 For a penetrating discussion of key differences between marked and unmarked culture, see Urban, "The Two Faces of Culture," 1–21.

17 Henry Louis Gates Jr., *Loose Canons: Notes on the Culture Wars* (Oxford: Oxford University Press, 1992), xv.

18 Gates, "The Master's Pieces: On Canon Formation and the African-American Tradition," 107.

19 Eve Kosofsky Sedgwick, "Pedagogy in the Context of an Antihomophobic Project," in *The Politics of Liberal Education*, 146.

20 Fraser, "Rethinking the Public Sphere," 124.

21 See, for example, Ernest Gellner, *Nations and Nationalism* (Ithaca, NY: Cornell University Press, 1983).

22 See also Greg Urban's discussion of alpha culture in Urban, "The Two Faces of Culture," 3–12.

23 *Gellner, Nations and Nationalism*, 31, 29.

24 Ibid., 33–34.

25 Ibid., 28.

26 Ibid., 3.

27 Jürgen Habermas, "Citizenship and National Identity: Some Reflections on the Future of Europe," in *Theorizing Citizenship*, ed. R. Beiner (Albany: State University of New York Press, 1995), 255–83.

28 Cited by Stanley Fish, "The Common Touch, or, One Size Fits All," in *The Politics of Liberal Education*, Politics of Liberal Education edited by D.J. Glad and Barbara Herrnstein Smith, (Duke University Press 1993), 244.

29 Cited by Gates, *Loose Canons: Notes on the Culture Wars*, xv.

30 See Thomas J. Scheff, "Toward a Sociological Model of Consensus," *American Sociological Review* 32 (1967): 32–46.

31 E.D. Hirsch, *Cultural Literacy: What Every American Needs to Know* (Boston: Houghton Mifflin, 1987).

32 Fish, "The Common Touch, or, One Size Fits All," 247.

33 "Hirsch, "Literacy, and the 'National Culture'" in *The Politics of Liberal Education*, 79.

34 See Graff, "Teach the Conflicts," 57–73. See also Gerald Graff, "Taking Cover in Coverage," *Profession* 86 (1986), 41–45; Gerald Graff, "What Should We Be Teaching – When There Is No 'We'?" *Yale Journal of Criticism* 1 (1987): 189–211.

35 Graff, "Teach the Conflicts," 58.

36 Ibid., 57.

37 Graff, "Taking Cover in Coverage," 42.

38 Ibid., 43.

39 Graff, "Teach the Conflicts," 68.

40 Ibid., 57.

41 Mette Hjort, *The Strategy of Letters* (Cambridge, MA: Harvard University Press, 1993).

42 Jürgen Habermas, *The Structural Transformation of the Public Sphere: An Inquiry into a Category of Bourgeois Society*, trans. Thomas Burger with the assistance of Frederick Lawrence (Cambridge, MA: MIT Press, 1991).

5 As his title suggests, Imre Szeman is concerned in this contribution with the relationship of globalization to culture, and more particularly with a prevailing view that whatever "culture" is or refers to, it has come conceptually undone in the wake of globalization's larger assault on autonomy and specificity. This rather pessimistic interpretation, cogent arguments against which may be found in David Novitz's and Christoph Brumann's essays in this volume, arises from critics' recognition of the important role played by such notions as unity, coherence, and privileged singularity in underwriting "culture's" humanistic and social scientific salience in the midst of nineteenth-century European and American culture wars. Although in some important respects reluctant to support stronger versions of this negative hypothesis, Szeman suggests that globalization has made it impossible to maintain many of the fictions surrounding the Western conception of culture, including those connoting its fixity, superiority, and inherent opposition to a pathologically novel and banal commodity culture. Likewise he urges caution against accepting the view, implicitly endorsed by Jacques Barzun earlier in this volume, that culture works to prevent the expansion of philistinism and barbarism.

Claims concerning "culture's" unravelling have important intellectual and political corollaries, especially for those working in the humanities, which were themselves organized in defence of a concept, "culture," the integrity of which, Szeman concedes, can no longer be assumed. But the precise terms of this unravelling are worth attending to, since it clearly makes a difference how "culture," caught up in globalization's reconfiguration of spatiality and temporality, has changed. Provocatively, Szeman sees "culture" as having changed very little under globalization, largely because its promises of unity and stasis were only ever ideologically convenient (and period-specific) illusions: part of a resonant, deeply political, and historically contingent, dream. Culture, in other words, "has always been other than what it claimed to be," and so, like Mark Twain's death, reports of its dissolution have been greatly and at times ironically exaggerated. Thus Szeman sees the challenge for scholars lying not in charting "culture's" demise but in recognizing how globalization has created important new opportunities for rethinking contemporary experience within an explicitly "critical" humanities, the analytical character of which supports new modes of engagement with, and definitions of, "culture."

Just what exactly do these "critical" humanities look like, though? Here Szeman is cautious, but he does suggest that they will assume their revised form only following the wholesale reappraisal of their critical assumptions, methods, and practices. Accordingly Szeman finds the following four matters particularly pressing. First, critical humanists must assume responsibility for confronting the problem of "affirmative culture," or the tendency to focus on (and celebrate) specific texts, practices, or genres at the expense of adequately considering the specific cultural processes necessary for their production. Second, they must take commodities and consumerism seriously and non-normatively, rather than simply viewing them as malign symptoms of the triumph of market capitalism, as corruptions of culture rather than culture itself (in virtue of the market's insistence on the equivalence of "aesthetic value" and "exchange value"). Third, the historical narratives responsible for legitimating what has become the "standard" view of culture in the humanities must be fully explored so as to unsettle what Szeman claims are "unproductive conjunctions" linking art and culture. And, fourth, "critical" humanists must historicize their own critical practice, must come to understand recent theory as itself historically contingent, as immanent rather than transcendent, and as importantly, ineluctably, cultural. Only in this way will we become able to dispense with the idea of the humanities as culture's guardians, and to find, to use Szeman's metaphor, beauty amongst the ruins.

CULTURE AND/IN GLOBALIZATION

IMRE SZEMAN[1]

It is self-evident that nothing concerning art is self-evident anymore, not its inner life, not its relation to the world, not even its right to exist. The forfeiture of what could be done spontaneously or unproblematically has not been compensated for by the open infinitude of new possibilities that reflection confronts. In many regards, expansion appears as contraction. The sea of the formerly inconceivable, on which around 1910 revolutionary art movements set out, did not bestow the promised happiness of adventure. Instead, the process that was unleashed consumed the categories in the name of that for which it was undertaken. – Theodor Adorno, *Aesthetic Theory*

The nation understands itself as its own theme park, and that resolves the question of what it means to live in Italy: it is to have been Italian once. – Bill Readings, *The University in Ruins*

As the range and number of books and articles exploring culture in the era of globalization should indicate, the concept of culture has undergone a significant change at the end of the twentieth and early twenty-first century – a shift that has necessitated new ways of thinking and writing about culture.[2] This is not only, or even primarily, due to the impact on culture of those forces now inextricably associated with globalization: the unprecedented intensification and extensification of electronically mediated culture on a worldwide scale; the effects of the growth of finance capitalism, that is, of obsessive speculation on capital itself in place of the attention once paid to the products of industry; a political shift from nation-state based sovereignty to a diffusion of sovereignty into international organizations, trade conventions, NGOs, and transnational corporations; and so on. While these forces, individually and collectively, *have* changed culture and cultures, what is more significant is the conceptual impact of these (thus far largely) empirical developments. Early work on globalization tended to claim that it constituted something like a genuine historical and epistemic break: on the other side of 1989 (the beginning of the end of the Soviet Empire), everything is supposedly different. It has now become more common to see through the rhetoric of newness that surrounds globalization and to insist on the development of these forces in the *longue durée*. As with the economy and politics, so, too, with culture: rather than creating anything genuinely "new" in the sphere of culture, globalization has produced the conditions that might permit us to rethink culture in a larger historical frame, a process that would allow us to see that the concept of culture has *always been other* than what it claimed to be.

But if globalization has raised this possibility, its actualization has been repeatedly blocked by the operations of culture itself. The typical discussions that emerge around culture in reference to globalization – the already tired talk of cultural mixing-and-matching, or the equally unoriginal worry about the threats (and possibilities) posed to this or that culture by (American) mass culture – merely continue the old game of culture in a new guise. What is original about globalization for culture is *not*, it seems to me, to be found in the sudden impact of cultures upon one another. Rather, it is that globalization has made it impossible to maintain any of the fictions that have continued to circulate around the Western concept of culture. This can be seen most acutely, I think, in the crisis facing the humanities, which is why any exploration of culture and globalization must ask the question of what globalization means for the humanities today and for the future. But before we can address this question, we need to consider the ways

in which the concept of culture has typically circulated in and alongside globalization discourses, in order to understand what is missing in
most explorations of culture in the era of globalization.

Culture and Space

Discussions of globalization and culture have typically focused on the
way in which both physical and immaterial *speed* – the movements of
goods and people, as well as money and electronic signals – has reconfigured the *space* of culture. In the study of national literatures or histories, languages or cultural traditions, or any form of what used to be
referred to as area studies, culture has long been intimately related to
geography. Even though it has also always been clear that culture must
be understood as fluid and unbounded, as something able to travel and
exert its force across boundaries, culture has nevertheless been understood primarily as something that exists in fixed, determinate spaces,
whether this is the space of the nation and the region, or villages,
groups and subcultures. Since at least the nineteenth century, and in
conjunction with the solidification of the nation as a political form,
there have been repeated attempts to define and differentiate national
culture and character (from Johann Gottfried Herder to Hippolyte
Taine, and from Fred Morley to Fred Lewis Pattee).[3] Though the shaky
logic of national culture has been repeatedly challenged, these theoretical linkages between culture and geography have persisted as a powerful conceptual commonplace, appearing as the subject of an annual
deluge of non-fiction books investigating the national character of the
United States and Canada, as well as forming the basis of countless
travel narratives and the animating substance of journalistic reportage.
In the wake of 9/11, what Theodor Adorno referred to as "the detest-
able jargon of war that speaks of the Russian, the American, surely also
of the German,"[4] has experienced a notable resurgence in the form of
a populist Orientalist discourse of the "clash of civilizations" between
the West and Islam, which has further reinforced the idea of absolute
cultural divides between peoples based on what Taine referred to as
"race, moment and milieu."[5]

Even though these recent anti-Islamicist discourses suggest that less
has changed than one may have thought, the speed associated with

globalization has been connected (for better and worse) to the obliteration of the spaces in which culture was once thought to "naturally"
or "normally" dwell, as well as to the destruction of the borders that
were once imagined as marking off cultures from another. In the era
of globalization, cultural boundaries are imagined as having become
porous, indefinite, and indeterminate: the "local" intersects with the
global (and vice versa), and culture becomes unsettled, uprooted, hybrid, mixed and impure. Globalization is the moment of mass migration, multiculturalism and cosmopolitanism; if the nation was once
imagined as a community through the aid of newspapers and novels,
the ubiquity of new forms of mass culture has led to new, transnational regimes of the imagination. With respect to culture, discourses
of globalization are thus often focused on border zones and on the
complex negotiations that take place as these borders are explored, re-
imagined and reasserted in a world of increasing, if unequal, cultural
interaction. Much of the analysis of borders has focused rightly on the
implications of these power differentials – differentials of scale as well
as speed – on the form that these cultural interactions take. As problematic as the discourse of cultural imperialism has been, discussions
of the globalization of culture in both academic and public spheres
nevertheless continue to imagine the conjunction of these terms as a
narrative about "Americanization" or of the threat posed by Western
cultural products to cultural autonomy of non-Western, still modernizing communities and regions.[6] A direct line can be drawn from one
of the first major works on cultural imperialism, Ariel Dorfman and
Armand Mattelart's *How to Read Donald Duck*,[7] to the authors of the
recently published *Key Concepts in Post-Colonial Studies*, who claim
that "the key to the link between classical imperialism and contemporary globalization in the twentieth century has been the role of the
United States," which is responsible for initiating "those features of
social life and social relations that today may be considered to characterize the global: mass production, mass communication and mass
consumption."[8]

What is interesting is that while there have been repeated claims that
globalization produces new conditions for culture – new and unprecedented forms of cultural intermingling and interconnection that, in

Canada at least, is celebrated as the coming-into-being of a paradoxically ethnicized post-ethnic state – culture is *still* imagined in virtually all of these formulations as connected to geography in a more or less Romantic fashion. After all, globalization can only pose a threat to cultural autonomy if cultures are conceptualized as being necessarily (for purposes of individual and collective self-identity) autonomous in the first place. The reason why it is possible for discourses of cultural mixing (as in multiculturalism) and radical cultural otherness (as in the swooping and uncritical return of Eurocentrism during the current war on terrorism) to exist side-by-side in globalization is that, to a large degree, the former presumes the later: hybridity necessitates conceiving of cultures as monadic to begin with, whether historically or conceptually, or both. While culture is thought to have entered a new situation in globalization, it seems to me that the concept of culture itself *hasn't* undergone a similar change or shift. The conceptual boundaries within which culture is able to move remain those first delimited by Herder and Taine centuries earlier. Globalization has forced theorists to think seriously about the implications of the dislocation or deterritorialization of culture, and to try to think about culture after its ties to blood, belonging, and soil have been severed. But it seems that most attempts to conceptualize what globalization means for culture have only gone half-way: once disembedded from geography, the function and meaning of culture needs to be redefined in a radical way if the concept is to continue to have any meaning at all. That this hasn't happened has more to do with institutional and disciplinary inertia than with the continued applicability or utility of the Western idea of culture to the conditions of the global present. Or rather, since the shifting meaning of "culture" has charted "within its semantic unfolding humanity's own historic shift from rural to urban existence, pig-farming to Picasso,"[9] the lack of a shift now needs to be probed and assessed to determine what culture still signifies.

Culture and Time

The contradictions that emerge from the persistence of an older concept of culture in the investigation of the conditions of its dissolution can be seen in the conflicting views that have been expressed – often at the same time – about the temporality of globalization. One of the important (and importantly contested) assumptions of the typical narrative of globalization and culture is that globalization constitutes an historical rupture, a break with the past that inaugurates a new era of cultural relations. This rupture is usually *not* imagined as something completely new, that is, as a whole new *episteme* that marks the end of modernity and the birth of something else. Rather, pre-existing tendencies and processes (economic, political, social, etc.) are thought to have simultaneously undergone an epochal intensification. Globalization is imagined, in other words, as that moment on a graph of a logarithmic equation where the line suddenly spikes skyward; it is the moment when this spike occurs everywhere at a same time, if with greater or lesser degrees of intensity. For these reasons, globalization has been employed primarily as a periodizing term, the name for a particular moment in history, though it has by extension also been used to describe the set of processes that have produced or which are contained in this moment. These narratives of historical rupture have been accompanied by critiques that have taken the form not of an outright rejection of this periodizing hypothesis, but of attempts to downplay both the intensity and extensivity of globalization through references to historical precedents and the *longue durée*. Such deflationary counternarratives have been articulated in the fields of economics, studies of migration, and the interaction of social communities, global politics, and even communication technologies.[10] With respect to culture, these critiques point out that culture and cultural forms have long travelled outside of their "natural" boundaries, that is, that the interaction and hybridization of culture associated with globalization is part of a longer process. As Christopher Clausen has put it, the process of breaking down boundaries between cultures "sometimes misindentified with the electronic age – began long before computers were invented, and whether we label it globalization, modernity, assimilation, cultural imperialism, the technological revolution, or the inexorable logic of capitalism, no culture is immune to it."[11]

The debates over the appropriate historical frame of globalization have significance for the concepts and theories that are employed to

make sense of the contemporary world. Theories that envision a historical rupture occurring with Bretton Woods, the Vietnam War, or the
end of the Soviet Bloc (and there are of course other possibilities) trum-
pet the need for new concepts and the reconfiguration or re-evaluation
of older ones. On the other hand, those that place globalization within
a longer history tend to see older theories and concepts as still having
utility. With respect to discussions of culture and globalization, *both*
of these scenarios have been played out, though along different axes of
analyses. In the first instance, new models for the *circulation* of culture
have been proposed in order to make sense of the apparently discontinuous spread and impact of contemporary culture, the most well-known
being the vocabulary of scapes, flows, and cascades developed by Arjun Appadurai in an effort to understand the "complex, overlapping,
disjunctive order" of the new global cultural economy.[12] Even in this
case, however, what seems to be untouched by any of the transformations produced by globalization *is our understanding of the concept of
culture itself.* For Appadurai, culture now moves differently, and its new
mode of circulation produces new kinds of cultural effects (e.g., "local-
ized" outbreaks of ethnic violence whose root cause lies in the financial support funnelled to extremists by extra-local or extra-national
migrant communities). Yet even here, culture continues to play the role
that it has long performed, acting as the primary site where individual
and collective identities are shaped and formed; if anything, his insistence on the new role played by the "imagination" in the global order,
reinforces a Romantic view of culture, even if he also argues that it is
important to "capture the impact of deterritorialization on the imaginative resources of lived, local experience."[13]

To summarize: on the one hand, globalization names a new condition for culture that is related to the sudden dissolution of culture's
boundaries and its increased global motility. And yet the culture that is
suddenly mobile and deterritorialized is still imagined largely in its old
guise of human expressivity – as something, strangely (and yet famil-
iarly) unaffected by the hurly burly of empirical social transformations
– or as its opposite: the debased culture of mass culture, now imagined
as disastrously writ large over the face of the entire globe, subsuming
everything in its path. Yet neither of these concepts of culture seem to

adequately express the conditions under which culture is produced and circulated today, much less how culture functions, what this category means or describes, and how it relates to or mediates social life more generally – or even *if* its role is one of mediation any longer.

The Humanities and the "Cultural Turn"

Perhaps counterintuitively, this is confirmed by the *increasing* significance of culture in discussions of globalization, and, indeed in the social sciences more generally (as witnessed in the innumerable discussions of the "cultural turn" that has placed culture back of the agenda of the social sciences). While the discourse of globalization began in the early 1990s as one focused primarily on economic and political change, culture has since become more and more important in thinking about the meaning and consequences of globalization. There are countless examples that one could draw upon. In perhaps the final suturing of the torn halves of base and superstructure, Fredric Jameson and Lawrence Grossberg have both described globalization as the moment in which the economic and the cultural fold into one another, becoming both empirically and heuristically inseparable.[14] On the other side of the political spectrum, Samuel Huntington's thesis on the "clash of civilizations" affirms in its own way the centrality of culture to an analysis of the new global situation. And what John Tomlinson has usefully described as the "complex connectivity" of globalization is expressed in and through culture in a way that places the register of culture at the centre of discussions of globalization. Tomlinson suggests that the complex connectivity of globalization has confused the division of human life into the familiar categories of the social sciences: the economic, the social, the political, the technological, etc. As the point of articulation of all these categories – the site or spaces of "meaning construction [that] informs individual and collective actions"[15] – culture is now championed as the key register within which globalization is both experienced and understood.

Such an interest in culture might suggest that the way is open for the humanities – the traditional site of the study of culture in the university – to reassert their importance. Yet the very opposite seems to have taken place. This is due in part to changes in both the ideology and social function of the university over the past few decades, a transformation of the university from secular clerisy to corporation that has been traced out by Bill Readings, Masao Miyoshi, Mary Poovey, and others. Over the past several decades, the humanities have endured funding cuts, a decline in student enrolment and interest, and an increasing functionalization of the curriculum, along with a gradual transformation of its labour pool into part-time and contract workers. These attacks on the humanities are not simply the result of disinterested, philistine politicians who don't understand the importance of the humanities (though in Canada, such readings are hard to resist in the age of Gordon Campbell and Ralph Klein), or the fault of humanities professors, who haven't asserted themselves enough in the public sphere to bring needed attention to the crucial role their work plays in social life. As surprising as this statement might seem to those engaged in cultural work today, the nation-state *isn't* opposed to culture. All one needs to do is to look at recent policy documents to see that it talks about culture incessantly, and does so in the most Romantic terms possible. To take just one example, the Executive Summary of the February 1999 report of the Cultural Industries Sectoral Advisory Group on International Trade, begins: "Culture is the heart of a nation. As countries become more economically integrated, nations need strong domestic cultures and cultural expression to maintain their sovereignty and sense of identity.... Cultural industries shape our society, develop our understanding of one another and give us a sense of pride in who we are as a nation."[16] While this might sound like discourse that could have emerged from an old-school humanities department, the reality is that the model or vision of culture produced in and by the humanities bears little relationship to the one championed by those globalization theorists for whom culture has become everything, or by the state for whom "culture is a nation's heart," or indeed by multinational media conglomerates beset by the crisis of a lack of cultural "content" to circulate through the communication networks that encircle the globe. The humanities have become marginalized as a result of their inability to continue to grasp the concept that they have committed themselves to understanding: the concept of culture *has* shifted, even if this has yet to be properly registered by the humanities or by intellectuals more generally.

How can this be? Over the past forty years, the legitimacy of the concept of culture that continues to underwrite the humanities has been under concerted attack – and not from without, but from *within* the humanities itself. Postcolonial studies has drawn attention not only to the blindspots of the Western academy in considering the culture and cultural production of other peoples, but also to the fundamental role played by culture in imperialism and colonialism. In the Western academy, the development of cultural studies has drawn attention to other blindspots, not the least of which has been the way in which "culture" has been used to exercise and legitimatize political domination. For example, in his discussion of the historical context of Matthew Arnold's seminal articulation of the relationship of culture to society, Raymond Williams makes clear the links between the assertion of "excellence and humane values" and Arnold's opposition to the "anarchy" of public demonstrations and protests over the extension of the franchise in Britain.[17] In a similar way, Pierre Bourdieu[18] and Terry Eagleton[19] have exposed the ruse of the aesthetic, showing how aesthetic value names a relation of power, rather than the special properties of specific objects (like literary texts or artworks) or dispositions of the subject. For both writers, the university was the site at which one learned appropriate modes of aesthetic distinction and cultural interpretation. This is one of the reasons why, as Etienne Balibar and Pierre Macherey argue, the very concept of "literature is inseparable from an academic or schooling practice that defines the conditions for both the consumption and production of literature."[20] Perhaps most importantly, in their crucial analysis of the coincident development of both culture and the state beginning in the late-eighteenth century as "sites of reconciliation for a civic and political society that is seen to be riven by conflict and contradiction,"[21] David Lloyd and Paul Thomas point to the ideological role that culture was to play in the West: "Culture … is not confined in its objects to the artistic, or, more narrowly, the literary, but aims rather at the harmonious cultivation of all the capacities of the human subject at a time when it was already apparent that the division of intellectual and manual labour was increasingly formative of specialized or partial individuals."[22]

This conjunction of state to citizen through the medium of culture was the product of a specific moment in history, a moment that we are now past. In the waning of the importance of the nation-state in the operations of global capitalism (and it has waned, even if the state played a crucial role in instigating and instituting the anti-statist regime of globalization), there becomes less of a need for a social institution geared towards the production of a national narrative or of a discourse which mediates the relationship between the populace and the state. It is this decline of the university, and of the humanities in particular, that Bill Readings outlines in *The University in Ruins*. He writes that "since the nation-state is no longer the primary instance of the reproduction of global capitals, 'culture' – as the symbolic and political counterpart to the project of integration pursued by the nation-state – has lost its purchase. The nation-state and the modern notion of culture arose together, and they are, I argue, ceasing to be essential to an increasingly transnational global economy."[23] Even as the ideology of the humanities gets spread over an increasingly larger sphere of concern (as suggested, for example, in Appadurai's appeal to the imagination), the function that this ideology was supposed to serve has disappeared along with the institutions that produced it. It's no wonder that the concept of culture is now open to all kinds of other uses, but also that there is so much confusion over its uses, as older definitions and sensibilities collide with new realities that they are unable to make sense of by means of it.

The Humanities in Ruins

Potentially, the crumbling of the socio-historical conditions that have produced the need for this particular ideology of culture – ideologies which have long masked the operations of social power in metanarratives of progress, humanity, and Enlightenment – opens the way for a new, less mystified understanding of culture. At the very least, it opens the way up for methodologies that have always stressed the need to see cultural objects in networks or systems of power to assume a more prominent place in the humanities and in definitions of its role and function. The *analysis* of culture – that is, of what occurs in the name of culture, of what forms of power and knowledge pass through those objects, practices and experiences that we describe as "cultural" – might replace *(e)valuation* as the dominant way of thinking of culture.

The spectre of value that has long provided the ground of humanities scholarship could give way finally to the examination of the modes and forms of the productivity of culture; globalization might be what brings culture back down to earth from the heavens, insisting on the immanence of what has long imagined itself as transcendent. From this perspective, what might be most significant about globalization – as concept and as empirical reality – is less the rapidity of the circulation of culture within it, or the intensified intersection of cultures with one another, than the fact that this circulation (and the historical circumstances that enable it) makes it difficult, if not impossible, to imagine any longer the function of culture and of the humanities is to express and defend the "best that has been thought and known." For what the emphasis on the mobility of culture insists upon is not just that this is a new condition of culture, but that culture has always been uprooted and hybrid, that is, culture *has never been what we believed it to be*, it has always had a different function than the guardians of the humanities would have liked to have assigned to it.

What has mitigated this radical rethinking of the concept of culture, and thus of a new role for the humanities even in the face of radical critiques of its ideological uses, is yet another aspect of globalization and its relationship to culture. If it has remained possible for the humanities to continue to imagine their role as being "the harmonious cultivation of all the capacities of the human subject," and of the university to maintain (at least in official pronouncements) its "grand narrative ... centered on the production of a liberal, reasoning subject,"[24] it is because in the humanities, global culture is widely conceived of as commodity culture, a form of culture conceived as constituting an attack on modern subjectivity itself. Instead of asking deep questions about the politics of the humanities and of the ideology of culture that sustains it, the combination of fears about commodity culture, along with a new fear of its dislocation of anything and everything once outside of it on a global scale, has allowed the humanities to assume a role with which it is imminently comfortable: the defender of truth and beauty against a philistinism or barbarism which, having become global, is now more dangerous than ever. It comes as no surprise that it is precisely at this point that there has been a return of a more or less classical discourse of "beauty," as reflected by books such as Elaine Scarry's *On Beauty and Being Just*,²⁵ Wendy Steiner's *Venus in Exile*²⁶ and James Elkins' *Pictures and Tears: People Who Have Cried in Front of Paintings*.²⁷ But the return of this discourse, and of other books which attempt to re-assert value in the face of commodity culture, must be seen as a further symptom of the ruin of humanities, as opposed to a valiant reclama-tion of its fundamental task: to express what is best and greatest about (an always unhistoricized) human Being.

Such recourse to Arnoldian or Romantic notions of culture in res-ponse to globalization are not only to be found in, for instance, the defence of literature or the fine arts against the encroachment of a predominately visual consumer culture. It is possible to find it as well in forms of apparently more political or politicized discourse, in which what is opposed to mass culture are those aspects of the subject and state that only high culture makes possible (or so it's asserted). With respect to the subject, this concerns the possibility of reason or critical thinking, which in turn is related to the possibilities of citizenship and civic virtues – a common enough connection of subject to state from Kant to Habermas. The humanities thus come to stand as guardians of critique itself, defenders of a barbarism characterized not by indus-trial culture and profit (as it was for Arnold), but now by an interest in mass culture (expressed paradigmatically in the form of that evil called television.) For example, Mark Crispin Miller, a former profes-sor of English who has since become one of the most virulent critics of contemporary media, offers the following account of the decline of critical thinking:

By the mid-Seventies, however, there was one demographic group now "totally into it" [television] for the first time: America's undergraduates, who watched much more and knew much less than any of the student cohorts that had preceded them. So it seemed, at least, to those of us now teaching. No longer, certainly, could you assume that your lit classes would recognize, say, Donne's Holy Sonnet XIII, or the Houyhnhnms, or the first sentence of *Pride and Prejudice*, or any of the other fragments that have once been common knowl-edge among English majors.²⁸

For Miller, the problem has as much to do with the decline of *reading* as with the lack of knowledge of English literary history:

Spectatorial "experience" is passive, mesmeric, undiscriminating, and therefore not conducive to the refinement of the critical faculties: logic and imagination, linguistic precision, historical awareness, and a capacity for long, intense absorption. These – and not the abilities to compute, apply or memorize – are the true desiderata of any higher education, and it is critical thinking that can best realize them.[29]

Such arguments are common enough. What is more interesting than whether they have any critical bite or not, is the way in which a certain vision of the critical faculties, itself a product of history rather than nature, is reified as the one and only mode of real critique. With images of the classical moment of the bourgeois public sphere dancing in their heads, the present can't help but seem as a wasteland to critics who measure the twentieth-first century by a whitewashed version of the nineteenth. What such critiques fail to do, of course, is to offer an account of just what function culture performs *now*. Instead, they oppose contemporary culture with their own already problematic vision of culture that they take as truth, in much the same way as, in a different context, György Lukács insisted on the political virtues of the realist novel in comparison to its decadent modernist counterparts. Bertolt Brecht's response to Lukács is appropriate in this case, too: it's not the good old days that we should be fascinated with, but rather the bad new ones, and in these bad new days, new forms of culture must necessarily replace the old ones.

Humanities without Value, Culture beyond Culture

The bad new days need not be so bad as they are usually thought to be (or maybe the right way to say this is that the present is always bad for those who have to live it). The typical link between globalization and culture tends to obscure first, the degree to which globalization has disturbed the concept of culture, and second, its impact on the humanities. Globalization has left the humanities in ruins, conceptually and materially. But there are two ways to think about these ruins. One is to see them as a sign of the lamentable end of forces and modes of being essential to democratic life and genuine individual experience; another is to see globalization as opening up the possibility for thinking about contemporary experience and culture in a more complex way than this defensive reassertion of the modern subject and state suggests – that is, as paving the way for a new form of critical humanities that is able to think about culture from perspectives adequate to the age. I have tried to argue for the limits of the former and the necessity of the latter.

What form would this new critical humanities take? And what role would the concept of culture play within it? Can the humanities do without the array of concepts that it has long associated with culture – concepts such as "genius," "imagination," "creativity," "beauty," and "value"? In what way would such a practice continue to be the humanities? It is admittedly more difficult to answer these questions than it is to identify the problematic circulation of an older vision of the humanities in the new circumstances of globalization. But at least the outlines of a critical humanities are, I think, easily grasped. There are no absolute beginnings: a humanities that takes seriously the analysis of its historical and ideological genesis will still have to draw on this history to make sense of the ways in which historical developments have reconstituted the grounds of its own practice. The humanities would continue to be defined as a practice that explores culture, but one that takes as a central principal of its practice the notion that culture is constituted in entirely different ways at specific moments in time. Strangely, contemporary literary history (for instance) has been better at achieving this than have studies of the contemporary moment itself. There are clear models for such a practice, including Walter Benjamin's "The Work of Art in the Age of Mechanical Reproduction," which begins with a challenge to the categories of "genius, eternal value and mystery"[30] in the arts, and Pierre Bourdieu's analysis in *The Rules of Art* of the emergence of the cultural sphere in its modern sense in nineteenth-century France.[31] By destabilizing the grounds of the humanities, globalization opens up the possibility of *generalizing* these kinds of critical practices, of moving them from the periphery to the core of the humanities' self-identity.

There is a great deal more that could be said here, but let me end by pointing to some of the theoretical grounds for this new humanities. In order to take advantage of the opening that globalization provides for a new conception of culture, I would like to highlight four interrelated dimensions along which the humanities have to reconsider their theoretical orientations and interpretive practices.

First, those involved in the study of culture need to think seriously about the problem of "affirmative culture," which arises out of the tendency to focus on objects (specific literary and cultural texts, cultural producers, genres, etc.) rather than cultural processes. Affirmative culture is a concept developed by Herbert Marcuse, who described it as the product of a process:

> ... in which the spiritual world is lifted out of its social context, making culture a (false) collective noun and attributing (false) universality to it. This ... concept of culture, clearly seen in expressions such as "national culture," "Germanic culture" or "Roman culture," plays off the spiritual world against the material world by holding up culture as the realm of authentic values and self-contained ends in opposition to the world of social utility and means. Through the use of this concept, culture is distinguished from civilization and sociologically and valuationally removed from the social process.[32]

It is not only traditional forms of humanistic study that affirm culture in this way: cultural studies, too, has a tendency to oppose culture to the world of utility in the same manner. While proclaiming to study the "everyday," the life of the popular and the mass, cultural studies nevertheless imbues the cultural commodities that it studies with a more traditional "cultural" character through its very insistence on the authenticity of non-traditional cultural forms. As Readings perceptively points out, "cultural studies does not propose culture as a regulatory ideal for research and teaching, so much as seek to preserve the structure of an argument from redemption through culture, while recognizing the inability of culture to function any longer as such an idea."[33] Furthermore, by accepting commodity culture *as* culture, and by consequently affirming the spiritual dimension of this culture as a site of meaning and significance, cultural studies circulates in a perpetual present in which the reality of present-day culture amounts to no more and no less than *all* that culture is and can be. The cultural past, dominated by what cultural studies considers to be the lumbering dinosaurs of bourgeois high culture, is closed off from it – but so is the future, since the present of culture is taken as fate. A critical humanities will have to side-step both traditional humanities study and cultural studies, by focusing not on authenticity but on the social process in and through which cultural objects are produced, circulated, and consumed.

Second, a critical humanities that wants to understand the contemporary function of culture needs to take commodities and consumerism seriously – not as deviations of some true idea of culture, and not primarily as a normative issue (shopping as bad, destructive, etc.), but as a significant transformation in the concept of culture that has had implications that we don't yet completely understand. It has become a critical commonplace to lament consumerism and commodity culture; indeed, it often seems that much of the energy of the humanities emerges out of this lament and the frequently made opposition between (for instance) reading versus watching. But such laments fail to interrogate the culture of consumer culture, being satisfied instead with the presumption that consumerism is either without culture or its opposite.

Taking consumerism seriously doesn't imply the negation of a politics of consumerism or consumption, of the kind outlined by Juliet Schor, who has explored the consequences of (among other things) the growing "aspirational gap" in the U.S. society.[34] It remains important to draw attention to the ways in which contemporary mass culture constitutes a concerted form of "public pedagogy" – a pedagogy of hopes, desires, beliefs, and identities – that now outweighs anything that might be taught in schools or homes. Henry Giroux in particular has articulated this point tirelessly in his work on education and mass culture. However, when these critiques devolve into demands for the reassertion of the now lost public sphere or place hope in re-formation of collectivities of an older kind, the contemporary terrain of culture is dangerously misread. Analyses of consumerism almost always get confused with the normative claims they also want to advance: a clear understanding of how consumer culture operates, for instance, is almost always blurred by the wish that things could be different than they are. It has become nigh impossible to suggest, for instance, that consumerism is itself political – not, in order words, the "other" of civic possibilities and virtues, but an example of their mutation into a radically different form. For all its problems, Nestor Garcia-Canclini's claim in *Citizens and Consumers* that "consumption is good for thinking"[35] has the effect of shaking up our pre-established sense of what consumerism is about. "To consume," he writes, "is to participate in an arena of competing claims for what society produces and the ways of using it."[36] Instead of imagining consumers and citizens as existing in an inverse relationship to one another, Garcia Canclini suggests that we investigate consumption as a site "where a good part of economic, sociopolitical, and psychological rationality is organized in all societies."[37] Whether or not Canclini is right in his sense of how consumption operates, an understanding of culture in the era of globalization cannot avoid seeing consumption as a site of rationality and of cultural experience which, whatever one thinks of it, has a constitutive role to play in contemporary culture.

Third, even after all of the explorations of the ideologies of the humanities, there remains a need for a more thorough investigation of the historical narratives that have legitimized the standard view of culture in the humanities. This is especially true of the narratives that established the modern sense of the mission of the humanities. One such narrative concerns the opposition of modernism to mass culture, an opposition which has elevated the monuments of modernism into exemplary expressions of a critique of the existing world within the realm of art and literature. The narrative that links modernism to revolution has transformed much of the writing on modernism into an elegy over lost political possibilities. This narrative has been challenged recently in Miriam Hansen's writings on "popular-reflexivity" of early cinema[38] and Susan Buck-Morss's explorations of the unexpected links between Soviet and American twentieth-century popular culture.[39] Perhaps most forcefully, Malcolm Bull has argued that, while modernism may have been against *modernity*, it was never against *capitalism*, which is evidenced in part by the seemless assimilation of modernist culture into museums and literary canons.

Bull claims that "modernists were not partisans resisting the present and pressing on eternity, they were negotiating the equally tricky but rather more mundane path between the two cultures of capitalism"[40] – classicism and commodity culture. Rather, "working between two antithetical cultures meant that resistance to the one almost always involved some degree of complicity with the other."[41] But his argument goes beyond the not uncommon assertion of modernism's incomplete rejection of either classicism or commodity culture. Bull suggests that modernism has to be seen as belated, as working a divide between one culture of capitalism and another that by beginning of the twentieth-century had already been crossed over once and for all:

For most people, the culture of modernity has been the culture of commodities; or, to put it more bluntly, "postmodernism" was the culture of modernity all along. This is true not just for the huge numbers of people in the twentieth century whose first experience of anything other than folk traditions has been American-style TV; but also for their predecessors who moved straight from agrarian communities to the world of the newspaper and the wireless.... Only for those steeped in the classical tradition did postmodernism require new forms of attention.[42]

Such re-narrativizations can help to dissipate what have become un-productive conjunctions between art and culture. It's not that Bull's arguments eliminate the political productivity or engagement of certain forms of modernist cultural production. Rather, by showing us a modernism that is always already contaminated by its historical situation, he helps us to avoid lamenting the irretrievable loss of this moment of supposed purity, which in turn prompts us to look at the politics of culture in our moment as one which not only need not but cannot be free of ideological contagion.

Finally, humanities scholars need to re-consider the history of recent theory as reactions to historically specific circumstances that may no longer hold today. When Hardt and Negri describe both postcolonial and postmodern theory as *symptoms* of the end of modern sovereignty – as kinds of critique that can only emerge once modern sovereignty is no longer the framework for control and domination – they do so not in order to deny the utility and importance of many of their formulations.[43] They are pointing, rather, to the way in which any theory expresses incompletely the moment that it is trying to analyze, relying on concepts and narratives that no longer or incompletely relate to empirical circumstances. The progressivist narrative in which we have tended to view theory, in which one theory builds on another and we slowly get closer and closer to the truth, tends to obfuscate the historicity of theory. Of course, the historicity of concepts is a central element of contemporary theory, such that no one who engages in theory would understand what they do as a project involving truth. Still, in the actual practice of theory, this fact is more often than not lost and theory becomes yet another narrative of modernity (which means, for instance, that there are more and less developed theoretical regions in the world, that theory can be imported from one country to another in the manner of high technology, or even that there can be strategies of import-substitution in the theoretical field).

In making these statements about what the humanities needs to do to reinvent itself in the context of globalization, I don't mean to advocate any particular methodology or interpretive practice. I merely want to suggest this: if the role of the humanities is to explore and to understand the circulation of forms of symbolic and culture production, if its task is to bring to the surface of social consciousness normally latent processes that take place in these forms – and to do so in a critical fashion, rejecting the commonplaces of the day – it needs to direct itself to the ways in which the profound transformation in circulation of culture that we have called globalization *has also been* accompanied by a profound transformation in culture itself. While there has been a great deal of attention paid to the new conditions for the circulation of culture, there is little movement to re-imagine the concept of culture as such. This is not a demand for that most precious of commodities – a whole new theory of culture – but a suggestion that one way forward is to reassert or reaffirm those theories that have long drawn attention to the shape of our ideologies of culture, while also giving up on the identity of the humanities as the guardian of the good against commodity culture and commodity aesthetics.

And this is more difficult than it might seem. Pierre Bourdieu made it part of his life's work to deny the importance of the aesthetic, focusing, for example, in *The Rules of Art* on a "scientific analysis of the social conditions of the production and reception of a work of art"[44] while never once addressing the question of value. However, in the attack that he launched on neoliberalism over the last part of his life, an attack based on the pernicious influence of the logic of neoliberalism over all social spheres, Bourdieu reverted to a vocabulary in which he defended (for example) the production of the great works of European literature, claiming that such masterpieces could only continue to be produced if the fields of cultural production were allowed to remain semi-autonomous.[45] The spread of the logic of neoliberalism across society (measurable, for instance, in the widespread application of the vocabulary of market efficiency in the operation of non-market sectors) demands a response. But is an appeal to aesthetic value an appropriate one? Such an appeal is at best a contradictory one, and one that cannot be seen to really oppose the cultural conservatism that makes up (in its own contradictory way) the dynamism of neoliberalism. What would be better would be a challenge that did not make recourses to the aesthetic at all, but which made an argument within the logic of contemporary culture; but since such a logic has yet to be mapped out, it is not surprising that the critics like Bourdieu remain stuck with a concept of culture that it no longer our own.

Notes

1   I want to thank Richard Cavell for giving me the chance to present an earlier version of this paper at the International Canadian Studies Centre at the University of British Columbia. This paper was written with the assistance of a Social Sciences and Humanities Research Council of Canada Standard Research Grant.

2   See Iain Chambers, *Culture after Humanism* (New York: Routledge, 2001), and John Tomlinson, *Globalization and Culture* (Chicago: University of Chicago Press, 1999), as just two examples of a large genre of books and articles in this field.

3   Morley and Pattee offered early and influential definitions of the fields of English and American literature. Morley described the connection between English literature and the English nation in 1873 in the following terms: "The literature of this country has for its most distinctive mark the religious sense of duty. It represents a people striving through successive generations to find out the right and do it, to root out the wrong and labour ever onward for the love of God. If this be really the strong spirit of her people, to show that it is so is to tell how England won, and how alone she can expect to keep, her foremost place among nations." The first professor of American literature, Fred Lewis Pattee, began his introductory text on the subject with a description of the relationship between litera-

ture and the nation that by the end of the century had become all but indisputable: "The literature of a nation is the entire body of literary productions that has emanated from the people of the nation during its history, preserved by the arts of writing and printing. It is the embodiment of the best thoughts and fancies of a people." Morley and Pattee cited in Christopher Clausen, "'National Literatures' in English: Toward a New Paradigm," *New Literary History* 25, no. 1 (1994): 64 and 65, respectively.

4   Theodor Adorno, "On the Question: 'What Is German?'" in *Critical Models: Interventions and Catchwords* (New York: Columbia University Press, 1998), 205.

5   Adorno suggests that such nationalist thinking "obeys a reifying consciousness that is no longer really capable of experience. It confines itself within precisely those stereotypes that thinking should dissolve." Ibid., 205. This is apt description of the work of many pundits on 9/11, including Samuel Huntington, writer Robert Kaplan, *New York Times* columnist Thomas Friedman and *Globe and Mail* columnist Margaret Wente.

6   For a critique of the concept of cultural imperialism, see John Tomlinson, *Cultural Imperialism* (Baltimore: Johns Hopkins University Press, 1991).

7   Ariel Dorfman and Armand Mattelart, *How to Read Donald Duck* (New York: International General, 1975).

8   Bill Ashcroft, Gareth Griffiths, and Helen Tiffin, *Key Concepts in Postcolonial Studies* (New York: Routledge, 1998), 112–13.

9   Terry Eagleton, *The Idea of Culture* (Oxford: Blackwell, 2000), 1.

10 On economics, see Paul Hirst and Grahame Thompson, *Globalization in Question: The International Economy and the Possibility of Governance* (London: Polity Press, 1999), Gary Burtless et al., *Globaphobia: Confronting Fears about Open Trade* (Washington: Brookings Institute, 1998), and Goran Therborn, "Into the 21st Century: The New Parameters of Global Politics," *New Left Review* 10 (2001): 87–110. On the long history of global migration and intercultural communities, see Martin Bernal, *Black Athena: The Afroasiatic Roots of Classical Civilization* (New Brunswick, NJ: Rutgers University Press, 1989). For a discussion of transformations in political modernity, see Michael Hardt and Antonio Negri, *Empire* (Cambridge: Harvard University Press, 2000), and Peter Taylor, *Modernities: A Geohistorical Interpretation* (Minneapolis: University of Minnesota Press, 1999). Finally, Mattelart has emphasized recently the long-term development of that most important figure in the narrative of globalization: communications technologies. Armand Mattelart, *Networking the World, 1794-2000*, trans. Liz Carey-Libbrect and James A. Cohen (Minneapolis: University of Minnesota Press, 2000). All of these works are, of course, examples drawn from a formidable body of texts and debates concerning claims about globalization's originality.

11 Christopher Clausen, "Nostalgia, Freedom, and the End of Cultures," *Queen's Quarterly* 106, no. 2 (1999): 234.

12 Arjun Appadurai, *Modernity at Large: Cultural Dimensions of Globalization*, vol. 1, *Public Worlds* (Minneapolis: University of Minnesota Press, 1996), 32.

13 Ibid., 52.

14 Lawrence Grossberg, "Speculations and Articulations of Globalization," *Polygraph* 11 (1999): 11–48, Fredric Jameson, "Finance Capitalism and Culture," in *The Cultural Turn: Selected Writings on the Postmodern, 1983-1998* (New York: Verso, 1998), 136–61.

15 Tomlinson, *Globalization and Culture*, 24.

16 Canada, "Cultural Industries Sectoral Advisory Group on International Trade," in *Canadian Culture in a Global World: New Strategies for Culture and Trade* (Ottawa: 1999), 1.

17 Raymond Williams, *Problems in Materialism and Culture: Selected Essays* (New York: Verso, 1980).

18 Pierre Bourdieu, *Distinction: A Social Critique of the Judgement of Taste*, trans. Richard Nice (Cambridge, MA: Harvard University Press, 1984).

19   Terry Eagleton, *The Ideology of the Aesthetic* (Malden, MA: Blackwell, 1990).

20   Étienne Balibar and Pierre Macherey, "On Literature as an Ideological Form: Some Marxist Propositions," in *Untying the Text: A Post-Structuralist Reader*, ed. Robert Young (London: Routledge & Kegan Paul, 1981), 46.

21   Ibid., 1.

22   David Lloyd and Paul Thomas, *Culture and the State* (New York: Routledge, 1998), 2.

23   Bill Readings, *The University in Ruins* (Cambridge, MA: Harvard University Press, 1996), 12.

24   Ibid., 9.

25   Elaine Scarry, *On Beauty and Being Just* (Princeton: Princeton University Press, 1999).

26   Wendy Steiner, *Venus in Exile: The Rejection of Beauty in Twentieth-Century Art* (New York: Free Press, 2001).

27   James Elkins, *Pictures and Tears: People Who Have Cried in Front of Paintings* (New York: Routledge, 2001).

28   Mark Crispin Miller, *Boxed In: The Culture of TV* (Evanston, IL: Northwestern University Press, 1988), 8.

29   Ibid., 6.

30   Walter Benjamin, "The Work of Art in the Age of Mechanical Reproduction," in *Illuminations: Essays and Reflections* (New York: Schocken Books, 1968), 218.

31   Pierre Bourdieu, *The Rules of Art: Genesis and Structure of the Literary Field*, trans. Susan Emanuel (Stanford, CA: Stanford University Press, 1996).

32   Herbert Marcuse, *Negations: Essays in Critical Theory*, trans. Jeremy J. Shapiro (London: Free Association Books, 1988), 94–95.

33   Readings, *The University in Ruins*, 17.

34   Juliet Schor, "Towards a New Politics of Consumption," in *The Consumer Society Reader*, ed. Juliet B. Schor and Douglas Holt (New York: The New Press, 2000), 446–62.

35   Néstor Garcia Canclini, *Consumers and Citizens: Globalization and Multicultural Conflicts*, trans. George Yúdice (Minneapolis: University of Minnesota Press, 2001), 39.

36   Ibid., 39.

37   Ibid., 5.

38   Miriam Hansen, "The Mass Production of the Senses: Classical Cinema as Vernacular Modernism," *Modernism/Modernity* 6, no. 2 (1999): 59–77.

39   Susan Buck-Morss, *Dreamworld and Catastrophe* (New York: MIT Press, 2001).

40   Martin Bull, "Between the Cultures of Capital," *New Left Review* 11 (2001): 102.

41   Ibid., 102.

42   Ibid., 100.

43   Hardt and Negri, *Empire*.

44   Bourdieu, *The Rules of Art*, xix.

45   Pierre Bourdieu, *Acts of Resistance: Against the Tyranny of the Market*, trans. Richard Nice (New York: The New Press, 1998), 339–44.

6 In his essay, one of the last written prior to his untimely death from cancer late in 2001, David Novitz inquires into the precise nature of art's contribution to the development of a cultural identity. What does art do or provide, he asks, that permits it to play any role at all in settling the terms of reference of the cultures within which it is created and interpreted? How or what does art, in virtue of its relationship to culture, contribute to identities? For Novitz these questions can only be answered after becoming clearer about what precisely is meant by the terms "art," "culture," and "identity."

Novitz begins to clarify these concepts by considering "culture," his explication of which closely mirrors Christoph Brumann's in his contribution to this volume. Like Brumann, Novitz views culture as an "aggregate" or "colligatory" concept, one which bundles together sequences or patterns of action, beliefs, desires, values, and institutions in a way capable of conceptually isolating groups of people in virtue of what they share. This view has several advantages, including its superior capacity for mapping varying degrees of integration within cultures, its provision of reliable predictive tools, and its incompatibility with the notion that "culture" means only "elite culture." Novitz also argues that a colligatory account diminishes pessimism concerning the wild semantics of "culture" of the sort expressed by Geoffrey Hartman in his contribution. For although the term may refer to many different kinds of phenomena, and many different instantiations of those kinds, its "sense" – the fact that as a collective noun it refers to some (but not any one specific) collection of institutions, values, beliefs, and practices – does not.

Novitz's colligatory account differs most remarkably from the "ghostly" or "Idealist" conception of culture associated with G.W.F. Hegel and his proponents, on the terms of which "culture" refers to that "Spirit" or "Geist" underlying and animating social phenomena. Culture on this view is that which is responsible for the achievements of a people as well as the source of social cohesion and the root of that identity – the sense of belonging to some larger whole – shared by members of a group. However, Novitz points out that several problems with the Hegelian view obtain, problems strikingly absent from the colligatory account. He argues that the hidden "entity" posited by Idealists and held responsible for phenomena cannot be considered apart from those phenomena, that the precise nature of its causal efficacy remains elusive, and that in order to "act" in and on the social system Geist must be presumed to possess a rationality even the most cursory reading of systems of social organization suggest it lacks. In virtue of these and other shortcomings Novitz proposes that the Idealist account be rejected.

Novitz explains cultural identity as a byproduct of human beings' attempts to make sense of their desires, values, ambitions, and hopes with reference to those of others around them. On this view, individuals come to possess or inherit a cultural identity as a result of recognizing in others an orientation towards the world they take themselves to share. This recognition lends salience to individuals' plans and aspirations by socially legitimating the values, practices, and activities underpinning them, a process by its very nature both provisional and political. It is in connection with this process that Novitz sees artworks playing a crucial role in the constitution of cultural identities. For belonging to a culture, feeling in some important sense at home in it, involves the acquisition of beliefs about others which art – films, novels, TV programs, paintings, etc. – fosters. In short, Novitz argues that art enables us to come to know others as well as ourselves, and by so knowing to identify with, to feel like we belong to, a group.

ART, CULTURE, AND IDENTITY

DAVID NOVITZ

Art and culture seem to go together. We speak of them in the same breath, rather in the way that we speak of a horse and cart, or (in times long past) of love and marriage. For most people, art is intimately related to culture, although quite what they mean by this is far from clear. Still, we like to think that there are clues. To be acquainted with art, its history, its current trends and developments, is, we are told, to be cultured. Furthermore, people often have a special interest in the high art of their own society, believing that it is in some way the bearer of their cultural heritage. By becoming acquainted with it, they take themselves to learn about their culture; by appreciating and valuing it, they feel a part of that culture and in some way identify with it.

My question in this paper is quite straightforward. How, I want to know, do works of art contribute to the development of a cultural identity? Even though the question is straightforward, finding a satisfactory answer to it is not. For unless one can give an adequate explanation of the concepts of a culture and an identity, one cannot hope to explain how works of art contribute to a cultural identity. Nor should we simply assume that "culture" is in some way co-extensive with art and its history, or that people become acculturated just by being exposed to both. "Culture," I shall argue, is a much richer concept than this suggests. Indeed, we will see that the tendency to associate culture with high art and its history is a peculiarly narrow, late nineteenth-century view of the concept "culture," that is badly in need of revision.

Culture: The Ghost in a Societal Machine?

One way of elucidating the concept "culture" is to explain how we count cultures, what we look to and take into consideration when distinguishing one culture from another. For if anything is plain, it is that cultures differ from one another. Germans participate in a culture that is radically different from that found among the Bengalis or the Thais. There is something distinctive about German culture, one wants to say; something that makes it home to Goethe but not Tagore. Indeed, the very same culture that distinguishes a nation, a society, a country, or a people may differ from one period to the next. Contemporary English culture is markedly different from its Elizabethan counterpart, although both count as stages in one and the same culture. However, English culture differs not just qualitatively but numerically from the cultures that distinguished the Celts, the early Saxons, and the Angles – even though all three cultures fed into and helped nurture what we now regard as a distinctively English culture.

What is it, then, that makes a culture distinctively one? Put differently, how are we to tell that any two people belong to one and the same culture? Normally we appeal to a range of social phenomena: to language, political and economic systems, values, beliefs, religion, dress, art, customs, traditions, conventions, leisure pursuits, and so on. The extent to which people do or do not participate in these, we are sometimes inclined to say, is a measure of their common culture.

This, I have argued elsewhere, is a reasonable way of answering our question, but one that has its own difficulties.[1] The Spanish, the Dutch, the Italians, and the English speak and behave differently; they have different customs, different languages, different religions, and different manners. This, presumably, inclines us to speak of distinctive Spanish, Dutch, Italian, and English culture. But we also speak of each as belonging to European culture, and we do so, presumably, because of what they have in common: similarities of language, art, religion, history, and values. Problematically, though, not all social similarities ensure a shared culture. The English and the Irish, to take just one example, speak the same language, share much of their history, have religions and have had monarchs in common, but even so, English and Irish cultures remain distinct.

Certain social similarities may be necessary in order to speak correctly of a shared culture, but there are no similarities that will always logically guarantee that people have a culture in common. Indeed, it is difficult to specify what social behaviour, values, and beliefs one absolutely must share with someone else in order to be described as belonging to the same culture. We need not share a religion in order to belong to British culture; nor is it clear that we must share a language, a philosophical outlook, or similar tastes in art.

Perhaps it was these difficulties that inclined G.W.F. Hegel to the view that there must be some substratum that unifies, controls, and is causally responsible for diverse social phenomena. On his view, Spirit or *Geist* underlies the various social phenomena that we naively think of as characterizing a particular culture. More accurately, a particular culture is to be identified as nothing more than a stage in the development of *Geist*. In *The Phenomenology of Mind*, for instance, Hegel maintains:

That which, in reference to the single individual, appears as his culture, is the essential moment of spiritual substance as such ... or, otherwise put, culture is the single soul of this substance, in virtue of which the essentially inherent (*Ansich*) becomes something explicitly acknowledged, and assumes definite objective existence.[2]

It is, then, a particular stage in the development of *Geist* that is causally responsible for the distinctive institutions, customs, and practices of any society (country, or nation), and that helps distinguish the society in the eyes of its members or citizens. This stage in the development of Spirit is what Hegel calls the *Volksgeist*. He sees it as a strong binding force – something that the individual can neither deny nor escape. And so he tells us that:

... the individual is an individual in this substance.... No individual can step beyond it; he can separate himself certainly from other particular individuals, but not from the *Volksgeist*.[3]

If Hegel is correct, we should individuate a culture not in terms of a set of distinctive social phenomena, but in terms of the *Volksgeist* that is causally responsible for those phenomena. It is this that guides the growth and development of a nation and furnishes its citizens with a clear sense of their own identity. This much emerges from his *Lectures on the Philosophy of History*, where he maintains that:

World history represents … the evolution of the awareness of Spirit of its own freedom.… Every step being different from every other one, has its own determined and peculiar principle. In history such a principle becomes the determination of Spirit – a peculiar National Spirit [*ein besonderer Volksgeist*]. It is here that it expresses all the aspects of its consciousness and will … ; it is this that imparts a common stamp to its religion, its political constitution, its art, and its technical skills. These particular individual qualities must be understood as deriving from that common peculiarity – the particular peculiarity that characterizes a nation. Conversely, it is from the facts of history that the general character of this peculiarity has to be inferred.[4]

Culture, on Hegel's view, is akin to a Cartesian ghost, this time in a societal, rather than a biologically human, machine. To some, this is a very attractive view of culture. For one thing, it offers a unifying principle that brings together a range of diverse social phenomena as manifestations of a single culture. For another, it explains culture as the driving force of a society; one, moreover, that infuses humans in a way that makes it impossible for them to step beyond its influence. Culture, as a Cartesian ghost, is responsible for the achievements of a nation as reflected in its technologies, artworks, customs, artefacts, practices, and political institutions – all of which come to be distinctive of that nation and give shape to its character. Much more, this notion of culture is also able to explain social cohesion as well as the sense of identity and belonging that members of a culture (sometimes) share. For although Hegel did not defend doctrines of cultural exclusivity, it is plain from what he says that *Geist*, hence culture, infuses and shapes individuals in ways that make it impossible for them to step beyond their own culture, or enter and participate fully in any other.

But ghostly accounts of culture are also deeply unsatisfactory. Not only do they posit a hidden entity as the causal source of all social phenomena, but it soon turns out that the entity in question cannot properly be identified apart from these phenomena. Much worse, it is difficult to understand the causal powers of this entity, for if it really is *Geist* – that is, a kind of spiritual substance – it is difficult to know how it intervenes causally in the world. Hegel, however, is not particularly worried about these objections. On his view, *Geist* is not an empirical entity, cannot be directly observed, but is revealed through philosophy, art, and religion – although quite how Hegel or anyone else can know this is far from clear.

Geist, it would seem, is an unobservable entity, and as such might appear to be totally useless in explanations of social phenomena. However, this need not follow. Unobservable entities can be, and often are, allowed a place in perfectly acceptable explanations. So, for instance, Daniel Dennett points out that we readily posit unobservable beliefs, intentions, and desires when explaining the behaviour of a chess-playing computer.[5] We do this because the physical state and design of a computer is too complex to be helpfully invoked in an explanation or prediction of the computer's moves.[6] Instead, we treat the computer as an intentional system – that is, as a system whose behaviour can be predicted and explained by assuming that it has certain beliefs, by supposing its behaviour to be directed by certain intentions, and then by calculating the most reasonable action for it to take relative to its beliefs and intentions.[7]

It can plausibly be argued that Hegel does something similar when he attempts to explain the behaviour of a society by appealing to an unobservable spiritual substance that is treated as the seat of various beliefs and intentions. Dennett, however, insists that in order to explain the behaviour of any system in terms of beliefs and intentions, one has to assume the rationality of that system.[8] One must assume, that is, that the system will pursue its goals, and so attempt to fulfill its intentions, in ways that are appropriate to the beliefs (or information) that it has.

The trouble, though, is that the assumption of rationality does not sit well with human societies. It seems perfectly reasonable, for instance, to assume that society has as a goal the welfare of its members. If it were ideally rational, then, given certain beliefs or information, it would pursue this goal by the most appropriate or reasonable means. And to do so is to be an intentional system. However, it is not difficult to show that societies frequently run counter to this aim, and that they do so even when they have at their disposal the information with which to secure their long-term goal. So, for instance, they stumble into wars, destroy their own economies, create mass poverty, epidemics, social dislocations, famines, environmental disasters, and so on. Given this repeated tendency in societies all over the world, it is difficult to assume that human societies behave rationally. As a result, it seems inappropriate to explain their behaviour as if they were intentional systems. But if we cannot do this, then it does, after all, appear to be inappropriate to explain cultural change in terms of the mental states of an unobservable spiritual substance.[9]

Perhaps one can defend the view that human societies are intentional systems by arguing that, although rational, they regularly operate on the basis of false beliefs. This would account for their failure to achieve their goals, while at the same time preserving the assumption of their rationality. Hence, on this view, societies pursue their goals in ways that are appropriate to the beliefs that they happen to have, and the fact that these beliefs turn out to be false does not make them any the less rational. After all, the complex information that societies need in order to secure the well being of their members is, as a matter of fact, very difficult to come by.

This, however, does little to preserve the rationality of human societies. For were it the case that a chess-playing computer were regularly to operate on the basis of false beliefs – that knights move like bishops, and castles like pawns – it would be odd to attest to its rationality in anything but the most extended sense of this term. We would be much more inclined to say that the computer is malfunctioning. The case is slightly different for persons, although the lesson is the same. We might scruple at ascribing cognitive malfunctions to people, and yet, if they regularly pursue their goals in terms of false beliefs, we would be forced to doubt their rationality. We would do so not because they are acting in ways inappropriate to their beliefs but because they are unable to interpret and assess the evidence. This, of course, is a vital criterion of a person's rationality; anyone unable to fulfill it would be regarded as irrational in a perfectly straightforward sense of the word. Hence, although a society that regularly pursues its goals in ways appropriate to false beliefs satisfies one criterion of rationality, it fails to satisfy another. And this makes it inappropriate to assume its rationality, and so treat it as an intentional system.[10]

The problem, then, with Hegelian attempts to explain culture as a ghostly entity that somehow motivates and guides social change is not just that culture itself becomes mysterious but also that one cannot get around this problem by treating culture as part of an intentional system. For, as we have now seen, there are very real difficulties that attend the assumption of a society's rationality. This is not to deny that some societies may be rational, hence amenable to intentional explanations. A golf club, a university, or a village council might all qualify. It could also turn out that the behaviour of certain larger societies – perhaps the state itself – is, for a certain time, largely rational. However, the weight of evidence suggests that we cannot simply assume this. Without such an assumption, though, one cannot treat society as an intentional system and so offer a mentalistic account of its culture.

A Colligatory Account of Culture

Even though an Hegelian or idealist view of culture has considerable popular appeal, it receives very little philosophical support. There is, however, another and a more adequate view of culture available to us – one, to extend my analogy, that takes us away from the Cartesian "ghost" to something like a Humean "bundle."

To the uninitiated, human behaviour is bewildering in its apparent diversity and randomness, so that we try, almost constantly, to make sense of it. By studying and observing human beings and the relationships into which they enter, we discover different sequences or patterns of action and interaction. Social scientists distinguish rituals, customs, traditions, manners, types of play, and modes of dress. They discern particular linguistic habits, distinctive political and economic systems, and, of course, distinctive religions and art forms. Each, in turn, is based on, or mediated by, certain values, systems of belief, and bodies of knowledge.

Importantly, such beliefs, values, and practices and the institutions founded upon them, come together in complex and varying ways.

Economic systems can reinforce or undermine moral and religious beliefs; the practice of artists can subvert hegemonic structures within a society or, as is sometimes the case, can strengthen them. Religion may affect the art of a society, the health system, the economic system, and so on. Crucially, all of these complex relations of interdependency can (and do) differ from one society, tribe, country, nation, or state to the next. And it is largely in order to distinguish these intricate and variable relationships that social scientists use the word "culture." Used thus, culture is what, following W. H. Walsh, I have elsewhere called a colligatory concept.[11] It is used to mark off groups of people by collecting together their characteristic and mutually dependent patterns of action and interaction, as well as the values, attitudes, beliefs, and knowledge that guide them.

A colligatory account of culture is not at all new. Most anthropologists subscribe to some or other version of it, beginning with Edward Tylor in 1871.[12] Even so, it is an account that stands in need of detailed elaboration and defence. In particular, one needs to show that it is capable of offering a satisfactory explanation of cultural identity, social change, cultural cohesion, and cultural knowledge in ways that avoid the pitfalls of an Hegelian or idealist approach. On an Hegelian view, for instance, cultures are always organic; they infuse individuals, make them what they are, and in this way bind them to the society, the tribe, or the state. What this fails to observe is that not all cultures can be construed on the model of an organism. African culture, for instance, is not very well integrated and consists of largely independent practices, institutions, values, and beliefs. Irish culture is rather more integrated, and Catholic culture can usefully be construed as an organic whole that consists of mutually interdependent parts. One clear advantage of a colligatory account of culture is that it allows us to distinguish and explain degrees of integration without implying, as an Hegelian account does, that weakly integrated cultures are in some ways ailing or deficient.

A colligatory account has the further, altogether obvious, advantage of enabling us to understand what is involved in coming to know a culture. Above all, there are no inferences to a mysterious *Geist*. Rather, in coming to know Italian culture, I learn about a particular pattern of values, behaviour, and beliefs – I learn, that is, that they hang together in specific ways. To be acquainted with different cultures, therefore, is to know about these different patterns. And such knowledge is a useful diagnostic and predictive tool, for it is in light of it that various actions and pronouncements assume a significance they would otherwise lack. So, for instance, we know that Ancient Greek and Zulu cultures include dance in their religious rituals, and that Protestant culture does not. As a result, we can gauge the significance that a Scottish protestant, a Zulu, or an ancient Greek would attach to dance during a religious ceremony.

There is a further advantage to a colligatory account of culture. Many theorists believe that there are different senses of the word "culture," so that on this view a unified theory of culture simply is not available to us.[13] James P. Spradley, for instance, contends that "social scientists have made it a regular practice to expropriate this term for their special purposes. As each new definition is added to the list, the semantic battle lines are drawn and verbal warfare continues."[14] A colligatory account of culture, when properly understood, offers a unified account that eliminates all need for such "verbal warfare." For the acrimony, it would seem, is the result of a failure to understand the colligatory function of the word "culture." The word, we have seen, is used to bring together different patterns of behaviour, values, belief, and knowledge in different ways. But this does not entail that the meaning of the word is constantly changing; what it is used to refer to may no doubt change, but its sense will remain unchanged.

Consider, for instance, the way in which the collective noun "team" functions. I may speak of the Manchester United soccer team, the Cirencester ladies' tennis team, and the All Blacks rugby team. In each case, the word "team" is used to mention, and to bring together, rather different entities – male soccer players who are of course different from female tennis players, who, in their turn, are singularly different from the members of the New Zealand first fifteen. But it would be quite wrong to suppose that the word "team" changes its meaning from one use to the next. It does not. In each case, it is used in precisely the same way, to collect together and to identify a group of sportsmen and women. Of course, when used referringly, the phrase "the team" may refer to different groups of people, but, as Frege pointed out a long time ago, we must avoid confusing sense with reference.[15] This is why I may speak of a pile of stones and a pile of used shoes, and use the word "pile" in each case in precisely the same sense even though the word "pile" brings different things together on each occasion.

The same applies to all collective nouns or colligatory concepts. When historians speak of the Elizabethan and the Napoleonic era, they clearly speak of different periods and events, but in each case the word "era" retains its sense. In just the same way, the word "culture" retains its meaning no matter what collection of institutions, behaviour patterns, values, beliefs or ideologies it is used to bring together. When we speak of contemporary German culture, we speak, among other things, of a capitalist economic system; when we speak of Catholic or Jewish culture, we speak of no economic system at all. But this, we can now see, does not mean that "culture" has a different sense on each occasion of use.

It is sometimes held that there is a distinctive sense of the word "culture" that confines it to high art and the customs, attitudes, and sensibilities that surround it.[16] On my view, though, when "culture" is used to bring these items together it does not acquire a peculiar and distinctive sense; on the contrary, it is used, as it always is, to bring together a range of social phenomena. The argument, if there is one, should not be about the sense of the term "culture," but about whether its colligatory function can usefully be limited in the way favoured by the advocates of high culture.

The Demarcation of Cultures

Collections always reflect the particular concerns and interests of the collector. Even the most committed philatelists do not collect all of the stamps that come their way. Rather, given their interests, they collect only certain types of stamps, and then only in rather special ways. They may collect according to years or countries of origin, pictorial motifs, printing techniques, printing errors, and so on. As a result, the collections will be distinguished not just by the kinds of stamps they contain, but also by the principles in terms of which these stamps are brought together.

Precisely the same is true when people gather, organize, and relate human phenomena under the banner of "culture." Examples are many and obvious. At times sentimental, perhaps political, interests dominate. A Caribbean scholar, for instance, might think it proper to inquire into the Caribbean contribution to British history, philosophy, art, education, moral values, commerce, science, technology – in short, to British culture. However, members of the National Front in Britain might very well deny both that there has ever been any Caribbean contribution to British culture or that the Caribbean people have any proper place in British culture.

Driven in this way by their interests, people often try to demarcate their own culture in a manner that casts it in a favourable light. So, for instance, a proud Briton may be reluctant to see racism, occultism, quackery, or prostitution as part of British culture, and may be outraged by the suggestion that war and its glorification are part of the British cultural heritage. The same desire to commend one's own culture prevents some citizens of Israel from treating racism and revenge as part of Israeli culture, or Indians from treating prostitution, bribery, and economic corruption as an integral part of its culture.

There are, needless to say, very many interests and concerns that affect the ways in which cultures are demarcated. High modernism, for example, and the consequent rise of esoteric art, so affected values and interests in the West that it brought successive generations to the view that the term "culture" was coextensive with the production and appreciation of "high" art.[17] An entirely different restriction on the scope of the word can be found among those anthropologists who are concerned to make their subject scientific. They confine the term "culture" to publicly accessible behaviour, thereby excluding non-observable, hence non-quantifiable, value systems or systems of belief from the culture of any tribe or people.[18]

Our allegiances, preferences, and prejudices clearly can influence the principles according to which we demarcate a culture. Even so, this does not entail that we are at liberty to include or exclude whatever social phenomena we wish when doing so. There are obvious constraints, both of evidence and consistency, on the ways in which we delineate and describe a culture. If, for example, someone chooses to demarcate British culture solely in terms of its imperial history, this will strongly influence what is and is not included under the British cultural banner. One is likely to attend only to those past events, institutions, values, and frames of reference that one regards as pertinent to the formation and defence of the British Empire. But one can rightly object to this principle of demarcation by pointing out that it reflects neither the intricacy nor the detail of British society. For in concentrating on military history, it fails to say anything at all about the contemporary detail of British society: its economic and political systems, its religions, languages and literature, its contributions to philosophy, painting, music, technology, and the like. It also leaves out of account British racism, prostitution, and organized crime. The evidence, therefore, suggests that *this* principle of demarcation is inadequate to the facts of British social life.[19]

Evidence, however, is not the only constraint on the demarcation of cultures. Consistency, I have already indicated, is another. A member of the Ku Klux Klan, for instance, may prefer to demarcate the culture of the United States in terms of its technological achievements but may insist that black people have no place in this culture. However, if a survey of the institutions and practices that the Klansman wants most to include under the banner of American culture reveals a continuous African American contribution to them, then it is simply inconsistent to say that black people have no place in this conception of American culture.

Issues of consistency also arise when we ask, as people often do, whether one culture can properly be regarded as part of another. There is, of course, no *a priori* reason why not, for, according to a colligatory account of culture, just as my jug collection can form part of my Victoriana collection, so we could find that Jewish culture is properly a part of European culture. However, one cannot infer this from the fact that Jewish individuals contribute to the institutions and art of European society. For a Jewish scholar could conceivably contribute to the corpus of Catholic theology, but this would not make Jewish culture a part of Catholic culture. Jewish culture, one wants to say, simply cannot be part of, and is entirely distinct from, Catholic culture.

Why should this be? Consider the task of collecting stamps according to their colour. Here the same principle is used to collect all stamps, although, of course, various stamps will satisfy the principle differently. As a result, there will be a collection of red stamps, blue stamps, green stamps, and so on. It is because each collection of stamps satisfies the same classificatory principle but does so differently that the resultant collections are necessarily exclusive of each other. A collection of green stamps cannot form part of a collection of red ones.

It is this rule of classificatory logic that makes it impossible for Jewish culture to form part of Catholic or Muslim culture. For in each case we colligate social phenomena according to the same principle – that is, according to the way in which groups of human beings conceive of, and worship, a divinity. If they do so differently – and Jews, Catholic, and Muslims do – then, on this principle of demarcation, they must constitute different and exclusive cultures. Consequently, it is only when two cultures are demarcated according to different principles that it becomes possible for the one to form part of another. If, then, we demarcate European culture in terms of the origin of the political, economic, religious, linguistic, and artistic institutions and traditions of Europe, there is no reason why Jewish culture cannot form part of it, for, as we have seen, it is demarcated according to an entirely different principle. Of course, whether or not it does as a matter of fact belong to European culture must depend on whether the Jewish culture actually contributed to these European traditions. And this is an empirical question to be decided by historical research.

On Cultural Identity

What is it that people look for when they search for their cultural identity? We know from our argument so far that they cannot coherently search for a spiritual entity – a *Geist* or a *Volksgeist* – in which they somehow inhere. Rather, a colligatory view of culture would have it that those who seek their identity hope, at root, to acquire a unified view of that cluster of human phenomena that they call their culture: a coherent way of thinking about it that makes sense of their lives, their values, projects, and aspirations. More than this, they hope that this view will somehow foster a sense of belonging, will make them feel at home in the world by legitimating their values and aspirations, and lending significance to their customs, traditions and practices.

The problem is that members of a group may have a range of different views about their culture, few of which are held in common. And in such a case it seems correct to say that the group as a whole lacks a cultural identity. What is wanted, therefore, is not just a unified view of a culture, but a unified view that individuals believe to be widely shared by many others within their community; a view, therefore, that helps unite the group and so ensures solidarity among its members. It is in this way that a cultural identity fosters what is often called the organic unity of the group.[20] It is not just that the individual serves, and is served by, his or her community in all sorts of ways but that such mutual support helps shape the image that individuals have of themselves and one another, of their mutual place in the world, and of the legitimacy and importance of their actions, projects, beliefs, and values.

Identities are not always acquired. Some people are born into a culture that fosters and perpetuates a particular view of itself. This, I think, is true of contemporary Maori culture in New Zealand, of Afrikaner culture during the apartheid years in South Africa, and of contemporary Palestinian and Israeli culture. In such cases, the acquisition of a well-formed identity is part of what is involved in being socialized by the group. Anyone who belongs to the culture, who is reared within it, and contributes to and participates in the human phenomena that are collected together under its banner, also acquires a unified and shared view of that culture, and thereby a cultural identity.

Other people, however, belong to cultures, usually urban and cosmopolitan, that do not foster any one view of their community or group. Such people sometimes search for, or else strive to create a cultural identity. Australians, Canadians, and New Zealanders often engage in this quest. They search endlessly and nervously for something distinctive about the human phenomena in which they participate; something that distinguishes Canadian culture from that of the United States, New Zealand culture from that of Australia; and Australian culture from that of Great Britain and the United States.

However, the search for distinctiveness is itself problematic. Earlier I argued that cultures that satisfy the same principle of cultural demarcation, but that do so differently, are necessarily different and exclusive of each other. But such differences, it should be stressed, need not amount to cultural distinctiveness. One can agree, for instance, that Canadian and Greek culture are necessarily exclusive of each other, but this does not entail that there is anything distinctive about Canadian culture, let alone that there is a Canadian cultural identity.

The quest for distinctiveness and, through it, for a cultural identity is a search not just for differences but for remarkable, extraordinary, and important differences that clearly distinguish one culture from all others. And the belief is that when these are taken into account, we will begin to think differently about our culture. Not only will we notice, perhaps for the first time, its strengths and weaknesses but we will be able to appeal to these traits in order to enlist loyalties, to summon a group or national pride, to articulate grievances, and, importantly, to alter the sense that we have of our place in the world. In light of this, we may re-think our role within the group and demand action that will either alter or strengthen the fabric of our society. We may come to understand, perhaps for the first time, the wider significance of our actions, the importance and legitimacy of our values, and because of this we may be inclined to formulate new projects and develop different social institutions.

The search, then, for cultural distinctiveness and identity is a political, not a scientific, search. It is one that sets its own criteria of success, which is just to say that there are no independent, objectively specifiable, criteria of success. It certainly is not as if one can find one's cultural identity lurking intact behind a bush or a boulder (as one might find the Abominable Snowman). Certainly, one's view of one's culture may be more or less accurate, but the success of one's search for an identity does not depend on its accuracy. Rather, as I have already intimated, it depends on whether or not it lends significance to one's projects and aspirations, whether it legitimates one's values, one's activities and practices in the world, and, most importantly, whether or not it is widely accepted by a designated population. And these are, in the broadest sense, political matters – not scientific ones.

It follows, I think, that the search for an identity can be ill-conceived and will be if one thinks that one can discover it in the way that Columbus discovered America. For to think this, we have seen, is to misunderstand the role that a shared identity is meant to play. In a rather different way, those who look only to the "ingredients" of their society – to its languages, institutions, rituals, religions, art forms, and technology – in order to find cultural distinctiveness, also misconceive the search for an identity. They fail properly to understand the concept "culture." For as we now know, "culture" is a colligatory concept: it brings different human phenomena together in different ways. A culture could be distinctive, therefore, not because of the nature of the phenomena that it brings together, but because of the special way in which it brings these together.

To use an example close to my home, the search among New Zealanders for a cultural identity has tended in the past to use a geographical principle of demarcation, according to which all social phenomena in a given geographical area constitute New Zealand culture. Thus demarcated, the culture is non-distinctive, so that the tendency is to hunt for increasingly idiosyncratic phenomena, and to add these to the collection in order to remedy the deficiency. But this does little, if anything, to create a widely shared view of New Zealand culture that makes the world a more accommodating place for individual New Zealanders.[21]

The fault has to do with an exclusive reliance on a geographical principle of cultural demarcation. This can rightly be seen as an Hegelian hangover, for, on Hegel's view, geographically (and temporally) delimited phenomena are invariably manifestations of the *Volksgeist*. What a colligatory account of culture enables us to do is discover distinctiveness not just by appealing to unusual social phenomena, but also by appealing to idiosyncratic ways in which social phenomena hang together in a particular society. So, for instance, one can argue that social phenomena in New Zealand cluster around an imperialist principle. On this view, the political and economic systems in New Zealand, its religions, language, art, philosophy, sport, and recreation, are to be seen as linked in a common colonial cause that directs the people of New Zealand to serve the material, strategic, and cultural ends of the imperial master. Thought of in this way, human phenomena in New

Zealand can be seen to be importantly, indeed remarkably, different from what we find in Britain or the United States. For whereas Britain and the United States are to be understood as the colonizers, New Zealand and its institutions are the colonized.

It is true, of course, that this particular way of demarcating New Zealand culture can properly be adopted only if there is evidence to support it. While the search for an identity is deeply political, this does not entail that identities are just political fictions and that we cannot or should not assess them for their accuracy. For unless an identity accurately reflects the way in which human phenomena hang together in a particular society, it will mislead us as to the actual nature of the culture, with potentially disastrous consequences. Many Germans, for instance, regarded racial superiority (during the years of the Third Reich) as the distinctive feature of their culture, and every attempt was made to organize German society around this assumed feature. Of course, it was never really a feature of that culture. Aryan people were not actually more intelligent, more athletic, healthier, hardier, or more beautiful than non-Aryan people. But even though it was false, the identity helped furnish German citizens with a powerful, unified, and widely shared view of their culture that stirred millions to military action and worse.

Art and Identity

We are at last in a position to speak informatively of the contribution that art makes to culture and identity. We now understand why it would be misleading to identify culture with high or popular art, and why a cultural identity, however acquired, cannot depend on art alone. But we are still left with the question: How, if at all, can works of art contribute to such an identity? The short answer, we shall see, is that they contribute differently, sometimes in ways that are explicitly didactic; at other times in ways that are intriguingly subtle, that offer no reasons or evidence or argument, but that nonetheless affect the view that we have of our culture.

Among the works that offer explicit messages about societies and their cultures are those that suggest principles of cultural demarcation, but do so even when there is no specific intent on the part of the artist to develop or advocate any particular identity. So, for instance, F. Scott Fitzgerald brings us, in *The Great Gatsby*, to think of American life as organized around the dream and promise of abundant wealth and the happiness supposedly bred of it. Despite this, there is no reason to think that Fitzgerald was thereby advocating a particular identity. His aim, we must suppose, was largely critical, and while some readers may indeed come to think of the culture of the United States in this way, their view is likely to be resisted by most citizens of that country. They will prefer a more positive image of their society, one that does more to endorse themselves, their values and their activities.

So while there are novels, plays, and films that explicitly suggest particular ways of viewing a culture, they tend in the more noteworthy cases to do so critically, with a view to exposing its defects and so altering the culture, but not with a view to developing or reinforcing an identity. In *A Portrait of the Artist as a Young Man*, for instance, James Joyce brings us to think of Irish culture as organized around the fearful and debilitating power of the priest. Then, too, through a series of novels published during the apartheid years, the rebel Afrikaner novelist André Brink encouraged readers to see Afrikaner politics, religion, education, art, and science as bound together in the promotion of an enormous illusion designed solely to preserve the material advantage of a privileged few. In New Zealand, authors like Bruce Mason and Jean Devanny have encouraged readers to think of the political and economic systems of that country, and the values that they subtend, as clustering around a ruthless slaughterhouse principle. On their view, the preparation of flesh for the tables of others is the primary colligatory principle that binds New Zealand culture and renders it distinctive. And in *The Poisonwood Bible*, Barbara Kingsolver gets her readers to think of American materialism as the binding force of a deeply corrupt, self-deceived, and morally bankrupt society. To understand the novel is at the very least to entertain the view that this society seeks its advantage through the ruthless exploitation of African societies, that it destroys their cultures and, with it, the basic freedoms that it pretends to advance.

In these cases, I have said, there is no attempt to foster a cultural identity. If anything, the artists concerned wish to shake the cultural complacency of their readers and to bring them to reassess the views that they unthinkingly hold of their cultures. However, there are novels, poems, plays, and films that do try to develop a shared view of a culture in a perfectly direct and non-critical way, by offering reasons of one sort or another for that view. Perhaps the most frequently cited and best regarded example of such works is Leni Riefenstahl's powerful film *Triumph of the Will* (1935) and her lesser known but very effective *Olympia* (1938) – both of which explicitly set out to convey a particular view of German culture during the time of the Third Reich.[22] Again, a good deal of early Soviet literature, architecture, sculpture, music, and painting was intended to convey an officially sanctioned view of the socialist state and, with it, of Soviet culture. Writers were urged to convey the idea of the Soviet Union as a prosperous, morally enriched, and contented country. Thus, for instance, Alexander Blok, in his most famous work, *The Twelve*, interprets the revolution of 1917 as the moral purification of what becomes a morally elevated Mother Russia. And during the period of so-called Industrial Literature, which began in 1928 with the Soviet Union's First Five Year Plan, writers (like Valentin Kataev in *Time, Forward!*) were expected to produce works concerning economic problems and the Soviet system's capacity, as a kind of economic and moral saviour, to overcome them.

Not only Stalin and Goebbels but many governments all over the world have been sensitive to the impression that certain works of art create of their society. Boards of censors not just in Iran, Iraq, South Africa, and Mobutu's Zaire, but also in Europe and America, have intervened in ways intent on cultural impression management.[23] The Italian government, for instance, regarded the treatment of social problems in Italian films like Vittorio de Sica's *The Bicycle Thief* (1948) as harmful to the country's image both at home and abroad, and in 1949 legislated against the export of such films. As a result, it effectively put an end to the Italian neo-realist movement in cinema.

We can now distinguish at least two ways in which works of art contribute to or affect a cultural identity. The messages contained in some works of art do suggest principles of cultural demarcation, but these, we have seen, are often intended critically and, given people's interests, are unlikely form the basis for a cultural identity. However, as our Italian example suggests, such works can subvert an identity, destabilize the view that people share of their culture, and can do so without replacing it with something more satisfactory. These works – works, one might say, of cultural criticism – are to be distinguished from those that explicitly set out to develop an identity. The latter are often baldly pedagogical, highly moralistic, lack all subtlety, and tend to be formulaic and unexplorative. As a result, they are often deeply flawed as works of art, but nonetheless furnish reasons for embracing a particular identity.

We need to contrast these two cases with the many excellent works of art – from those of Shakespeare and Goethe to Michelangelo and Manet – that also contribute to our cultural identity, but do so in much subtler ways. They are not explicitly pedagogical, do not moralize or depend on explicit messages in the work, and do not cite any reasons or evidence for the views of a culture that they convey. Their contribution to cultural identity, and the fact that they make any, is genuinely puzzling.[24]

In order to understand how such works of art achieve their cognitive effects, it is important to see that people may, as a matter of fact, share many values, beliefs, practices, and aspirations without recognizing that these are held in common, and without being able to articulate them. It may well be the case, for instance, that millions of Australians or Canadians have a shared idea of what is worthwhile, appropriate, fair, helpful, and harmful in their society, and that they have this without knowing that these ideas are shared. In just this way, they may unwittingly share views about the importance of certain institutions – schools, the stock market, the military, the church, the health and postal systems, the Internet – and have some idea of how these support one another and hang together in the advancement of the core values of their society. But they need not be very articulate about their shared view, and were it to be spelled out in some sociological detail, most of those who subscribe to it would quickly fall asleep.

For the most part, people are unaware of the extent to which their values, beliefs, and aspirations are shared by others in their society; they are unaware of the extent to which they are members of, and of the ways in which they participate in, a culture. And yet, part of belonging to a culture and of feeling at home within it and the world at large, involves knowing – or at the least believing – that one's values, beliefs, and understandings are shared or endorsed by others, that one contributes to their world as they contribute to yours. My claim is that the acquisition of such beliefs and knowledge is aided and abetted at every turn by movies, novels, plays, poems, music, song, paintings, sculptures, buildings, monuments, and memorials – many of which are of considerable artistic merit. The more obviously commercial arts figure as well. Advertisements in our newspapers and on television, the gloss of our fashion magazines, the design of our motor cars and bathrooms, embody values, beliefs, insights, and shared knowledge that enter into and endorse the view that we have of our social world.

Such works of art do not deliberately set out to impart a particular view of a culture. Most, however, set out to enrich our lives, for works of art characteristically have, and are expected to have, what I have elsewhere called a eudaimonistic function.[25] According to Monroe Beardsley, "in creating works of art we humanize the earth as we can in no other way, we warm it for ourselves, make it a place where we belong."[26] Beardsley in fact overstates the case, for we know from the heated nature of the many disputes that surround art, that the works that make one person feel at home in and supported by the world may make another feel alien, overlooked, even violated.[27] Art can both endorse and challenge our values, but in either case – and this is the important point – it does so by embodying and so objectifying certain values at the expense of others.

Generally speaking, then, an artist will exploit those values and beliefs that a chosen audience takes for granted in their everyday lives. As a result, these become embodied in the work, which, because of its public and privileged status, imparts to the social environment a significance and an order that legitimates and endorses the values and the beliefs of the individual. At once the world becomes a friendlier, more accommodating, place for those individuals who subscribe to the values and the beliefs in question. To the extent, moreover, that the work finds general approval, it not only gives substance to the culture to which we belong, but makes it publicly available in ways that lead us to believe that certain of our values, beliefs, and aspirations are both widely shared and supported.

In this way, such works of art plainly foster a sense of belonging, of identification with a group, and do so even when they do not set out to demarcate and afford a unified view of a culture. Surprisingly, they can do so as well by challenging our values and by making us feel discomfited, alien, and violated. For in so doing they force us to formulate our values and our knowledge of how one should act in the world, and of the ends that are worth pursuing.[28] Our common disapproval of the work, and the consequent articulation of our values, beliefs, and knowledge, helps strengthen cultural bonds by assuring us that others share these with us. And this, in its turn, helps shape the view that we have of our culture.

All of this helps explain why some art – the art that endorses our beliefs and values – can be so deeply satisfying and enriching. It also explains why other works of art can be so profoundly disturbing and disorienting. It is not that the latter works must be offensive. Indeed, the term "offensive" hardly does justice here. Rather, the sense of outrage that these works occasion arises because such works are wholly alien in the sense that they celebrate what one finds altogether wrongheaded and unacceptable.[29] There is a sense, then, in which such art enables us to know ourselves. For if we are curious enough, we will try to understand precisely why we find the work so alien, and in so doing we will be forced to articulate our values and our goals, and thereby aspects of the cultures that have shaped us.

We are now in a position to understand how works of art can encourage certain views of our culture, and how they can do so without the benefit of reasons, argument, or evidence. Some works of art, we saw earlier, convey a view of a culture explicitly, often because of the messages that we find in it.[30] In this way, messages in a work furnish reasons for a particular view of one's culture, which one can assess rationally in the light of independent evidence. But to be too explicit about one's reasons for challenging or promoting another's deeply held values may be to incur resistance on their part. William Blake, I have argued elsewhere, was just too explicit in advancing reasons for what was a particularly bleak view of English culture in his *Songs of Innocence and Experience*.[31] The result, it is well known, was that his contemporaries were outraged, preferred to think of him as mad, and declined to take his views seriously.

There is, though, another way in which Blake could have contrived to convey his view of English culture, for art that is foreign to our values and cultural understandings need not always result in outrage or a sense of violation. Sometimes, even as they bring us to modify our outlook, such works successfully anaesthetize the emotions that would normally accompany challenges to our fundamental beliefs and values.[32] The artistry involved in this is complex and dangerous, and while I will not pursue its detail here, it is important to observe that broadly speaking it involves seductive rather than rational persuasion.[33] Whereas rational persuasion tenders reasons for adopting certain beliefs, values, or strategies, and so places one in an epistemically stronger position regarding them, seduction is starkly different. For to have been seduced is quite often not to know, and is at times to wonder, how one has come to hold specific beliefs and perform particular actions. Just by pressing the right emotional buttons, by displays perhaps of great beauty, or by presenting an audience with very attractive and life-like imaginative scenarios, artists may lure their audiences into the uncritical acceptance of beliefs and values that they would otherwise have shunned.[34] The fact, moreover, that we expect works of art to make the world a friendlier place for us, that we think of them as harmlessly beneficent, makes us more rather than less likely to be lured by the beliefs and values that it advocates.

Sometimes, moreover, works convey messages that do not properly attach to, and cannot be derived from, their content at all. These are not messages "in" the work of art; rather, they may be thought of as messages "through" art.[35] Nor need it be the case that those who designed the works intended such messages. Rather, a message "through" a work of art is one that is a function of certain widely held beliefs, values, or presupposed attitudes that surround its production and display, and to which the artist appeals, either deliberately or inadvertently. So, for instance, the Vermeer in my bedroom at home may tell people how wealthy I am. Michelangelo's artworks in the Vatican may bring people to recognize just how powerful Pope Julius II was. And an André Brink novel written in English, after the banning of his Afrikaans-language novels, may serve to accuse the one-time Afrikaner government of South Africa of having betrayed its own culture. These are messages that cannot be taken from the content of any of these works, but are the function of certain widely held beliefs and values that surround their production and display. Messages "through" art have to do with the social space that works of art occupy, and the clever artist may exploit this "space" in ways that convey messages that are not properly part of the content of the work, and for which the work gives no reason or evidence. It is in conveying these messages that works of art sometimes add to, reinforce, or even subvert the view that we have of our culture.

Conclusion

Art, we can now see, is linked in a variety of different, sometimes very complex, ways to the development of a cultural identity. As a cultural artefact, a work of art invariably privileges some values at the expense of others, and this may either reinforce or undermine particular views of the culture. How it does this has much to do with the cognitive and affective powers of art; a topic shamefully neglected in contemporary epistemology.

Whatever the mechanisms at work, it should be clear from my argument that the claims made about the relation of art to culture and cultural identity remain incurably vague until we know what to understand by the terms "culture" and "identity." Part of my aim in this paper has been to demystify these concepts, to reject a ghostly account of culture in favour of a vastly more accessible colligatory account. By doing so, I have given substance to my claim that art affects culture, and that individual works can shape the ways in which we construe our culture. There is no longer anything mysterious or particularly elevated about this, although much more needs to be said about the precise ways in which art contributes to our understanding of our own and other cultures.

Notes

1 See David Novitz, *Knowledge, Fiction & Imagination* (Philadelphia: Temple University Press, 1987), ch.10. The account of culture and identity defended in this paper differs only in minor respects from the account offered there. However, a very different account is offered of the ways in which works of art contribute to a cultural identity.

2 G.W.F. Hegel, *The Phenomenology of Mind*, trans. J.D. Baillie (London: Allen & Unwin, 1949), 516.

3 Cited by Charles Taylor, *Hegel and Modern Society* (Cambridge: Cambridge University Press, 1969), 86.

4 G.W.F. Hegel, "Vorlesungen über die Philosophie der Geschichte," in *Sämtliche Werke*, ed. Herman Glockner (Stuttgart: Friedrich Fromann Verlag, 1971), vol. 11, 101.

5 Daniel C. Dennett, *Brainstorms: Philosophical Essays on Mind and Psychology* (Sussex: Harvester Press, 1981), ch. 1.

6 Ibid., 3–5.

7 Ibid., 6.

8 Ibid., 6, 9–12.

9 I have developed these criticisms of Hegel's idea of culture in more detail in Novitz, *Knowledge, Fiction & Imagination*, 209–12.

10 This point is developed in detail in ibid., 211–12.

11 See W.H. Walsh, "Colligatory Concepts in History," in *The Philosophy of History*, ed. Patrick Gardiner (Oxford: Oxford University Press, 1974), 127–44. See, as well, Novitz, *Knowledge, Fiction & Imagination*, 213–16.

12 Edward B. Tylor, *Primitive Culture*, 2 vols., vol. 1 (London: John Murray, 1871), 1–7. See as well, A. L. Kroeber and Clyde Kluckhorn, *Culture: A Critical Review of Concepts and Definitions*, vol. 47 (Cambridge, MA: Harvard University, Peabody Museum of American Archaeology and Ethnology Papers, 1952), no. 1, 181; Bronislaw Malinowski, "Culture," *The Encyclopedia of the Social Sciences* 4 (1931): 621–45; Edward Sapir, "The Unconscious Patterning of Behaviour in Society," in *Selected Writings of Edward Sapir in Language, Culture and Personality*, ed. David G. Mandelbaum (Berkeley: University of California Press, 1958), 544–59; Morris E. Opler, "Component Assemblage and Theme in Cultural Integration and Differentiation," *American Anthropologist* 61 (1959): 955–64.

13 See, by way of example, R.A.D. Grant, "Culture," in *A Companion to Aesthetics*, ed. David Cooper (Oxford: Blackwell, 1992), 99–104.

14 James P. Spradley, ed., *Culture and Cognition: Rules, Maps and Plans* (San Francisco: Chandler, 1972), 6.

15 G. Frege, "On Sense and Reference," in *Translations from the Philosophical Writings of Gottlob Frege*, ed. Peter Geach and Max Black (Oxford: Blackwell, 1966), 56–78.

16 See Matthew Arnold, *Culture and Anarchy*, ed. J. Dover Wilson (Cambridge: Cambridge University Press, 1963). Raymond Williams, *Culture* (Glasgow: Fontana, 1981), 11; and Terry Eagleton, *The Idea of Culture* (Oxford: Blackwell, 2000), who sets out to discriminate different meanings of "culture" – a term that he regards as one of the most complex in the English language. See, as well, Grant's "Culture," where he distinguishes "high" culture as the fifth of six meanings of the word "culture."

17 I explain and discuss the emergence of "high" culture in David Novitz, "Ways of Artmaking: The High and the Popular in Art," *British Journal of Aesthetics* 29 (1989): 213–29.

18 Ward Goodenough, ed., *Explorations in Cultural Anthropology* (New York: McGraw Hill, 1964), 11. Of course, such systems of value and belief are included in the scope of the term if they are manifested behaviourally. What is rejected is the idea that one can understand a culture by asking people about their values, attitudes, traditions, and beliefs.

19 I do not, of course, mean to suggest that the discernment of evidence is unproblematic. On this, see Novitz, *Knowledge, Fiction & Imagination*, 218.

20 Here I am indebted to Adam Muller for his perceptive comments on an earlier draft of this paper.

21 For more on this, see David Novitz and Bill Willmott, eds., *Culture and Identity in New Zealand* (Wellington: GP Books, 1989).

22 See Mary Devereaux, "Beauty and Evil: The Case of Leni Riefenstahl's the Triumph of the Will," in *Aesthetics and Ethics: Essays at the Intersection*, ed. Jerrold Levinson (Cambridge: Cambridge University Press, 1998), 227–56, esp. 227–41.

23 See David Novitz, *The Boundaries of Art* (Philadelphia: Temple University Press, 1992), 116–27.

24 A comprehensive solution to this puzzle will need to look closely at human psychology, studies in cognitive dissonance, motivated irrationality, and the persuasive devices of political propaganda. These issues cannot be addressed here, although I have touched on them in ibid., ch. 6.

25 See David Novitz, "Disputes About Art," *Journal of Aesthetics and Art Criticism* 54 (1996): 153–63, esp. 155.

26 Monroe C. Beardsley, "Art and Its Cultural Context," in *The Aesthetic Point of View: Selected Essays*, ed. Michael J. Wreen and Donald M. Callen (Ithaca, NY: Cornell University Press, 1982), 352–70, esp. 370. A similar but more precise view is taken by Roger Scruton in Roger Scruton, *The Aesthetics of Architecture* (London: Methuen, 1979), 248–49, where he writes that "the aesthetic sense ... is precisely devoted to the task of endowing the world with an order and meaning of that kind. Not only the man who builds but the man who lives with the product, must see the building in relation to himself ... in that process his humanity may be either rebutted or confirmed."

27 See Novitz, "Disputes About Art," 154–55.

28 On this, see Roger Scruton's excellent article, "Emotion and Culture," in *The Aesthetic Understanding: Essays in the Philosophy of Art and Culture* (London: Methuen, 1983), 138–52.

29 This inclines some to the view that these artefacts are not really works of art. On this, and on ways of resolving disputes of this sort, see Novitz, "Disputes About Art."

30 On this, see Jerrold Levinson, "Messages in Art," in *The Pleasures of Aesthetics*, ed. Jerrold Levinson (Ithaca: Cornell University Press, 1996), 224–41.

31 Novitz, *The Boundaries of Art*, ch. 10.

32 How this occurs, and the implications of it, are discussed in David Novitz, "The Anaesthetics of Emotion," in *Emotion and the Arts*, ed. M. Hjort and S. Laver (Oxford: Oxford University Press, 1997), 246–62. The topic is also addressed in Novitz, *The Boundaries of Art*, ch. 9.

33 For more on seduction through art, see Novitz, *The Boundaries of Art*, ch. 10.

34 For an account of what precisely this involves, see Novitz, "The Anaesthetics of Emotion," 247–51. For a more general account of the issues involved, see David Novitz, "Participatory Art and Appreciative Practice," *Journal of Aesthetics and Art Criticism* 59 (2001): 153–65, esp. section 5.

35 See David Novitz, "Messages 'in' and Messages 'through' Art," *Australasian Journal of Philosophy* 73 (1995): 199–203, esp. 199.

7

In his contribution, Robert Stecker works to provide a robust account of what he terms "historical contextualism," an approach to major questions in the philosophy of art which emphasizes the importance of context in settling a diverse assortment of interpretive and other disputes. According to Stecker, these questions variously concern the definition of art, the interpretation of artworks, aesthetic value, and the ontology of artworks, the latter differing from the definition of art insofar as it seeks specification of the properties of artworks (and thus a set of classificatory heuristics) and not to identify the essence of art as such (the rules for distinguishing artworks from non-artworks). All of these questions can, for Stecker, be satisfactorily resolved only with reference to an artwork's context of creation or origin, the moment(s) in space and time during which an artwork comes into being in the world, including any social, psychological, biographical, political, art-historical or otherwise "cultural" conditions directly or indirectly affecting what that artwork is, does, or can be made to do.

So, for example, historical contextualists maintain that the identity of artworks and their meaning is partly determined by the context of their creation, a view which Stecker defends with reference to the "pragmatic" philosophy of language developed by Paul Grice and exemplified by the essays comprising the latter's *Studies in the Way of Words*. For Grice the meaning of an utterance such as "the cat is on the mat" is at least partly a function of the context in which these words were uttered, so that whether or not "cat" in this case refers to a feline or to a human being will depend on such things as whether or not the one who makes the utterance is a beatnik speaking in a Greenwich Village coffee house in the 1950s, what he intends the word "cat" to mean, what the word can conceivably mean given prevailing linguistic conventions (including accepted denotations and connotations), and so on. Likewise the identity of an utterance is contextually sensitive, since for many utterances including the one above whether or not it is, say, declarative or interrogative may only finally be resolved by appeal to who, what, and where the utterer was when it was made. Stecker argues that as with utterances so too with artworks, which are likewise meaningful expressions of individual (in this case artistic and creative) intent. So construed, historical contextualism may be seen to entail the rejection of (at least) strong forms of anti-intentionalism and related psychological antirealisms such as that championed by Roland Barthes in his essay "The Death of the Author." Historical contextualism also proves incompatible with essentialism and constructivism, two metaphysical orientations towards the ontology of art, the latter of which lies at the heart of some of the most influential recent theoretical work in literary and cultural studies.

Although there will always be some disagreement, even amongst historical contextualists, concerning what exactly an artwork's "context of origin" is, Stecker rightly argues that this context must largely be understood culturally. What this means is that "culture" – which Stecker does not define as such but which may be assumed to be the particular amalgamation (or "colligation," to use David Novitz's term) of all manner of conventions, traditions, political and societal concerns, formal and stylistic matters specific to the functioning of relevant artworlds, and much, much more – plays a crucial role in determining not just what artworks are and mean but also how they are valued and come to be understood as "art." It is important to recognize, as a number of thinkers including Pierre Bourdieu and, in this volume, Jacques Barzun have done, that the relationship between art and culture is not static but reciprocal, with culture influencing artworks and their meanings just as artworks influence culture in their turn. Hence the political significance of such literary works as Upton Sinclair's *The Jungle* and Harriet Beecher Stowe's *Uncle Tom's Cabin*.

AESTHETICS AND CULTURE

ROBERT STECKER

Let us begin with some stipulations about "aesthetics." For present purposes it will simply refer to the philosophy of art without prejudice as to what conclusions should be reached concerning its central issues. In making this stipulation, I am intentionally distancing myself from two other uses of the word. One refers to the study of a purportedly special type of experience, properties that deliver the experience when attended to, and value associated with the experience. The experience can be had, and the properties can be found, most think, in artworks but also in many other things, so aesthetics in this sense is not peculiarly tied to art. The second sense of aesthetics that I am distancing myself from is tied to the study of art, but primarily as a source of such experiences, a bearer of such properties, and a provider of the relevant value.[1] I do not deny that artworks provide something we could aptly call aesthetic experience and have aesthetic value, but I do claim that this is just one way artworks can be appreciated as art, and so the philosophy of art should not be focused exclusively on "aesthetics" in either of the above two senses.

I mentioned above the central issues of aesthetics (in my stipulated sense), and let me now say what I understand them to be. There are four.[2] The first is raised by the question "What is art?" and one attempts to resolve it by giving a definition, or non-definitional conception, of art. This would give us attempts to identify the nature of art if art has an essential nature, or at least principles of classification for distinguishing art from non-art. The second issue concerns what it is to understand artworks, assuming, as I do, that they are the kind of thing in need of understanding. A good chunk of this issue involves giving a theory of interpretation. Artworks are among the things commonly in need of interpretation, and we come to better understand and appreciate such works by interpreting them. However, I would argue that not all understanding of art is interpretive.[3] The third issue concerns the value of art as art. Not every valuable property of a work is part of its artistic value or its value as art. For example, most people don't think that a work's monetary value is part of its artistic value. Similarly, the fact that a work has sentimental value for me because it was present at a significant moment in my life does not enhance its artistic value. So how do we distinguish artistically valuable properties from other valuable properties? Do the artistically valuable properties justify the great cultural importance given to art? Are the artistically valuable properties among the defining properties of art? Are there properties that a work must have to be artistically valuable? The fourth issue concerns the ontology of art. What type of object is an artwork? This question should not be confused with the one raised earlier: what is art? At least one way of answering this latter question is to identify a set of properties shared by all artworks and by no non-artworks. However, if there is a *type* of object such that, if something is an artwork, it is an object of that type, it hardly follows that no non-artworks belong to that type. Consider a candidate answer. Artworks belong to the type: physical object. Obviously if this answer were correct, there would be many non-artworks that belong this type of object too. It also shouldn't be assumed that the sample question just asked to characterize the fourth issue – What type of object is an artwork? – is the right question to ask with regard to this issue. This is because the question presupposes that there is one type of object that all artworks fall under, and this is far from obvious. Paintings may be one type of object; novels a different type. The issue is to identify the relevant type *or types*. The issues are interrelated. For example, the fourth issue has an important bearing on the second. Artworks are, presumably, the objects we are attempting to understand and interpret when we are engaged in art interpretation, and what this involves might be different given different types of objects. Later we will see how this pans out in practice.

Finally, these are not the only issues addressed in the philosophy of art, and given that, it should not be surprising if there was some disagreement about which issues are most central. There are those who think that some of the issues mentioned above are played out, and so are no longer fruitfully pursued. This is especially true of the issue raised by the question: what is art? Some place greater weight on other issues. Some focus on the fictionality of much art and the make-believe mandated by the fiction. Others concentrate on the imagination, on the expressiveness of art, on our emotional reactions to it, on formal or representational features. In my scheme of four central issues, these others just mentioned are by no means ignored, but they are not the chief cogs turning the aesthetic machinery.

To be distinguished from issues are theoretical stances with respect to them, which is not to deny that one's theoretical stance will influence which issues are taken as central. I will now set out how one particular stance, historical contextualism, situates art in culture with respect to the four central issues set out above. I will then compare this approach to two others found in recent aesthetics – essentialism on the one hand, constructivism on the other. Finally, I will briefly compare the aesthetics as defined above with the way the discipline known as cultural studies situates art in culture.

Historical Contextualism

Historical contextualism is the view that the four central issues of aesthetics, among others, can only be satisfactorily resolved by appealing to the context in which a work comes into existence: the context of origin or creation.[4] So, it claims that the identity of artworks depends, in part, on the context in which it is created. Further, reference to this context is equally crucial for understanding works and for a proper assessment of their artistic value. Finally, historical contextualists believe that a satisfactory definition of art, or nondefinitional conception, must be historical. Hence, all four central issues of aesthetics are resolved by appeal to the context of origin of the work. To get a better sense of this view, we have to become clearer on what is meant by context of origin and see in more detail how it handles these issues.

The context of origin contains anything that is (in part) determinative of meaning in a work, of what the artist does in the work, or of significant artistic properties of a work, and that exerts an influence no later than the time the work comes into existence, i.e., when it is completed by the artist or artists who make it. Context contains conventions or traditions in place when the work is created, the artist's intentions, any relevant circumstances: biographical, social, cultural, art-historical, and so on. In some writing, including some of my own, "context" is used to refer only to surrounding circumstances and is contrasted with intentions and conventions. However, this is not the way "context" is used here.

Returning to the way the historical contextualist handles the central issues of aesthetics, let us begin with the ontology of art. Here, this view asserts that artworks are a type of object whose identity depends on context of origin, and, even if, among the artworks, there are different types of objects, they would all share this feature in common. To illustrate, consider a musical work on the one hand and painting on the other. It is widely believed, both by historical contextualists and their opponents that musical works, not only belong to a type but that they are types: types of sound structures or sound events. This is because, while musical works are most commonly presented through performances, or, these days, recordings, and while a performance or playing of a recording presents an instance of a piece of music, neither the performance, the CD, nor the instance they present is the musical work per se. The musical work, being repeatable, cannot be identified with a concrete individual either physical or mental. So the musical piece must be an abstract entity of some kind and this is usually thought to be a type. What the historical contextualist says is that just identifying an abstract structural type or event type is not enough to identify a musical work. What we need, in addition, is to identify certain features of the context in which the type is "identified" or pieced together and used to do something musical. This is the context of composition.

One reason given in support of this claim is that we can imagine two composers writing scores indicating identical sound structures. However, especially if the composers live in different historical periods, their respective works would have some very different artistic properties. One might be amazingly original, the other derivative. One might be full of discord; the other may be unchallenging to the ear. One may initiate a new style; the other might allude to an older style. They might express very different moods or emotions. So it seems plausible that each composer produced a different work despite using the same sound structure, in virtue of having different artistic properties. This suggests a more general reason for the historical contextualist's claim that reference to abstract types is not enough to identify musical work: namely that structure by itself cannot account for many important artistic properties of musical works. But when we add to this the idea that we are dealing with a structure that is put to use in a particular cultural context, we can account for these properties.

Paintings seem to be quite different types of objects than musical works. While there can be many instances or performances of the same musical work, this is not so for paintings. Copies of paintings are just that: copies of a unique object. Since this object – consisting of paint arranged on a surface – has many physical properties, it's plausible that a painting is a physical object. However, just as with musical works, many crucial artistic properties derive from the context of creation of the painting. This has been amply illustrated in Arthur Danto's numerous discussions of the different properties of visually indistinguishable works.[5]

While all historical contextualists agree that the identity of an artwork in part depends on its context of creation, they don't agree among themselves on the features of the context necessary for this identity. Some claim that the identity of the artist is crucial so that, while different mathematicians might prove the same theorem, different artists never produce the same work. Others find this counterintuitive, believing different artists working in every other respect in the same context – with the same traditions and conventions, at the same time period, in the same country, with similar cultural backgrounds – could produce the same work.

I look at it this way. We should think of artworks as utterances of the artist or artists who produce them. A linguistic utterance is a use of language on an occasion to say or do something. However, utterances are by no means confined to linguistic ones.[6] Identifying a work is much like identifying an utterance. Consider an utterance of a single sentence on a specific occasion. Suppose I say "George does not have a heart." Notice I can't identify what utterance I make simply by appeal to the structural type – the sentence – I use to make the utterance. The same sentence can be used on different occasions to make many different utterances. So with the sentence "George does not have a heart." I can on different occasions be speaking of many different Georges, and saying of them many different things: that he lacks the organ that pumps blood, that the organ is in very bad shape, that he is callous and uncaring, that he lacks even a single member of a certain suit of cards, that he did not get the item that he was supposed to dissect, and so on. On a particular occasion I don't say all these things with my utterance, but probably just one; or perhaps I say something that does not correspond to a literal meaning of the sentence at all. This will depend on features of context – perhaps my intention in using those words, appropriate conventions, or the situation I'm in. It won't, however, depend on who I am: my identity. We know this because we know that someone else can make the same utterance that I made, and this would be impossible if the utterance I make depends on who I am. So those who deny that the identity of the work absolutely depends on the identity of the artist are right in theory. However, the more complicated an utterance, the less likely it is that anyone else will make it. Consider the Gettysburg Address. It's so unlikely as to be a practical impossibility that anyone else said what Lincoln said on the occasion of his giving this speech, except perhaps when intentionally repeating Lincoln's words. So while not a theoretical necessity, a good rule of thumb is: different artist, different work.

The introduction of the utterance model is also useful in explaining the historical contextualist's conception understanding artworks. If artworks are like utterances, the meaning of an artwork, if it has one, will be like the meaning of an utterance.[7] It is obvious that the meaning of an utterance is highly context-dependent, and that the context that this meaning depends on is the context in which the utterance is issued. Suppose Sally utters "George doesn't have a heart." in the context of her kindergarten class on the day when they are making Valentine's Day cards from paper hearts. That she is referring to another member of her class, and not, say, the president of the United States, and that she is speaking to his lack of a paper heart rather than his blood pumping internal organ, his treatment of others, his possession of playing card suits, etc., is determined by the context of utterance. As it is with utterances, so it is with artworks, according to the historical contextualist.

Again, proponents of this view don't agree on what features of context determine the meaning of a work. Some think that it is conventions which do this, conventions in place when the work is created; some think it is the artist's intention; some claim that it is the best hypothesis about this intention regardless of whether this corresponds to the artist's actual intention; and some think it is some combination of factors including intentions, conventions, and circumstances.

It also should not be thought that historical contextualists claim that identifying what I have been calling "the meaning of a work," on the analogy with utterance meaning, is the only interpretive enterprise we engage in with respect to artworks. Some may think this, but others recognize interpretive enterprises of different kinds. For example, some recognize that we may be interested in what works could mean, or ways in which they could be taken, relative to certain assumptions or points of view, rather than what they actually do mean. It is also frequently recognized that some interpretations legitimately aim to show how a work is relevant to the concerns of some group, and to explore the significance of the work with respect to those concerns. Doing this may place the work in a context other than its context of origin.

However, historical contextualism claims that works have a core meaning that can only be identified by seeing the work in its original context. Further, what is true of meaning is true of value. This too will have a core that is in fact revealed by a work's core meaning. After all, the core meaning of a work tells us what the artist does in the work that is of artistic significance. Identifying this enables one to grasp the artistically valuable properties of a work and to experience the work in a way that enhances one's appreciation of it.

It is worth pausing over some examples that the historical contextualist would claim illustrate this point both about core meaning and value. Consider "London," a poem by William Blake, the first two stanzas of which go as follows:

> I wander thro' each charter'd street,
> Near where the charter'd Thames does flow,
> And mark in every face I meet
> Marks of weakness, marks of woe.
>
> In every cry of every Man,
> In every infant's cry of fear,
> In every voice, in every ban,
> The mind-forg'd manacles I hear.

In these lines, the speaker of the poem represents London as a prison and its inhabitants as chained to and made miserable by human institutions ("mind-forg'd manacles"). We don't have to think of the speaker of the poem as Blake himself, but we do have to decide whether Blake endorses the speaker's sentiments. Since "London" is part of a larger work, *The Songs of Innocence and Experience*, and is in particular one of the songs of experience, its relation to other poems in this group will in part contribute to the way we should take it. We could also ask whether London, as the poem describes it, is *merely* a metaphor for a type human condition or whether Blake is commenting on the city of his day. How we answer these and other questions about what Blake does in the poem, what he represents, what feelings and attitudes are expressed, the conception of life in London, and of various institutions forging that life (including the church and marriage), will according to the historical contextualist determine (part of) the core meaning of the poem. This in turn will determine our appreciative experience of the poem, and the value we find in it.

Next consider any one of a number of novels from the nineteenth century. The works of Dickens have to be anchored in the context of the England of his day, the social ills of the time portrayed in his works and their influence on the outlook and character of members of the society.

Other works from this era – a good example is the writing of the Swiss novelist Gottfried Keller – have to be understood in terms of the transformation from a traditional to a modern society brought about by several different forces converging at this time: industrialization, nationalism, science, and so on. Part of the value of these works lies in their offering readers vivid conceptions of these things, and in allowing readers an imaginative experience of those conditions or developments as conceived in the works. Of course, this reference to broad historical conditions is only one contextualist consideration among many others, although it happens to be quite important in the works just mentioned. Also, this contextualized understanding and appreciation of these works does not preclude them from speaking to other people living in other times, although the contextualist claims that they speak more eloquently if they are first anchored in their own.

The question "What is art?" raises different issues because it shifts our focus from individual works that are the objects of understanding and evaluation to works of art in general. Attempting to answer this question cannot be a matter of putting an individual work in its historical context. Rather it is a matter of seeing individual works as part of and appropriately related to other artworks belonging to a history of art. Something is a work of art because it stands in the right historical relation to earlier works, or because it belongs to a form and fulfills functions that are so related. Here is one definition of art – probably the best known – that operates strictly according to this model. "An artwork is a thing that has been seriously intended for … regard in any way pre-existing artworks are or were correctly regarded."[8] As it stands, this definition is incomplete in several respects. For one thing, it doesn't cover the very first instances of art which do not, because they cannot, look back to earlier art. Second the notion of intending something for regard as earlier works are correctly regarded needs refinement on several fronts (refinement which Levinson carefully bestows on it). Just to mention one such front, as it stands it is not entirely clear why this definition does not imply that intending something to be regarded as red would not suffice to make it an artwork since there are earlier works that are correctly regarded as red. Yet such a result would clearly be unacceptable. If I paint my house red, intending for it to be regarded as red, I don't thereby create art. However, my point here in mentioning this definition is to illustrate the historical contextualist approach. Something that comes into existence now is an artwork because of a relation it bears to earlier works. In the case of Levinson's definition, the relation is being intended for regard in a way earlier works are correctly regarded.

My own approach to this issue is slightly different, but still lies within the historical contextualist fold. I say that something is an artwork if it is in a central art form at a certain time T (a time no earlier than the time the item comes into existence) and is intended to fulfill a function that the form has at T, or it is an artefact that fulfills with excellence such a function. Here it is a relation to a gradually evolving set of functions and forms that is responsible for the present item being art. There is still a historical-cultural backdrop here, and it is the situation of the item against this backdrop that makes it art. As with Levinson's definition, this one can (and has been) improved with further refinement, but those details need not trouble us here.

Historical Contextualism and Culture

This completes a thumbnail sketch of the historical contextualist approach to the four central issues of aesthetics. Culture plays a crucial role in the handling of these issues primarily because the context of origin is, in large part, defined culturally. Conventions, traditions, widespread ideas or concerns, the state of politics and society, artistic styles and movements, the work of others, and the artist's own oeuvre are all cultural aspects of original context. So are the art forms and functions that are central at any given time. Because of the large role of culture in creating art-historical contexts, culture plays an equally large role in determining the identity of individual works, their meaning and value, as well as in shaping what art is and, as it evolves, what it becomes.

There are other ways that art and culture interact on this view. I mention two here. Just as culture shapes art, art shapes culture. Each individual artwork (although some much more than most others) adds to the context of origin of subsequent works and other cultural arte-facts. The value of the art of a society is a substantial part of the value to be found in the culture. It is in part by revolutionary works that art forms and functions change.

The way historical contextualism handles this last point needs a bit of explaining because it is not unusual for it to be criticized for being unable to account for revolutionary art. The source of the criticism is easy to understand. Historical contextualism is primarily backward-looking. When we try to understand and appreciate an artwork, this view tells us to look back to the context of the work's creation. When we want to understand why something is art, we are told to look back to its relation to earlier art. So what room is there for revolutionary art, art the breaks from the past? Actually, there is quite a lot of room. First, no work that I know of completely breaks from the past, so there always seems to be some connecting strand. Later works can be related to earlier ones in virtue of being a repudiation or reaction against them. Second, this doesn't mean that these later works don't contain some-thing new which eventually or immediately creates new functions or "regards" that further art's evolution. For example, many novels (such as those of Woolf and Joyce) of the early twentieth century react against the realism of some of their predecessors and contemporaries (such as Galsworthy and Bennett).

Nevertheless, one can see a continuity of concerns. For the explora-tions of consciousness and perspective in the more avant garde works is continuous with the psychological investigations of earlier novels, despite the perceived differences looming larger when the former works were produced. Finally, as noted earlier when speaking of art interpre-tation, historical contextualism permits art to be thought about in rela-tion to contexts other than the context of origin. In fact, it's inevitable that a work's audience will be concerned with ways it is relevant to them, ways it interfaces with their cultural context. So a work is constantly being brought to new contexts in thought, and for that reason plays new roles in the evolving culture. What historical contextualism denies is that this implies that the core meaning of the work changes as it plays these new roles, or that the work is in flux because of the new cultural contexts into which it enters.

Alternatives to Historical Contextualism: Essentialism and Constructivism

I now more briefly turn to two stances within aesthetics that are alternatives to historical contextualism. One of these is essentialism; the other is constructivism.

Essentialism is not actually incompatible with historical contextualism. There are, in fact, essentialist versions of this view. Essentialism is an alternative stance simply because it does not imply historical contextualism and because there can be *versions* of essentialism that are incompatible with it. According to these versions (acontextual essentialism), we can define art independently of its history by identifying certain unchanging essential properties shared by all artworks, and only by artworks. Such views often hold that distinctively artistic value is equally ahistorical, unchanging, and derived from properties possessed only by artworks or possessed only by them to a significant degree. Since, on such a view, the most important thing to understand about an artwork is the degree to which it has such properties, such understanding also seems context-independent. It is just possible that, while the sort of properties that define art, that make it valuable and that need to be identified to understand a work do not change from one context to another, a work still needs to be placed in context to recognize its properties. For example, just which expressive, formal, or, more generally, aesthetic properties a work has plausibly depends on its style, its period, and what other works made at the same time were like. So a degree of context-dependence might be incorporated into an otherwise acontextual essentialism. On such a view, what makes something art and what is responsible for its possessing artistic value does not *evolve* with a changing context, but context still helps to determine which properties are crucial. This is an intermediate view. There are still versions of essentialism that are completely ahistorical and acontextual.

The sort of views that tend to fit the acontextual, essentialist profile I have elsewhere called simple functionalist.[9] They not only make the claims mentioned above about the definition of art and the value of art, but they make the further claim that the properties essential for artistic value are the defining properties of art. Some formalist theories, expression theories, and aesthetic theories of art are examples of this type of essentialism. Consider Clive Bell's version of formalism, in which art is defined as significant form – form that elicits aesthetic pleasure.[10] This is also what makes artworks valuable as art. Finally, this is the aspect of art *least* tied to context for Bell. It is pretty much the same sort of thing in ancient Chinese, renaissance, and post-impressionist painting, and its recognition requires the right perceptual attitude, but not historical knowledge.

For the acontextual essentialist, art may contribute mightily to culture, but culture does not contribute much to art. This is because art inhabits a separate world from the rest of culture. Art is a wonderful cultural compartment, but to bring other compartments of a culture to bear on its art is to muddy one's perception of the former rather than to enhance one's understanding.

What constructivists have in common is the belief that the context of origin does not pin down the artwork once and for all. Hence constructivism is always incompatible with at least some of the theses held by historical contextualists. However, like the other stances we have considered, constructivism comes in different versions. I distinguish two such versions here. Moderate constructivists claim that artworks undergo changes as they receive new interpretations, as they enter new cultural contexts, or conceptual environments.[11] Furthermore, these changes are not peripheral ones that occur around a stable core fixed by the work's origin. The distinction between core meanings and peripheral ones is rejected. Hence works are things that are much more in flux than they are thought to be under historical contextualism, and there is consequently a difference in views about the understanding and value of art. Some moderate constructivists claim that the boundary between properties that belong to artworks and properties that do not is indeterminate. Interpretive properties are imputed to works rather than discovered in them.

Radical constructivists believe that works are created, not merely altered, in the process of interpretation.[12] Of course, this raises the question: the interpretation of what? The answer cannot simply be the interpretation of the created object, since an interpretation must begin with some object it is directed at, and the created object is an end product not in existence until the interpretive activity is complete, or at least well under way. There must be an object that initially prompts and guides the interpretation, and this must be different from the created object. Hence for radical constructivists, there are always three objects involved in art interpretation: the initial object, the interpretation, and the created or subsequent object.

For constructivists, what occurs after an artist makes an artefact is at least as important for the creation and meaning of an artwork as the context of origin. For many constructivists, the evolving culture shapes the work at least as much as the artist does. Art is the product of culture, for these theorists, as much or more than it is the product of creative individuals, including critics and interpreters as well as artists.

Evaluating Stances

I have given above thumbnail sketches of three stances that have been taken concerning the central issues of aesthetics. Each would need to be and, in fact, has been developed in far greater detail so as to be made over from stances into philosophical theories. However, the question I turn to now is whether anything can be said to evaluate the stances just sketched considered as stances rather than as full-blown philosophical theories. Is there a way of estimating in advance which stance is most likely to produce a satisfactory theory, or is one's estimation at this level of generality simply to remain a matter of sensibility?

Before turning directly to evaluation, let me say a word about the somewhat different issue of acceptance. Currently, acontextual essentialism is probably the least accepted, and constructivism probably the most widely accepted, of the three views. The latter, while having many adherents within analytic philosophical aesthetics, has even more supporters elsewhere. Gadamer's hermeneutics, Derrida's deconstruction, and many more general forms of postmodernism originating in France and Germany which have achieved widespread popularity across humanities disciplines in the United States and elsewhere, are constructivist in character. These constructivist views are self-consciously fashioned to be alternatives to the two other stances discussed here. They not only reject permanent essences, but perhaps even more so historical views that focus on the origin of works. Is there a connection between such popularity and plausibility?

The unpopularity of acontextual essentialism has a basis in plausible, if not completely decisive, objections to that view. For example, the views classified above as simple functionalist, such as formalist, expressivist, and aesthetic conception of art, offer definitions of art that are highly prone to counter-examples both in the direction of excluding bona fide artworks and including non-artworks. Similarly, they offer an overly narrow conception of artistic value and understanding. Although the anti-essentialists of the 1950s and 1960s[13] were wrong to claim that essentialism per se cannot accommodate the production of novel works and forms, they correctly saw that the simple (and not so simple) functionalisms on offer at that time were too rigid and narrow to accommodate such change. The most promising attempts to meet the anti-essentialist challenge have been historical in character.[14] Hence, the lack of promise in *acontextual* essentialism.

The most important debate today concerning the stance one should take in aesthetics is one between historical contextualism and constructivism. Is there reason to think one of these views is superior to the other?

Despite its popularity, constructivism faces serious problems of its own. Consider the sort of object constructivists take artworks to be. I shall focus here on the more moderate version of constructivism, which I take to be the more plausible. The moderate constructivist takes a work of art, along with its semantic properties, to be in constant flux as it receives new interpretations and enters into new contexts. The idea of an object with constantly changing properties is not in itself problematic. Problems arise when we look more closely at some characteristic moderate constructivist claims, such as the claim that interpretations bring about such changes in a work's properties. How can an interpretation change a work? Interpretations typically contain assertions or conjectures about the properties of a work. If the assertion or conjecture is true, then it seems that the work already has the property ascribed to it. If the assertion or conjecture is false, the work does not have the property and no amount of saying it does can change this. So it seems that interpretations cannot change their objects.[15]

There are many proposals on offer to meet this objection. One of these accepts the idea that interpretive statements are assertive but denies that they have bivalent truth values, i.e., the values true and false and no other alethic values. Rather, it is claimed that interpretative statements, while sometimes false, are never true, but have multiple truth-like values such as "plausible," "apt," and "reasonable."[16] The problem with this response to the above argument is two-fold. First, while there are coherent multi-valent logics, one needs a very good reason to depart from standard logic, which is bivalent. Saving constructivism is not in itself a sufficiently good reason for this departure. More important still, rejecting bivalence does not by itself secure the claim that interpretations change their objects. In fact, it is much more obscure what the claim could mean if we reject bivalence. What the claim seems to say is that before an interpretation is offered, the object lacks property F, but afterwards and in virtue of the interpretation, the object has F. If these claims are not *true*, it's not clear what is meant by property change.

A second proposal attempts to meet the original objection to constructivism by postulating two different objects of interpretation. Suppose I am looking at Van Eyck's "Arnolfini Marriage" and, as a result of wondering about the significance of the sundry objects represented in the painting – a pair of shoes, a dog, a mirror, some fruit – I arrive at the interpretation that these objects are symbols that reveal the allegorical meaning of the painting. On the present view, the painting I see, or at least the painting I initially conceive as containing puzzling representations, is one object. I *construct* a subsequent object that has symbolic, allegorical significance. About this constructed object, I assert the said significance.[17] This is an extremely clever proposal to explain how interpretations can be both constructive and assertive, which is what the initial argument essentially denies. It is ultimately unconvincing, however, for the following reasons. First, there is the idea that there are three objects involved in interpretation: the initial object, the interpretation itself, and the subsequent object. This looks like an ad hoc proposal to save constructivism, unless there is an independent argument for the existence of the subsequent object capable of persuading those who are not already predisposed to the constructivist view. The three-object view is initially counterintuitive. If I am puzzled by Van Eyck's painting, I want an interpretation of it, not of some other object constructed from it. If an interpretation does not make an assertion about the painting, it changes the subject rather than resolve my puzzle. Second, to suppose there is a subsequent object is not only ad hoc but confused. The subsequent object is a way of conceiving or representing the initial object (the painting) by a process "of selection, suppression, highlighting and contextualizaton."[18] But this is just what the interpretation itself is; interpretations are just such representations of their objects. When I assert that the "Arnolfini Marriage" is an allegory in which the dog symbolizes fidelity, I represent the painting in a certain way by selecting certain features of it and giving them special salience. But that representation is the interpretation, not a third object constructed by it. Finally, note that this proposal does not explain how interpretations change their objects (a moderate constructivist thesis) but purports to explain how interpretations construct subsequent objects from initial objects. This is a radical constructivist thesis. This in itself does not disqualify it but does illustrate the fact that moderate constructivism tends to devolve into the more radical view, which for the reasons just mentioned is ultimately unconvincing.

A third, and for our purposes, final proposal to meet the original objection to moderate constructivism claims that interpretations change their objects not all at once, but through a gradual process of social uptake. Something like this certainly happens in some domains outside the arts. The word "Madagascar" once referred to a part of the African mainland. Through a process of what must have initially been misapplication, but which received subsequent social uptake, the reference of the word eventually shifted to the island, Madagascar. The present proposal is that interpretations bring about changes in their objects not simply by being asserted, but by receiving uptake of some sort, such as being found acceptable within a critical community.[19]

This is the most promising among the proposals we have considered, but I am not convinced it is ultimately workable. There is an important difference between linguistic change and artwork change through a process of interpretation and uptake, and for this reason the two processes do not necessarily lead to the same result. The meaning of words ultimately depends on how they are used in a community. As this use changes, word meaning changes. But an assertion or conjecture does not become true or even more reasonable just because it is widely accepted. Whether it is reasonable depends on the evidence that supports it. Whether it is true depends on whether the work is as it is asserted or conjectured to be. Even if an interpretation is not merely accepted but has become part of the cultural consciousness of a community, if it turns out to be based on a false belief about the work in question, the interpretation would be called in question. For example, many paintings were attributed to Rembrandt but were later discovered to be painted by lesser members of his school. This required not just a change in attribution but other changes in the understanding and assessment of the works. Acceptance does not guarantee property possession.

Space does not permit a detailed exploration of other objections to constructivism, but let me mention in passing one other problem it perennially faces: the problem of work identity. Moderate constructivists, like most other theorists of interpretation, want a common object that multiple interpretations address. Yet if different interpretations bring about different changes in an initial object, we either have one object with inconsistent properties possessed at the same time or we end up with different objects. The first situation is impossible. The second is undesirable if we are after different interpretations of the same initial object (the artwork). The best strategy if the constructivist is to meet this problem is the strategy of rejecting bivalence because, on that view, it would at most be plausible to some degree that the initial object has one of the properties and plausible to some degree that it has the other, but not strictly true that the initial object has either of the inconsistent properties. Hence interpretations can be about a single, self-identical artwork without making inconsistent claims about it. However, denying that bivalence holds in the domain of art interpretation does not solve this problem all by itself. Whether it provides a satisfactory solution depends on the details of the multi-valued logic adopted, which constructivists in this area of philosophy rarely consider. In addition, the choice of this logic would need independent justification.

We are therefore left with historical contextualism. Does this stance face equally daunting objections? I shall consider two possibilities.

Many people object to the historical contextualist's account of what it is to understand artworks, in particular to the idea that there is such a thing as the meaning of a work that derives from its context of origin. Some of these objections are based on mere misunderstanding. For example, there is a fairly widespread, though by no means universal, assumption that there is such a thing as the intentional fallacy: the idea that any reference to an artist's intention when attempting to identify meaning in artworks is illegitimate. If one holds this assumption and supposes that historical contextualism commits one to intentionalism, then one would also believe the intentional fallacy implies the falsity of this view. However, historical contextualism is not per se committed to intentionalism. The latter is just one view among many about the historical origins of meaning. Hence it is just a misunderstanding to believe that one must reject historical contextualism if one accepts the idea of an intentional fallacy.

One may also be disturbed by the historical contextualist conception of work meaning because one might think it undermines the idea, to which many theorists and critics are committed, that the same artwork can receive many acceptable interpretations that cannot be conjoined to form a single, uniquely correct interpretation. I will call this view critical pluralism. Since the historical contextualist believes that there is such a thing as *the* meaning of a work determined by context of origin along with other properties of the work, it might seem that historical contextualism is incompatible with critical pluralism. However, this is not so, primarily because the historical contextualist is not committed to accepting the idea that the identification of work meaning is the only legitimate interpretive project. There are several other projects that can be just as important: there are projects that concern what a work *could* mean or how it *could* be taken. We might consider this in connection with making the work relevant to a certain audience, with enhancing one's appreciative experience, defamiliarizing an overly familiar work, seeing the work in terms of certain important ideas or certain later works and so on. Related to projects like these is the attempt to bring out the potential significance of the work for one audience or another.

A final objection to historical contextualism attempts to show that the move made in the previous paragraph to accommodate critical pluralism is not really available. This is so, according to the present objection, because the move is inconsistent with the ontological commitments of the historical contextualist. Here is the argument. According to historical contextualism, the identity of a work is in part determined by its context of origin. For this reason, certain properties it has in virtue of this context are essential properties of the work, i.e., properties without which *this* work would not exist. Now when we ask what a work could mean, where this is something other than what a work does mean, we are supposing it is possible in some sense that something about the work is different from the way it actually is. If the difference depends on context of origin, we are supposing that the context of origin would be different. However, for the historical contextualist, context of origin could not be different, since it is essential to the work's identity. Hence, a work could not mean anything other than what it does mean, at least where this meaning derives from context of origin. This appears to cut off the route to critical pluralism sketched in the previous paragraph.[20]

Fortunately for historical contextualism, this argument is invalid. First, historical contextualism does not imply that *every* feature of the context of origin is essential to the work, or that *only* context of origin determines meaning. Hence it is consistent with this view that a work could have been different in various ways, and in virtue of this mean things other than it actually means. More important, even if a work's meaning is essential to it, so that we would not have the same work with a different meaning, this rules out questions about what a work could mean only if we assume we are concerned with one among several different senses of "possibility." The sense in question is called metaphysical possibility by philosophers. If a property is essential to a work, it is metaphysically impossible for it to be without that property or, in other words, it has the property in every possible world in which the work exists. However, when critics wonder what works could mean, it is not clear they are always concerned with whether it is metaphysically possible for any of its semantic properties to be different. They may be talking about what meanings are possible relative to the evidence they actually possess (epistemic possibility). Alternatively, they may intentionally bracket off certain facts about a work, including some facts about origin, and see what a work could mean after such bracketing has occurred (call this pragmatic possibility). A work could mean things incompatible with their essential natures relative to the latter two senses of possibility. So if critics are concerned with these kinds of possibility, as I believe they are, the historical contextualist's route to critical pluralism is not cut off.

My own view, as is no doubt already evident, is that among the three stances considered in this essay, historical contextualism is the most plausible. There are objections to all of these stances, but historical contextualism has the best answers in response to them. Of course, I haven't actually demonstrated that here, for to do so would be impossible in anything less than a book-length project. Here I must leave it to the reader to consider what further objections, and what replies, might be offered with respect to these stances.

Aesthetics and Cultural Studies

With the same sketch pencil used throughout this paper, I will conclude by briefly situating aesthetics with respect to the movement known as cultural studies, which is just as concerned with art and culture as some of the stances resident in aesthetics.

Cultural studies, however it should be positively characterized, is different from aesthetics in a number of respects. First, it is not simply a philosophy of art. It is an interdisciplinary movement that is just as concerned with sociological and political issues as with philosophical ones. Second, it is not simply concerned with art and its institutions, as aesthetics, understood as the philosophy of art, necessarily is. The scope of cultural studies extends to the practices and institutions of society at large. Third, at least the dominant view within cultural studies embraces a specific ideology and political program. "Cultural studies is shaped by postcolonial inquiries into colonial strategies of cultural oppression, and also by tactics for resisting those practices."[21] Finally, while all the stances in aesthetics discussed above are heavily influenced by the Anglo-American analytic tradition in philosophy though, especially in the case of constructivism, not only by that tradition, the intellectual sources of cultural studies are almost uniformly continental: Marxist, structuralist, and post-structuralist.

These differences might seem to create a huge gap between aesthetics and cultural studies. In a good deal of practice, the gap manifestly exists. Many within cultural studies look with suspicion at aesthetics, practised as I have described it as just another conservative strategy of oppression. This is true of its subject matter: "These [aesthetic] value judgments [underlying the concept of literature] themselves have a close relation to social ideologies. They refer ... not simply to private taste, but to the assumptions by which certain social groups exercise power over others."[22] It is also true of the discipline itself: "academic institutions were locked directly into structures of technological dominance, military violence, and ideological legitimation."[23] Many who adopt one of the above aesthetic stances look in their turn on the ideological aspect of cultural studies as something dogmatic which is itself oppressive.

Yet I think these differences are not as great as they appear. First, though aesthetics as I have stipulatively defined it is necessarily concerned with art and only with art, philosophers of art do not typically believe that the stances they take toward art apply or have implication only within that domain. So their focus is not necessarily narrower than that of those who work in cultural studies. Second, for the last thirty years, philosophy has become increasingly interdisciplinary. Philosophers of science have immersed themselves in the history and practice of science. Philosophy of mind contributes to cognitive science, where philosophers, psychologists, linguists, and brain and computer scientists work and debate common issues. Aesthetics is no exception. Criticism, theory, and philosophy of particular art forms are often practised in tandem, and in tandem with work of related disciplines. Ideology is the one area where differences can be bridged only by accommodation and not by a recognition of intellectual and methodological proximity. But I think accommodation is reasonable. On the one hand, those who practice aesthetics can reasonably be expected to recognize that their philosophical positions on central issues might somehow be enmeshed in ideology, however unconsciously. Some consciousness raising might be appropriate without its being the case that views should be evaluated simply on this basis. On the other hand, those in cultural studies who think of institutions exclusively as forces of oppression, whose existence is to be explained solely in hegemonic terms, should realize that this view is over-simplistic and reductive. I hope we are already on the way to this accommodation, progress towards which would be manifest if my description of the ideological divide itself appears over-simplistic or passé.

The fourth aforementioned difference between aesthetics and cultural concerns its intellectual sources. Here one should not confuse source and substance. When we turn to the philosophical core underlying views maintained in cultural studies, we find interesting parallels with some stances taken in aesthetics. Cultural studies has its own brand of historical contextualism. After all, it is a tenet of much writing within cultural studies that works of art and their meaning are shaped by cultural forces, typically oppressive colonial and neo-colonial forces, of which artists themselves may be unaware. There is certainly room in any reasonable historical contextualism to acknowledge the expression of attitudes in works unbeknownst to their creators, and some recent work on the topic of interpretation and artistic value has done this.[24] So here is a substantial and important common ground. Interestingly, there is an equally forceful constructivist element within the philosophical foundations of cultural studies. This arises from the assumption that interpreters (at least those outside the movement) are as prone to be as culturally determined as artists, and so meanings attributed to artworks are constructed rather than discovered.

This creates a tension in the foundation of cultural studies, manifested in the way it combines historical contextualism and constructivism. How this tension should be resolved is an open question, and one which philosophical aesthetics can help to answer.

Notes

1   The most important, though by no means the only, champion of the philosophical study of art in terms of aesthetic value and experience is Monroe Beardsley, *Aesthetics: Problems in the Theory of Criticism* (New York: Harcourt, Brace and World, 1958). For more than thirty years now, the philosophy of art has been moving beyond aesthetics in the narrower senses. Nearly all the leading figures in this area during this period have promoted this broader conception: Nelson Goodman, Richard Wollheim, Joseph Margolis, Arthur Danto, George Dickie, Kendall Walton, Noel Carroll, and Jerrold Levinson, among others.

2   See Robert Stecker, *Artworks: Definition, Meaning Value* (University Park: Pennsylvania State University Press, 1997), for a more elaborate discussion of the central issues of aesthetics.

3   Where meaning is obvious or can be made obvious by a "mechanical" procedure like looking up a word in a dictionary or consulting a chart, interpretation is not required in order to grasp meaning.

4   The seminal works of historical contextualism are Arthur Danto, "The Artworld," *Journal of Philosophy* 61 (1964): 571–84; Kendall Walton, "Categories of Art," *Philosophical Review* 79 (1970): 334–67. Other proponents of this view in contemporary aesthetics include Noel Carroll, *Beyond Aesthetics: Selected Essays* (Cambridge: Cambridge University Press, 2001), Stephen Davies, *Definitions of Art* (Ithaca, NY: Cornell University Press, 1991), Jerrold Levinson, *Art, Music and Metaphysics* (Ithaca, NY: Cornell University Press, 1990), and Robert Stecker, *Artworks*.

5   See Arthur Danto, *The Transfiguration of the Commonplace* (Cambridge, MA: Harvard University Press, 1981).

6   This point was emphasized by Paul Grice in "Utterer's Meaning and Intentions," *Philosophical Review* 78 (1969): 147–77.

7   This thought has been developed by a number of authors including William Tolhurst, "On What a Text Is and How It Means," *British Journal of Aesthetics* 19 (1979): 3–14. Jerrold Levinson, "Intention and Interpretatation in Literature," in *The Pleasures of Aesthetics* (Ithaca, NY: Cornell University Press, 1996), 175–213, and Robert Stecker, *Interpretation and Construction* (Cambridge, MA: Blackwell, 2003).

8   Jerrold Levinson, "Refining Art Historically," *Journal of Aesthetics and Art Criticism* 47 (1989): 21.

9   Stecker, *Artworks: Definition, Meaning Value*, 31–47.

10   Clive Bell, *Art* (London: Chatto and Windus, 1914).

11   The leading proponent of moderate constructivism is Joseph Margolis in numerous works including, but by no means confined to, *Art and Philosophy* (Brighton: Harvestor Press, 1980), *Interpretation Radical but Not Unruly* (Berkeley: University of California Press, 1995) and *What, After All, Is a Work of Art?* (University Park: Pennsylvania State University Press, 1999). A proponent of a rather different version of this view is Graham Mcfee, "The Historicity of Art," *British Journal of Aesthetics* 38 (1980): 307–24.

12   An example of a radical constructivist is Paul Thom, *Making Sense* (Lanham, MD: Rowman and Littlefield, 2000).

13   See, for example, Morris Weitz, "The Role of Theory in Aesthetics," *Journal of Aesthetics and Art Criticism* 15 (1956): 27–35, Paul Ziff, "The Task of Defining a Work of Art," *Philosophical Review* 62 (1953): 58–78.

14   Another promising approach that we have not discussed here is the institutional approach best exemplified in the work of George Dickie such as *The Art Circle* (New York: Haven Publications, 1984).

15 A more elaborate version of this problem for constructivism is presented in Robert Stecker, "The Constructivist's Dilemma," *Journal of Aesthetics and Art Criticism* 55 (1997): 43–51.

16 See the works of Joseph Margolis cited in note 11.

17 This view is presented by Thom, *Making Sense*.

18 Paul Thom, "Review of Michael Krausz's *Rightness and Reasons: Interpretation in Cultural Practices," Literature and Aesthetics* 7 (1997): 183. This review also discusses Joseph Margolis' *Interpretation Radical but Not Unruly* (1995) and my own "The Constructivist's Dilemma."

19 This proposal derives from Philip Percival, "Stecker's Dilemma: A Constructive Response," *Journal of Aesthetics and Art Criticism* 58 (2000): 51–60.

20 This objection is based on an argument given in David Davies, "Interpretive Pluralism and the Ontology of Art," *Revue Internationale de Philosophie* 50 (1996): 577–91.

21 Robert Con Davis and Ronald Schliefer, *Contemporary Literary Criticism: Literary and Cultural Studies* (White Plains, NY: Longman, 1994), 597. This way of expressing what I call cultural studies' ideology reflects some of developments in that discipline which have occurred since it became a popular international movement especially in the United States. Reference to "post-colonial inquiries" would be foreign to the original work of its British founders. However, the early proponents and more recent proponents of cultural studies share the idea that cultural institutions and their products, including works of art, are made possible by and help to maintain oppressive political power.

22 Terry Eagleton, *Literary Theory: An Introduction* (Minneapolis: University of Minnesota Press, 1983), 16.

23 Terry Eagleton, *The Significance of Theory* (Oxford: Blackwell, 1990), 30.

24 As examples, see Noel Carroll, "Anglo-American Aesthetic and Contemporary Criticism: Intention and the Hermeneutics If Suspicion," in *Beyond Aesthetics* (Cambridge: Cambridge University Press, 2001), 180–90. See also Robert Stecker, *Aesthetics and the Philosophy of Art* (Lanham, MD: Rowman and Littlefield, 2005), 133–38, 208–10.

8 In several noteworthy respects Martin Roberts' contribution represents a practical exemplification or enactment of the requirements of "critical" humanistic inquiry specified by Imre Szeman in his article in this anthology. Roberts' discussion of film culture, in other words, refuses to shirk responsibility for addressing the problem of affirmative culture, it takes commodities and consumerism seriously, it places the contemporary fact of film cultures in its historical context, and by so doing reveals the many different (and theoretically variable) ways in which culture and film may be linked. It also thereby acknowledges the historical contingency, the deep historicity, of intellectuals' and other commentators' interpretations of such linkages, and of their efforts to operationalize as irreducibly multifaceted a term as "film culture." What Roberts does not do, however, is go so far as to provide a thorough account of film culture; indeed providing one on his terms would clearly require space beyond that available to anyone involved in a collective undertaking of this sort. Instead he offers us a guide to what any such account must necessarily include, in the process briefly surveying some of the more substantial recent developments and trends affecting film's "cultural" significance.

Roberts begins by proposing that we understand "film culture" organically, as comprised of a set of dynamically related practices and processes mirroring the chronological "life-cycle" of film itself, beginning with film production, evolving through film exhibition, and concluding in film conservation. Mediating each of these developmental moments, giving them shape and their larger cultural meanings, are a wide variety of actors, processes, and interests, including the nation state, various taste publics and critical communities, and a number of important new technologies. It is with reference to these constitutive parts that we become aware of how any understanding of "film culture" must necessarily distinguish between it, as a largely (and increasingly) cosmopolitanized phenomenon, and "national cinema," with which it shares very few economic and aesthetic *raisons d'être*.

Focusing attention on the nation and national culture serves to foreground the relationship linking film and the state, a complex and decisive nexus insofar as matters of culture are concerned. Roberts explains how the state both encourages and inhibits film production via, respectively, subsidies and support for such national filmmaking agencies as Canada's National Film Board (NFB), and trade tariffs and various forms of censorship. Roberts also reveals the ways in which states exert a strong influence on the distribution of films, and notes the power that distributors have to shape national film cultures by deciding which films, in which formats (dubbed or not; edited so as to conform to local norms or not) will be available within a given distributional domain.

And yet this power, whether of private-sector distributors or of governments, has in recent years been unsettled by the spread of new technologies, particularly digital technologies and the Internet, which have altered film's formal characteristics as well as its modes and sites of distribution and exhibition. As Roberts carefully shows, these changes have not just altered what films are, their genres, how they are made, and where they are seen, they have resulted in the further diversification of subcultures associated with film production and reception, in the process of which film's "cultural" character – the ways in which the medium is theorized, discussed, and comes to mean something to us – has itself been radically changed.

FILM CULTURE

MARTIN ROBERTS

In his preface to the *Film Cultures Reader*,[1] Graeme Turner observes that one of the most important shifts within film studies over the past decade has been the disciplinary impact of cultural studies, television studies, ethnographic studies of media audiences, and social history. One form this impact has taken, according to Turner, has been a shift of emphasis away from analysis of film texts to "the cultural contexts in which the consumption of film takes place, as well as the industrial contexts in which it is produced."[2] Accordingly, one of the book's focal points is "the study of film as culture,"[3] in particular "the part that movies play in the construction of social identities."[4]

While its focus is ostensibly the cultural dimension of film, one of the most curious aspects of the *Film Cultures Reader* is that the concept of "film culture" itself remains unexamined, although the book is certainly not exceptional in this regard. While references to film culture are ubiquitous in writing on film, the meaning of the term itself is usually treated as taken-for-granted and self-evident. The aim of this essay, then, is to scrutinize the concept of film culture more closely and to suggest some possible ways of approaching it. What exactly do we mean when we speak of "film culture"? How is film culture constituted, and by what forces? What inclusions and exclusions does it involve? More generally, what is the relationship between film and culture?

Depending on the particular disciplinary standpoint we choose to adopt (political economical, sociological, ethnographical, historical, aesthetical), there are, of course, many ways of attempting to answer such questions. Given the multi-dimensional nature of film culture, however, it seems advisable to adopt a correspondingly interdisciplinary approach. If we treat film not just as an archive or corpus of texts but as a field of cultural production, in Pierre Bourdieu's sense of the term,[5] a new set of questions opens up: who are the primary agents within this field, and what are the relations of power between them? What are the key determinants of and constraints on cultural production within it? Since there is no satisfactory way of analyzing such a multi-dimensional concept as film culture, my discussion will broadly follow the chronological life-cycle of film itself, from production to distribution, exhibition, reception, and conservation. In the course of this discussion, I focus on some key issues relating to film culture, including the role of the state and the culture industries in film production; censorship and regulation; piracy and intellectual property; the impact of new media technologies and computer networks on film culture; and film subcultures. Before proceeding, however, some preliminary observations are first necessary.

Historically, film industries have tended to be (and in many cases, still are) nationally based, and film scholarship has correspondingly tended to approach film culture in national terms, with attention focusing on, for example, cinema's place within national culture and its role in the formation of national identities.[6] In approaching the concept of film culture, however, it should be recognized from the outset that the boundaries of a national cinema are by no means co-extensive with those of a national film culture, the former typically being only a component of the latter. If film industries have historically been nationally based, film distribution has been international since the Lumière brothers' camera operators first began travelling the world to show *actualité* films a century ago. Thus French film culture has never been constituted exclusively by French films, but also by non-French (and specifically Hollywood) films, which have in turn played a role in the direction taken by French cinema itself. European art cinema has historically largely defined itself in opposition to the commercial cinema of Hollywood, while the Third Cinema movement which arose in Latin America and Africa in the 1960s and 1970s defined itself in opposition to Hollywood and, to a lesser degree, the European New Wave. In West Africa, film culture has only relatively recently begun to include African cinemas (ironically as a result of the success of African filmmakers abroad), having until then been largely constituted by American, French, and Asian cinemas. Even U.S. film culture – if such a vast field can be spoken of in such monolithic terms at all – today increasingly includes non-U.S. films, as the popular success of films such as *Life Is Beautiful* or *Crouching Tiger, Hidden Dragon* attests.

A second issue concerns objections to the category of film culture itself. While in certain historical contexts (say, France in the 1950s) it might have made sense to speak of a national film culture, film culture today is arguably so fragmented that we must speak at the very least of a multiplicity of film cultures and subcultures, from Hollywood blockbusters to avant-garde film and independent film. As we will see later, the Internet is both accelerating and globalizing this process of fragmentation.

A third issue concerns the technological infrastructure of film culture. Since network television began broadcasting movies in the 1950s, it has no longer been possible to discuss film culture in terms of theatrical exhibition alone. Television plays a key role in the production of film culture today, not just as a market for film distribution and exhibition, but also because television is itself actively involved in film production, whether for theatrical or broadcast (made-for-TV movies) release. With the advent of new media technologies and broadband networks capable of distributing digital video on a computer screen, it arguably makes more sense today to speak of screen culture rather than film culture. Having said that, the impact of digital technologies remains historically quite recent, and for much of its history, film culture has been organized around the production and consumption of film texts. While taking account of the contemporary transformation of film culture by new media technologies, then, the discussion which follows is equally concerned with the continuing presence of film as a medium and of film culture today, including the paradoxical use of new media technologies to arrest its impending disappearance.

Production

One question which immediately arises when we consider film culture from the standpoint of production concerns the medium of film itself. While 35 mm and 70 mm have been standard gauges in film production for much of its history, they are far from being the only ones. Large bodies of film production have also taken place on smaller gauges, often associated with particular social groups and communities. Documentary filmmakers, for example, have shown a predilection for 16mm cameras and film, more portable and cheaper than the larger formats used in feature-film production. Among non-professionals, 8 mm and Super-8 cameras have been used for decades to produce home movies documenting family vacations, weddings, and other social rituals, and their importance has been increasingly recognized by historians and film scholars.[7] Experimental filmmakers, thirdly, have drawn upon the entire repertoire of film and media formats as well as more esoteric formats such as Pixelvision. In recent years, each of these groups has begun to make extensive use of digital cameras, further blurring the line between professional and amateur production. Notwithstanding the issue of film formats and their cultural dimensions, however, the bulk of film production for theatrical exhibition has taken place on 35 mm, and in what follows I will accordingly focus primarily on production of this type.

From the standpoint of film culture, my next set of questions relates to the institutional and economic bases for film production: what kinds of films are made, and why? What are the respective roles of the state and the commercial sector in film production in a given national or transnational context? Who decides which films are produced, which are not, and why? What degree of creative control do filmmakers exercise over the films which will eventually reach their audience? What opportunities are available, what constraints are placed on film production by the respective forces of the state and the market, and the dynamics between them?

The impact of the state on film culture can operate either positively or negatively, in the form of financial support or censorship. In many nations, cinema has long been seen both as a national cultural institution and a means of promoting national culture abroad. In such cases, states have accordingly taken an active role in providing institutional support for a national film industry through national film schools, institutes, boards, and commissions. While such state-supported film production potentially affords filmmakers greater creative independence by freeing them from the economic constraints of the market, it arguably only replaces these with a different set of constraints in that it enables the state to regulate film discourses about and representations of the nation.[8]

Similar ideological and political agendas can operate in the relationship between former imperial powers and their ex-colonies. While few would disagree, for example, that the development of cinema in Francophone West Africa in the 1960s and 1970s could not have taken place without the support of the French Bureau du Cinéma,[9] this support necessarily set limits over the kinds of discourses African filmmakers could engage in, most notably about colonial history itself. As a result of conflicts with the Bureau over his film *Mandabi* (1968), for example, the Senegalese director Ousmane Sembene refused to work with French funding, yet this also provided him with greater freedom to deal with politically "sensitive" subjects: arguably, his anti-colonialist films of subsequent decades such as *Xala* (1975) or *Camp de Thiaroye* (1987) might never been made if they had relied on French funding. Less-established filmmakers, unable to afford such creative independence, have had to work within the constraints which necessarily accompany French institutional support for their work.

In addition to financial and logistical support, state support for domestic film industries may also take the form of protection from foreign imports through quotas and other measures, as in the case of France's long-running dispute with Hollywood from the 1920s to the GATT negotiations.[10] In other cases, a state may seek to harness economic forces, as with Brazil's revival of its film industry in the 1990s through a series of fiscal incentives.[11]

On the negative side, a state may regulate its film culture through various forms of censorship of domestic film production (as well as of imported films, as I will discuss in the next section on distribution). Historically, boards of film censors have played a key role in shaping film cultures around the world, although filmmakers have proved no less adept at circumventing the restrictions placed upon them. Censorship of foreign films is today proving increasingly unworkable because of the multiplicity of delivery systems, from satellite TV to broadband computer networks, and the difficulty of policing these. While a nation such as Iran may officially prohibit ownership of satellite dishes, in practice they are quite widely available and censorship efforts have to shift to the international arena in attempts to stop satellite feeds themselves.

Commercially produced films in some ways enjoy greater autonomy than state-produced ones, but are subject to a different set of constraints – most notably those of the market, with its imperative of maximizing audiences – which are arguably even more limiting. The film culture of state-supported film industries looks very different from those shaped solely by the cultural logic of capitalism. At least in principle, cinema in state-based film industries is conceived more as a form of cultural patrimony than a commercial product, an art form more than a commodity, whose primary function is more edification than entertainment. In state-based film industries, notions of artistic quality take priority over commercial success, and such industries are able to produce films which would never see the light of day in a commercial system. In practice today, however, such distinctions are becoming less and less clear-cut, with states proving increasingly reluctant to fund films unlikely to attract large domestic and international audiences, as well as prioritizing those most likely to garner prestige abroad through awards at international film festivals and other venues.

An important aspect of the film-culture relationship with regard to production is the increasing capacity of transnational capital today to influence the cultural policy of nation-states. The most obvious example here is the continuing battle between France and the U.S. over film quotas. Film production, especially that of Hollywood, has over the past decade increasingly shifted overseas to nations such as Canada, Australia, Mexico, or the Czech Republic, which offer cheaper labour, tax concessions, and other incentives.[12] This internationalization of production has many cultural dimensions, not least in its creation of a new kind of transcultural contact zone between Hollywood cultural producers and local ones. This cultural encounter can often be seen as a form of neo-colonialism, as the controversial production of *The Beach* in Thailand amply attests.[13]

Finally, new technologies of production and promotion have radically altered the political economy of filmmaking, with independent production becoming a more viable possibility today than it has ever been before. The advent of digital video (DV) formats, with their affordable cameras and desktop editing software, have spawned a host of subcultures of digital filmmakers, with its own festival circuit, publications, and cult directors.[14] *The Blair Witch Project*, shot on 16 mm film and DV, not only had a surprise impact on mainstream U.S. film culture in the summer of 2000, but also rewrote the rules of film promotion through its use of the web as free advertising. As in the case of the music industry and its relation to independent production, Hollywood is no longer the only force driving mainstream film culture and is increasingly having to be responsive to initiatives and innovations within the independent sector.

Distribution

Broadly speaking, the history of film distribution may be thought of as a struggle between national institutions and transnational corporations for control of film distribution and exhibition. As with film production, ownership is key: whoever owns the means of film distribution and exhibition in a given part of the world can exercise considerable control over the local film culture there. While historically, states and commercial distributors have at different times each held greater power over distribution than the other, neither has ultimately succeeded in monopolizing distribution and exhibition in a given national context.

In its strongest form, state control over distribution and exhibition takes the form of state ownership of movie theatres, as was the case in China until recently. Weaker forms include state regulation of corporate ownership, import quotas, and censorship. In the studio era in the U.S., vertical integration guaranteed studios distribution and exhibition of any film they produced. The U.S. Justice Department's dismantling of this system after the Second World War broke the studios' stranglehold on U.S. film culture and separated film production from distribution and exhibition. The studios have spent much of their time since to trying to recover their former monopoly but today the picture is more complicated because the means of distribution and exhibition now include not just movie theatres but television networks and cable channels, home video, and the Internet. Monopolizing distribution and exhibition thus requires horizontal as well as vertical integration.[15]

Censorship constitutes a third way in which many states continue to regulate the distribution both of domestically produced films and international ones. Although often ideologically motivated, censorship may also have a cultural basis, in that it is related to dominant identities and belief-systems within a society. An article in *Res* magazine about the first digital film festival held in the Philippines, for example, noted that one film had been excluded from competition "because of pubic hair exposure."[16] Leaving aside the reviewer's impatience with such prudery, this small example shows how as films circulate in increasingly global markets today, they encounter and must negotiate local cultural resistance in various forms.

State censorship of, for example, pornographic film is notoriously difficult to enforce, and today has to reckon not only with film prints but new distribution technologies, from satellite TV to DVD. While commercial distributors are primarily concerned with optimizing distribution of their films, their profits also depend on successfully protecting their properties by preventing the circulation of pirated copies. Corporate institutions, or governments acting on their behalf, thus often pressure national governments to crack down on video piracy, albeit with varying degrees of success.[17] It need hardly be emphasized that digital media formats and global computer networks have made it increasingly difficult today for either national governments or commercial distributors to regulate the films that people have access to.

Commercial film distributors may be divided into several categories: they may distribute film prints for theatrical exhibition, videotapes, or (increasingly, today) DVD transfers of films for home viewing, or a combination of all three. The format of film distribution itself is a controversial issue for aesthetic reasons, since watching a movie on a TV or computer screen necessarily changes how it is experienced. While it would never occur to most people that the "film" they rent from a Blockbuster outlet is in actuality a miniaturized videotape copy rather than the film "itself," certain film critics and professors still insist on the specificity of the medium and may refuse to watch or show films other than in their projected form.[18]

As market-places for film distributors and meeting-places for producers developing new projects, film festivals play a central role in shaping film cultures around the globe.[19] While it might be assumed that securing a distributor in a particular country is the first step to exhibition, this is not necessarily true. In his polemic against the U.S. film industry *Movie Wars*, the *Chicago Reader*'s film critic Jonathan Rosenbaum is especially critical of the business practices of Miramax:

Because Miramax picks up over twice as many films as it releases – keeping most of its unreleased pictures in perpetual limbo, shaping and re-cutting most of its favorites, and marginalizing most of the others so that only a handful of people ever get to see them – there's statistically *less* chance of the public ever having access to a movie if Miramax acquires it.... It's been speculated that one reason why Miramax picks up so many films is in order to prevent other distributors from acquiring them; if this is true, then I guess we're supposed to conclude that Miramax's profit motive is more important than the desire of many people to see these and other films that are kept out of reach.[20]

While national distributors play a valuable role in distributing foreign cinemas, the films they distribute may largely define what constitutes those cinemas for domestic audiences. The case of California Newsreel is instructive in this regard. The major distributor of African films in the U.S., it distributes subtitled versions of over a hundred African films. Because it largely monopolizes U.S. distribution of African films, however, California Newsreel has more or less single-handedly invented the category of African Cinema in the U.S. It has defined this in exclusively auteurist terms, as a primarily academic phenomenon (as evidenced by the study-guides it also publishes). Its library of African cinema is strikingly selective when compared with other international distributors of African film such as the Paris-based Médiathèque des Trois Mondes.

Another anomaly of film distribution is how nationally based it remains, even in an age of economic globalization: a Canadian distributor of a certain foreign film, for example, cannot legally sell that film to a customer resident in the United States, even if the film in question has no U.S. distributor. The Médiathèque des Trois Mondes cannot legally distribute a certain African film in the U.S., even if California Newsreel does not do so. Moreover, since it distributes these films in France and the films themselves are subtitled in French, most U.S. viewers would not be able to watch them anyway. Even in a globalized world, then, it is clear that we are still far from a global film market, and given existing legal systems and cultural differences, the situation is unlikely to change in the near future.

When films cross national borders, they also have to be altered. As Rosenbaum notes, Miramax routinely re-edits the films it distributes to optimize them for the U.S. market. Cuts commonly have a cultural basis, involving scenes with sexual or violent content, and may be more or less stringent depending on the moral codes of the nation in question. Films in languages other than that of the importing country must also be either subtitled or dubbed, both practices with a strongly cultural dimension.[21] Different nations have different practices with regard to dubbing and subtitling, and their cultural meaning varies accordingly. In European countries such as Spain, dubbing (*doblaje*) of foreign films has been standard practice for decades and has been incorporated into Spanish film culture: dubbing actors who supply the voice for the same movie stars from one film to another become indissociable from them and even celebrities in their own right, as in the case of Woody Allen's Spanish alter ego, Joan Pera. By contrast, Miramax's decision to release Roberto Benigni's Oscar-winning film *Life Is Beautiful* (1998) in a dubbed version after the success of the original subtitled one was a subject of controversy.[22] In the U.S., subtitling of foreign films has long been the norm, with dubbing reserved for popular genres such as martial-arts movies or *anime*. Miramax's move was in accordance with industry orthodoxy about subtitling, which has long served as an alibi for U.S. audiences' supposed disinterest in foreign films. Rosenbaum disputes this claim, maintaining that it is condescending towards audiences and merely provides an excuse for U.S. distributors' reluctance to distribute foreign films. The fact remains, however, that with certain exceptions subtitled films in U.S. film culture are associated with the art films and auteurs rather than the mass-cultural cinema of the multiplex. Lastly, it is worth mentioning that, in the home video market, new media technologies are rendering such debates increasingly beside the point today, since DVD editions of films increasingly include dubbed or subtitled versions in multiple languages. For this reason alone, the future careers of dubbing actors such as Joan Pera seems assured.

Exhibition

The role of exhibition in shaping film culture can be approached in a number of ways. On the one hand, we might focus on the historical dimension of theatrical exhibition in all its many forms, from the nickelodeon to the multiplex, drive-in movies to simulation rides, Cinerama to IMAX. A relevant issue here would be the transformation of U.S. film culture by the advent of television in the 1950s, and the new forms of film experience which were developed in response to it (3-D movies, Technicolor). Since the film cultures around these historical forms of exhibition have already been widely studied, however, I will focus here on exhibition in the contemporary world.[23]

The subject is an especially complex one because of the multitude of ways in which films are exhibited today. In addition to theatrical exhibition, home video, and television, we can add in-flight movies, movies in Greyhound buses and SUVs, laptops playing DVDs or streaming video from websites, and portable "movies" on PDAs and even mobile phones.[24] Collectively, these technologies have transformed film culture in modern societies by disembedding cinema from the relatively circumscribed cultural contexts in which it was previously experienced and making it ubiquitous. DVD editions of films today are typically packages including multiple versions of the same film (director's cut, letterbox), making-of documentaries and interviews with filmmakers and cast members, problematizing the status of the film text itself as the unique, definitive version of a particular film. The availability of and access to such exhibition technologies remains very uneven, however, and films are exhibited in many other ways today which compensate for this and have often been overlooked to date. Since these alternative forms of exhibition also play a key role in shaping local film cultures, they merit closer attention.

Film is often regarded as one of the defining cultural institutions of modernity, and discussions of film culture even in partially modernized or modernizing nations tend to privilege urban contexts: geographically speaking, film culture is treated as if it exists only where movie theatres or television are available, but this is not the case. In many parts of the world today, mobile cinemas play an important role in exhibiting films in rural, traditional communities.[25] Little is known about this form of exhibition, but it plays an important cultural function. The films exhibited by mobile cinemas vary in different countries, but they are clearly not the same as the Hollywood blockbusters being watched by the cosmopolitan middle classes in urban multiplexes, nor the auteurist art films which represent "Indian cinema" or "Indonesian cinema" at international film festivals. They are the kinds of popular films encountered when one ventures beyond the mall or the museum, in movie theatres with garishly painted billboards above their entrances, noisy audiences, and temperamental equipment. These popular cinemas in themselves represent a little-studied sector of film culture in many parts of the world today, and this is even more true of mobile cinemas.[26] The films exhibited are not necessarily local fare, as the longstanding popularity of Hindi musicals or kung-fu movies in Africa attests, but they are more likely to be popular genres produced by national film industries: musicals, action adventures, westerns, or some combination of these. While the genres may be transnational, mobile cinemas play a key role in constructing a national film culture by incorporating local, rural communities into the imagined community of the modern nation-state.

Throughout Asia, Africa, and the Indian subcontinent, in nations lacking either the infrastructure of theatrical exhibition or which restrict foreign film imports, video parlours provide another alternative exhibition system. As in the case of "mobile cinemas," the term "video parlour" is a generic one covering a wide range of exhibition environments, from a VCR and monitor in a village shack to large-screen projection of DVDs in an upscale bar. The popularity of video parlours is partly attributable to technological factors: in many Asian countries, for example, films have long been available in a variety of digital formats, with the enhanced image and sound quality these provide. Elsewhere, however, it may be related to other factors: in Nigeria or Ghana, where video is the dominant format for local film production, video parlours provide an alternative public sphere where local audiences can watch films about their own lives and concerns, rather than the imports which typically dominate local movie theatres.[27] In China, which until recently restricted U.S. film imports to about ten per year, video parlours provide an unofficial exhibition system for international films, which, although officially illegal, the state has tended to turn a blind eye to.

Since many of the films shown in video parlours are pirated, they have understandably been at the centre of controversy over video piracy and are subject to regular crackdowns by national governments responding to pressure from Western business interests or the governments representing them. The shady reputation of video parlours is also related to the fact that they are also often at the centre of local pornography industries, screening movies which may be officially illegal. While many feature cubicles for individual use, video parlours are also widely used as love hotels in societies where sexual activity between unmarried partners is prohibited for cultural reasons. Because they often operate at the margins of legality, video parlours typically attract similarly illegal activities, while their failure to meet safety standards can sometimes be fatal.[28]

Both mobile cinemas and video parlours resemble theatrical distribution in that they remain essentially place-based, bringing film audiences together in a shared space of collective viewing. Over the past decade, the Internet has emerged as a new exhibition medium, while at the same time deterritorializing it by disembedding it from the space-time contingencies of a particular locale. What we might call exhibition "proper" remains rudimentary at this stage – while films are widely available in streaming format (on sites such as iFilm.com or Atom-Films.com), most computers are presently too limited in bandwidth, processor power, and screen resolution to be able to compete with the movie screen or even television. On the other hand, these very limitations have made the Internet an attractive distribution medium for the short film, long relegated to late-night television, which has been undergoing something of a renaissance in recent years.[29] An article by Jonathan Rosenbaum on Internet film culture does not even bother to mention exhibition,[30] so it is ironic that Resfest, a digital film festival which is one of the cheerleaders of the so-called iFilm movement, still takes place in theatrical venues and provides only short clips on its website.

If the Internet still leaves much to be desired as an exhibition medium, it has nevertheless spawned a multitude of online subcultures organized around film genres. Such communities pre-date the Internet, of course, but the Internet has deterritorialized and globalized them. Fans of Japanese *anime* movies, for instance, have had an online presence for some time, trading videotapes by mail with friends on the other side of the world. New media facilitates this process: as the shelves of blank DVD-R and DVD-RW disks available at retail electronics stores amply attest, movies ripped from commercial DVD releases or recorded from television onto hard drives via systems such as TiVo, today are routinely shared via peer-to-peer (P2P) networks, in spite of increasingly futile industry efforts to regulate such practices.[31] This may be one reason for the movie industry's reluctance to shift to digital distribution and exhibition: while it may be technically feasible and economically desirable, new films distributed in their old-fashioned format of reels in tin cans are still easier to protect from piracy than digital copies distributed via broadband networks. Arguably, such concerns are beside the point today, since the digital genie is manifestly already out of the bottle; as the movie industry executives continue to resist moving to digital distribution, hackers are doing it for them.

The cultural consequences of such developments are difficult to determine. It seems clear, however, that film cultures and subcultures will become increasingly deterritorialized and cosmopolitan, their tastes and range of options less dictated by film-cultural elites. Much of this emerging cosmopolitanism of film culture is already evident in the proliferating webzines and resource sites devoted to different film genres, national cinemas, cult movies and directors, or film in general. These proliferating discourses on cinema lead us to the question of reception and film culture.

Reception

Reception is where films finally meet their audiences, where they begin to play a role in people's everyday lives, and where the process of constructing their meanings and value begins in earnest. In his work *Globalization and Culture*, John Tomlinson defines "culture" as the ongoing process by which societies incorporate objects and symbols into their lives in existentially meaningful ways,[32] and film clearly plays a significant role in this process. While for many, watching movies is primarily a leisure practice, it is widely recognized that much of the appeal of watching films is that they provide narratives which enable us to make sense out of our own experience. Some argue that the process extends beyond this, a case in point being the long-running controversy over film violence,[33] reactivated in the U.S. in the wake of the massacres at Columbine High School in Littleton, Colorado, in April 1999.

The cultural dimension of film reception may in part be approached as a set of culturally specific social practices, the most obvious being the practice of movie-watching itself. One way of thinking about film culture from the standpoint of reception, for example, is in terms of the ethnography of film audiences, and the cultural differences in audience behaviour in different ethnographic and sociological contexts. The social etiquette of speaking during film screenings is an interesting issue here: while even popular theatres in the Western world enforce a norm of silent viewing, typically via the reminders before a screening begins, in many other parts of the world reacting verbally to and discussing a film while it is in progress are an equally accepted part of the viewing experience. Food is another issue: if popcorn is the staple of the global multiplex today, it is far from universal; visitors to a movie theatre in Madrid, for example, are likely to find the floor carpeted with the discarded husks of sunflower seeds consumed at the previous screening. Another key issue – as in public spaces outside the movie theatre – is the practice of making or accepting cellphone calls during screenings. While in corporate theatre chains around the world patrons are now routinely requested to turn off cellphones as a courtesy to others, this is often ignored and standards of what is acceptable practice are as varied as cultural attitudes to the public use of cellphones in general.

In approaching film reception and its role in constituting film culture, we might also think of it as a discursive field, an array of discourses which construct frameworks and categories for the classification, interpretation, and evaluation of film texts and practices. Taxonomic categories such as "art films," "summer blockbusters," or "world cinema"; analytical ones (shot/reverse shot; lap dissolve; jump cut); film genres; the analytical category of "film genre" itself – these terms are all discursive constructs, the result of a long and complex negotiation between film texts and the discourses generated around them. Collectively, they constitute a discursive field into which all new film-cultural practices are inserted and acquire meaning and value, and which in turn defines the horizon of possibilities for future practices. While this discursive field does not pre-determine new forms of film-cultural production, any film-maker today necessarily works within it and positions his or her work, even oppositionally, in relation to it.[34]

The discursive field of film culture itself is deeply hierarchical, raising political and sociological questions about both the constitution of the field itself (the social construction of taste) and the positioning of agents and practices within it. It is useful here, following Nestor García Canclini, to differentiate between three discursive arenas: the cultured, the mass-cultural, and the popular.

The discourse of academic film theorists and scholars, film curators, and other specialists, first of all, occupy the domain of the cultured. They play a key role in the formation of analytical-theoretical categories, but circulate only in elite discursive arenas (e.g., academic conferences), and although their work is popularized by film journalists it is little known by the general public.

In the arena of mass culture, secondly, we can differentiate between the discourse of film journalism and the promotional discourse of media reportage. Because it circulates widely through print and broadcast media, film journalism plays a key role in shaping public tastes, and no doubt for this reason film journalists are treated carefully by the film industry, receiving privileged access to production locations, interviews with filmmakers and cast members, and invitations to advance screenings and premieres. If the role of film journalists is, broadly speaking, to inform the public of which films are worth seeing and why, the media reportage of TV networks, cable channels such as E! Entertainment, or *People* magazine serves a largely promotional purpose. Perhaps the most egregious example is the annual feeding frenzy of the Academy Awards, which, although ostensibly a celebration of the aesthetic merits of films and actors, is notoriously more preoccupied with what the stars are wearing. Such media reportage arguably serves mainly to naturalize the culture of celebrity and promote the agendas of the film industry.

Popular discourses about film, thirdly, were until recently marginal in relation to cultured and mass-cultural discourses, but in recent years the Internet has been a catalyst for a multitude of popular discourses about film, from discussion forums on the Internet Movie Database to precocious teenage film critics. Some amateur or freelance critics have extensive archives of film reviews and critical articles, and have become frequent reference points in professional film journalism.[35]

More generally, the Internet has become a breeding-ground for film fan clubs and subcultures of every kind, organized around cult movie genres, directors, specific movies, and stars. Film fan culture probably reaches its furthest extent in the massive subculture organized around George Lucas's *Star Wars* trilogy (given further momentum by the new series of *Star Wars* prequels). As with other fan cultures, such as the one organized around *Star Trek*,[36] the original reference text has generated new, proliferating forms of cultural production, including fan fiction, artwork, and most interestingly, fan films, inspired by Kevin Rubio's brilliant *Star-Wars*-meets-COPS-meets-*Fargo* spoof, *Troops*.[37]

Conservation

Cinema today is little more than a hundred years old. In the course of the past century, however, film culture has grown increasingly aware of its historical dimension, of cinema's contribution to cultural patrimony, and of the need to preserve this for future generations. Although there were calls for a permanent archive of film images as early as 1898, such archives did not begin to be established until the 1930s. It is estimated that the number of films surviving from the first three decades of the cinema's history constitutes less than 20 per cent of the number of films actually made.[38] France claims to have established the first film museum in 1972, and it was quickly followed by Britain and the United

States. Today, national film archives such as those of the CNC (Centre National de la Cinématographie) in France or the BFI (British Film Institute) in Britain have acquired large collections of film negatives and prints and are actively involved in the conservation and restoration of films. Because of the highly unstable nature of the cellulose nitrate film stock used throughout the first half of the twentieth century, this is neither easy nor cheap: negatives are highly flammable and have to be stored at low temperatures and in low humidity to slow the decomposition process. In recent decades, digitization has emerged as the most viable (albeit far from satisfactory) solution to the perishability of film as a medium, and many archives today are transferring their early-film collections to digital formats. Whether these formats will prove any more durable than the material ones remains to be seen, but an interesting aspect of digitization is that film libraries can be made available via the Internet, thus deterritorializing the film archive itself: the Library of Congress or the Prelinger Archives, for example, already offer large collections of historical films online. Just as print-based national libraries such as the new Bibliothèque de France are moving towards online distribution of their collections, as the capacity of broadband networks increases it is likely that film archives such as the Cinémathèque Française or the National Film Theatre will do the same.

One area in which new media technologies play an increasingly important role in shaping film-cultural production is that of film restoration and reconstruction. A deteriorating celluloid film print can be digitized, processed to improve image and sound quality, then exported either to a new celluloid print for theatrical or, more commonly, DVD release. The preference for home video over theatrical exhibition is largely economic: since audiences for cable channels such as TMC or home video are larger than those for theatrical releases, it is simply more profitable to re-release films that way. DVD editions of silent films may also include additional features such as explanatory voice-overs (as in Bertrand Tavernier's commentary on the DVD edition of the Lumière brothers' early films), re-recorded soundtracks of musical accompaniments or completely new performances, as in the case of the Alloy Orchestra's soundtracks on DVD editions of Vertov's *Man with a Movie Camera* (1929) and Eisenstein's *Strike!* (1924). In some cases, such projects have fed back into theatrical exhibition: the Alloy Orchestra's live performances at screenings of restored prints of *Strike!* and other films is an interesting development in contemporary film culture.

The possibilities offered by new media technologies are not limited to film restoration, however. Among the most interesting examples are Rick Schmidlin's 239-minute reconstruction of Erich von Stroheim's mutilated masterpiece *Greed* (1924) – premiered on the Turner Movie Classics (TMC) network on 5 December 1999 – which uses video animation of over 650 production stills to flesh out the truncated version originally released by MGM.[39] Another of Schmidlin's projects, a theatrical re-release of Welles's *Touch of Evil* (1958), re-edits the film in accordance with a memo submitted by Welles requesting a re-edit but never implemented by the studio, as well as a digitally restored soundtrack.[40] Such reconstruction projects have fuelled excitement about more ambitious future ones, from a resurrected "lost" silent film about the Titanic to the insertion of full-motion video scenes or even entire films never actually produced. Such projects raise questions about the integrity of film texts and authorial authority over them. They feed into the larger ongoing debate about the new digital censorship of DVD editions of movies, such as Warner Home Video's much-criticized R-Rated release of Kubrick's *Eyes Wide Shut*, or the right of directors such as George Lucas or Steven Spielberg to issue digitally "corrected" versions of their films (brilliantly satirized in a *South Park* episode). Both such expurgated versions and the inclusion of alternative endings and deleted scenes exemplify how the integrity of the film text itself has become an increasingly political issue in digital film culture.

The memorialization and museification of film culture reached its height toward the end of both the century and the millennium with the centenary of the birth of motion pictures in the mid-nineties, which triggered a spate of commemorative projects in the form of retrospective screening series, publications, and new film projects reflecting on the history of motion pictures, its global dimension, and its uncertain future in the brave new digital world. At the turn of the millennium, film culture arrived at the point of self-reflexivity, constituting itself as a historical object of collective memory. A striking aspect of this self-reflexivity, symptomatic of a larger tendency over the past decade, was a recognition of the global dimension of cinema, and corresponding attempts to encompass this within the equally all-encompassing attempts to take in a century of film history.[41] The emergence of the category of "World Cinema," now ubiquitous in college film-studies curricula and film catalogues, is itself symptomatic of perhaps the most significant development in film culture at the millennium: its globalization and cosmopolitanism.

Towards a Cosmopolitan Film Culture

To suggest that we are moving towards a cosmopolitan film culture today may seem heretical: what of the Cannes and Venice film festivals, European co-productions of the 1960s such as *Doctor Zhivago*, Omar Sharif and David Niven, Marcello Mastroianni and Anita Ekberg, Sophia Loren and Capucine, spaghetti westerns, or the globe-trotting films of Herzog and Wenders, Jarmusch and the Käurismäki brothers?[42] Has not cinema itself been cosmopolitan from its inception, in the global travels of the Lumière camera operators and the images of the world they brought back with them? From a different perspective, it could be suggested that cosmopolitanism is far from new in non-western societies, accustomed to decades of Hollywood blockbusters, Hong Kong martial arts movies, and Hindi musicals.[43] While acknowledging these objections, I would still like to suggest that film culture today is increasingly global and cosmopolitan, the consequences of which are visible in new film production.

A good example of what I am referring to is the globalization of the star system. That system has long been international, of course, but until recently it has been dominated by Hollywood and European stars. In recent decades, however, the Euro-American star system has become increasingly entangled with those of other global cinemas, notably those of Asian cinemas. An actress such as Maggie Cheung, for example, was a star of Hong Kong action movies for years before crossing over into the Euro-American system through her role in *Irma Vep*. Jackie Chan's emergence as a Hollywood star (and director) is an even more striking case in point. The cosmopolitanism of contemporary film culture can also be observed in film soundtracks: Ali Farka Toure in Olivier Asseyas's *Fin Août, Début Septembre*, or any of Wong Kar-Wai's films, to name but two examples.

The factors accounting for the cosmopolitanism I am referring to here are complex but can be seen as resulting from a number of larger tendencies. One is the increasing presence in North American and European film cultures of non-western cinemas or "World Cinema," which now includes not just Bollywood and Hong Kong martial arts movies, but also Middle Eastern, African, and other Asian cinemas. As in other sectors of popular culture today, a cosmopolitan familiarity with exotic film cultures is a source of cultural capital and social distinction, especially in contemporary global youth cultures. A second factor underlying the emergence of a cosmopolitan film culture is the globalization of film distribution, in response to the commercial imperative of maximizing box-office revenues, and the transformation of film production which this entails. Film distribution has always been international, but film production today is increasingly structured around this end. One strategy is the foregrounding of cultural and historical specificity characteristic of heritage cinema, from Merchant-Ivory's stiff-upper-lip Britishness to the Taiwanese costume dramas of Hou Hsiao-Hsien, or the national self-stereotyping of *Chocolat* or *Amélie*. At the other end of the spectrum we find a global cinema optimized to succeed in the maximum number of international markets worldwide. To elaborate this point more fully, I will conclude by briefly considering three films which have achieved both critical acclaim and box-office success in global markets, each of which in different ways exemplifies the emergent cosmopolitan film culture I have been discussing.

A result of the cross-cultural collaboration between Taiwanese-born, New York-based director Ang Lee and the founder of the production company Good Machine, James Schamus, *Crouching Tiger, Hidden Dragon* (2000) features an all-star cast well known both in Hong Kong and Chinese cinema and increasingly in the West: Chow Yun-Fat, Michelle Yeoh, and rising star Cheng Pei-Pei. As is well known, the film was far more profitable in the U.S. than in Asian markets (although it was not exactly a failure there either). Much of the film's success can be attributed to its astute self-positioning as a hybrid of multiple global film genres: most obviously, the Hong-Kong martial arts movie; the heritage cinema of internationally (if not nationally) acclaimed Chinese directors Zhang Yimou and Chen Kaige; and the digital martial-arts movie, piggy-backing on the success of *The Matrix*. Interestingly, the film's strategy of being all things to all audiences proved more successful in the U.S. than in Asia, largely for cultural reasons: Hong Kong actress Michelle Yeoh's Cantonese-accented Mandarin was reportedly the source of much amusement among Mandarin-speaking audiences, for example, a fact lost on Western audiences. The film's digitally enhanced combat sequences, which impressed Western audiences unfamiliar with Hong Kong martial arts movies, were less impressive to Asian audiences, where such digitally enhanced choreography is valued less than the virtuosic performance of stars such as Jackie Chan.

In a very different way, Australian director Baz Luhrmann's *Moulin Rouge* (2001) can be seen as similarly hybridized and cosmopolitan. A postmodern retelling of the classic story of the nineteenth-century Parisian music hall immortalized in the paintings of Toulouse Lautrec, the film's nostalgic bohemianism is laced with a retro-pop soundtrack featuring songs by Marc Bolan, David Bowie, Elton John, and Madonna. Its stars include Scottish Ewan MacGregor and Australian Nicole Kidman. The film's updating of the musical genre and the bohemian trope of the starving artist (familiar from one of the film's countless intertexts, Gene Kelly's *An American in Paris*), lent it popular appeal, but its campy visual excess has also made it a cult favourite for queer audiences. Lastly, its unabashed exoticism, most apparent in the pastiche of a Bollywood dance number, both appeals to multicultural (specifically South Asian and South-Asian diaspora) audiences and Anglo-Americo-Australian exoticist ones.

New York-based Indian director Mira Nair began her career in documentary with films such as *India Cabaret* (1985), a study of Bombay nightclub dancers, before moving into commercial feature films such as *Mississippi Masala* (1991), on South Asian diasporic identities in the U.S. and the sumptuous *Kama Sutra* (1996), which was widely criticized as auto-exoticist/eroticist pandering to western Orientalism. Her film *Monsoon Wedding* (2001) is in many ways a synthesis of her previous work, but it again exemplifies the emergent cosmopolitan film culture I have been describing. Whereas Nair's earlier films were targeted either at South Asian diaspora or cosmopolitan white audiences in the U.S. and UK, *Monsoon Wedding* was also distributed in India and is clearly also addressed to domestic audiences there, whether of the working class or the more affluent and cosmopolitan urban middle class. Neither documentary, art film, nor Bollywood musical, it combines all three in a hybridized mix of musical numbers, tasteful eroticism, and social commentary (notably the theme of child abuse). While the main characters belong to the conspicuously cosmopolitan Indian middle classes, jetting in from various corners of the globe for the wedding of the film's title, their romantic entanglements are counterpointed (in classic Bollywood fashion) by the parallel romance involving two of the household servants, as a point of access for the less affluent members of the film's audience. For non-Indian audiences, the film provides plenty of the exotic attractions familiar from the Indochic craze inspired by Madonna's Indian phase. The strategy of addressing multiple international audiences appears to have paid off, especially in the multicultural UK, where the BFI sponsored an eight-month national tour of Bollywood cinema called ImagineAsia.[44] British film culture, indeed, is becoming increasingly multicultural, as Bollywood movies gain in popularity among non-Asian audiences and the work of diaspora filmmakers such as Gurinder Chadha (whose film *Bend It Like Beckham* was a runaway success) become increasingly national figures. Similar patterns can be observed in the popularization of North African *beur* cinema in France over the past decade.

One of the ironies of contemporary film culture is that as the film industries of nations such as France or Britain continue to export films perpetuating essentialist myths of national identity abroad, the postcolonial film culture within those nations themselves is increasingly multicultural. At the transnational level, on the other hand, the pattern is clearly towards a cosmopolitan cinema, produced in multiple locations, with a cast of international stars, multiple cultural, social, and sexual identities, densely intertextual narratives – something for everyone, in other words. This conspicuously cosmopolitan film culture is emblematic of the culture industries in general, from fashion to popular music, where the commercialization of non-Western and non-U.S. cultural identities and practices requires a rethinking of older models of cultural imperialism. While what Salman Rushdie might describe as the mongrelization of film culture today may seem like a positive

development overall, however, we would do well to remember the political and economic assymetries on which it is founded, and the place
of global Hollywood within those assymetries. From this perspective,
the work of today's documentary filmmakers, such as Stephanie Black's
account of the impact of global economic forces in Jamaica in *Life and
Debt* (2001), while less eye-catching than the commercial films I have
discussed, provides a timely reminder of the realities of the new world
order, and a much-needed counterweight to the cosmopolitan pleasures
of the global culture industry.

Notes

1   Graeme Turner, ed., *The Film Cultures Reader* (New York: Routledge, 2002).
2   Ibid., ix.
3   Ibid., 8.
4   Ibid., xx.
5   Pierre Bourdieu, *The Field of Cultural Production: Essays on Art and Literature*, ed. Randal
    Johnson (New York: Columbia University Press, 1993).
6   For an overview of the question of national cinema and theoretical issues associated with
    it, see Cinema and Nation, ed. Mette Hjort and Scott MacKenzie (New York: Routledge,
    2000).
7   A noteworthy example here are the series of videos produced by the Media Arts Center
    of the Japanese American National Museum in Los Angeles over the past decade, which
    includes extensive footage of home movies made by Japanese Americans during their
    internment in concentration camps during World War II. (See http://www.janm.org/
    mediaartscenter/production.html.) On the avant-garde tradition in 8 mm film produc-
    tion, see the film series co-produced by the Museum of Modern Art and San Francisco
    Cinematheque from February 1998 to December 1999, and its accompanying catalogue:
    MOMA and San Francisco Cinematheque, *Big as Life: An American History of 8mm Films*
    (San Francisco: Foundation for Art in Cinema, 1998).
8   Writing on the Australian film industry, for example, Graeme Turner comments: "It is
    ironic to note that as government support became less important to the Australian film
    industry and the influence of private investment stronger, the variety of Australian films
    being made widened to range from the low-budget art film of Paul Cox's *Cactus* to the
    slyly engaging mainstream fare of *Crocodile Dundee*." Graeme Turner, *Film as Social
    Practice* (New York: Routledge, 1999), 145–46.
9   Manthia Diawara, *African Cinema: Politics and Culture* (Bloomington: Indiana Univer-
    sity Press, 1992).
10 Armand Mattelart, *Networking the World, 1794–2000*, trans. Liz Carey-Libbrecht and
    James A. Cohen (Minneapolis: University of Minnesota Press, 1996).
11 See Randal Johnson, "The Brazilian Film Industry," in *The International Movie Industry*,
    ed. Gorham Kindem (Carbondale: Southen Illinois University Press, 2000), 257–72. See
    also Randal Johnson, "Notes on the Re-Emergence of Brazilian Cinema," in *Brazil E-Jour-
    nal* (Washington: Brazilian Embassy, 2000).

12   Aida A. Hozic, *Hollyworld: Space, Power, and Fantasy in the American Economy* (Ithaca, NY: Cornell University Press, 2001). Toby Miller, *Global Hollywood* (London: British Film Institute, 2001).

13   John Vidal, "Dicaprio Filmmakers Face Storm over Paradise Lost," *The Guardian*, 29 October 1999.

14   A major international showcase for the digital cinema movement is the annual ResFest festival (http://www.resfest.com) and its accompanying magazine *Res* (http://www.res.com).

15   Edward S. Herman and Robert W. McChesney, *The Global Media: The New Missionaries of Global Capitalism* (Washington: Cassell, 1997).

16   Todd Verow, "Mov: The First Philippines Digital Film Festival," *Res* 5, no. 3 (2002): 73.

17   Annette Hamilton, "Video Crackdown, or, the Sacrificial Pirate: Censorship and Cultural Consequences in Thailand," *Public Culture* 5, no. 3 (1993): 515–31.

18   One of the few film critics to have addressed the issue of how television changes the nature of the film text is Serge Daney, former editor of *Cahiers du Cinéma* and founder of the film journal *Trafic*, in his untranslated work *Devant la recrudescence des vols de sacs à mains* (1991). The work's equally untranslatable title is a reference to a message traditionally displayed in French movie theatres, warning patrons of thefts of personal property during film screenings.

19   On film festivals, see Kenneth Turan, *Sundance to Sarajevo: Film Festivals and the World They Made* (Berkeley: University of California Press, 2002).

20   Jonathan Rosenbaum, *Movie Wars: How Hollywood and the Media Conspire to Limit What Films We Can See* (Chicago: A Cappella, 2000), 118.

21   On dubbing, see István Fodor, *Film Dubbing: Phonetic, Semiotic, Esthetic, and Psychological Aspects* (Hamburg: Buske, 1976). See also Antje Ascheid, "Speaking Tongues: Voice Dubbing in the Cinema as Cultural Ventriloquism," *The Velvet Light Trap* 40, no. 3 (1997): 32–41. On subtitling, see Atom Egoyan and Ian Balfour, eds., *Subtitles: On the Foreignness of Film* (Cambridge, MA: MIT Press, 2004). See also Abé Mark Nornes, "For an Abusive Subtitling," *Film Quarterly* 52, no. 3 (1999): 17–34.

22   Anthony Kaufman, "Life Isn't Beautiful Anymore, It's Dubbed," in *Indiewire* (23 August, 1999).

23   For an overview of the history of film exhibition, see Ina Rae Hark, ed., *Exhibition: The Film Reader* (New York: Routledge, 2002).

24   On the miniaturization of cinema by digital media technologies, see Vivian Sobchack, "Nostalgia for a Digital Object: Regrets on the Quickening of Quicktime," in Jeffrey Shaw and Peter Weibel eds., *Future Cinema: The Cinematic Imaginary after Film* (Cambridge, MA: MIT Press, 2003), 66–73. See also Martin Roberts, "Variable Cinema: Portable Movies and the Pleasures of Reinvention" (*Society for Cinema Studies Conference*, May 23–26, 2002).

25   Two interesting documentaries about mobile cinemas in China and India respectively are Hervé and Renaud Cohen's *Porteurs d'ombres éléctriques* [*Carriers of Electric Shadows*] (France 1993) and Andrej Fidyk's *Battu's Bioscope* (Poland 1998). On mobile cinemas (*bioskop keliling*) in Indonesia, see Krishna Sen, *Indonesian Cinema: Framing the New Order* (Atlantic Highlands, NJ: Zed Books, 1994), 72–73.

26   Over the past decade, more studies of non-Western popular cinemas have begun to appear. Examples include: on Indonesian cinema, Karl G. Heider, *Indonesian Cinema: National Culture on Screen* (Honolulu: University of Hawaii Press, 1991); on Hong Kong cinema, Stephen Teo, *Hong Kong Cinema: The Extra Dimensions* (London: BFI, 1998) and David Bordwell, *Planet Hong Kong: Popular Cinema and the Art of Entertainment* (Cambridge, MA: Harvard University Press, 2000); and on Indian cinema, Vijay Mishra, *Bollywood Cinema: Temples of Desire* (New York: Routledge, 2002).

27 N. Frank Ukadike, "African Video-Films: An Alternate Reality," *Correspondence: An International Review of Culture and Society* 8, no. 3 (2001): 3–14.

28 In March 2000, seventy-four people died in a fire at a pornographic video parlour in a city in central China. See John Gittings, "Fire Kills 74 Locked in Porn Cinema," *The Guardian*, 1 April 2000.

29 Haidee Wasson, "Blinking, Stammering, Stuttering, Gone: The Size and the Speed of Web Movies," (*Society for Cinema Studies Conference*, May 23–26, 2002).

30 Jonathan Rosenbaum, "Internet Film Culture," in *Correspondence: An International Review of Culture and Society* (2001): 14–17.

31 The increasing availability of region-free and multi-system DVD players, as well as DivX-capable players, which can play movies in computer formats (.avi, .wma), are rendering the DVD zoning system and national video formats (NTSC, PAL) increasingly ineffective as a means of regulating the transnational exchange of pirated film and video texts.

32 John Tomlinson, *Globalization and Culture* (Chicago: University of Chicago Press, 1999), 17–22.

33 David Slocum, ed., *Violence and American Cinema* (New York: Routledge, 2001).

34 Discursive fields will of course vary according to the particular cultural contexts in which they are produced; the discursive field of French film reception, for example, will not be the same in the United States, Japan, or India, although as I will suggest shortly, the internationalization of film culture is arguably leading to the emergence of a more globalized field of film reception.

35 Perhaps the best-known example is Harry Knowles, whose Ain't-It-Cool website became a magnet for industry insiders after Knowles began leaking advance information about forthcoming studio releases, much to the displeasure of the studios themselves. Knowles himself became an instant celebrity, receiving an invitation to Sundance, an interview with Siskel and Ebert, and the inevitable book contract. For Knowles's own self-congratulatory account of his rise to stardom, see Harry Knowles, Paul Cullum, and Mark Ebner, *Ain't It Cool? Hollywood's Redheaded Stepchild Speaks Out* (New York: Warner Books, 2002).

36 Henry Jenkins, *Textual Poachers: Television Fans and Participatory Culture* (New York: Routledge, 1992). Roger Nygard, *Trekkies* (Paramount Pictures, 1997).

37 Downloadable from http://www.theforce.net/theater/shortfilms/troops/.

38 Paolo Cherchi Usai, "Origins and Survival," in *The Oxford History of World Cinema*, ed. Geoffrey Nowell-Smith (New York: Oxford University Press, 1996), 12.

39 Jonathan Rosenbaum, "Fables of the Reconstruction," *Chicago Reader*, 26 November 1999.

40 Fred Camper, "Out of the Shadows," *Chicago Reader*, 18 September 1998.

41 Peter Cowie, ed., *World Cinema: Diary of a Day. A Celebration of the Centenary of Cinema* (Woodstock, NY: Overlook Press, 1994). Geoffrey Nowell-Smith, *The Oxford History of World Cinema* (New York: Oxford University Press, 1996). Judy Stone, *Eye on the World: Conversations with International Filmmakers* (Los Angeles: Silman-James Press, 1997).

42 On the history of the Cannes film festival, see Schwartz, "Le Festival de Cannes."

43 Efforts have been underway for some time now to rehabilitate the concept of cosmopolitanism – long an object of suspicion on the left because of its elitist associations – by re-thinking it along more egalitarian lines as an actually existing condition of global postmodernity. See Bruce Robbins, *Secular Vocations* (London: Verso, 1993). Bruce Robbins and Pheng Cheah, eds., *Cosmopolitics: Thinking and Feeling Beyond the Nation* (Minneapolis: University of Minnesota Press, 1998). Carol A. Breckenridge et al., eds., *Cosmopolitanism* (Durham, NC: Duke University Press, 2002).

44 For details, see the ImagineAsia website: http://imagineasia.bfi.org.uk/index.html.

9 In his contribution to this volume, Jim Parry works to locate Olympism – an ideology of sport developed in the late nineteenth century and predicated on the possibility of athletic competition improving the bodies, minds, and dispositions of those more and less directly involved in it – within the matrix of a number of key anthropological and philosophical debates. Together these debates lend considerable moral and political significance to various aspects of Olympic competition, though of particular concern to Parry is Olympism's apparent universalism: its commitment to a cluster of values which are claimed to promote international understanding, peaceful cooperation and coexistence, and moral refinement. These values, which include fairness, justice, respect, and excellence, and which emphasize the role of sport in global culture, are universal to the extent that they are held to be valued by all people at all times. They are also, Parry notes, values which lie at the heart of liberal humanism, and herein lies an important complication. For to the extent that liberal humanism is anything but universally accepted, and indeed is more properly considered temporally and culturally contingent, important questions inevitably arise concerning Olympism's universalist ambitions. Particularly when considered alongside the history of the modern Olympic movement, itself a byproduct of the superimposition of nineteenth-century values over those of ancient Greece, the claim that Olympism speaks to and for a "common humanity" begins to seem rather doubtful.

In response to concerns over Olympism's veiled particularism, Parry proposes that we distinguish between, respectively, the "concept" and various different "conceptions" of Olympism. This distinction permits him to claim for Olympism a high level of generality as a concept, so much so that it readily admits of a broad range of attendant conceptions. For while any number of cultures might readily endorse values such as justice and excellence when construed broadly enough, the precise meaning assigned to these terms will inevitably vary from group to group, place to place, and from one time period to another. Parry's thought here is that much as liberalism, or what we might follow John Rawls and call "procedural" or "thin" liberalism, remains critically agnostic concerning the particular conception of the good life which members of a culture choose for themselves, it is nonetheless deeply invested in articulating and defending a core set of principles upon which any such particularistic conception rests, and which even those in illiberal societies would endorse. Among such core principles Parry identifies peace, the idea of a common good, a sense of social responsibility, and the freedom of conscience and thought.

Of course, even these general principles are far from universally accepted, and Parry wrestles with the question of how to resolve conflicts between liberal and illiberal cultures. He follows Yaël Tamir in endorsing "rights-based liberalism" which, unlike "autonomy-based liberalism," promises respect for decent and respectful but nonetheless illiberal cultures. Rights-based liberalism offers a tolerant and cosmopolitan alternative to more explicitly assimilationist versions of political liberalism and is thus better suited to the untidy sorts of compromises upon which intercultural cooperation and peaceful coexistence typically depends. Olympic sport has an important role to play in promoting precisely this sort of cooperation. Sport is, after all, a deeply ethical activity as well as a social practice predicated on antagonists' ability to understand and come to respect one another, and to peacefully resolve their conflicts in accordance with a mutually agreed upon set of rules. Olympism is the most coherent systematization of the ethical and political values informing sport more generally and may by extension be understood as one of the signal ways in which human beings express their optimism concerning the future of the world.

SPORT, UNIVERSALS, AND MULTICULTURALISM

JIM PARRY

We live in a world of universalizing tendencies, where the economic and political forces of globalization meet the ethical and cultural imperatives generated by our need to co-exist in a shrinking and increasingly inter-connected global society. Sport is not immune to these tendencies. Rather, in the experience of many millions of people, it is a prominent example of them, graphically illustrating them in the processes of global dissemination and participation, commercialization, sponsorship, athlete migration, equipment production and distribution, media/sport symbiosis, politics/sport relations, and increasing rules clarification, together with their progressively universal interpretation and application.

Through our participation in, or consumption of, sport such widespread tendencies and processes are rendered visible and potentially intelligible. Critics have often noted the conservative effect of sports in their "naturalizing" of human capacities and relations ("of course men and women are not equal – look at tennis or athletics"). But I suggest that this effect need not be conservative. It is also possible for radical restatements of capacities and reconceptualizations of human relations to be naturalized through sport. One example is the current re-examination of racism in Europe sparked by the racist chanting of football spectators in the European Champions Cup. European football (especially English football) is now so thoroughly international and interracial that it foregrounds the unacceptability of racism in society in a way unthinkable even twenty years ago.

Sport thus presents us with opportunities to encounter political sociology in the demystifying context of the "natural" and the "playful." To understand what might be the possible effects of this – the cultural manifestations and potential cultural development involved – we need to examine in some detail a contemporary example, and we shall make reference to the largest and probably most well-known sporting manifestation in the modern world: the Olympic Games.

Globalization

To begin with, we must understand the context within which the universal (and universalistic) pretensions of "Olympism" could have made sense – that is, the context of globalization. Globalization refers to a process of increasing interdependency amongst societies and individual humans at the economic, political, cultural, and social levels.

Ties of trade, warfare, migration and culture are of long standing in human history. More recent globalization processes have unleashed new sets of interdependency chains that have interconnected people from distant parts of the globe.[1]

Joe Maguire claims that we are now experiencing an intensification of the unfolding globalization process, which speeds up time and shrinks space and gives us a greater degree of interdependence and an increased sense of the world as a whole. Modern sport is bound up in this global network of interdependency relationships and cannot be understood unless it is seen in that context.

Firstly, Maguire urges us to adopt an historical and comparative approach in order to appreciate the context within which the pattern of global sport has emerged. Then he suggests five dimensions of "intermingling":

- the international movement of people (athletes);
- the flow of technology (equipment and facilities);
- economic issues (prize money, endorsements, marketing);
- the flow of media images (transnational sports "stars");
- the ideological dimension (ideas which seek universal application and acclaim – which transcend national or "state" ideologies).

Maguire also develops a five-stage model of the emergence and global diffusion of sport. Despite the well-documented existence of cultic activities, folk games and recreations in earlier societies, "modern sport, like the steam engine, emerges first in England."[2] The stages are as follows:

Stage 1: In the seventeenth and eighteenth century, cricket, fox-hunting, horse racing and boxing emerge as modern sports.

Stage 2: In the nineteenth century, football, rugby, tennis and track and field begin to take on modern forms.

Stage 3: From about 1880, English sport forms begin to be diffused to continental Europe and the British Empire.

Stage 4: From 1920–1960 there emerges a sporting hegemony of the West (the U.S.A. and Europe), despite resistance from indigenous sport forms and successful competition from (formerly) colonized regions.

Stage 5: From the late 1960s, Euro-American control of sport has diminished both on and off the field, evidencing a "de-centering of the West." This is indicative of the globalization of sport as practised, as consumed and as represented in the media.

Accepting this account, or something very close to it, I would like to concentrate here on just one dimension and one stage: the ideological dimension at Stage 5. I shall explore the ideology of Olympism, which provides a "universalizing" account of sport in culture and education, and which is both global and also locally instantiated. And I shall characterize Stage 5, which posits a de-centring of the West, as requiring a re-evaluation of ethnocentrism and an understanding of multiculturalism as a value and as a practice.

Olympism

For most people, I suppose, the word "Olympic" will conjure up images of the Olympic Games, either ancient or modern. The focus of their interest will be a two-week festival of sport held once in every four years between elite athletes representing their countries or city-states in inter-communal competition.

Most people, too, will have heard of an "Olympiad," even though it is sometimes thought to refer to a particular Games. In fact it refers to a four-year period, during which a Games may or may not be held. So: the Beijing Games of 2008 are properly referred to not as the XXIX Games (since there have been only twenty-five so far, including Athens 2004, three having been cancelled due to World Wars) but as the Games of the XXIX Olympiad, the "modern" series having begun in Athens in 1896.

Fewer, however, will have heard of "Olympism," the philosophy developed since the 1890s by the founder of the modern Olympic Movement, Baron Pierre de Coubertin, a French aristocrat who had been much influenced by the British Public School tradition of sport in education. This philosophy has as its focus of interest not just the elite athlete, but everyone; not just a short truce period, but the whole of life; not just competition and winning, but also the values of participation and co-operation; not just sport as an activity, but also as a formative and developmental influence contributing to desirable characteristics of individual personality and social life.

For Olympism is a social philosophy which emphasizes the role of sport in global culture, international understanding, peaceful co-existence, and social and moral education. De Coubertin understood, towards the end of the nineteenth century, that sport was about to become a major growth point in popular culture – and that, as physical activity, it was apparently universalizable, providing a means of contact and communication across cultures.

De Coubertin founded the International Olympic Committee at the Sorbonne in Paris in 1894, and its present-day headquarters are in Lausanne, Switzerland. There are now over two hundred National Olympic Committees, which means that only the United Nations rivals the Olympic Movement as a global institution.

A universal philosophy by definition sees itself as relevant to everyone, regardless of nation, race, gender, social class, religion or ideology, and so the Olympic movement has worked for a coherent universal representation of itself. The principles of Olympism, to be universal, must be unchanging, and yet they must apparently be everywhere different. They must not change over time, but at all times we see rule changes reflecting social changes. How are these paradoxes to be resolved?

What I have argued elsewhere[3] is that, of course, they do change – there are indeed fundamental differences between the ancient and modern games, and between de Coubertin's revivalist ideas and those which are current today. The ancient Games had developed over a thousand years, as an expression of the values of a developing archaic community. The modern Games, however, were created by a set of nineteenth-century ideas which sought to impose a modern ideology onto ancient values so as to affect contemporary social practice for the better.

Such differences are inevitable, over time and space. Social ideas, or ideas inscribed in social practices, depend upon a specific social order or a particular set of social relationships for their full meaning to be exemplified. This seems to suggest that such meanings are culturally relative and that therefore there could be no such thing as a universal idea of Olympism. But are we doomed to relativism? Are we doomed to a situation in which we must continue to misunderstand one another, since we inhabit different cultures, languages, and values (and therefore generate different meanings for "Olympism")?

The distinction between concepts and conceptions is useful here. The *concept* of Olympism may be at a high level of generality, although this does not mean that it will be unclear. What it means is that the general ideas which comprise its meaning will admit of possibly contesting interpretations. Thus, naturally, the concept of Olympism will find different expressions in time and place, history and geography. That is to say, there will be differing *conceptions* of Olympism, which will interpret the general concept in such a way as to bring it to real life in a particular context. We may compare this, say, to the concept of democracy, which spawns many conceptions, as diverse societies attempt to enact it.

So we need to make a preliminary attempt to identify a concept of Olympism which identifies a range of values to which each nation can sincerely commit itself whilst at the same time finding for the general idea a form of expression which is unique to itself, generated by its own culture, location, history, tradition, and projected future.

De Coubertin, being a product of late nineteenth-century liberalism, emphasized the values of formal equality, fairness, justice, respect for persons, and excellence. These are values which span nearly three thousand years of Olympic history, although some of them may be differently interpreted at different times. They are, basically, the main values of liberal humanism – or perhaps we should say simply humanism, since socialist societies have found little difficulty in including Olympic ideals into their overall ideological stance towards sport and culture.

The contemporary task for the Olympic Movement is to further this project: to try to see more clearly what its Games (and sport in wider society) might come to mean. This task will be at the level of both ideas and action. If the practice of sport is to be pursued and developed according to Olympic values, the theory must strive for a conception of Olympism which will support that practice. The ideal should seek both to sustain sports practice and sports culture and to lead sport towards a vision of Olympism which will help to deal with the challenges which are bound to emerge.

The official position of the International Olympic Committee is expressed in the *Olympic Charter*,[4] which states simply the relationship between Olympic philosophy, culture, and education:

Fundamental Principle 2 says:

Olympism is a philosophy of life, exalting and combining in a balanced whole the qualities of body, will and mind. Blending sport with culture and education, Olympism seeks to create a way of life based on the joy found in effort, the educational value of good example and respect for universal fundamental ethical principles.[5]

Fundamental Principle 6 says:

The goal of the Olympic Movement is to contribute to building a peaceful and better world by educating youth through sport practised without discrimination of any kind and in the Olympic spirit, requires mutual understanding with a spirit of friendship, solidarity and fair play.[6]

Chapter IV deals with National Olympic Committees, and again states simply and prominently the pre-eminent duties of NOCs with regard to Olympic culture and education:

The mission of the NOCs is to develop and protect the Olympic Movement ... [and to] propagate the fundamental principles of Olympism at national level within the framework of sports activity and otherwise contribute, among other things, to the diffusion of Olympism in the teaching programs of physical education and sport in schools and university establishments ... [and to] see to the creation of institutions which devote themselves to Olympic education.[7]

If we add to this de Coubertin's famous dicta "all sports for all people"[8] and "All games, all nations,"[9] we seem to have a recipe for the core values of Olympism: respect for universal ethical principles, fair play, mutual understanding, anti-discrimination, education through sport, and multiculturalism.

Taken together, the promotion of these values will be seen to be the educative task, and sport will be seen as a means. Each one of these values, being articulated at a high level of generality, will admit of a wide range of interpretation. But they nevertheless provide a framework which can be agreed upon by social groups with very differing commitments. This raises the questions of the relationships between such differing cultural formations, and of our own attitudes towards cultural difference. One way of addressing these questions is via a consideration of the key liberal idea of multiculturalism.

Liberalism and Multiculturalism

In an earlier paper[10] I looked at the contemporary importance for liberalism of the idea of multiculturalism. The liberal state sees itself as deliberately not choosing any particular conception of the Good Life for its citizens to follow. Rather, it sees itself as neutral between the alternative conceptions of the Good to be found in most modern liberal democracies. In this it sharply distinguishes itself from "illiberal" states, which embody and enforce one view of the Good Life. Rather than promoting one culture over others, the liberal state sees itself as multicultural – citizens can choose their own version of the Good and pursue their own aims and values, independently of the state.

Some authors[11] address the suggestion that we have reached "the end of history" – that is, that liberal democracy has won the battle for global political hegemony. If this is true (and even, I suspect, if not), attention to such multicultural ideals as recognition, respect, and equal status for different cultures will become increasingly important.

Multiculturalism, says Raz, "requires a political society to recognize the equal standing of all stable and viable communities existing in a society."[12] However, some of these may be authoritarian, illiberal, and oppressive – so does "multiculturalism" apply equally to all communities? In order to address this question, Tamir distinguishes two concepts of multiculturalism: thin and thick.

Thin multiculturalism involves differences between different liberal cultures, where consensus over foundational values means that there will be no serious problem of cultural relativism. Thick multiculturalism involves differences between liberal and illiberal cultures. Thin multiculturalism leads to an interest-group politics. Thick multiculturalism leads to a stand-off, where an illiberal point of view seeks to secure its own existence within liberal society.

Tamir's claim is that we all need induction into the discourse of rights and rationality, since without such "thin civic education," cross-cultural discussions based on equal respect and concern for all will be impossible. This kind of consideration is not based on assimilation, but on a valuing of diversity. "It is a respect for and a belief in the importance of belonging to thick cultures that motivates the search for a thin layer of agreement."[13]

This calls for a compromise between liberal and illiberal views. Here questions of cultural relativism may indeed arise. For example, the wearing of special headgear is not allowed in French public educational institutions, but such items may be worn in the private sphere, which liberals see as the proper sphere in which to express identities. But what French officials see as imposing neutrality, Muslims see as a campaign against Islam (since Muslims don't see religion as something that can remain in the private sphere – God's commands apply everywhere).

Nagel sees a deep problem here: "When a conflict involves systems of values so opposed that the adherents of each not only think the other completely wrong, but they cannot accord the others freedom to act on their values without betraying themselves,"[14] then the matter cannot be resolved by an agreement on general principles or by achieving overlapping consensus.

Multiculturalism, though, is a fact nowadays for most Western societies, requiring a political society to recognize the equal standing of all stable and viable communities existing within it. It outlaws discrimination against groups and individuals on the grounds of ethnicity, race, nationality, religion, class, gender, or sexual preference. However, some of these communities themselves may be authoritarian, illiberal and, oppressive – so do the benefits of "multiculturalism" apply equally to all communities or only to the liberal ones? Can a multicultural society find a way to counter cultural conflict?

Rawls attempts to draw guidelines for a Law of Peoples[15] acceptable to members of both liberal and illiberal cultures, by introducing the notion of "reasonable societies." These societies, though illiberal, follow certain core principles:

- Peace (pursuing their ends through diplomacy and trade);
- Common Good (a conception of justice);
- Consultation (a reasonable hierarchy thereof);
- Responsibility (citizens recognize their obligations and play a part in social life);
- Freedom (some freedom of conscience and thought).

"Reasonable societies," even illiberal ones, could agree to a Law of Peoples based on such a "thin liberalism" as this – and this could be seen very positively: as offering learning experiences both ways, as each culture learns from the other.

However, aren't most illiberal societies "unreasonable" ones, too? Even if they are, the attempt to bring them under a Law is important, since it draws the limits of a possible compromise. Such a compromise is possible due to the distinction between *Rights-based* Liberalism and *Autonomy-based* Liberalism.

Rights-based Liberalism (RBL) can express tolerance and respect for *decent* illiberalism, but Autonomy-based Liberalism (ABL) can respect only autonomy-supporting cultures (namely, liberal ones). It thus cannot avoid the trivialization of pluralism. Since ABL takes autonomy as paramount, it ranks societies by their potential contribution to the conditions of autonomy and therefore judges illiberal cultures to be inferior. As members of such cultures insist on "bringing up their children in their own ways," Raz writes, they are "in the eyes of a liberal like myself, harming them." Liberals of this persuasion see themselves as justified in seeking to assimilate those cultures, even at the cost of letting them die.

But assimilation is not the necessary conclusion of RBL, which places at its core a commitment to equal concern and respect for individuals, their preferences and interests, regardless of whether they were formed autonomously. This is important for multiculturalism: ABL endorses toleration of illiberal cultures only as a means to the slow liberalization of them; whereas RBL protects all cultures which provide their members with a decent environment and life-chances. It is more "cosmopolitan."

For RBL the question is not which societies allow individuals the better to develop their autonomy, but which societies individuals would like to live in. As Mendus argues, ABL prevents us from appreciating other cultures, since our autonomy-valuing gets in the way of a proper appreciation of their virtues. RBL might be more open-minded about the set of values offered by another; multiculturalism might be seen as a way of enriching the liberal perspective, of "de-centring and coming to terms with otherness."[16] Feinberg argues that this is the major task for the education of a democratic public in a multicultural society.[17]

Illiberal groups, however, are likely to regard such encounters as threatening. In the Mozert case discussed by Macedo, Christian fundamentalists in the U.S.A. objected to a reading program which interfered with the free exercise of their religion by "exposing the children to a variety of religious points of view in an even-handed manner, thus denigrating the truth of their particular religion."[18] Similarly, in the case of sports, some Muslim societies refuse to participate in women's competitions on Western terms. Instead they reserve a separate sphere of practice and competition for women, so that their activities can take place away from the scrutiny of men. Their claim is that there is no injustice here – women are separate, but are treated equally in terms of opportunity to participate and access to resources. To compete internationally, however, they would have to do so in public, and so they decline.

In cases such as these, members of illiberal groups often feel that they have been forced to join a liberal game, which places such liberal values as pluralism and diversity at its core. Liberals present the game as a concession to the demands of illiberal groups, celebrating all their beliefs, ways of life, and conceptions of the good. But the game's central procedural values are external to illiberal traditions, asking them to compromise their beliefs and face the risk of assimilation.

So how are we to approach illiberal groups? At present they often co-operate simply out of fear – they are, for example, minorities, and if they were majorities they would impose their own ways if they could. It is not even a principled *modus vivendi* (live and let live), but a conditional one, based on fear. Tamir's conclusion is that thick multiculturalism makes it impossible to achieve a political agreement which could be seen as ideal by either party, and liberals should limit their demands and expectations of illiberal groups. Probably the best that can be achieved is an untidy compromise. There is no right solution, but maybe some reasonable ones, the products of continuing negotiations.

Multiculturalism, then, has its limits, and those limits are drawn by the universalistic claims of thin liberalism, supported by some form of Human Rights theory. As Hollis says, liberal societies "must fight for at least a minimalist, procedural thesis about freedom, justice, equality and individual rights."[19]

In the short term, in the interests of peace and development (or of political or economic gain), such basic moral commitments may be temporarily diluted or shelved, but they are the inalienable bedrock of the possibility of a global multiculturalism. There are limits to toleration. Liberal democracy is (still) an exclusionary system – some cultures are beyond the pale.

I believe that the distinction between thick and thin multiculturalism is a clever, accurate, and useful one, and I think it directly applies to the explication and justification of the concept of Olympism. Above, I outlined the distinction between concepts and conceptions and argued that the concept of Olympism will be at a high level of generality. In fact, it sets out a range of "thin" liberal values. However, the values which comprise its meaning will admit of contesting interpretations, exhibiting a range of "thick" values as the concept of Olympism finds different expressions in time and place, history and geography.

In terms of promoting its aims of international understanding and multiculturalism, it is most important that the Olympic movement continues to work for a coherent universal representation of itself – a concept of Olympism to which each nation can sincerely commit itself whilst at the same time finding for the general idea a form of expression (a conception) which is unique to itself, generated by its own culture, location, history, tradition, and projected future.

Why Be Multiculturalist?

Why should we be multiculturalists? Because we want to honour and respect the widest variety of human culture. Why? Because it enriches us all. We value diversity because every culture expresses a form of human life and helps us to appreciate the full range of difference and choice. It is the same reason that we value knowledge of the history of human social evolution: to help us to understand more fully our identity as humans.

But this means that we have to tolerate difference, and we have to accept that sometimes other people's views will hold sway over our own. The liberal citizen permits democracy – people can see the reason for (and therefore accept) decisions even if they don't agree with them. Such a "rational pluralism" is characteristic of Liberalism, but "unreasonable" doctrines will not accept such a pluralism. Liberals see the problem as resting with those who object to the valuing of anything other than their own culture. In these circumstances we can still believe in "live and let live" – but we must defend the liberal values that permit such tolerance. Central to our concern is the defence of individual rights against illiberal groups. We have two motivations:

(a) to preserve a valuable heritage, central to the identity of a group of people; and
(b) to defend the liberal rights of the individual.

For example, imagine Aztec society, now long disappeared. Its achievements (in common with the astonishing achievements of other indigenous meso-American cultures) cause us to think again about the capacity of humans to organize themselves into social groups that can build, think, create, organize, maintain, etc. But it also promoted the ritual sacrifice of some of its members to propitiate its gods.

So we disapprove of forced sacrifice, ritual murder, cannibalism, etc. – but this does not prevent us from valuing those cultures for their achievements, and for their reminders to us of the great variety and flexibility of possible human social arrangements. So what do we do? Internally, we seek to liberalize illiberal cultures, at least to some small extent, e.g., to enforce basic liberal rights within illiberal states. So, in minority cultures, we permit no slaves, no mutilation, no forced marriage, no child prostitution, etc. – or we permit individuals to escape from those circumstances if they want to; to deny others the right to "harness" individuals to their ends. Externally, we pursue foreign policies that seek to contain hostile illiberal societies in ways that minimize their threat to liberal ones. So long as they are far away, pose no external threat, collaborate with (or at least do not obstruct) commerce, we may express disapproval or criticism of their arrangements, but we often leave them to do as they wish, even in cases where the majority of the population is obviously oppressed.

Is Universalism Ethnocentric?

Critics of the liberal project put forward the objection that the idea of liberal democracy is a historical product, a kind of western ethnocentrism, a kind of post-colonial imperialism, foisting local western values on the rest of the world. The kind of "universalism" to which both liberalism and Olympism pretend is just an ethnocentric smoke-screen. There is no basis for such a universalism of values, because all values arise within cultures, and therefore do not apply across cultural boundaries – they are culturally relative.

We may call this thesis "the Anthropologist's Heresy": liberalism for the liberals; cannibalism for the cannibals.[20] All cultures are equally valid, because they can only be judged on their own "internal" terms – norms and principles that apply only to themselves. There are many objections to the Anthropologist's Heresy:

1. It cannot account for moral criticism across cultures, for how can we criticize unjust practices if that's all they are – the practices of others?
2. Relativism itself is a kind of concealed ethnocentrism. It is not true that to respect other cultures is to abstain from criticizing them. Rather it is a kind of disrespect – failing to apply to others (denying to others) the standards of justification and argument we apply to ourselves.
3. Relativism is self-refuting. It is a theory that claims that there are no cross-cultural truths. But we can ask: does relativism apply to itself? If so, relativism is not true (because it says that there are no cross-cultural truths; so relativism is just a cultural practice of western anthropologists, with no claim to truth, and therefore nothing to say to outsiders). So: even if relativism could be true, it would make itself false (or, at least, merely relative). But relativism can't be true, since it claims that there is no such thing as Truth.
4. The concept of "culture" is a tricky one here, too. Relativism, says Lukes, trades on "poor man's sociology," according to which cultures are homogeneous, coherent wholes. But

cultures are not "windowless boxes." Conflicts arise within cultures as well as between them, but relativism gives us no way of making progress.

5. Finally, adherence to the Anthropologist's Heresy means a rejection of all those organizations that pretend to universalist values, including the United Nations, the World Health Organization, and Amnesty International. It means that there is no such thing as Human Rights, an idea which, of course, is rooted in notions of our universally common humanity. I don't think that there will be too many of us willing to accept such a radically disastrous conclusion.

So Lukes and Hollis dismiss relativism as a sensible response to diversity. Of course, there is considerable diversity, and the job of the anthropologist is to seek it out and describe it for us. But the anthropologist exceeds his occupational remit when he seeks to convert his experiences into an ethical theory. The importance of such research cannot be overestimated. It continually reminds us that we should recognize the value of modesty or restraint in moral judgment and criticism, and avoid the dangers of abstract moralizing. But anthropological experience is not a sufficient basis for ethical theory. The facts of diversity require theoretical explanation – but the facts alone do not explain it.

The Philosophical Anthropology of Olympism

We must now return to the concept of Olympism, and examine a little more closely its origins and meanings. My guiding thought lies in the status of Olympism as a social, political, and educational ideology. Based on its heritage and traditions, any such ideology necessarily appeals to a philosophical anthropology – an idealized conception of the kind of person that that society (or ideology) values, and tries to produce and reproduce through its formal and informal institutions.

Social anthropology is the investigation of whole cultures, which are preferably, from the point of view of the researcher, quite alien to the researcher's own society. A social anthropologist investigates the living instantiations of human nature – the apparently quite different kinds of human nature that are to be found around the world – practically, scientifically, through observation and social scientific methodology.

A philosophical anthropologist, however, tries to create a theory about human nature by thinking about the human being at the most general level. Hoberman writes about differing political conceptions of sport but finds it necessary to refer to several levels of explanation and theorizing:

[Different societies] … have distinct political anthropologies or idealized models of the exemplary citizen which constitute complex answers to the fundamental question of philosophical anthropology: "What is a human being?"[21]

He quotes John F. Kennedy as a representative of "centrist neo-Hellenism":

… the same civilization which produced some of our highest achievements of philosophy and drama, government and art, also gave us a belief in the importance of physical soundness which has become a part of Western tradition; from the *mens sana in corpore sano* of the Romans to the British belief that the playing fields of Eton brought victory on the battlefields of Europe.[22]

In order to try to fill out just what were the ideas that have been handed down from classical times, to be reinterpreted and re-specified (by de Coubertin and others) we need to examine two central ideas.

The Ideas of Kalos K'agathos and Areté

Lenk says that "Many representatives of the Olympic movement combine these values together to form a picture of the human being harmoniously balanced intellectually and physically in the sense of the Greek 'kalos k'agathos.'"[23] This is also a theme in Nissiotis, who writes that:

… the Olympic Ideal is what qualifies sport exercise in general as a means for educating the whole man as a conscious citizen of the world…. The Olympic Ideal is that exemplary principle which expresses the deeper essence of sport as an authentic educative process through a continuous struggle to create healthy and virtuous man in the highest possible way ("kalos k'agathos") in the image of the Olympic winner and athlete.[24]

Eyler pursues the meaning of the Olympic virtue of excellence in performance and in character, through Homer, early philosophers, Pindar and Pausanias. He concludes:

In summary, arete has several meanings – distinction, duty (primarily to oneself), excellence, fame, glorious deeds, goodness, greatness, heroism … valour and virtue. Some of the many implications of these meanings contextually are: man is born, grows old, and dies; performance is not without risks; winning is all; man achieves by his own skills … human performance is the quintessence of life; and finally, man is the measure of all things and the responsible agent.[25]

He quotes Kitto, who notes that:

… what moves a Greek warrior to heroism is not a sense of duty as we understand it, i.e. duty towards others, it is rather a duty towards oneself. He strives after that which we translate virtue or excellence, the Greek "arête" (The Right Stuff).[26]

Lenk emphasizes the centrality of the ideas of action and achievement:

The Olympic athlete thus illustrates the Herculean myth of culturally exceptional achievement, i.e. of action essentially unnecessary for life's sustenance that is nevertheless highly valued and arises from complete devotion to striving to attain a difficult goal.[27]

Paleologos echoes the mythical origins of the Ancient Games in the deeds of Hercules, one of the great heroes of antiquity. He writes:

With the twelve labors depicted by the bas-reliefs on the two metopes of the Temple (of Zeus), the world is presented with the content of the moral teachings which Olympia intended with the Games.[28]

The idea is that the sculptures of the demi-God Hercules in Olympia performed a morally educative function, standing as role models, especially for the athletes who were there to train for the Games, of physical, moral, and intellectual virtue:

Hercules is shown bearded, with beautiful features, ... a well-trained body, fine, proportioned muscles, ... as a representative of the 'kalos k'agathos' type, where the body is well-formed and harmonious, the expression of a beautiful soul, and the face radiates intelligence, kindness and integrity.[29]

Nissiotis concludes that:

The Olympic Idea is thus a permanent invitation to all sportsmen to transcend ... their own physical and intellectual limits ... for the sake of a continuously higher achievement in the physical, ethical and intellectual struggle of a human being towards perfection.[30]

So: a philosophical anthropology is an idealized conception of the human. If we ask ourselves what the Olympic Idea is, it translates into a few simple phrases which capture the essence of what an ideal human being ought to be and to aspire to. From the above, and drawing on conceptions of Olympism presented in the previous section, I think we might suggest that the philosophical anthropology of Olympism promotes the ideals of:

- individual all-round harmonious human development;
- towards excellence and achievement;
- through effort in competitive sporting activity;
- under conditions of mutual respect, fairness, justice, and equality;
- with a view to creating lasting personal human relationships of friendship;
- international relationships of peace, toleration and understanding;
- and cultural alliances with the arts.

That's the general idea: a conception of the human being who is capable of being and doing those things.

Sport and Universalism

However, Olympism achieves its ends through the medium of sport, and so it cannot escape the requirement to provide an account of sport which reveals both its nature and its ethical potential.

Although sports are widely considered to be pleasurable, their likelihood of gaining wide acceptance lies rather in their intrinsic value, which transcends the simply hedonic or relative good. Their ability to furnish us with pleasurable experiences depends upon our prior recognition in them of opportunities for the development and expression of valued human excellences. They are widely considered to present such opportunities because, even when local instantiations, their object is to challenge our common human propensities and abilities.

Let me briefly suggest a set of criteria which might begin to indicate the fundamentally ethical nature of sport.

- physical (so that *effort* is required);
- contest (suggesting a "*contract to contest*"; valuing *competition* and *excellence*);
- rule-governed (requiring an *obligation* to abide by the rules, *fair play, equality,* and *justice*);
- institutionalized (suggesting "*lawful authority*");
- shared values and commitments (such that *due respect* is owed to opponents as co-facilitators).

Thus, it is difficult even to state the characteristics of sport without relying on terms that carry ethical import, and such meanings must apply across the world of sports participation. Without agreement on rule-adherence, the authority of the referee, and the central shared values of the activity, there could be no sport. The first task of an International Federation, for example, is to clarify rules and harmonize understandings so as to facilitate the universal practice of its sport.

Olympism in Practice

Above, I outlined the distinction between concepts and conceptions and argued that the concept of Olympism will be at a high level of generality. In fact, it sets out a range of "thin" liberal values, allied to the thin values underlying the concept of sport. However, the values which comprise its meaning will admit of contesting interpretations, exhibiting a range of "thick" values as the concept of Olympism finds different expressions in time and place, history and geography.

In terms of promoting its aims of international understanding and multiculturalism in a practical way, it is most important that the Olympic movement continues to work for a coherent universal representation of itself – a concept of Olympism to which each nation can sincerely commit itself whilst at the same time finding for the general idea a form of expression (a conception) which is unique to itself, generated by its own culture, location, history, tradition and projected future.

The provision of multicultural education in and for modern democracies is a new and urgent task, and one that must succeed if we are to secure a workable political heritage for future generations. In the present global political context, this means promoting international understanding and mutual respect, and a commitment to the peaceful resolution of conflict – both goals of Olympism.

In the case of Olympism, I think that the "thin" values underpinning the rule structures of sport, acceptance of which by all participants is a pre-condition of the continuing existence of sporting competition, support at the educational and cultural levels such political efforts. Children who are brought into sporting practices, and who are aware of international competitions such as the Olympic Games and the World Cup, are thereby becoming aware of the possibilities of international co-operation, mutual respect, mutual valuing, and the resolution of conflict under agreed rules.[31]

Two Examples

I believe that there is a close relationship between ethics and structures, inasmuch as structures encapsulate and express values. It is possible to "read off" working values from structures and compare them with professed values. Conversely, the test of the sincerity with which professed values are held is whether or not they are represented in working practices. What the Olympic Movement means by its values should be written into its practices; and its sincerity may be interrogated through the reality of its practices. There follow two examples.

1. THE OLYMPIC PROGRAM

Firstly, let's apply this test to the Olympic Program. The main principles of selection of sports for the Games are popularity and universality: and unity of time and place is an important principle of organization during their celebration. However, it also affirmed that one of the missions of the Olympic Movement is to contribute to the development of sport in all its forms. I believe that there is a contradiction here: the present criteria, though reasonable, tend to produce a list of sports which have already attained world popularity, which means, in effect, those which reflect the earlier cultural hegemony of the West.[32] This has the effect of reducing the popularity and influence of traditional and regional sports in favour of those on the Olympic program.[33]

The underdevelopment of those sports is therefore *produced* by Olympic criteria (a parallel with the "development of underdevelopment" thesis within development economics, which says that underdevelopment is not simply a *condition* of a society, but rather a condition that is *produced* by development elsewhere). Eichberg has described this as "the non-recognition of non-Western sports," corresponding to neo-colonization.[34] However, in the fifth stage of the globalization process, we should surely be thinking of ways in which we can de-centre Western practices within Olympic ideology and recognize significant sporting forms and practices from around the world. There are many ways of doing this. The most radical suggestion might be to rethink entirely the Olympic program of sports and events.

Let me make a simple provocative suggestion: why not implement a compensatory policy, according to which (for example) one popular sport from each continent should be included in the official program? This would help to promote regional sports which have hitherto received little exposure (kabbadi is one example from India), and it would be a practical way of affirming a commitment to multiculturalism – an exemplar of the way in which Olympic values might be enshrined in its structures, and an example of how radical sports reform could exemplify a radical sports politics.

2. THE OLYMPIC MOVEMENT AND INTERNATIONAL UNDERSTANDING

Secondly, let me draw attention to the emerging relationship between the Olympic Movement and the United Nations, two global organizations facing similar problems in regard to universality and particularity. The general problem faced by both is how they are to operate at a global (universal) level whilst there exist such apparently intractable differences at the particular level.

Some seek to resolve such difficulties in the sportsworld by speaking of sport as a universal language; but this seems to me to under-represent the case. Not just sport, but Olympism itself seeks to be universal in its values: mutual recognition and respect, tolerance, solidarity, equity, anti-discrimination, peace, multiculturalism, etc. This is a quite specific set of values, which are at once a set of universal general principles; but which also require differential interpretation in different cultures – *stated* in general terms whilst *interpreted* in the particular.

This search for a universal representation at the interpersonal and political level of our common humanity seems to me to be the essence of the optimism and hope of Olympism and other forms of humanism and internationalism. In the face of recent events in Europe and elsewhere it seems a fond hope and a naive optimism, but I don't see why we should not continue to argue for and work towards a future of promise, and I still see a strong case for sport as an efficient means. I believe that sport has made an enormous contribution to modern society over the past hundred years or so and that the philosophy of Olympism has been the most coherent systematization of the ethical and political values underlying the practice of sport so far to have emerged.

It also has radical political potential. Despite the U.S.-led boycott, the Olympic Games went to Moscow in 1980, and it was impossible to prevent the penetration of ideas into a previously closed society.

Maybe it goes too far to claim a direct relation of the Games to the dramatic, spectacular, and incredible events of 1989, when "the Wall came down" – but maybe not. Now, many of the former "Eastern bloc" countries have formally joined the European Union. A generation ago this was unthinkable. The question arises: What will be the lasting results of the 2008 Beijing Games?

The very idea of a "closed society" is under threat everywhere – the people are no longer reliant on restricted and controlled forms of information. The Internet, satellite TV, and global forms of communication are all contributing to a democratization of information, and the extensive migration of people across continents is producing a new cosmopolitanism. It will require increasingly high levels of dogmatism, authoritarianism, isolationism, and extremism to sustain closed, exclusivist societies. Their life is limited. This, at any rate, has to be our hope, and the hope of any kind of peaceful internationalism based on the idea of individual freedom and human rights.

Does all this matter? Is it just abstract academic theorizing? I think it matters a great deal, and our commitment to the development of global forms of cultural expression such as sport, and to international understanding through ideologies such as Olympism is one way that we as individuals can express our commitments, ideals, and hopes for the future of the world.

Notes

1 J. Maguire, *Global Sport: Identities, Societies, Civilisations* (Cambridge: Polity Press, 1999), 187.

2 Ibid., 6.

3 J. Parry, "Olympism at the Beginning and End of the Twentieth Century," *Proceedings of the International Olympic Academy* 28 (1988): 81–94.

4 IOC, *The Olympic Charter* (Lausanne: International Olympic Committee, 2004).

5 Ibid., 7.

6 Ibid.

7 Ibid., 31.

8 Quoted in B. During and J.F. Brisson, "Sport, Olympism and Cultural Diversity," in *For a Humanism of Sport*, ed. B. Jeu et al. (Paris: CNOSF-Editions, 1994), 187.

9 P. de Coubertin, "Forty Years of Olympism (1894/1934)," in *The Olympic Idea: Pierre de Coubertin, Discourses and Essays*, ed. Carl-Diem-Institut (Stuttgart: Olympischer Sportverlag, 1934), 127.

10 J. Parry, "Globalisation, Multiculturalism and Olympism," *Proceedings of the International Olympic Academy* 39 (1999): 86–97.

11 For example, Y. Tamir, "Two Concepts of Multiculturalism," *Journal of the Philosophy of Education* 29, no. 2 (1995): 161–72.

12 J. Raz, *Ethics in the Public Domain* (Oxford: Oxford University Press, 1994), 69.

13 See M. Walzer, "Education, Democratic Citizenship and Multiculturalism," *Journal of the Philosophy of Education* 29, no. 2 (1995): 181–90.

14 T. Nagel, *Equality and Partiality* (Oxford: Oxford University Press, 1991), 169.

15 J. Rawls, "The Law of Peoples," in *On Human Rights: The Oxford Amnesty Lectures*, ed. S Shute and S. Hurley (New York: Basic Books, 1993): 41–82.

16 S. Mendus, "Tolerance and Recognition: Education in a Multicultural Society," *Journal of the Philosophy of Education* 29, no. 2 (1995): 191–201.

17 Joel Feinberg, "Liberalism, Community, and Tradition," *Tikkun* 3 (1988): 38–41; 116–20.

18 S. Macedo, "Multiculturalism for the Religious Right? Defending Liberal Civic Education," *Journal of the Philosophy of Education* 29, no. 2 (1995): 224.

19 M. Hollis, "Is Universalism Ethnocentric?" in *Multicultural Questions*, ed. S. Lukes and C. Joppke (Oxford: Oxford University Press, 1999), 42.

20 See S. Lukes, *Liberals and Cannibals* (London: Verso, 2002). See also Hollis, "Is Universalism Ethnocentric?", 36.

21 J. Hoberman, *Sport and Political Ideology* (London: Heinemann, 1984), 2.

22 Ibid., 21.

23 H. Lenk, "Values, Aims, Reality of the Modern Olympic Games," *Proceedings of the International Olympic Academy* 4 (1964): 206.

24 N. Nissiotis, "Olympism and Today's Reality," *Proceedings of the International Olympic Academy* 24 (1984): 64.

25 M.H. Eyler, "The Right Stuff," *Proceedings of the International Olympic Academy* 20 (1981): 165.

26 H.D.F. Kitto, *The Greeks* (Harmondsworth, UK: Penguin, 1951), 166.

27 Lenk, "Values, Aims, Reality of the Modern Olympic Games," 166.

28 K. Paleologos, "Hercules, the Ideal Olympic Personality," *Proceedings of the International Olympic Academy* 22 (1982): 63.

29 Ibid., 67.

30 Nissiotis, "Olympism and Today's Reality," 66.

31 See Parry, "Olympism at the Beginning and End of the Twentieth Century." See also J. Parry, "Physical Education as Olympic Education," *European Physical Education Review* 4, no. 2 (1998): 153–67.

32 See F. Landry, "The Olympic Games & Competitive Sport as an International System," *Proceedings of the International Olympic Academy* 24 (1984): 157–67.

33 There is an interesting discussion of traditional games and regional identities in During and Brisson, "Sport, Olympism and Cultural Diversity," 188–89.

34 H. Eichberg, "Olympic Sport: Neocolonisation and Alternatives," *International Review for Sociology of Sport* 19, no. 1 (1984): 98.

10 In her contribution to this volume, Martha Nussbaum intervenes in one of the thorniest and longer-
standing debates bedeviling work in the humanities and social sciences, that over relativism and
universals. In his aptly entitled essay "Relativism
and Universals," Ernest Gellner identifies two ques-
tions at the heart of this debate – "Is there one kind of man, or many?" and
"Is there one world, or many?" – and argues that the problem of relativism
and the problem of human universals are in fact distinct. This distinctiveness arises for Gellner from relativism's primary emphasis on the singularity
of worlds, on the question of whether or not vastly different impressions of
reality are finally just different "takes" on the same objective world against
which differences as such assume their epistemological and phenomeno-
logical salience. The problem of human universals, on the other hand, arises
when trying to determine what within the world might remain the same for
all people, in all places, at all times. The problem of universals is thus closely
tied to ideas about what human beings are or could be, and it is precisely
in virtue of its attempt to navigate this gulf between the normative and the
descriptive, particularly insofar as the condition of women are concerned,
that Nussbaum's argument derives its considerable moral force.

Briefly, Nussbaum aims to show that there exist certain universal norms
governing human functioning to which we should appeal when ascertaining the relative wellbeing of members of different societies, when assessing what we might otherwise call their varying "quality of life." For these
assessments to have the right sorts of political and moral value, Nussbaum
argues, they must reveal not only the existence of specific manifestations of
social and political inequality, but also provide some measure of their harm
relative to what individual human beings minimally require in order to live
free and dignified lives (i.e., in order to be "fully" human). Nussbaum maintains that, properly interpreted, critical inquiry into human "capabilities" –
to live a life of normal length, to be adequately nourished, to have the sovereignty of one's body respected, to be allowed to cultivate the imagination,
to be allowed attachment to other people and to things, to engage in critical
reflection, to love others and to have one's dignity respected by others, to

harmonize one's relationship to the natural world, to play, and to have political and material control of one's environment – provides us not just with a sense of what might be wrong with a society, but also with concrete ideas concerning how to go about bettering the lives of those living in it. Unlike, say, Gary Becker's utilitarian model of the family, which measures quality of life in terms of some aggregate accounting of a family's resources, Nussbaum's "capabilities approach" is more finely attuned to the asymmetrical distribution of resources within groups like families, inequalities often the most damaging to women.

Note that these capabilities are simply the material and psychological prerequisites for free rational action, and not in themselves constitutive of a particular way of life. In this way Nussbaum's account, like Mette Hjort's and like Gellner's, manages to walk an important line between universalism and particularism. Although she believes that everyone should possess at least the capabilities listed above, Nussbaum remains a pluralist concerning the specific modes of political and social organization necessary for nurturing and protecting them. Her universalism rests on a conception of the human person that even those living in other (i.e., non-Western, non-democratic, non-secular) cultures should accept, thereby guaranteeing maximum freedom for those with different conceptions of the good to seek it by their own lights. Against this capacious liberal view of human social relations, criticisms from relativists and paternalists, when not simply counterintuitive, seem either dangerous, demeaning, or small.

IN DEFENCE OF UNIVERSAL VALUES*

MARTHA NUSSBAUM

I found myself beautiful as a free human mind. – Mrinal, in Rabindranath Tagore's "Letter from a Wife"[1]

It is obvious that the *human* eye gratifies itself in a way different from the crude, non-human eye; the human *ear* different from the crude ear, etc.... The *sense* caught up in crude practical need has only a *restricted* sense. For the starving man, it is not the human form of food that exists, but only its abstract being as food; it could just as well be there in its crudest form, and it would be impossible to say wherein this feeding activity differs from that of *animals*. – Marx, *Economic and Philosophical Manuscripts of 1844*

I.

An international feminism that is going to have any bite quickly gets involved in making normative recommendations that cross boundaries of culture, nation, religion, race, and class. It will therefore need

* A longer version of this essay appears in Martha Nussbaum's *Women and Human Development: The Capabilities Approach*. It has been significantly edited for publication here and appears with the permission of the author and Cambridge University Press.

to find descriptive and normative concepts adequate to that task.[2] I shall argue that certain universal norms of human capability should be central for political purposes in thinking about how the basic structure of a society can promote its citizens' quality of life, and that these norms are legitimately used in making comparisons across nations, asking how well they are doing relatively to one another in promoting human quality of life. My project, then, commits itself from the start to cross-cultural comparisons and to developing a defensible set of cross-cultural categories. This enterprise is fraught with peril, both intellectual and political. Where do these categories come from, it will be asked? And how can they be justified as appropriate ones for lives in which those categories themselves are not explicitly recognized? The suspicion uneasily grows that the theorist is imposing something on people who surely have their own ideas of what is right and proper. And this suspicion grates all the more unpleasantly when we remind ourselves that theorists often come from nations that have been oppressors, or from classes in poorer nations that are themselves unusually privileged. Isn't all this philosophizing, then, simply one more exercise in colonial or class domination?

Now of course no normative political theory uses terms that are straightforwardly those of ordinary daily life. If it did, it probably could not perform its special task as theory, which involves the systematization and critical scrutiny of thoughts and perceptions that in daily life are jumbled and unexamined. For this task theory needs overarching analytical concepts that may not be at all familiar in daily conversation, although the theorist should be able to show that they respond to reality and help us to scrutinize it. Germans of the eighteenth century did not walk around talking about "the Kingdom of Ends," nor did Greeks of the fourth century B.C. speak readily of "a disposition lying in a mean." Some thinkers indeed hold that all philosophical theorizing in ethics is suspect just on that account, that we would all be better off without these departures from the language of the everyday.[3] Though I cannot argue the point fully here, I am convinced that this wholesale assault on theory is deeply mistaken, and that the systematic arguments of theory have an important practical function to play in sorting out our confused thoughts, in criticizing unjust social realities, and in preventing the sort of self-deceptive rationalizing that frequently makes us collaborators with injustice. It's perfectly obvious, too, that theory has great practical value for ordinary non-philosophical people, in giving them a framework in which to view what is happening to them, and a set of concepts with which to criticize abuses that otherwise might have lurked nameless in the background of life.

But even if one defends theory as valuable for practice, it may still be problematic to use concepts that originate in one culture to describe and assess realities in another – and all the more problematic if the culture described has been colonized and oppressed by the describer's culture. Such a history does not, of course, entail that the particular describer has colluded with colonization and oppression; she may be a determined critic of colonialism, just as an indigenous woman may be a supporter of it.[4] Despite this fact, however, any attempt by international feminists today to use a universal language of justice, of human rights, or of human functioning to assess impoverished lives is bound to encounter charges of Westernizing and colonizing – even when the universal categories are introduced by feminists who live and work within the nation in question itself. For, it is standardly said, such women are alienated from their culture, and are faddishly aping a Western political agenda. The minute they become critics, it is said that they cease to belong to their own culture and become puppets of the Western elite.[5]

Interestingly, such charges were rarely made against Marxism, which was usually understood to have powerful indigenous roots in people's experience of economic exploitation, although the theory itself, obviously, was created within elite Western culture, using its cultural resources. Sometimes accusations of "Westernizing" are made today against those who struggle for democracy and political liberties in totalitarian societies – but we usually know to greet such accusers with scepticism, asking whose interests are served by branding those concepts as alien Western intrusions into a culture's traditions. For example, when Lee Kuan Yew proclaimed that the concept of freedom is alien to Asian culture, he did find some support, but he also encountered vigorous criticism.[6] But when feminists appeal to notions of equality and liberty – even when those notions are actually in the constitutions of the nations in which they live, as they are, for example, in the Indian constitution – they do standardly get accused of Westernizing and of insufficient respect for their culture, as if there were no human suffering, no reasons for discontent, and no criticism until aliens invaded the peaceful landscape. We should ask whose interests are served by this nostalgic image of a happy harmonious culture, and whose resistance and misery are being effaced. Describing her mother's difficult life, Indian feminist philosopher Uma Narayan writes, "One thing I want to say to all who would dismiss my feminist criticisms of my culture, using my 'Westernization' as a lash, is that my mother's pain too has rustled among the pages of all those books I have read that partly constitute my 'Westernization,' and has crept into all the suitcases I have ever packed for my several exiles."[7]

In one way, then, the charge of "Westernizing" looks like a shady political stratagem, aimed at discrediting forces that are pressing for change. Surely opponents who claim that women were all happy in India before Western ideas came along to disrupt them hardly deserve the time of day. They are ignoring tremendous chunks of reality, including indigenous movements for women's education, for the end of *purdah*, for women's political participation, that gained strength straight through the nineteenth and early twentieth centuries in both Hindu and Muslim traditions, in some ways running ahead of British and U.S. feminist movements.[8] Similarly out of touch with reality is any opponent who today denies that the ideas of political liberty, sex equality, and non-discrimination are Indian ideas – for such a person is simply saying that India should not have the constitution it does have, one that was adopted, ultimately, by overwhelming consensus despite the sharp political divisions that existed and that continue to exist. It's perfectly clear, fifty years later, that no proposal to repeal any of the enumerated Fundamental Rights would meet with serious political support. So the opponent seems to be saying that even though the Founders took women's equality and other basic liberties seriously enough to fight to get them into the Constitution, these ideas were just alien colonial ideas. What an implausible and condescending story to tell about Nehru and his fellow freedom fighters – all nothing but dupes of colonial powers, even when they thought that they had risked their lives for independence and were writing a Constitution for an independent India! This objection, then, shows such ignorance of Indian history and Indian law that it should not be taken seriously; only ill-informed and guilt-ridden Westerners are likely even to entertain it. How absurd, too, to take credit for sex equality as an American idea when America has not been able to pass an equal rights amendment, something that India did in 1951.

On the other hand, when we make a concrete proposal for a universal framework to assess women's quality of life, we will face a somewhat more respectable form of this objection that does deserve to be seriously answered. For it will be suggested that the particular categories we choose are likely to reflect our own immersion in a particular theoretical tradition, and may be in some respects quite the wrong ones for the assessment of Indian lives. So at the very least we need to ask whether it is correct to use a universal framework at all, rather than a plurality of different though related frameworks. And we also need to ask whether the framework we propose, if a single universal one, is sufficiently flexible to enable us to do justice to the human variety we shall certainly find.

This challenge is serious because international development projects have often gone wrong through insufficient attunement to cultural variety and particularity. When, for example, development workers proceed on the (typical Western) assumption that families are the primary units of personal solidarity and that women relate to other women primarily as members of heterosexual couples, existing traditions of female solidarity and group membership, often highly productive for economic development, will be ignored.[9] Even where there are no local traditions of female group solidarity and women are to a great extent cut off from the company of other non-family women, an approach based on the Western-style nuclear family ignores fruitful possibilities for change that can be created by the construction of local women's collectives, possibilities that good development projects in India and Bangladesh have recently exploited.[10] Again, if Western feminists speak of Indian issues such as *sati* and dowry deaths, they will only do so productively if they understand the issues fully in their historical and cultural context.[11] Similarly, if they make criticisms of

Hindu or Islamic traditions regarding women, they will be both wrong and offensive if they neglect the variety and complexity of those traditions, equating them with their most stridently misogynistic elements. In general, any productive feminism must be attentive to the issues that people really face and to their actual history, which is likely to be complex.

But it is one thing to say that we need local knowledge to understand the problems women face, or to direct our attention to some aspects of human life that middle-class people tend to take for granted. It is quite another matter to claim that certain very general values, such as the dignity of the person, the integrity of the body, basic political rights and liberties, basic economic opportunities, etc., are not appropriate norms to use in assessing women's lives in developing countries. How might one argue this more contentious point?

II.

As I have said, the claim that there is a global difference between Western and Eastern values, and that Indian culture simply does not value the rights and liberties cherished by the West, is not a serious contender. But when we propose a universal framework to assess women's quality of life, we face three more respectable arguments that deserve to be seriously answered.

First is an *argument from culture*. A more subtle and sincere version of the anti-Westernizing argument, it says that Indian culture contains, in both Hindu and Muslim traditions, powerful norms of female modesty, deference, obedience, and self-sacrifice that have defined women's lives for centuries. We should not assume without argument that those are bad norms, incapable of constructing good and flourishing lives for women. Western women are not so happy, the objector adds, with their high divorce rate and their exhausting careerism. Feminists condescend to third-world women when they assume that only lives like their own can be fruitful.

My full answer to this point will emerge from the proposal I shall make, which certainly does not preclude any woman's choice to lead a traditional life, so long as she does so with certain economic and political opportunities firmly in place. Indeed, my proposal protects spaces within which women may make such choices, and in which parents may teach the value of tradition to their children. But we should also note that the objector, once again, oversimplifies tradition, ignoring counter-traditions of female defiance and strength, ignoring women's protests against harmful traditions, and in general forgetting to ask women themselves what they think of these norms, which are typically purveyed, in tradition, through male texts and the authority of male religious and cultural leaders, against a background of almost total economic and political disempowerment for women. In addition, if divorce and career difficulties are painful, as they surely are, they are a lot less painful than the systematic malnutrition, physical abuse, and ill health to which traditions of modesty and purity have consigned many women, against their will. And even when women appear to be satisfied with such customs, we should probe more deeply. If someone who has no property rights under the law, who has had no formal education, who has no legal right of divorce, who will very likely be beaten if she seeks employment outside the home, says that she endorses traditions of modesty and purity and self-abnegation, it is not clear that we should think this the last word on the matter. Female protest against unfair treatment by males is, moreover, a very old theme in Indian tradition, going straight back to Draupadi's eloquent protest against sexual harassment in *Mahabharata,* Book 11, when, lost by one of her Pandava husbands[12] in a dice game, she is dragged by her hair into the hall and undressed by the winners, who gloat and call her a slave. She gains justice in a miraculous way: her sari keeps growing new yards of cloth, so that she remains fully clothed no matter how eagerly they try to undress her. This story serves, in fact, as a touchstone for the women of the Self-Employed Women's Association (SEWA)[13] who invoke it to compare the struggles of their founder Ela Bhatt (a deeply religious Brahmin woman) against the humiliating treatment she suffered at the hands of male labour-union leaders.[14] This, too, is Indian tradition, as is the more general idea of human dignity that underlies the story.

And if Draupadi's protest against sexual violence may seem in some ways a confirmation of deep-seated customs of female purity,[15] there are other even more radical norms of female independence in the Hindu tradition. Mrinal, in Rabindranath Tagore's story "Letter from a Wife," declares her independence from her husband in a way that shows the influence of nineteenth- and early twentieth-century humanist thought[16]; and of course Tagore's fiction is obsessed with the damage done by ossified custom to the human search for self-expression and love. In general, the Bengal Renaissance was based not only on independent moral argument but also on a close interpretation of tradition, and called on Hindus to reject contemporary superstitions and rigid rules in order to return to what is finest in the tradition.[17] But Mrinal invokes a much older exemplar: Meerabai, the sixteenth-century Rajput queen who left her marriage and her royal status to become a singer, performing "joyfully rebellious songs." "Meerabai too," she tells her husband, "was a woman like me."[18]

Such critical thinking is old in the Muslim tradition as well. In 1905, Muslim feminist Rokeya Sakhawat Hossain mocked the seclusion of women in her fantasy *The Sultana's Dream*, whose characters maintain that, since men are the dangerous ones, they are the ones who should be shut up in purdah:

"Where are the men?" I asked her.

"In their proper places, where they ought to be" [Sultana tells her that in her country it is women who are secluded.]

"But, dear Sultana, how unfair it is to shut in the harmless women and let loose the men.... Suppose some lunatics escape from the asylum and begin to do all sorts of mischief to men, horses, and other creatures: in that case what will your countrymen do?"

"They will try to capture them and put them back into their asylum."

"And you do not think it wise to keep sane people inside an asylum and let loose the insane?"

"Of course not!" said I, laughing lightly.

"As a matter of fact, in your country this very thing is done! Men, who do or at least are capable of doing no end of mischief, are let loose and the innocent women shut up in the zenana! ... You have neglected the duty you owe to yourselves, and you have lost your natural rights by shutting your eyes to your own interests."[19]

This articulate protest relies on a long tradition of thought about sex equality in the Indian Muslim tradition and defines that tradition further. By now, such norms of self-cultivation and rights-seeking have caused widespread re-examination of the basis of norms of female deference; women have urged other women to ask what is really important in the tradition, and whether the really important features justify seclusion and veiling.

At times, in fact, it may be the uncritical veneration of the past that is more "foreign," the voice of protest that is more "indigenous" or "authentic," if such terms have any meaning at all. Chinese women I met at a 1995 conference on feminism in Beijing[20] reacted to a paper praising Confucian values of care as good norms for feminists by saying, "That was a Western paper. She would not have said that had she not come from Hong Kong" (as indeed the young speaker did). What they meant was that for her the traditions could look beautiful, since she had never had to live in the world they constructed. For them, Confucian values were living excuses for sex discrimination in employment and other things they didn't value at all. This is also the way many Indian women, though by no means all, view the norms of the "good" or "pure" woman to which traditionalist Hindu and Muslim leaders are currently giving enormous emphasis, construing control over female sexuality as a central aspect of cultural continuity.[21]

More generally, we should say that any story that attributes to India only a single set of cultural norms, even for women, is bound to be bizarrely inadequate. Few American feminists make such generalizations about "American culture" – or, insofar as they do, they are well aware that the culture contains much else besides the norms they attack (including, of course, themselves). But India is probably the most diverse single nation in the modern world, if there is any such coherent notion. With ten national languages, four prominently institutionalized religions with their own legal systems (and others that are smaller), huge regional differences and differences of class and caste, differences between urban and rural, differences between matrilineal and patrilineal tradition, between secularism and religiosity, between rationalism and mysticism – all these would have to be included in any adequate story of the stock of tradition out of which Indian women may select their norms. As Indira Karamcheti writes, "Neither I nor anyone else can deliver a representative, authentic Third-world woman to academia or elsewhere. Even in India, there is no such thing as the Indian woman – there are only Indian women. And the individuals are far more interesting than any assumed stories of authenticity."[22]

One might try to refurbish the argument from culture by an appeal to the idea of cultural relativism: the idea, that is, that normative criteria must come from within the society to which they are applied. I believe such an attempted salvage operation would be totally unsuccessful. As a descriptive thesis about how people really do make moral judgments, relativism is clearly false. People are resourceful borrowers of ideas. The ideas of Marxism, which originated in the British Library, have influenced conduct in Cuba, China, and Cambodia. The ideas of democracy, which are not original to China, are by now extremely important Chinese ideas. The ideas of Christianity, which originated in a dissident sect of Judaism in a small part of Asia Minor, have by now influenced conduct in every region of the globe, as have the ideas of Islam. As Aristotle said, "In general, people seek not the way of their ancestors, but the good."

As a normative thesis, about how we should make moral judgments, relativism has several problems. First, it has no bite in the modern world, where the ideas of every culture are available, internally, to every other, through the Internet and the media. The ideas of feminism, of democracy, of egalitarian welfarism, are "inside" every known society. Many forms of moral relativism, especially those deriving from the cultural anthropology of a previous era, use an unrealistic notion of culture. They imagine homogeneity where there is really diversity, agreement or submission where there is really contestation. My observations about India apply here: there is little that is not "internal" to India, once we get a sufficiently complex idea of its traditions. Second, it is not obvious why we should think the normative thesis true. Why should we follow the local ideas, rather than the best ideas we can find? Finally, normative relativism is self-subverting: for, in asking us to defer to local norms, it asks us to defer to norms that in most cases are strongly non-relativistic. Most local traditions take themselves to be absolutely, not relatively, true. So in asking us to follow the local, relativism asks us not to follow relativism.

Many people, in particular students, confuse relativism with toleration of diversity, and find relativism attractive on the ground that it shows respect for the ways of others. But of course it does no such thing. Most cultures have exhibited considerable intolerance of diversity over the ages, as well as at least some respect for diversity. By simply making each culture the last word, we deprive ourselves of any more general norm of toleration or respect that could help us limit the intolerance of cultures. Once we see this, our interest in being relativists should rapidly diminish.

The cultural argument fails; nor can it be rescued by an appeal to moral relativism. At this point, however, two other objections to universal values need to be heard. I shall call them the *argument from the good of diversity* and the *argument from paternalism*.

The argument from the *good of diversity* reminds us that our world is rich in part because we don't all agree on a single set of categories but each speak a different language of value. Just as we think the world's different languages have worth and beauty, and that it's a bad thing, diminishing the expressive resources of human life generally, if any language should cease to exist, so too we may think that cultural systems each have a distinctive beauty, and that it would be an impoverished world if everyone took on the value system of America, or even of Europe.

Here we must be careful to distinguish two claims the objector might be making. He might be claiming that diversity is good as such; or he might simply be saying that there are problems with the value system of America, and that it would therefore be too bad if the rest of the world emulated our materialism and aggressiveness. This second claim, of course, doesn't yet say anything against universal values, it just suggests that their content should be critical of some American values. So the real challenge to our enterprise lies in the first claim. To meet it we must ask how far cultural diversity really is like linguistic diversity, or the diversity of species. The trouble with the analogy is that languages don't harm people, and cultural practices frequently do. We could think that Cornish or Breton should be preserved, without thinking the same about Nazism, or Stalinism. In the end, then, the objection doesn't undermine the search for universal values, it requires it: for what it invites us to ask is whether the cultural values in question are among the ones worth preserving, and this entails at least a very general universal framework of assessment, one that will tell us what is and is not beyond the pale. I will be offering just such a very general framework, one that allows a great deal of latitude for diversity, but one that also sets up some general benchmarks that will tell us when we are better off letting a practice die out. Traditional practices like the division of labour in a brick kiln site are not worth preserving simply because they are there, or because they are old; to make a case for preserving them, we have to assess the contribution they make and the harm they do. And this requires a set of values that gives us a critical purchase on cultural particulars. So the argument does give us good reasons to seek to preserve types of diversity that are compatible with human dignity and other basic values; but it does not undermine and even supports our search for a general universal framework of critical assessment.

We might add that it is not terribly clear that there is interesting diversity exemplified in the practices of male dominance that feminists have most contested. Getting beaten up and getting malnourished have depressing similarities across all cultures; denials of land rights, political voice, and employment opportunities do also. Insofar as there is interesting cultural diversity worth preserving in the varied cultures, it is perhaps not in traditions of sex hierarchy, any more than in traditions of slavery, that we should search for it.

Finally, we have the *argument from paternalism.* This argument says that when we use a set of universal norms as benchmarks for the world's varied societies, we show too little respect for people's freedom as agents (and, in a related way, their role as democratic citizens). People are the best judges of what is good for them, and if we prevent people from acting on their own choices, we treat them like children. This is an important point, and one that any viable cross-cultural proposal should bear firmly in mind. But we can say already that a commitment to respecting people's choices hardly seems incompatible with the endorsement of universal values. Indeed, it appears to endorse explicitly at least one universal value, the value of at least having the opportunity to think and choose for oneself. Thinking about paternalism gives us a strong reason to respect the variety of ways citizens actually choose to lead their lives in a pluralistic society, and therefore to prefer a form of universalism that is compatible with freedom and choice of the most significant sorts. But religious toleration, associative freedom, and the other major liberties are themselves universal values. They seem to require a universalist account for their recognition and their protection against people who don't necessarily want people to choose what they think good for themselves.

The issue of paternalism arises in different ways when we think about a national state's relation to its citizens, and when we think about the relationship between a system of international law to the various national states. The latter raises complex issues of accountability, and even strong universalists about rights may legitimately worry about the democratic credentials of international human rights bodies when they seek to enforce norms against democratically accountable nation states. I shall therefore focus from now on on the first issue, that of a nation state's treatment of groups within the nation who have traditional practices that treat women unequally. Thinking of this problem, then, we can insist that universal norms of religious toleration, freedom of association, and the other liberties are essential in order to prevent illiberal subgroups from threatening legitimate forms of pluralism. India remains a highly pluralistic society only because it has committed itself to a menu of fundamental rights and liberties.

We should and can make a further claim: many existing value systems are themselves highly paternalistic, particularly toward women. They treat them as unequal under the law, as lacking full civil capacity, as not having the property rights, associative liberties, and employment rights of males. If we encounter a system like this, as we certainly do in India, in the form not only of traditional practices but also of the various religious systems of personal law, it is in one sense paternalistic for a state to say, sorry, that is unacceptable under the universal norms of equality and liberty that we would like to defend. In that way, any bill of rights is "paternalistic," vis-à-vis families, or groups, or practices, or even pieces of legislation, that treat people with insufficient or unequal respect, if paternalism means simply telling people that they cannot behave in some way that they have traditionally behaved. The Indian Constitution is in that sense "paternalistic" when it tells people that it is from now on illegal to treat women as unequal in matters of property and civil capacity, or to discriminate against them in employment on grounds of sex. More generally, any system of law is "paternalistic" in keeping some people from doing some things that they want. But that is hardly a good argument against the rule of law, or, more generally, against opposing the attempts of some people to tyrannize over others. We dislike paternalism, insofar as we do, because there is something else that we like, namely each person's liberty of choice in fundamental matters. It is fully consistent to reject some forms of paternalism while supporting those that underwrite these central values, on an equal basis. Even strong opponents of paternalism with respect to private choices that do no harm to others, such as John Stuart Mill, have countenanced state interference as soon as the conduct does harm others; and Mill clearly thought that many forms of traditional sex hierarchy fell afoul of the "harm principle."[23]

Beyond this, we should note that the various liberties of choice have material preconditions, in whose absence there is merely a simulacrum of choice. Children in the desert areas of Andhra Pradesh have the right to go to school – but there aren't any schools or teachers, since nobody has decided to spend money on creating them. All citizens of India have the right to exercise their religion freely, on an equal basis; the Constitution says so. But in an area torn by communal violence, where police are either impotent or corrupt, where rape in police custody is generally agreed to be a very serious problem,[24] it doesn't mean a whole lot to point to the Constitution. All women in India have equal rights under the Constitution; but in the absence of effective enforcement, and of programs targeted at increasing female literacy, economic empowerment, and employment opportunities, those rights are not real to them. In short, liberty is not just a matter of having rights on paper, it requires one being in a position to exercise those rights. And this requires material resources. The state that is going to guarantee people rights effectively is going to have to take a stand about more than the importance of these basic rights themselves. It is going to have to take a stand on the distribution of wealth and income, and their use to guarantee to citizens what John Rawls has called the "equal worth" of the various liberties – for example by raising revenue through taxation in sufficient quantity to make schools available to all. That requires yet more universalism and in a sense paternalism, meaning interference with activities that people choose; but we could hardly say that those rural children, living in a state of virtual anarchy, are especially free to do as they wish.

The argument from paternalism indicates, then, that we should prefer a universal normative account that allows people plenty of liberty to pursue their own conceptions of value, within limits set by the protection of the equal worth of the liberties of others. It does not give us any good reason not to endorse any universal account, and some strong reasons why we should do so, including in our account not only the liberties themselves, but also forms of economic empowerment that are crucial in making the liberties truly available to people. And the argument suggests one thing more: that the account we search for should preserve liberties and opportunities for each and every person, taken one by one, respecting each of them as an end, rather than simply as the agent or supporter of the ends of others. The idea that the individual person should be the focus of political thought has sometimes been given dismissive treatment by feminists as entailing neglect for care and community, as involving a male Western bias toward self-sufficiency and competition, and away from cooperation and love. We could argue for a long time over whether particular Western liberal theorists are indeed guilty of neglecting cooperation and community. I would maintain that a lot of what communitarian thinkers have said in criticism of figures such as Rawls and Kant, and even Mill, is mistaken.[25] But rather than pursue that agenda here, I simply point out that there is a type of focus on the individual as such that requires no particular metaphysical tradition, and no bias against love and care. It arises naturally from the recognition that each person has just one life to live, not more than one, that the food on A's plate doesn't magically nourish the stomach of B, that the pleasure felt in C's body does not make the pain experienced by D less painful; that the income generated by E's economic activity does not help to feed and shelter F; in general that one person's exceeding happiness and liberty doesn't automatically make another person happy or free. So, programs aimed at raising general or average well-being do not improve the situation of the least well off in that region unless they go to work directly to improve those people's life quality, among others. If we combine this observation with the thought, which all feminists share in some form, that each person is valuable and worthy of respect as an end, we must conclude that we should look not just at the total or the average, but at the functioning of individuals.[26]

It has been claimed by Veena Das that even this very intuitive idea that each person has her own dignity and that questions of well-being should be considered one by one, rather than in the aggregate, is a Western intrusion, and that Indian women are simply unable to form the concept of their own personal well-being as distinct from the well-being of family members.[27] If Das simply means that Indian women frequently judge sacrifice for the family to be a good thing, and frequently subordinate their own well-being to the well-being of others, it is plausible enough, but hardly an objection to the type of political individualism I have recommended; there is no incompatibility between the idea that politics should treat each person as an end and the idea that some people may choose to make sacrifices for others. If, however, Das really means to say that Indian women can't tell their own hunger apart from the hunger of a child or a husband, can't really distinguish their own body and its health from someone else's body and its health, then she doesn't have a leg to stand on. It is difficult to believe that Das has not had many conversations with Indian women in her own social surroundings that emphasize the tensions between a woman's well-being and the well-being of someone else. But extremely poor people are likely to be especially keenly aware of the separateness of each person's well-being – for hunger and hard physical labour are great reminders that one is oneself and not someone else. Bengali author Manik Bandyopadhyay put it this way, in his short story "A Female Problem at a Low Level":

A slum girl and daughter of a laborer cannot mentally depend on her father or brother, like the daughters of the babu families who even as grown women see individual disaster in any family mishap. She is used to fending for herself, relying on her own wits.[28]

On this account, the perception of the organic connectedness of interests in the family is more likely to be an upper-middle-class ("babu") mode of consciousness, alien to those who are really struggling to survive. (Has Das, not at all from a peasant background, mistaken her own background for a special "Indian essence"?)

One might, of course, come to accept religious beliefs, in particular Buddhist beliefs, that do hold that people aren't really separate individuals at all, and that the whole idea that objects and people are distinct from one another is an illusion. It must be remembered, however, that Buddhist metaphysics is hardly typical of non-Western religion as a whole,[28] and many traditions take the individual very seriously as loci of purity, self-discipline, and spiritual achievement. Buddhism, furthermore, self-consciously portrays itself as a radical critique of ordinary practices, and as making demands that take people, in meditation, far away from the world of physical objects they must continue to inhabit in their daily lives. So empirical individualism isn't even insulting or unfair to Buddhists, since it is meant to supply a basis for politics in the daily world, not in the world of enlightened meditation and reflection. The Buddhist can accept the appropriateness of relieving the suffering of bodies one by one, even though she believes that at some level bodies as such are an illusion, and that the more correct description of the goal would be to minimize the quantity of suffering in the world as a whole.[29]

If we agree that citizens are all worthy of concern and respect, and grant that they live separate lives in the sense just characterized, then we ought to conclude that politics should not treat people as agents or supporters of other people whose mission in the world is to execute someone else's plan of life. It should treat them as ends, as sources of agency and worth in their own right, with their own plans to make and their own lives to live, and therefore as deserving of all necessary support for their equal opportunity to be such agents. To treat someone as an equal we do have to take a stand on some values that will be made central for political purposes, and we do have to take a stand against some very common ways of treating women – as childlike, as incompetent in matters of property and contract, as mere adjuncts of a family line, as reproducers and care-givers rather than as having their own lives to live. But when we take a stand in this way, that should not raise the charge of paternalism, since we do so in order to treat each and every citizen as an end.

III.

Let me recapitulate. The *argument from culture* reminded us that we should leave space for women who may wish to choose a traditional hierarchical way of life. But it said nothing against using a universal account to criticize unjust cultural practices; indeed, we were reminded that the activity of criticism is deeply internal to Indian culture itself. The *argument from the good of diversity* told us something important about any proposal we should endorse: that it ought to provide spaces in which valuably different forms of human activity can flourish. We should not stamp out diversity, or even put it at risk, without a very strong reason. But in light of the fact that some traditional practices are harmful and evil, and some actively hostile to other elements of a diverse culture, we are forced by our interest in diversity itself to develop a set of criteria against which to assess the practices we find, asking which are acceptable and worth preserving, and which are not. As for the *argument from paternalism*, it nudges us strongly in the direction of what might be called *political* rather than *comprehensive liberalism* in the sense that it urges us to respect the many different conceptions of the good citizens may have and to foster a political climate in which they will each be able to pursue the good (whether religious or ethical) according to their own lights, so long as they do no harm to others. In other words, we want universals that are facilitative rather than tyrannical,[30] that create spaces for choice rather than dragooning people into a desired total mode of functioning. But understood at its best, the paternalism argument is not an argument against cross-cultural universals. For it is all about respect for the dignity of persons as choosers. This respect requires us to defend universally a wide range of liberties, plus their material conditions; and it requires us to respect persons as separate ends in a way that reflects our acknowledgment of the empirical fact of bodily separateness, asking how each and every life can have the preconditions of liberty and self-determination.

We have some good reasons already, then, to think that universal values are not just acceptable, but badly needed, if we really are to show equal respect for all citizens in a pluralistic society. But we can now approach this question from another direction, by looking at three of the most prominent approaches in international development work to assessing a nation or region's quality of life. For the defects of these approaches, both in general and as approaches to the situation of poor women in developing countries, give us yet further reasons for turning to a universal normative account.

The most prominent approach to quality of life assessment used to be simply to ask about GNP per capita, treating the maximization of this figure as the most appropriate social goal and basis for cross-cultural comparison. It has by now become obvious that this approach is not very illuminating, because it does not even ask about the distribution of wealth and income, and countries with similar aggregate figures can exhibit great distributional variations. In Charles Dickens's *Hard Times*, circus girl Sissy Jupe is asked by her economics teacher to imagine that her schoolroom is a nation, "and in this Nation are fifty millions of money." Next, she is asked to say whether this isn't a prosperous nation, and whether she herself isn't in "a thriving state." Sissy replies, in tears of confusion, that she doesn't see how she can answer the question until she knows "who has got the money, and whether any of it is mine." But that, as she soon learns "is not in the figures" – and so it wasn't, for a long part of the subject's history. Sissy's intuitive sense of the distinctness of one person from another informs her that aggregate data aren't enough for a normative assessment of prosperity: we need to know how each one is doing. And, we might add, we need to know still more, since we also need information about important goods that are not always well correlated with wealth and income such as life expectancy, infant mortality, educational opportunities, employment opportunities, political liberties, the quality of race and gender relations. Countries that do very well on GNP per capita have often done egregiously badly on one of these other distinct goods: South Africa under apartheid; Singapore under its extremely constraining political regime. And, of particular importance for our project, countries with similar GNP performance exhibit great variation in their performance on various aspects of gender equality. Thus Pakistan, Zimbabwe, and Honduras have almost exactly the same GNP per capita, while the female literacy rate is 23% in Pakistan, 60% in Zimbabwe, 71.6% in Honduras; the proportion of income earned by women is 20% in Pakistan, 24% in Honduras, 35% in Zimbabwe. India and Kenya have the same GNP per capita, while the female literacy rate is 36% in India, 67.8% in Kenya, and the earned income share that goes to women is 25.7% in India, 42% in Kenya.[31] Seeing what is absent from the GNP account nudges us sharply in the direction of mapping out other basic goods in a universal way, so that we can use a list of basic goods to compare quality of life more fruitfully across societies.

Suppose, instead, we take a more straightforwardly utilitarian approach, asking about the total or average utility of the population, as measured by expressions of satisfaction. Here again, we run into the problem of respect for the separate person – for an aggregate figure doesn't tell us where the top and the bottom are. In that sense, it doesn't tell us "who has got the money and whether any of it is mine" any more than does the crude GNP approach. Suppose a majority of citizens of Andhra Pradesh express satisfaction with their educational opportunities in a hypothetical poll: such a result does not give us the information that things are disastrously bad out in the desert areas, where there are no schools at all. We could imagine getting a similar average satisfaction figure in Kerala, where the bottom is far better situated with respect to education.[32] Nor, of course, does such an aggregate inform us about the different views of men and women, and it can conceal an extremely bad situation for women within a total or average that looks pretty good. We may or may not want to improve the lot of the worst off, or of women; but we certainly shouldn't make decisions without knowing how they are doing. Average utility is an imprecise number which doesn't tell us enough about different types of people and their relative social placement. This makes it an especially bad approach when we are focusing on the situation of women, whose placement in a hierarchy of power is a critical part of any good description.

What is more, utilitarians typically aggregate not only across distinct lives but also across distinct elements of lives. Thus, within the total or average utility will lie information about liberty, about economic well-being, about health, about education. But these are all separate goods, which vary to some extent independently of one another;[33] and there are reasons to think that they all matter, that we should not give up one of them simply in order to achieve an especially large amount of another. John Rawls's central argument against utilitarianism was that because of its commitment to trade-offs among diverse goods, it offers insufficient protection for political and religious liberty. It encourages trade-offs between those goods and others, in order to produce the largest social total (or average).[34] Once again, this will create problems for thinking well about marginalized or deprived people, for whom some of the opportunities that utilitarianism puts at risk may have a specially urgent importance.

There is a further problem with the reliance on utility. This is that it doesn't even include all the relevant information. One thing we want to know is how individuals feel about what is happening to them, whether dissatisfied or satisfied. But we also want to know what they are actually able to do and to be. Debating this issue well certainly requires looking at people's satisfaction and dissatisfaction; but it will also require using everything known about the connections between education and population control, education and political empowerment, education and employment opportunities. Confining our inquiry to the space of utility prevents us, then, from using some information that seems highly relevant to the resolution of the question before us.

Thinking about the defects of utilitarian approaches to development pushes us in the direction of a substantive account of certain central goods, as the relevant space within which to make comparisons of quality of life across societies, and also the relevant benchmark to use in asking what a given society has or has not done for its citizens. The suggestion is that such a list will contain a plurality of distinct items, and that it will not treat these items as simply offering different amounts of a single homogenous good. Nor will the assessment focus solely on how people feel about their relation to these goods; it should look, as well, for information about what they are actually able to do and to be.

Before we turn to the third major approach to quality of life assessment, we should mention a variant on the utilitarian approach that has had enormous influence on modelling and information gathering the world over: Gary Becker's model of the family. Becker does think (for descriptive, not normative purposes) that the goal of the family as unit is the maximization of utility, and that utility (construed as the satisfaction of preference or desire) is the relevant space of comparison when we are asking how families (and, presumably, larger groups such as nations) are doing. But inside the family he takes a different line. The family, he holds, should be understood as a group held together by motives of altruism. In particular, the head of the household is assumed to be a beneficent altruist who will adequately distribute resources and opportunities to the family's members.[35] The upshot of this assumption is that we need not ask how each and every individual in the family is doing, even in respect of utility: we just ask about the whole, and assume that the distribution has been altruistic. For this reason, development people influenced by Becker's model have standardly sought information about households, rather than about individual household members; it is difficult to find data, for example, on how widows in India are doing, since in the data they usually appear as members of a household headed by someone else. Although Becker's model has only descriptive and predictive purposes, when used by others in this way it has clear normative implications: for we can hardly make things better for widows unless we can first of all attend to them as distinct persons, and ask how they are doing.

Becker made an immensely valuable contribution when he put the whole question of the family on the agenda of the economics profession. But his model is inadequate in some crucial ways. It assumes a picture of the family that is romance more than reality. In real life families contain all sorts of struggles over resources and opportunities. Some people get milk in their tea, some only sugar; some go to school and some do not; some get life-sustaining health care and some do not. Such conflicts for resources among members of a putatively cooperative body are now familiar in the economic literature. Called "cooperative conflicts," their existence has given rise to a new way of thinking about the family that has increasingly displaced the organic Becker approach.[36] The new "bargaining model" of the family has marked advantages over the more organic approach.

What is important here is to note that the Becker model, like the other two approaches we have discussed, fails in large part because it is not individualistic enough: it does not look at each person one by one to see how each one is doing. This wouldn't be a good way to proceed even if the assumption about the head of the household were true: for seeing other family members as recipients of the largesse of a beneficent altruist is not the same thing as to see them as agents, each with a life to live, deserving of both respect and resources. But it is even more fatal when we see that the head of the household does not allow all its members what they need, and is sometimes quite indifferent to their well-being.[37] The deficiencies in Becker's approach remind us, once again, that we need to ask about the opportunities of individuals taken one by one; and when we do so, we need to ask not just what they feel about their situation, but what they are actually able to do and to be.

Distinctly more promising is our third major alternative, an approach that looks at a group of basic resources and then asks about their distribution, advancing criteria for a fair social allocation. The most famous such approach is that of John Rawls, who, in *A Theory of Justice* and subsequent works, advanced a list of the "primary goods," items that all rational individuals, regardless of their more comprehensive plans of life, would desire as prerequisites for carrying out those plans.[38] Rawls's list is heterogeneous. It includes liberties, opportunities, and powers, which are capacities of citizens in their social environment;[39] structurally similar is the social basis of self-respect, a feature of society in relation to the powers of persons. At the same time, however, the list includes thing-like items, above all wealth and income, and these items have a particularly central role on the list, since they are used to define the class of the least well off.[40] The basic idea is that, whatever else citizens pursue, they should be able to arrive at a working political consensus about the central importance of these basic resources and about some rough criteria for their fair distribution.

Rawls's approach is very promising in terms of all our concerns to date. It is highly attentive to concerns about pluralism and paternalism, and yet at the same time it takes a stand about the importance of basic liberties and opportunities for all citizens, and about the importance of the material basis of these central areas of choice. In all these respects, Rawls's model seems to provide an excellent basis for further thought about quality of life in the international arena. Rawls himself pulls back at this point, preferring to regard the political conception of the person, together with the picture of primary goods, as grounding a consensus only within a particular Western tradition of political philosophy.[41] In reality, however, there seems no reason to think that any of the primary goods is particularly Western, nor that the power of forming and revising a plan of life expresses a distinctively Western sense of what is important. The idea of being able to plan and to execute a plan arises without any philosophical backing, out of the struggle of human beings to live in a hostile environment. Certainly these ideas have indigenous roots in the Indian women's movement, where no concepts are more centrally stressed than those of reflection, choice, planning, and control, and where it is perfectly clear that these activities have a material basis in property rights, land rights, access to employment, and so forth. As Ela Bhatt says, women don't just want a piece of the pie; they want to choose its flavour themselves and to know how to make it themselves.

Far from being a Western import, this idea, insofar as it was inspired by anything outside women's daily situation, has Gandhian roots. It translates the Gandhian idea of India's self-sufficiency in the colonial struggle against Britain onto the plane of the family and the village, where women, too, struggle to be free from a quasi-colonial oppression. John Stuart Mill emphasized that struggling against the subjection of women in the family is isomorphic to, and expressive of, the same concerns as the struggle waged by democracy against feudalism.[42] The women of SEWA (and many other working women in similar movements throughout India) independently make the same connection: far from being colonialist, ideas of individual life-control and life-planning are an expression of the struggle against colonialism. People don't need Western philosophers to tell them that they don't like to be pushed around by the world, or to live in a condition of helplessness.

But Rawls's approach, even though more promising as a basis for international thinking than Rawls himself is willing to suggest, nonetheless has some grave defects. By measuring who is better and who worse off in terms of resources, the Rawlsian neglects a salient fact of life: that individuals vary greatly in their need for resources and in their ability to convert resources into valuable functionings. Some of these differences are straightforwardly physical. Nutritional needs vary with age, occupation, and sex. A pregnant or lactating woman needs more nutrients than a non-pregnant woman. A child needs more protein than an adult. A person whose limbs work well needs few resources to be mobile, whereas a person with paralysed limbs needs many more resources to achieve the same level of mobility. Many such variations can escape our notice if we live in a prosperous nation that can afford to bring all individuals to a high level of physical attainment; in the developing world we must be highly alert to these variations in need. Again, some of the pertinent variations are social, connected with traditional hierarchies. If we wish to bring all citizens of a nation to a given basic level of educational attainment, we will need to devote more resources to those who encounter obstacles from traditional hierarchy or prejudice: thus women's literacy will prove more expensive than men's literacy in many parts of the world. The resource-based approach doesn't go deep enough to diagnose obstacles that can be present even when resources seem to be adequately spread around, causing individuals to fail to avail themselves of opportunities that they in some sense have (such as free public education, or the vote, or the right to work). If we operate only with an index of resources, we will frequently reinforce inequalities that are highly relevant to well-being. This is an especially grave defect when it is women's quality of life we want to consider; for women who begin from a position of traditional deprivation and powerlessness will frequently require special attention and aid to arrive at the same level of capability that the more powerful can more easily attain.

Thus even the Rawlsian approach, in the end, doesn't sufficiently respect the struggles of each and every individual for flourishing. To treat A and B as equally well off because they command the same amount of resources is, in a crucial way, to neglect A's separate and distinct life, to pretend that A's circumstances are interchangeable with

B's, as may not be the case. To do justice to *A*'s struggles, we must see them in their social context, aware of the obstacles that context offers to the struggle for liberty, opportunity, and material well-being. In his discussions of liberty and opportunity, Rawls shows himself well aware that a theory of justice must be cognizant of the different situations of distinct lives, in order to distribute not only liberty, but also its equal worth; not only formal equality of opportunity, but also truly fair equality of opportunity. His emphasis on wealth and income as primary goods central to the task of indexing, however, sells short his own respect for the individual.

To sum up: We want an approach that is respectful of each person's struggle for flourishing, that treats each person as an end and as a source of agency and worth in her own right. Part of this respect will mean not being dictatorial about the good, at least for adults and at least in some core areas of choice, leaving individuals a wide space for important types of choice and meaningful affiliation. But this very respect means taking a stand on the conditions that permit them to follow their own lights free from tyrannies imposed by politics and tradition. This, in turn, requires both generality and particularity: both some overarching benchmarks and detailed knowledge of the variety of circumstances and cultures in which people are striving to do well. The shortcomings of both the utilitarian and the resource-based approaches suggest that we will take a stand in the most appropriate way if we focus not on satisfaction or the mere presence of resources, but on what individuals are actually able to do and to be. General benchmarks based on utility or on resources turn out to be too insensitive to contextual variation, to the way in which circumstances shape preferences and the ability of individuals to convert resources into meaningful human activity. Only such a broad concern for functioning and capability seems capable of doing justice to the complex interrelationships between human striving and its material and social context.

IV.

The most interesting worries about universals thus lead us to prefer universals of a particular type. I shall now argue that a reasonable answer to all these concerns, capable of giving good guidance to governments and international agencies, is found in a version of the *capabilities approach* – an approach to quality of life assessment pioneered within economics by Amartya Sen,[43] and by now highly influential through the *Human Development Reports* of the UNDP.[44] My own version of this approach (which got its start independently of Sen's work through thinking about Aristotle's ideas of human functioning and Marx's use of them[45]) is in several ways different from Sen's, both in its emphasis on the philosophical underpinnings of the approach and in its readiness to take a stand on what the central capabilities are.[46] I shall not comment on those differences further here, but shall simply lay out the approach as I would currently wish to defend it. Like any universal approach, it is only valuable if developed in a suitably relevant way, so we need to worry not just about the structure of the approach, but also about how to flesh out its content in a way that focuses appropriately on women's lives. Otherwise promising approaches have frequently gone wrong by ignoring the problems women actually face. But the capabilities approach directs us to examine real lives in their material and social setting; so there is hope that it may overcome this difficulty.

The central question asked by the capabilities approach is not "How satisfied is this woman?" or even "How much in the way of resources is she able to command?" It is, instead, "What is she actually able to do and to be?" Taking a stand for political purposes on a working list of functions that would appear to be of central importance in human life, we ask: Is the person capable of this, or not? We ask not only about the person's satisfaction with what she does, but about what she does, and what she is in a position to do (what her opportunities and liberties are). And we ask not just about the resources that are sitting around, but about how those do or do not go to work, enabling her to function in a fully human way.

Having discovered the answers to this question, we now put the approach to work in two closely related ways. First, it is in terms of these capabilities to function, in certain core areas, that we would measure a woman's quality of life, comparing her quality of life with that of others. When we aggregate the data from different lives to produce accounts of regional, class, and national differences in quality of life, it is always in the space of the central capabilities that we will make those comparisons, defining the least well off and the best off in this way.

Second, we then argue that in certain core areas of human functioning a necessary condition of satisfactoriness for a public political arrangement is that it deliver to citizens a certain basic level of capability. If people are systematically falling below the threshold in any of these core areas, this should be seen as a tragic situation, in need of urgent attention – even if in other respects things are going well.

The intuitive idea behind the approach is twofold: first, certain functions are particularly central in human life, in the sense that their presence or absence is typically understood to be a mark of the presence or absence of human life. Second, and this is what Marx found in Aristotle, these functions are performed in a truly human, not merely an animal, way. We judge, frequently enough, that a life has been so impoverished that it is not worthy of the dignity of the human being, that it is a life in which one goes on living, but more or less like an animal, not being able to develop and exercise one's human powers. In Marx's example, a starving person doesn't use food in a fully human way – by which I think he means a way infused by practical reasoning and sociability. He or she just grabs at the food in order to survive, and the many social and rational ingredients of human feeding can't make their appearance. Similarly, he argued that the senses of a human being can operate at a merely animal level – if they are not cultivated by appropriate education, by leisure for play and self-expression, by valuable associations with others; and we should add to the list some items that Marx probably would not endorse, such as expressive and associational liberty, and the freedom of worship. The core idea seems to be that of the human being as a dignified free being who shapes his or her own life in cooperation and reciprocity with others, rather than being passively shaped or pushed around by the world in the manner of a "flock" or "herd."[47] A life that is really human is one that is shaped throughout by these human powers of practical reason and sociability.

At one extreme, we may judge that the absence of capability for a central function is so acute that the person isn't really a human being at all, or any longer – as in the case of certain very severe forms of mental disability, or senile dementia. But I am less interested in that boundary (important though it is for medical ethics) than in a higher one, the level at which a person's capability is what Marx called "truly human," that is, *worthy* of a human being. Note that this idea contains, thus, a reference to an idea of human worth or dignity. Marx was departing from Kant in some important respects, by stressing (along with Aristotle) that the major powers of a human being need material support and cannot be what they are without it. But he also learned from Kant, and his way of expressing his Aristotelian heritage is distinctively shaped by the Kantian notion of the inviolability and the dignity of the person.

Notice that the approach makes each individual a bearer of value, and an end. Marx, like his bourgeois forebears, holds that it is profoundly wrong to subordinate the ends of some individuals to those of others. That is at the core of what exploitation is, to treat a person as a mere object for the use of others. Thus it will be just as repugnant to this Marxian approach as to a bourgeois philosophy to foster a good for society considered as an organic whole, where this does not involve the fostering of the good of individuals, taken one by one. What this approach is after is a society in which individuals are treated as each worthy of regard, and in which each has been put in a position to live really humanly.

My claim is that we can arrive at an enumeration of these elements of truly human functioning that can command a broad cross-cultural consensus. Although this list of basic capabilities is somewhat different in both structure and substance from Rawls's list of primary goods, it is offered in a similar, political-liberal spirit: as a list that can be endorsed for political purposes by people who otherwise have very different views of what a complete good life for a human being would be. (In part, as we shall see, this is because the list is a list of capabilities or opportunities for functioning, rather than of actual functions; in part it is because the list leaves spaces for people to pursue other functions that they value.) The list is supposed to provide a focus both for quality of life assessment, demarcating the space within which comparisons will most revealingly be made, and also for political planning, providing the materials for an account of the basic social minimum that any nation should secure to its people. For both purposes, it isolates those human capabilities that can be convincingly argued to be of central importance in any human life, whatever else the person pursues or chooses. The central capabilities are not just instrumental to further pursuits: they are held to have value in themselves, in making the life that has them fully human. But they are held to have a particularly pervasive and central role in everything else people plan and do. In that sense, they play a role analogous to that of primary goods in Rawls's political-liberal theory: they have a special importance in making any choice of a way of life possible, and so they have a special claim to be supported for political purposes in a pluralistic society.[48]

A list of the central capabilities is not a complete theory of justice. Such a list gives us the space within which we may, through suitable devices of aggregation,[49] index the quality of life in a society. It also gives us a set of benchmarks for evaluating whether a society has given its citizens a decent minimum standard of living.[50] The structure of social and political institutions should be chosen, at least in part, with a view to promoting human capabilities. Indeed, in many respects the capability minimum can be viewed like a set of constitutional guarantees or entitlements. But in order to describe how a threshold level of capability might best be secured, much more needs to be said about the appropriate role of the public sphere vis-à-vis incentives to private actors, and also about how far the public sphere is entitled to control the activities of private actors in the pursuit of the capabilities on the list. We could agree that the space of capabilities is the relevant space in which to make such comparisons, and that a basic social minimum in the area of the central capabilities should be secured to all citizens, while disagreeing strongly about the role to be played by government and public planning in their promotion. Since a general answer to this question requires us to answer economic questions that are not in the province of my inquiry, I shall not give a general answer to this question here. Many other questions treated by theories of justice are also left undecided by this account of capability.

The list represents the result of years of cross-cultural discussion, and comparisons between earlier and later versions will show that the input of other voices has shaped its content in many ways. Thus it already represents what it proposes: a type of *overlapping consensus* on the part of people with otherwise very different views of human life. Elsewhere I argue that this fact about how the list has evolved helps to justify it in an ancillary way, although the primary weight of justification remains with the intuitive conception of truly human functioning and what that entails. Since that conception of human functioning demands continued reflection and testing against our intuitions, we should view any given version of the list as a proposal put forward in a Socratic fashion, to be tested against the most solid of our intuitions as we attempt to arrive at a type of reflective equilibrium for political purposes.

Some items on the list may seem to us more fixed than others. For example, it would be astonishing if the right to bodily integrity were to be removed from the list; that seems to be a fixed point in our considered judgments of goodness.[51] On the other hand, one might debate what role is played by literacy in human functioning, and what role is played by our relationship to other species and the world of nature. In this sense, the list remains open-ended and humble; it can always be contested and remade. Nor does it deny that the items on the list are to some extent differently constructed by different societies. (Indeed part of the idea of the list is that its members can be more concretely specified in accordance with local beliefs and circumstances.) The threshold level of each of the central capabilities will need more precise specification, as citizens work toward a consensus for political purposes. This can be envisaged as taking place within each constitutional tradition, as it evolves through interpretation and deliberation. Finally, in its relatively concrete remarks about matters such as literacy and basic scientific education, the list is intended for the modern world rather than as timeless.[52]

Here is the current version of the list:[53]

Central Human Functional Capabilities

1. LIFE
Being able to live to the end of a human life of normal length; not dying prematurely or before one's life is so reduced as to be not worth living.

2. BODILY HEALTH
Being able to have good health, including reproductive health;[54] to be adequately nourished; to have adequate shelter.

3. BODILY INTEGRITY
Being able to move freely from place to place; having one's bodily boundaries treated as sovereign, i.e., being able to be secure against assault, including sexual assault, child sexual abuse, and domestic

violence; having opportunities for sexual satisfaction and for choice in matters of reproduction.

4. SENSES, IMAGINATION, AND THOUGHT

Being able to use the senses, to imagine, think, and reason – and to do these things in a "truly human" way, a way informed and cultivated by an adequate education, including, but by no means limited to, literacy and basic mathematical and scientific training. Being able to use imagination and thought in connection with experiencing and producing self-expressive works and events of one's own choice, religious, literary, musical, and so forth. Being able to use one's mind in ways protected by guarantees of freedom of expression with respect to both political and artistic speech, and freedom of religious exercise. Being able to search for the ultimate meaning of life in one's own way. Being able to have pleasurable experiences, and to avoid non-necessary pain.

5. EMOTIONS

Being able to have attachments to things and people outside ourselves; to love those who love and care for us, to grieve at their absence; in general, to love, to grieve, to experience longing, gratitude, and justified anger. Not having one's emotional development blighted by overwhelming fear and anxiety, or by traumatic events of abuse or neglect. (Supporting this capability means supporting forms of human association that can be shown to be crucial in their development.)

6. PRACTICAL REASON

Being able to form a conception of the good and to engage in critical reflection about the planning of one's life. (This entails protection for the liberty of conscience.)

7. AFFILIATION

A. Being able to live with and toward others, to recognize and show concern for other human beings, to engage in various forms of social interaction; to be able to imagine the situation of another and to have compassion for that situation; to have the capability for both justice and friendship. (Protecting this capability means protecting institutions that constitute and nourish such forms of affiliation, and also protecting the freedom of assembly and political speech.)

B. Having the social bases of self-respect and non-humiliation; being able to be treated as a dignified being whose worth is equal to that of others. This entails, at a minimum, protections against discrimination on the basis of race, sex, religion, caste, ethnicity, or national origin.[55]

8. OTHER SPECIES

Being able to live with concern for and in relation to animals, plants, and the world of nature.[56]

9. PLAY

Being able to laugh, to play, to enjoy recreational activities.

10. CONTROL OVER ONE'S ENVIRONMENT

A. *Political.* Being able to participate effectively in political choices that govern one's life; having the right of political participation, protections of free speech and association.

B. *Material.* Being able to hold property (both land and movable goods), and having property rights on an equal basis with others; having the right to seek employment on an equal basis with others; having the freedom from unwarranted search and seizure.[57] In work, being able to work as a human being, exercising practical reason and entering into meaningful relationships of mutual recognition with other workers.

The list is, emphatically, a list of separate components. We cannot satisfy the need for one of them by giving a larger amount of another one. All are of central importance and all are distinct in quality. The irreducible plurality of the list limits the trade-offs that it will be reasonable to make, and thus limits the applicability of quantitative cost-benefit analysis. One may, of course, always use cost-benefit analysis; but if one does so in connection with this approach, it will be crucial to represent in the weightings the fact that each and every one of a plurality of distinct goods is of central importance, and thus there is a tragic aspect to any choice in which citizens are pushed below the threshold in one of the central areas. That tragic aspect could be represented by a huge cost; but it is hard to represent clearly in this way the fact that a *distinctive* good is being slighted. One should not suppose, for example, that the absence of the political liberties would be made up for by tremendous economic growth, and the use of a single measure might easily make one think in this way.[58]

At the same time, the items on the list are related to one another in many complex ways. One of the most effective ways of promoting women's control over their environment, and their effective right of political participation, is to promote women's literacy. Women who can seek employment outside the home have exit options that help them protect their bodily integrity from assaults within it. Reproductive health is related in many complex ways to practical reason and bodily integrity. This gives us still more reason not to promote one at the expense of the others.

Some of the items on the list are or include what John Rawls has called "natural goods," goods in whose acquisition luck plays a substantial role. Thus, governments cannot hope to make all citizens healthy, or emotionally balanced, since some of the determinants of those good states are natural and luck-governed. In these areas, what government can aim to deliver is the *social basis* of these capabilities. The capabilities approach insists that this requires doing a great deal to make up for differences in starting point that are caused by natural endowment or by power, but it is still the social basis of the good, not the good itself, that society can reliably provide. Take women's emotional health. Government cannot make all women emotionally healthy; but it can do quite a lot to influence emotional health, through suitable policies in areas such as family law, rape law, and public safety. Something similar will be true of all the natural goods. But factors we cannot control may still interfere to keep some people from full capability. When we use capabilities as a comparative measure of quality of life, we must therefore still inquire about the reasons for the differences we observe. Some differences in health among nations or groups are due to factors public policy can control, and others are not.

Among the capabilities, two, practical reason and affiliation, stand out as of special importance, since they both organize and suffuse all the others, making their pursuit truly human. To use one's senses in a way not infused by the characteristically human use of thought and planning is to use them in a merely animal manner.[59] To plan for one's own life without doing so in complex forms of discourse, concern, and reciprocity with other human beings is, again, to behave more like a beast than like a human being.[60] To take just one example, work, to be a truly human mode of functioning, must involve both practical reason and affiliation. It must involve behaving as a thinking being, not just a cog in a machine; and it must be done with and toward others, in a way that involves mutual recognition of humanity.[61] Women's work frequently lacks this feature.

The basic intuition from which the capability approach begins, in the political arena, is that human abilities exert a moral claim that they should be developed. Human beings are creatures such that, provided with the right educational and material support, they can become fully capable of all these human functions. That is, they are creatures with certain lower-level capabilities (which I call "basic capabilities"[62]) to perform the functions in question. When these capabilities are deprived of the nourishment that would transform them into the high-level capabilities that figure on my list, they are fruitless, cut off, in some way but a shadow of themselves. If a turtle were given a life that afforded a merely animal level of functioning, we would have no indignation, no sense of waste and tragedy. When a human being is given a life that blights powers of human action and expression, that does give us a sense of waste and tragedy – the tragedy expressed, for example, in Mrinal's statement to her husband, in Tagore's story, when she says, "I am not one to die easily." In her view, a life without dignity and choice, a life in which she can be no more than an appendage of someone else, is a type of death, the death of her humanity. "I have just started living," she ends her letter – and signs it, "This is from Mrinal – who is torn off the shelter of your feet."

The capabilities framework, when used to evaluate lives lived in other cultures, does not appear to be an alien importation: it seems to square pretty well with the things Indian women are already thinking about, or start thinking about at some time in their lives, and want when they think about them. Insofar as it entails criticism of traditional culture, these women are already full of criticism; indeed, any framework that didn't suggest criticism wouldn't be adequate to capture what they want and aim for. In particular, the ideas of practical reason, control over environment, and non-humiliation (including sexual non-humiliation) seem especially salient in their thought, alongside more obvious considerations of nutrition, health, and freedom from violence.

Many women in India and in the rest of the world have lacked support for many of the most central human functions, and that lack of support is to at least some extent caused by their being women. But women, unlike rocks and trees and even horses, have the potential to become capable of these human functions, given sufficient nutrition, education, and other support. That is why their unequal failure in capability is a problem of justice. It is up to all human beings to solve this problem. I claim that a universal conception of human functioning gives us excellent guidance as we pursue this difficult task.

Notes

1   Published in Bengali in 1914; translated by Kalpana Bardhan in Kalpana Bardhan, *Of Women, Outcastes, Peasants and Rebels: A Selection of Bengali Short Stories* (Berkeley: University of California Press, 1990), 96–109.

2   For earlier articulations of my views on matters contained in this article, see Martha Nussbaum, "Nature, Function, and Capability: Aristotle on Political Distribution," *Oxford Studies in Ancient Philosophy*, suppl. vol. 1 (1988): 145–84; Martha Nussbaum, "Aristotelian Social Democracy," in *Liberalism and the Good*, ed. R. B. Douglass et al. (New York: Routledge, 1990), 203–52; Martha Nussbaum, "Non-Relative Virtues: An Aristotelian Approach," in *The Quality of Life*, ed. M. Nussbaum and A. Sen (Oxford: Clarendon Press, 1993), 242–69; Martha Nussbaum, "Aristotle on Human Nature and the Foundations of Ethics," in *World, Mind and Ethics: Essays on the Ethical Philosophy of Bernard Williams*, ed. J.E.J. Altham and Ross Harrison (Cambridge: Cambridge University Press, 1995), 86–131; Martha Nussbaum, "Human Functioning and Social Justice: In Defense of Aristotelian Essentialism," *Political Theory* 20 (1992): 202–46; Martha Nussbaum, "Human Capabilities, Female Human Beings," in *Women, Culture, and Development: A Study of Human Capabilities*, ed. M. Nussbaum and J. Glover (Oxford: Clarendon Press, 1995), 61–104; and, more recently in Martha Nussbaum, "The Good as Discipline, the Good as Freedom," in *The Ethics of Consumption: The Good Life, Justice, and Global Stewardship*, ed. D. Crocker and T. Linden (New York: Rowman and Littlefield, 1997), 312–41; and Martha Nussbaum, "Women and Cultural Universals," in *Sex and Social Justice* (Oxford: University Press, 1999), 29–54, and Martha Nussbaum, "Capabilities and Human Rights," *Fordham Law Review* 66 (1997): 273–300.

3   See Bernard Williams, *Making Sense of Humanity and Other Philosophical Papers, 1982–1993* (Cambridge: Cambridge University Press, 1995), and Martha Nussbaum, "Why Prac-

tice Needs Ethical Theory: Particularism, Principle, and Bad Behavior," in *The Path of the Law in the Twentieth Century*, ed. S. Burton (Cambridge: Cambridge University Press, 1998), 50–86. See also my Martha Nussbaum, "Public Philosophy and International Feminism," *Ethics* 108, no. 4 (1998): 762–96, and Martha Nussbaum, "Still Worthy of Praise: Comments on Richard Posner's the Problematics of Legal and Moral Theory," *Harvard Law Review* 111 (1998): 1776–1795.

4 For an account of Western women who supported Indian nationalism, see Kumari Jayawardena, *The White Woman's Other Burden: Western Women and South Asia during British Rule* (New York and London: Routledge, 1995); she shows that the Western women shared many of the viewpoints taken by Indian women, and that in both cases there was a multiplicity of perspectives. On the role of David Hare and Drinkwater Bethune in the Bengal Renaissance, see "Introduction" in Bardhan, *Of Women, Outcastes, Peasants and Rebels*, 43. Hare, who came to Calcutta in 1800 as a watch trader, set up schools for boys beginning in 1816–17, and Hindu College in 1817, which became the renowned Presidency College in 1855. When he died of cholera, five thousand Indians followed his hearse. Susobhan Sarkar writes, "His statue on the lawn of the Presidency College is surely the one monument to a foreigner in the city which even the most fanatic of nationalists would not dream of removing" (in Susobhan Sarkar, *Notes on the Bengal Renaissance*, [Jadavpur, Calcutta: The National Council of Education, 1958]), 28.

5 See the excellent discussion of these attacks in the essay by Uma Narayan, "Contesting Cultures," in *Dislocating Cultures: Identities, Traditions, and Third-World Feminism* (New York: Routledge, 1997), 1–40.

6 See, for example, Amartya Sen, "Human Right and Asian Values," *The New Republic* July, no. 10/17 (1997): 33–41.

7 Narayan, "Contesting Cultures."

8 For two good overviews, see Barbara Metcalf, "Reading and Writing about Muslim Women in British India," in *Forging Identities: Gender, Communities and the State in India*, ed. Zoya Hasan (Delhi: Kali for Women, and Boulder, CO: Westview Press, 1994), 1–21, and Faisal Fatehali Devji, "Gender and the Politics of Space: The Movement for Women's Reform, 1857–1900," in *Forging Identities*, ed. Zoya Hasan, 22–37; also Imtiaz Ahmad, ed., *Modernization and Social Change among Muslims in India* (Delhi: Manohar, 1983). For the special situation of Bengal, which in some ways developed progressive educational ideas earlier than other regions, under the influence of the reforms of Rammohun Roy and the Brahmo movement, see Susobhan Sarkar, *On the Bengal Renaissance* (Calcutta: Papyrus, 1979). Both in East and West Bengal, schools for girls were well established by 1850, and Bethune College, which opened in 1849, in 1888 became the first college in India to teach women through the MA level.

9 On the role of such assumptions in undermining African development projects, see Nkiru Nzegwu, "Recovering Igbo Traditions: A Case for Indigenous Women's Organizations in Development," in *Women, Culture, and Development*, ed. M. Nussbaum and J. Glover (Oxford: Clarendon Press, 1995), 444–66.

10 See Martha Alter Chen, *A Quiet Revolution: Women in Transition in Rural Bangladesh* (Cambridge, MA: Schenkman, 1983), describing women's collectives organized by the Bangladesh Rural Advancement Committee (BRAC). Another such project is the Mahila Samakhya Project created by the government of India to create women's collectives in four regions of the country, teaching women how to mobilize to demand their rights from local government and from their employers. Similar techniques of female group solidarity are employed by SEWA (see note 13) and other women's employment/credit groups.

11 See Uma Narayan, "Cross-Cultural Connections, Border-Crossings, and 'Death by Culture,'" in *Dislocating Cultures: Identities, Traditions, and Third-World Feminism* (New York: Routledge, 1997), 81–118.

12   Draupadi has five husbands (the Pandava brothers). She is described as "supremely happy with her five heroic husbands, as is the river Sarasvati with her elephants." Only one of the husbands questions the dice game itself on grounds of the damage done to Draupadi.

13   An organization with more than 50,000 members which for over twenty years has been helping female workers in the informal sector to improve their living conditions through credit, education, and a labor union.

14   See Kalima Rose, *Where Women Are Leaders: The Sewa Movement in India* (New Delhi: Vistaar Publications, 1992), 83–4 and 74–82, describing Bhatt's ouster from the National Labour Association and her humiliating treatment at a national meeting. The conflict arose over an issue of caste closely related to women's struggle against hierarchy: Bhatt opposed all compromise on the issue of affirmative action for lower castes in medical schools, out of concern for the lack of medical treatment for lower-caste women in rural areas, whom higher-caste doctors are not interested in treating. Bhatt (the Brahmin daughter of a judge, who married a lower-caste man) compared her own experience to that of Draupadi, saying "I felt like I was being stripped in front of the people I had respected most, with no one speaking up for me." Significantly, the SEWA version of the story has Draupadi prevail by praying to Krishna, whereas in the original epic she prevails by appealing to the idea of Law. Presumably Bhatt had not gotten very far through Law, and judged that a higher power was more likely to be on her side.

15   A pervasive problem in Indian legal feminism is the need to fight for feminist goals, for example protections against sexual harassment, using notions of female modesty and purity that are in some ways inimical to women's progress. Thus in 1996 a landmark sexual harassment case was won in the Supreme Court, argued by Indira Jaising, India's leading feminist lawyer; but the statute invoked was one that made it illegal to "outrage the modesty" of a woman, and the judgment involved elaborate interpretation of the concept of modesty (including its OED definition). See *Mrs. Rupan Deol Baja and Another V. Kanwar Pal Singh Gill and Another*, 309 AIR (1996). The case concerned a female civil servant who was repeatedly physically harassed by an Inspector General of Police, who blocked her exit at a party, pressed his body against hers, and eventually slapped her rear end, despite her vocal protests against his behaviour throughout the incident.

16   Especially influential for Tagore (1861–1941) is the thought of Bengali thinker and social reformer Rammohun Roy (1772–1833). On the "Bengal Renaissance," see "Introduction," in Bardhan, *Of Women, Outcastes, Peasants and Rebels*, 4–8, 42–44; also Sarkar, *On the Bengal Renaissance*.

17   See Bardhan, *Of Women, Outcastes, Peasants and Rebels*, 42, discussing Rammohun Roy, who based his campaign against *sati* on religious texts, and Iswarchandra Vidyasagar (1820–92), who used his scriptural knowledge to campaign against child marriage and polygamy and for widow remarriage.

18   "Letter from a Wife," trans. Bardhan, *Of Women, Outcastes, Peasants and Rebels*, 109.

19   Rokeya Sakhawat Hossain, *Sultana's Dream and Selections from the Secluded Ones*, ed. Roushan Jahan, trans. Roushan Jahan (New York: Feminist Press of the City University of New York, 1988).

20   This was not the large Beijing meeting in August 1995, but a small academic conference sponsored by the Ford Foundation in June 1995.

21   See Elizabeth A. Mann, "Education, Money, and the Role of Women in Maintaining Minority Identity," and Huma Ahmed-Ghosh, "Preserving Identity: A Case Study of Palitpur," in Zoya Hasan, *Forging Identities: Gender, Communities, and the State in India* (Boulder, CO: Westview Press, 1994), 130–67; 169–87.

22   In "The Graves of Academe," in Women of South Asian Descent Collective, *Our Feet Walk the Sky: Women of the South Asian Diaspora* (San Francisco: Aunt Lute Books, 1993), 274–77.

23 See John Stuart Mill, *The Subjection of Women*, ed. S. M. Okim (Indianapolis: Hackett, 1988), objecting to the failure to prosecute rape within marriage, the unequal legal conditions of marriage, etc. See also David Dyzenhaus, "John Stuart Mill and the Harm of Pornography," in *Mill's On Liberty: Critical Essays*, ed. Gerald Dworkin (Lanham, MD: Rowman and Littlefield, 1997), 31–54, arguing that there is a strong Millean case to be made for some legal regulation of pornography.

24 In the law of rape in India, the burden of proof has recently been shifted for police-custody rape accusations: there is a presumption of guilt. The reason for this change is to deter police misconduct by ensuring that police will not be alone with female prisoners, but will keep witnesses around to testify to their conduct. Obviously this will only work if the relevant parties do not collude to protect one another. Another change is that rape cases are now frequently heard in special women's courts with female judges.

25 For some examples, see my Martha Craven Nussbaum, "The Feminist Critique of Liberalism," The Lindley Lecture (Lawrence: Dept. of Philosophy, University of Kansas, 1997), and Martha Nussbaum, *Sex and Social Justice* (New York: Oxford University Press, 1998).

26 For this interpretation of individualism, see further "Feminist Critique of Liberalism."

27 Veena Das and Ralph Nicholas, "'Welfare' and 'Well-Being' in South Asian Societies," ed. Social Science Research Council (New York: ACLS-SSRC Joint Committee on South Asia, 1981). Although this paper has been circulated as a pamphlet, Das has never published it.

28 Bardhan, *Of Women, Outcastes, Peasants and Rebels*, 155.

29 On the close relationship between Buddhist and utilitarian ideas of aggregation, see Damien Keown, *The Nature of Buddhist Ethics* (New York: St. Martin's Press, 1992), ch. 7, "Buddhism and Utilitarianism." The idea of reducing suffering plays a central role in Buddhist political discourse, but usually not in its more severe metaphysical form, in which the sufferings of individuals would be treated simply as elements in a global total. The stricter form might have radical implications for policies, such as public provision of health care, that most Buddhists would agree in supporting.

30 For the charge that international human rights norms are tyrannical, see Wendy Brown, *States of Injury* (Princeton: Princeton University Press, 1995).

31 United Nations Development Programme, "Human Development Report" (New York: 1997).

32 This might be so, for example, if middle and upper classes were dissatisfied with the system of higher education.

33 For one compelling argument about this, see the regional comparisons Amartya Sen and Jean Drèze, *The Amartya Sen and Jean Drèze Omnibus* (New Delhi: Oxford University Press, 1999).

34 John Rawls, *A Theory of Justice* (Cambridge, MA: Harvard University Press, 1971), 156–73, discussing average utility and its difficulties.

35 Gary S. Becker, *A Treatise on the Family* (Cambridge, MA: Harvard University Press, 1981).

36 See Amartya Sen, "Gender and Cooperative Conflicts," in *Persistent Inequalities*, ed. I. Tinker (New York: Oxford, 1991), 123–49; Partha Dasgupta, *An Inquiry into Well-Being and Destitution* (Oxford: Clarendon Press, 1993), ch. 11. For other useful examples of bargaining approaches, see Bina Agarwal, *A Field of One's Own: Gender and Land Rights in South Asia* (Cambridge: Cambridge University Press, 1994) and "'Bargaining' and Gender Relations: Within and Beyond the Household," *Feminist Economics* 3 (1997): 1–51; Shelly Lundberg and Robert A. Pollak, "Bargaining and Distribution in Marriage," *Journal of Economic Perspectives* 10 (1996): 139–58; L.L. Chen, E. Huq, and S. D'Souza, "Sex Bias in the Family Allocation of Food and Health Care in Rural Bangladesh," *Population and Development Review* 7 (1981): 55–70.

37 Becker now admits that his assumption of altruism was incorrect: "Many economists, including me, have excessively relied on altruism to tie together the interests of family members." Motives of "obligation, anger, and other attitudes usually neglected by theories of rational behavior" should be added to the models; elsewhere, he mentions guilt, affection, and fear of physical abuse: see Gary S. Becker, "The Economic Way of Looking at Behavior," in *The Essence of Becker,* ed. Ramón Febrero and Pedro S. Schwartz (Stanford, CA: Hoover Institution Press, 1995), 647–48.

38 Rawls, *Theory of Justice,* 62, 90–95, 396–97. Rawls later qualified the view of primary goods by stating that they are to be seen not as all-purpose means, but as the needs of citizens understood from a political point of view, in connection with the development and expression of their "moral powers." He stressed that the account of the moral powers (of forming and revising a life plan) is itself one important part of the political theory of the good: see John Rawls, *Political Liberalism* (New York: Columbia University Press, 1993 expanded paperback edition 1996), 178–90.

39 In his later work Rawls added freedom of movement and the free choice of occupation: *Political Liberalism,* 181.

40 Rawls, *Theory of Justice,* 97: "taking these individuals as specified by levels of income and wealth, I assume that these primary social goods are sufficiently correlated with those of power and authority to avoid an index problem.... On the whole, this assumption seems safe enough for our purposes." The problem is all the greater when we recognize that Rawls's parties are heads of households who bargain, Becker-fashion, on behalf of their entire household; and yet the relation between the income/wealth of a household and women's powers and opportunities may be highly insecure. Self-respect may be insecurely correlated with all of the other primary goods; thus Jews in Europe in many cases did well enough on income and wealth, but very poorly on the social bases of self-respect.

41 Rawls, *Political Liberalism,* and John Rawls, "The Law of Peoples," in *On Human Rights: The Oxford Amnesty Lectures,* ed. S. Shute and S. Hunley (New York: Basic Books, 1993), 50ff. In the latter work, the equality of women is one value that Rawls is prepared to affirm cross-culturally.

42 Mill, *The Subjection of Women,* 16–18 and passim; see Nussbaum, "Feminist Critique of Liberalism."

43 The initial statement is in Amartya Sen, "Equality of What?" in *Tanner Lectures on Human Values 1,* ed. S. McMurrin (Cambridge: Cambridge University Press, 1980), reprinted in Amartya Sen, *Choice, Welfare, and Measurement* (Oxford and Cambridge, MA: Blackwell and MIT Press, 1982), 353–69; see also various essays in Amartya Sen, *Resources, Values, and Development* (Oxford and Cambridge, MA: Blackwell and MIT Press, 1984); Amartya Sen, *Commodities and Capabilities* (Amsterdam: North-Holland, 1985); Amartya Sen, "Well-Being, Agency and Freedom: The Dewey Lectures, 1984," *Journal of Philosophy* 82 (1985): 169–221; Amartya Sen, "Capability and Well-Being," in *The Quality of Life,* ed. M. Nussbaum and A. Sen (Oxford: Clarendon Press, 1993), 30–53; Amartya Sen, "Gender Inequality and Theories of Justice," in *Women, Culture, and Development,* ed. J. Glover and M. Nussbaum (Oxford: Clarendon Press, 1995), 153–98; Amartya Sen, *Inequality Reexamined* (Oxford and Cambridge, MA: Clarendon Press and Harvard University Press, 1992).

44 *Human Development Reports: 1993, 1994, 1995, 1996, 1997* (New York: United Nations Development Programme).

45 See Nussbaum, "Aristotle on Human Nature." For a very interesting related discussion of the early Marx, see Daniel Brudney, *Reclaiming the History of Ethics: Essays for John Rawls* (Cambridge: Cambridge University Press, 1997).

46 For a discussion of differences between our approaches, see David Crocker, "Functioning and Capability: The Foundations of Sen's and Nussbaum's Development Ethic, Part I,"

Political Theory 20 (1992): 584–612 and … "Part II," in Amartya Sen, "Gender Inequality and Theories of Justice," in *Women, Culture, and Development*, ed. J. Glover and M. Nussbaum (Oxford: Clarendon Press, 1995), 153–98.

47 Compare Amartya Sen, "Freedoms and Needs," *The New Republic* (January 10 & 17, 1994): 38: "The importance of political rights for the understanding of economic needs turns ultimately on seeing human beings as people with rights to exercise, not as parts of a 'stock' or a 'population' that passively exists and must be looked after."

48 Obviously, I am thinking of the political somewhat more broadly than does Rawls, for whom the nation state remains the basic unit. I am envisaging not only domestic deliberations but also cross-cultural quality of life assessments and other forms of international deliberation and planning.

49 The approach urges a focus on how each and every individual is doing. Obviously enough, however, social planning needs aggregate figures. The important thing will be to aggregate in a revealing rather than an obscuring way, for example by defining the position of the least well off clearly in terms of the various capabilities, and by allowing the ten separate capabilities to show up in the account that is produced, even if for some purposes we also use a figure that aggregates across several distinct capabilities (such as the Human Development Index and the Gender Empowerment Measure of the *Human Development Reports*).

50 To perform this function in a useful way, the list must have a more clearly demarcated account of the threshold level than is currently present.

51 I borrow the phrasing, of course, from Rawls, *Theory of Justice*, substituting "goodness" for "justice."

52 Some of the items are more timeless than others, clearly. Literacy is a concrete specification for the modern world of a more general capability that might have been realized without literacy in other times and places. All the large general rubrics appear rather timeless, though I do not claim, or need to claim, that human life exhibits an unchanging essence throughout history.

53 The current version of the list reflects changes made as a result of my discussions with people in India. The primary changes are a greater emphasis on bodily integrity and control over one's environment (including property rights and employment opportunities), and a new emphasis on dignity and non-humiliation. Oddly, these features of human "self-sufficiency" and the dignity of the person are the ones most often criticized by Western feminists as "male" and "Western," one reason for their more muted role in earlier versions of the list. See my "Feminist Critique of Liberalism."

54 The 1994 International Conference on Population and Development (ICPD) adopted a definition of reproductive health that fits well with the intuitive idea of truly human functioning that guides this list: "Reproductive health is a state of complete physical, mental and social well-being and not merely the absence of disease or infirmity, in all matters relating to the reproductive system and its processes. Reproductive health therefore implies that people are able to have a satisfying and safe sex life and that they have the capability to reproduce and the freedom to decide if, when, and how often to do so." The definition goes on say that it also implies information and access to family planning methods of their choice. A brief summary of the ICPD's recommendations, adopted by the Panel on Reproductive Health of the Committee on Population established by the National Research Council specifies three requirements of reproductive health: "1. Every sex act should be free of coercion and infection. 2. Every pregnancy should be intended. 3. Every birth should be healthy." See Amy O. Tsui, Judith N. Wasserheit, and John G. Haaga, eds., *Reproductive Health in Developing Countries* (Washington: National Academy Press, 1997), 14.

55 This provision is based on Indian Constitution Article 15, which adds (as I would) that this should not be taken to prevent government from enacting measures to correct the history of discrimination against women and against the scheduled tribes and castes. Non-discrimination on the basis of sexual orientation seems to me to be of central importance as well, but I reserve it for separate argument, since there is no political consensus on this topic at present, and especially not in India. I discuss this issue in Lecture 4 of my Seeley Lectures, arguing that discrimination on the basis of sexual orientation is deeply linked to sex discrimination, and should be opposed by anyone who opposes sex discrimination.

56 In terms of cross-cultural development, this has been the most controversial item on the list. Government can do quite a lot about this capability, through its choices of policy regarding endangered species, the health and life of animals and the ecology. Norway, for example, places tremendous emphasis on this capability. In Oslo one may build only within five miles of the coast; past that "forest line," the inland mountainous region is kept free of habitation to preserve spaces for people to enjoy solitude in the forest, a central aspect of this capability, as Norwegians specify it.

57 Nussbaum, "Aristotelian Social Democracy," argued that property rights are distinct from, for example, speech rights, in the sense that property is a tool of human functioning and not an end in itself. The current version of the list still insists that more property is not ipso facto better, but it expands the role of property rights, seeing the intimate relationship between property rights and self-definition. Most obviously, property rights should not be allocated on a sex-discriminatory basis, as they currently are under some of the systems of personal law in India. But it is also important to think of their absolute value, as supports for other valuable forms of human functioning. Thus all citizens should have some property, real or movable, in their own name. The amount requisite will properly be deliberated by each state in the light of its economic situation. Land is frequently a particularly valuable source of self-definition, bargaining power, and economic sustenance, so one might use the list to justify land reforms that remove surplus land from the rich in order to give the poor something to call their own. For example, the reform in West Bengal took wealthy landowners' second homes for this purpose. See also "Capabilities and Human Rights." *Fordham Law Review* 66 (1997): 273–300.

58 Thus phrases such as "Singapore success story" might have been harder to use had the measure of quality of life in terms of GNP per capita not been dominant in development policy.

59 See Nussbaum, "Aristotle on Human Nature"; Nussbaum, "Aristotelian Social Democracy."

60 See Nussbaum, "Aristotle on Human Nature," on the role of this idea in myths of transformations to and from the human.

61 On Marx's view, see Brudney, *Reclaiming the History of Ethics.*

62 See Nussbaum, "Nature, Function, and Capability," with reference to Aristotle's ways of characterizing levels of *dunamis.*

11

As many of the papers in this volume in one way or another make clear, "incommensurability" is a concept the specification of which is vital to our efforts to understand "culture" and its discontents. Whether pertaining to matters of translation, cross-cultural evaluation, subjectivity, disciplinarity, or distinction, "incommensurability," which may be broadly taken as the view that there exists no neutral "space" within which competing claims as to the truth of some condition of the world may be rationally evaluated, plays an important descriptive role. For example, strong criticisms of incommensurability lie at the heart of Nussbaum's rejection of the relativism central to the anti-universalist theses she terms the arguments "from culture" and "from paternalism," both of which maintain that the ship of universal values, piloted by fools, is doomed to founder on the rocks of cultural particularism. Relativists, in other words, hold that values can (at most) only reflect the moral orientation of some people at some times and cannot be assumed to comprise "universally" valid bases for cross-cultural comparison.

However, for incommensurability to have any theoretical bite it must be properly understood, since it remains unclear, important work by Feyerabend, Kuhn, and Laudan notwithstanding, what precisely hinges on incommensurability, what its consequences are in such domains as cultural studies, moral philosophy, and the history of the philosophy of science. In their contribution to this volume, Martens and Matheson give us some idea of what these consequences might be. They begin by distinguishing between two kinds of incommensurability, "semantic" incommensurability, or the view that the proponent of one theory cannot use the language of his or her own theory to explain the content of other theories, and "values" incommensurability, according to which the rational resolution of debates between individuals committed to different explanatory paradigms are undermined to the extent that each paradigm is organized around different explanatory objectives or goals. According to Martens and Matheson, neither account works well: the former lacks support from a plausible philosophy of language; and the latter, if at all empirically a feature of real scientific disputes, is deaf to the other possible causes of disputants' desire to fight.

With reference to three historically significant scientific arguments – between Johannes Kepler and Christoph Clavius, Michael Maestlin, and David Fabricius, respectively – Martens and Matheson work to develop an alternative "pragmatic" account of incommensurability. What their careful analysis of Kepler's arguments reveals is the sheer diversity of causes underlying his disagreements with his contemporaries, causes related to a great number of psychological, scientific, institutional, theological, historical, ideological – in short, *cultural* – phenomena. These phenomena, inevitably related to one another in highly complex, contradictory, and "elastic" ways, cannot comfortably be considered matters simply of value or of meaning. Therein lies the primary limitation to both of the aforementioned accounts of incommensurability: neither can properly explain the rich plurality of reasons why disputants disagree or, for that matter, refuse to change their minds. Accordingly, Martens and Matheson urge us to understand "incommensurability" as in some strong sense tied to the practical difficulties scientists and others with different theoretical outlooks face when attempting to reach a rational consensus, difficulties such as the opportunity cost of learning new theories, and the kinds of generic distinctions according to which institutional and other lifeworlds are organized. By attending to these difficulties at the level of description, by viewing incommensurability in the largest possible historic-descriptive frame, Martens and Matheson argue that it becomes possible to gain greater insight into such matters as the rationality of ignoring others, variations in cultures' tolerance of difference, the nature of "respect," and the difference between what a culture and what an individual knows.

INCOMMENSURABILITY PRAGMATIZED

RHONDA MARTENS AND CARL MATHESON[1]

The death of civil culture. The liberation of science. These verdicts represent opposing attitudes towards the notion of incommensurability, or the rational inadjudicability of scientific theories. Paul Feyerabend, who first discussed the concept, regarded it as an unassailable feature of scientific practice, and proceeded to argue that recognition of the pervasiveness of incommensurability could free scientists and philosophers of science from the shackles of scientific method. Some of those who responded, such as Israel Scheffler, took it to be a conceptual mirage,[2] albeit a threatening one, whereas others tried to provide theories of scientific rationality that allowed for substantial incommensurabilist intrusions. In hindsight, we can say that incommensurability constituted a vital port of entry into analytic philosophy for what might now be called the postmodern crisis of authority. It led Thomas Kuhn away from the idea that there could be rule-governed rationality[3] and it was vital in paving the way for the sociological accounts of knowledge propounded by, among others, Bloor.[4] However, as we shall see, incommensurability rests on shaky conceptual ground. In spite of this, the history of science abounds with cases of different theorists either talking past one another or even refusing altogether to talk to one another. In this paper, we would like to (1) set out and briefly evaluate the main types of incommensurability as it has been characterized to date, (2) examine three key case studies for the presence of incommensurability or something like it, and (3) propose a new account of incommensurability that is both conceptually well-founded and sensitive to the complexities of the historical data.

We will be focusing on incommensurability as it applies to scientific subcultures rather than to larger cultures. One concern that needs to be addressed is whether incommensurability in scientific subcultures functions in a sufficiently analogous way to how it functions in larger cultures. There is some reason to suppose it does, at least at the most general level. One thing we have noticed in the literature on culture is that some of the same issues keep coming up regardless of whether the culture clash is between academic cultures (e.g., Kimball),[5] geographically and linguistically remote cultures (e.g., Taylor's discussion of the rationality of the Zande's use of witchcraft),[6] or cultural groups divided (in part) by differing ideas about human rights (e.g., Nussbaum's article in this volume on the rights of women). The common issues that keep coming up revolve around difficulties with cross-cultural communication and conflict resolution. Problems with conflict resolution are exacerbated when one either acknowledges the difficulties associated with justifying objective and universal principles or abandons the idea that there can be such principles at all. While we intend to respect the current trend of resisting generalizing from specialized examples, the common threads across the different debates about culture open conceptual space for cross-fertilization. One of our goals in this essay is to develop an analysis of incommensurability in science that illuminates analogous problems in culture studies more generally. More on this at the end of the essay.

Incommensurability

Try this rough initial definition of "incommensurability": two theories are incommensurable just in case they can't be rationally evaluated with respect to each other. We can best hone this definition by considering the two main types of incommensurability, namely semantic and axiological incommensurability. We will be focusing on the arguments

for these positions that are given in the Anglo-American philosophical literature, but the conclusions reached (that incommensurability
renders either communication or rational adjudication impossible) are
echoed in other literatures.

Semantic Incommensurability

Semantic incommensurability or incommensurability of meaning, was
championed in the late 1950s and early 1960s by Paul Feyerabend[7] and
Thomas Kuhn.[8] Semantic incommensurability holds to the extent that
proponents of different theories are unable to express the content of rival
theories in the language associated with their own theories. Because
the proponents of theory A can't even understand theory B (and vice
versa) a rational comparison of A and B is impossible. Consider the
term "mass" as it occurs in Newton's classical mechanics and Einstein's
Special Theory of Relativity. For Einstein, but not for Newton, the mass
of an object depends on the object's velocity with respect to the observer's reference frame. Incommensurabilists take this difference to be a
difference between the two theories in the meaning they assign to the
term "mass." Einstein's claims do not contradict Newton's. They are
simply different claims about different properties.

At this point the incommensurabilist must justify her claim that the
term "mass" has a different meaning across the two theories. It would be
quite reasonable to suppose that Einstein and Newton meant the same
by "mass" and that they merely disagreed about the features of bodies
possessing mass. The hypothesis of difference in meaning is largely
based on a denial of the analytic/synthetic distinction, in other words,
of the position that sentences can be divided into those which are true
or false in virtue of the meaning of their terms (analytic sentences) and
those for which their truth or falsity is not solely a matter of meaning. Thus, to use the standard philosophical example of analyticity "All
bachelors are unmarried" is an analytic sentence, because we simply
define a bachelor as an unmarried male. On the other hand "All bachelors are dashing" is not analytic; to determine its truth we would have
to canvas the class of bachelors. Following Quine, many philosophers
have rejected this distinction, and the breakdown of the analytic/

synthetic distinction led Feyerabend and other incommensurabilists to conclude that *all* of the features associated with a term are part of its definition – in essence, that every sentence is analytic. Consequently, since Einstein and Newton associate different features with the term "mass," that is since they make different theoretical claims about mass (e.g., velocity dependence vs. the absence of velocity dependence), the term is not synonymous across the two theories. Furthermore, one could use the same sorts of reasons to show that Newton and Einstein would mean different things by all of their major theoretical terms, like "momentum" (which is partially defined in terms of mass), "energy," and "force." Therefore, their theories would be semantically opaque to each other.

At this point one could still object, however, that, even if we grant the non-synonymy of "mass" and other such terms for Newton and Einstein, the two theorists can still understand each other sufficiently to agree on a relative evaluation of their theories. They can at least compare the observational predictions made by their theories so that they can choose the theory possessing the greatest degree of observable adequacy, and they can do this even if they can't understand the claims made in the theoretical cores of each other's theories. However, the incommensurabilist will reply that, because observable terms are theory-laden in that they take some of their meaning from the theory in which they occur, Newton and Einstein will also be unable to understand each other's claims concerning observables. Feyerabend writes, "In short: introducing a new theory involves changes of outlook both with respect to the observable and the unobservable features of the world, and corresponding changes in the meanings of even the most 'fundamental' terms of the language employed."[9]

Feyerabend's arguments essentially rest on a thoroughgoing semantic holism, according to which (a) the meaning of any term as it occurs in a theory is determined by all the ways in which it is linked to other terms in the theory and (b) every term in a given theory is directly or indirectly semantically linked to every other term in the theory. Some comments are in order concerning this thoroughgoing holism. First, it does not follow immediately from a denial of the analytic-synthetic distinction, so even those people who deny the distinction will require additional reasons to be forced to accept it.[10] Second, if this strength of holism holds, then not only will Newton be unable to understand Einstein, but no two people who differ in even a single belief will be able to understand each other. Metaphorically speaking, in order for any term to be synonymous across two theories, the semantic webs of the theories would have to correspond exactly: any difference in a single strand or node would lead to a difference in meaning for all the terms in the theories. Suppose I acquire a new perceptual belief, for instance, that there is a beach ball in front of me. According to thorough-going holism, this single change in belief will lead to a shift in mean-ing, not just for "beach ball," but for all of my terms, and hence I will not be able to understand the theory of the world I had prior to seeing the beach ball. Clearly, cases like the beach ball case go against the original spirit of incommensurabilism, which tended to restrict fail-ures of comprehension to confrontations between representatives of very different theories (paradigms, research programs, etc.), and did not intend for incommensurability to arise with every change of belief. Third, a consequence of thoroughgoing holism which is underlined by the case of the beach ball is that radical shifts in meaning will often be undetected by the agents who fall victim to them. I will certainly not be aware that the meaning of all my terms has changed with the acquisition of the belief that there is a beach ball in front of me. Newton and Einstein will believe that they can understand each other: they will take their discussion about mass to be a disagreement rather than an instance of talking past one another.

Feyerabendian incommensurability is, therefore, under-justified, too widespread, and, from a practical point of view, utterly toothless. In order to be plausible, semantic incommensurability must be based on decent arguments in the philosophy of language or some related field, be largely confined to differences between significantly different theo-ries, and be such that the proponents of different theories will actually be able to notice it when it does occur. In addition to being conceptu-ally troubled, semantic incommensurability is empirically useless for the historian and philosopher of science, because her acceptance of standard semantic incommensurability will force her to relinquish the idea of meaningful disagreement between the proponents of different theories.

Here, we should also distinguish between semantic incommensurability as standardly construed, which entails an *impossibility in principle* for the proponents of different theories to understand each other, and a more pragmatic form of incommensurability, according to which the proponents of different theories will find it difficult to understand each other initially, but can in principle come to understand each other if they work hard enough at it. At the moment the prospects for standard semantic incommensurability are not good, for lack of a plausible philosophy of language to support it. We will further discuss the pragmatic form of incommensurability later in this paper.

Incommensurability of Values

In *The Essential Tension*, Kuhn shifts his focus from incommensurability of meaning to incommensurability of values, claiming that a rational resolution between the proponents of different paradigms (where "paradigm" is basically Kuhn's term for a large-scale theoretical unit)[11] is made difficult by a disagreement over the fundamental goals of science. Kuhn lists several possible goals of science, including accuracy, scope, simplicity, consistency, and fruitfulness.[12] Paradigms can differ over what they admit as permissible goals for science, or even in the weighting they assign to different goals. Thus paradigm *A* can include simplicity while paradigm *B* doesn't, or it can take simplicity to be more important than accuracy, while *B* doesn't.

The above differences will constitute sources of incommensurability (i.e., the rational inadjudicability of theories) only if the rational assessment of scientific goals, or of a complex of features including those goals, is impossible. Of course, within one's paradigm, a rational choice seems usually possible: the paradigm that favours simplicity over accuracy will choose the simpler theory, while its opponent will choose the more accurate. For the incommensurabilist, the important question is whether there is a way to choose between those theories (or those theory/value complexes) which is independent of one's paradigm, or which is at least paradigm-invariant. Despite the existence of contrary readings of his work, and while denying the existence of a rule-based decision process or algorithm for making choices about value, Kuhn himself stresses his faith in the ability of scientists to make rational choices in this area. For Kuhn, a major scientific choice is not rule governed, but it is rational because, after serious debate, a community of trained scientists generates a community-wide consensus.[13] Opponents of Kuhn can, however, plausibly claim that, in the absence of rules for rationality, how can we tell that the choice is rational, and not corrupted by the political interests of the participants or even simply arbitrary?

Sensitive to the objections raised against rationality by consensus, Larry Laudan has tried to provide rules for decisions concerning scientific goals. Laudan divides the Kuhnian paradigm (and the generic large-scale theoretical unit) into theoretical, methodological, and axiological components, which we shall call T, M, and A. T consists of the claims made by the theory about its area of study, M of methodological rules and experimental protocols (e.g., "always perform double-blind experiments where possible"), and A of the fundamental goals pursued by the paradigm and their relative weights. He then claims that in certain cases T, M, and A will conflict. For instance, physicists in the twentieth century had to come to grips with the fact that their best T (quantum mechanics) was incompatible with their A, which included the provision of a coherent and unified true description of the physical universe at all levels.[14] Their rational response, according to Laudan, was to revise their A, that is to give up on truth as a goal for science. Of course, in other cases, the best course might be to give up T or M.

Laudan's account is open to several objections. First, even in cases of an absolute incompatibility between T, M, and A, there is no principled way of telling which to reject. Laudan states that there are certain cases in which A can be found to be unacceptable, such as cases in which it can be shown either that A was unattainable or that we could never be aware of its attainment. However, Laudan's arguments are dubious even for these special cases. Second, even if correct in certain special cases, Laudan's theory would only directly apply to strict incompatibility between goals and theory and not to the incommensurability of goal/

value selection and weighting discussed by Kuhn. Third, many philosophers of science claim that there is no historical basis for value incommensurability, simply because the history of science has revealed an absence of shifts in or disagreements over fundamental scientific value. Apparent disagreements over fundamental scientific value are best seen as disagreements over instrumental values, for instance over the value of the pursuit of simplicity as a means to attaining what is intrinsically valuable. In other words, according to these critics, disagreements that are putatively at the A level are really at the M level. As such, not only do they fail to be differences in fundamental value, but, taken against an invariant axiological background, they are empirically decidable.

Because this objection does not so much respond to Laudan's defence against Kuhn as show that there is no case whatsoever to be made for value incommensurability, it is of the greatest interest to those who are interested in the general topic of incommensurability, and it is prey to significant objections. Have there really been no cases of fundamental shifts in value? Laudan argues that there have.[15] Kitcher for instance, argues that there haven't.[16] The matter is not easy to decide, because there is hardly an algorithm for sifting axiological commitments from methodological ones on the basis of historical data. Furthermore, those who believe that the history of science is axiologically unified tend to disagree on the nature of the unified axiology, positing fundamental goals as different from one another as empirical adequacy (van Fraassen)[17] and significant explanatory truth (Kitcher).[18] Finally, one could argue that, in order to defuse value incommensurability, it is not enough to show merely that scientific communities have pursued a single goal; one must show that this goal is the only possible acceptable goal for science. However, this debate inevitably leads us into the trench warfare characteristic of the long-standing debate over whether rationality is historically and contextually constituted.

What, then, are we to say concerning the prospects of value incommensurability? On the one hand, the presence of suggestive cases in the history of science and of tempting philosophical foundations lend it a greater degree of plausibility than we have accorded to semantic incommensurability. On the other hand, the existence of value-invariant ways of interpreting the historical data bids us to be cautious. Value incommensurability may exist, but it is probably far from prevalent. Furthermore, a fixation on value incommensurability or on semantic incommensurability would blind us to the many other ways in which scientists can talk and act past one another, and also to the equally numerous reasons that rival scientists may have for declining to debate and converse with one another. Clearly, something like incommensurability that does not easily fall under the rubrics of semantic or value incommensurability is frequently instantiated in the history of science. We want to determine the other ways in which incommensurability can manifest itself. In the next section we will consider some possible cases of incommensurability during the revolution in astronomy. In our concluding section we shall outline our reconfiguration of the concept of incommensurability.

We can already see how these philosophical positions, though they were developed in the context of examining scientific revolutions, have bearing on issues of culture more generally. In the case of semantic incommensurability, if this is right, then differing cultural norms and practices will suffice to make unintelligible any attempt at cross-cultural communication (let alone conflict resolution). Value incommensurability allows for the possibility of communication but cuts against the possibility of objectively fair or right conflict resolution. In both cases, the practical implications are dire, too dire. One reason we wish to examine historical case studies in detail is based on the concern that the above notions of incommensurability are driven more by theoretical considerations than by examining practice. This echoes Gramsci's concern that philosophy is too highbrow to guide action.[19] One way to make philosophy more accessible to practice is to start theorizing from practice.

Historical Case Studies

Johannes Kepler's (1571–1630) work provides an ideal case study of how the various forms of incommensurability raise barriers to effective theory evaluation and theory choice. Kepler was a Copernican at a time when not only was Copernicanism unpopular, but there was no unambiguous evidence available that would decide between the

Copernican and Ptolemaic (and Brahean) systems. Moreover, Kepler's brand of Copernicanism was radically at variance with the astronomical conventions of the day. Kepler grounded his astronomy in physics, which was in defiance of the standard disciplinary boundaries. In addition, the physics Kepler introduced invoked causal principles that were considered (most notably by Galileo) to be illegitimate.[20] Though Kepler's reform of astronomy improved dramatically its empirical accuracy, Kepler's contemporaries nonetheless had tremendous difficulties accepting the principles upon which the reform was based.

Since we only have space for three case studies, these case studies should not be taken as evidence that the history of science follows the pattern of these cases (the sample size is clearly too small). Rather, these cases serve as explanatory examples of two main points we wish to make. The first case, the Kepler-Clavius dispute, seems a clear-cut example of Laudan's goal-based version of incommensurability, but as we shall show, there are conceptual problems of interpretation. The remaining two cases, Kepler versus Fabricius and Kepler versus Maestlin, are examples of a type of incommensurability that has not yet been discussed. In particular, they show that various pragmatic, social, and political reasons can inhibit satisfactory debate resolution. While Kuhn certainly allows for a central role for these factors, his versions of incommensurability do not easily account for these cases. Kepler, Fabricius, and Maestlin have far too much in common to count as belonging to different paradigms, nor are these cases clearly a problem of disagreeing on the weighting of scientific virtues like simplicity and accuracy. Our point in bringing up these cases is to show the way in which even small points of difference can cause difficulty in debate resolution *without* entailing the sort of large-scale incommensurability of which Kuhn wrote. For that reason we will develop a different account of incommensurability in the final section of this paper.

Kepler vs. Christoph Clavius

Christoph Clavius (1538–1612) is known as one of the last great defenders of Ptolemaic astronomy. Clavius argued, among other things, that the Copernican theory is methodologically unsound, and, in particular, has not been properly tested. What is striking is that Clavius's methodological arguments for Ptolemaic astronomy are (at least on the surface) very similar to Kepler's methodological arguments for Copernicanism. We don't know whether Clavius and Kepler corresponded, but we do know that they had correspondents in common (e.g., Galileo, Giovanni Magini), and we also know that Kepler had great respect for Clavius (Kepler approvingly mentioned Clavius on a number of occasions).[21]

Philosophically Kepler and Clavius held much in common. Of interest here is their shared belief that it was possible to develop a causal account of the heavens, and that they both thought it possible to answer an important sceptical challenge levelled at astronomy.[22] We will discuss these in turn.

Kepler and Clavius agreed that a coincidence of effects indicates a cause. One of the coincidences that they both found striking is the dependence of planetary models on the sun.[23] In the Copernican system, the dependence is obvious – the sun is in the centre of planetary orbits. In the Ptolemaic system, the dependence is less obvious (the earth is in the centre), but no less striking. The planets appear to travel in a complicated path – most of the time they travel eastward through the stars, but at times they slow down and reverse directions before resuming their original course. The loop they trace out is known as retrograde motion. To account for this, the Ptolemaic system placed the planet on an epicycle, which is a small circle placed on a larger circle (known as the deferent). The deferent rotates, carrying around the epicycle, which also rotates. (figure 1)

The result is that the planet at p traces out loops. By varying the sizes and rotational velocities of the two circles, one can construct a variety of closed curves. The dependence on the sun comes out when one makes this system empirically adequate. One of the features of the inferior planets (Venus and Mercury, the planets inside the solar sphere) is that they never travel very far from the sun. To ensure this in the Ptolemaic system, the centre of the planet's epicycle is on the line between the earth and the sun. (figure 2)

For the superior planets (Mars, Jupiter, and Saturn, the planets outside the solar sphere), retrograde motion occurs only when in opposition, that is, when the sun, the planet, and the earth are all in a line. To

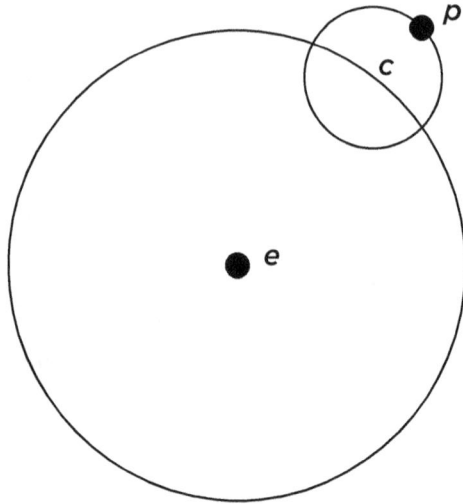

Figure 1 The Epicycle. The planet is at *p*, which rotates on circle *c*. Circle *c* rotates on the larger circle around *e*. The resulting path traced out by *p* is a series of loops.

ensure this, the line between the centre of the epicycle to the planet is kept parallel to the line between the earth and the sun. (figure 3)

Kepler and Clavius did not disagree about these features of the Ptolemaic and Copernican systems; their disagreement was whether this was *evidence* for the Copernican or the Ptolemaic hypothesis. Clavius held that these coincidences were evidence that the solar orbit was between the superior and inferior planets, a feature that is lost in the Copernican system (in the Copernican system, the earth's orbit is between the superior and inferior planets).[24] Kepler, by contrast, argued that these coincidences are explained only by the Copernican system. The inferior planets never stray far from the sun because they orbit it closely, and the superior planets go into retrogression only in opposition because retrograde motion is an appearance caused by the earth's passing or being passed by the planet. Thus both Kepler and Clavius agreed that these coincidences signalled the sun's causal role, but they disagreed on what this role should be.

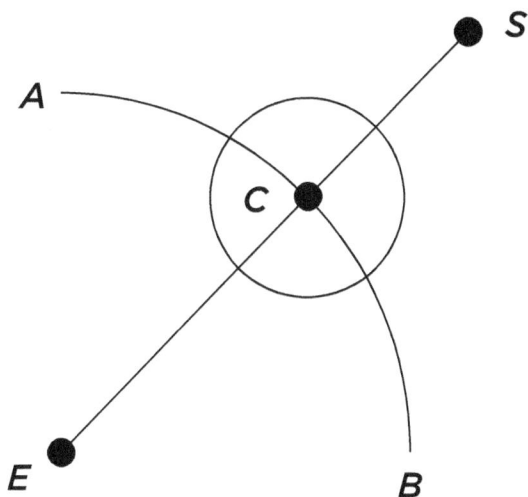

Figure 2 The Inferior Planets. Circle *C* is the epicycle of the planet. Arc *AB* is part of the larger circle that orbits the earth at *E*. The sun is at *S*.

The next point of departure between Clavius and Kepler involves different interpretations of the problem with ad hoc theory construction. A well-known sceptical problem in astronomy at the time is that since it is possible to generate the same predictions from competing models (e.g., the Copernican and the Ptolemaic), predictive accuracy does not warrant believing a theory to be true. Both Clavius and Kepler held this problem could be addressed by requiring that theories not be constructed in an ad hoc manner. But again, they reached different conclusions on which theory to accept.

Clavius argued that it is a simple matter to construct a false theory that gives true predictions if one knows in advance what the prediction should be. To avoid this, it is important to test a theory against *future* predictions, that is, before one knows the correct outcome.

Whence knowing the truth of some proposition, false premises can be arranged in such a form that by necessity, from the power of the syllogism,

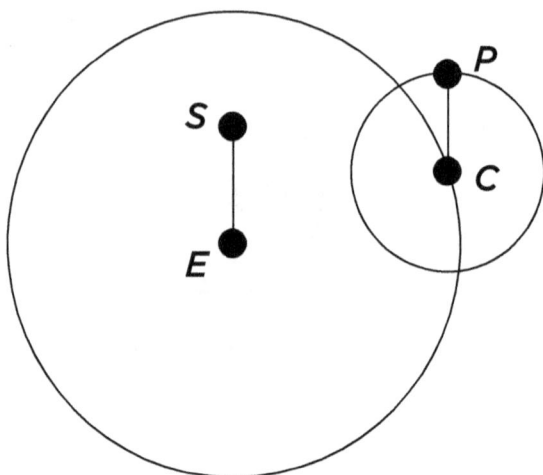

Figure 3: The Superior Planets. The planet is at *P*, the earth at *E*, and the sun at *S*. The line from the earth to the sun is parallel to the line from the centre of the epicycle to the planet.

that true proposition is concluded ... but from ... [Ptolemaic astronomy] ... not only the appearances of past things already known are defended, but also future things are predicted, the time of which is completely unknown.[25]

The Ptolemaic system, thus, had been properly tested to guard against the sceptical problem. The reason the Copernican system is suspect is because it can be generated using as a guide the predictions given by the Ptolemaic system. Indeed, the matter is more straightforward than that. One can generate a Copernican system by rearranging the geometrical features of the Ptolemaic system. In Figure 2 to convert this Ptolemaic model into a Copernican model, all one need do is move the sun into the centre of the epicycle and transfer the motion of the sun to the earth (i.e., move *S* to *C*, and draw arc *AB* through *E*). A similar but more complicated procedure holds for the superior planets. Thus, the two systems are geometrically equivalent, which is why they make the same solar and planetary predictions. Because of this, Clavius argued, the Copernican system is parasitic on the Ptolemaic, and thus has not been properly subjected to testing.

Kepler also believed that the key was to test theories against previously unknown data, or, at least, data the theory was not constructed to explain. Further, he added a proviso that this would be an effective test only if one is prohibited from responding to recalcitrant data by modifying the hypothesis.

The conclusion from false premises is accidental, and the nature of the fallacy betrays itself as soon as it is applied to another related topic ... [unless] you gratuitously allow the exponent of that argument to adopt an infinite number of other false propositions, and never in arguing forwards and backwards to reach consistency. That is not the case with someone who places the Sun at the center. For if you tell him to derive from the hypothesis ... any of the phenomena which are observed in the heavens ... he will have no difficulty with any point ... he will return with complete consistency to the same assumptions.[26]

And just as in the proverb liars are cautioned to remember what they have said, so here false hypotheses, which together yield the truth once by chance, do not in the course of a demonstration in which they have been combined with many others retain this habit of yielding the truth, but betray themselves. Thus in the end it happens that because of the linking of syllogisms in demonstrations, given one mistake an infinite number follow.[27]

Here the point is not whether one knows the outcome of the predictions ahead of time. Rather, it is whether the theory has some kind of internal coherence – whether the syllogisms are properly linked. Why does Kepler think the Copernican theory wins on this front? One of the key differences between the Copernican and Ptolemaic theory is that the Ptolemaic theory constructs the models for each planet individually. If one changes the model for one planet, this has no implications for the models of the other planets. This is not the case with the Copernican system. The appearances of the retrograde motions are the results of a single cause – the motion of the earth. Thus, if one encounters a problem with the predictions for the retrograde motion of one planet, and responds by changing the parameters of the earth's orbit, this will have implications for the predictions of all of the other planets. Kepler's point is that the systematic links between planetary models provide a series of independent ways of checking for errors.[28] One can set up the parameters of the earth's orbit using the observations of one planet, and then test these parameters by using the predictions they generate for the other planets. This is a very different position than Clavius's, since his depends on which theory was constructed first.

How deep does this incommensurability go, and what sort is it? At first blush it seems that Kepler is on better footing, *even on Clavius's own terms.* Consider the causal argument. While it is a nice feature of the Ptolemaic system that the solar orbit is the dividing line for the two types of planets (the sun is clearly a significant body), one cannot predict planetary phenomena from this feature. Under the Copernican system, by contrast, once one places the sun in the centre of all of the orbits, the phenomena are predicted. The planets close to the sun will not appear far away from it, and the more distant planets will have to wait for the earth to line up with them to show retrograde motion. This automatically follows from the basic features of the system. This should appeal to Clavius given the importance he gave to predictive power. Notice, however, that the predictions that follow from the Copernican theory that do not from the Ptolemaic are not *future* predictions, but retrodictions or explanations. Given that Clavius was not impressed by the prediction of data already known, no matter how nicely, it seems he is not required to concede the point to Kepler. On the second disagreement, again, since Kepler and Clavius differ on what constitutes adequate testing, it is difficult to see how they might have a quickly resolvable rational debate.[29]

The debate between Clavius and Kepler seems to be a classic case of methodological incommensurability. They both seem to agree on the aim of science (to provide a true picture of the world), but they disagree on the means of achieving this aim. Nonetheless, we face several problems of interpretation. If this is a classic case of methodological incommensurability, and if Laudan is right, then we should be able to determine which method best brings about this aim. If we address the matter conceptually, the problem we face is that philosophers today still can't reach consensus either on how to interpret the restriction on ad hoc modifications or on whether explanation is as important as prediction. But philosophers are famous for never resolving debates.

If we address the matter historically, while it is true that Kepler eventually won in that Copernicanism overthrew Ptolemaic astronomy, the reasons for this outcome (as many historians have pointed out) are varied and complex. The standard story is that the matter was resolved with Newton's grand unification of physics and astronomy. But this isn't a straightforward matter of determining that Kepler's method best fit with the goals. For one thing, Newton was not the same breed of realist as Kepler and Clavius. Both Kepler and Clavius followed Aristotle in holding that one requirement of a true description of reality is that it included an account of the causes at work. Newton famously refrained from postulating causes (*hypotheses non fingo*), focusing instead on the effects.[30] Perhaps both Kepler and Clavius would have argued that Newton did not provide sufficient warrant for believing his physical system to be true (and thus, Newton's success did not resolve the debate between Kepler and Clavius).

This is all on the assumption that the Clavius-Kepler debate is a debate over which method best achieves the same goal. But we have done very little to justify that claim. It could also be interpreted as a debate over how to best defend the theory to which the disputants were committed respectively. Kepler was initially attracted to Copernicanism because it was more mathematically elegant and became committed to Copernicanism because it best fit his metaphysical and aesthetic conception of the kind of world he believed God to have created.[31] Clavius was committed to the astronomical system that was established and the one that fit most easily with the dominant interpretation of the scriptures at the time. These are powerful psychological/socio-political factors that cannot be ignored in our examination of the debate. Moreover, this can (and should) filter into our interpretation of what the actual goals of science were at the time. If we straightforwardly interpret their debate as being about which method best achieves the goal of providing a true picture of the universe, we run the risk of interpreting their debate in the terms with which we are comfortable today. But in the historical period in question there was not the same distinction drawn between theology and science. Indeed, Kepler on occasion spoke of the job of the natural philosopher (scientist) as interpreting the Book of Nature in a manner that would comport with the proper interpretation of the Book of Scripture.[32] Given the period, perhaps the goal is to conduct science to the glory of God, regardless of the realism/antirealism question. Perhaps this was Kepler's but not Clavius's goal, or the reverse. The point here is that it is not clear what the goals actually were. We are saying nothing new; these are standard problems of historical interpretation.

Moreover, if Laudan is right, Kepler and Clavius should disagree either on T, M, or A. But it seems they disagree on components of M, aspects of T, and possibly on A. The debate cannot be characterized in such a tidy fashion. Granted, this is probably an excessively rigid reading of Laudan. We take the spirit of Laudan's paper to be that if they agree on enough elements, then those elements can be used to resolve the debate. But even this does not seem to be the case.

Kepler vs. Maestlin and Fabricius

Kepler's correspondences (collected in *Johannes Kepler Gesammelte Werke*) provide a useful resource on how his contemporaries reacted to his new astronomy. In this section we will discuss the response of two of his contemporaries – Michael Maestlin and David Fabricius – to his proposal to ground astronomy in physics. Both Maestlin and Fabricius were important astronomers in their own right, and both were sympathetic and supportive of Kepler's work.[33] Nonetheless, they both took issue with Kepler's method in the *Astronomia nova* (where he introduced his first two planetary laws) of using physics to further astronomy.[34]

There are a number of reasons why physics was considered a distinct discipline from astronomy. One has to do with the sceptical problem discussed in the previous section. A standard explanation of why astronomy was plagued with the problem of empirical equivalence is that it studies the motion of bodies mathematically. This was in violation of the standard Aristotelian account of knowledge given in the

Posterior Analytics.[35] In order to obtain knowledge, one needed to study the object's essence, and the mathematical features of physical systems in motion were considered accidental rather than essential properties. Thus, astronomy is especially vulnerable to scepticism. One could prevent the spread of scepticism to physics by divorcing the two, and thus, while Aristotle himself viewed physics and astronomy as closely related disciplines, sixteenth-century Aristotelians did not.[36]

Another reason for the disciplinary boundary is that the best physics of the day (Aristotelian physics) was incompatible with any of the empirically adequate astronomical models. Aristotelian physics require that the earth be in the centre of the planetary spheres. The Copernican system clearly violates this by placing the sun in the centre. The Ptolemaic system also conflicts with Aristotelian physics because to get the predictions right, the earth had to be placed a short distance from the centre.[37] The conventional solution to this tension was to assign the two disciplines different goals. The job of astronomy was to provide accurate predictions, and the job of physics was to provide knowledge of the heavens. This division was reinforced by the sceptical problem just discussed.[38]

Further, the division was entrenched at the institutional level. Physics and astronomy were separate in the curriculum (indeed, the institutional status of mathematical disciplines like astronomy was quite low). Osiander, in his famous preface to Copernicus's *De revolutionibus*, argued that if the Copernican system were interpreted as a real physical account, the liberal arts would be thrown into disarray.[39] So there was considerable official opposition to Kepler's new astronomical method, in addition to the conceptual barriers.

In light of this, Maestlin and Fabricius's resistance to Kepler's method is quite understandable. Also understandable is Kepler's response to Fabricius when Fabricius developed a non-physical astronomical model Kepler believed to be empirically equivalent to his own (Voelkel argues, however, that Fabricius's model is confused):[40]

You say that geometry bore you a daughter. I looked at her, she is beautiful, but she will become a very bad wench who will seduce all the men of the many daughters which mother physics has borne me. Your theory will attract lecturers and philosophers; it will offer a way out to the enemies of the physics of the sky, the patrons of ignorance.[41]

Given the general resistance to Kepler's program, Fabricius's model would have been very threatening (Kepler did not write to Fabricius for eight years, at which time he also sent a letter to Maestlin defending once again the need to ground astronomy in physics).[42]

How can one possibly resolve such a fundamental dispute? In light of Fabricius's alternative, Kepler couldn't appeal to how his approach provides superior results. What he needed to do was to argue that it was permissible to use physics in astronomy. The manner in which he did so was clever – he simply drew on ideas common at the time to support his position. First, he pointed out that despite the official distinction between physics and astronomy, the boundary was crossed on a regular basis. He pointed out that Aristotle himself used physics in astronomy (at one point Kepler commented sarcastically that Aristotle "is, indeed, to be censured because he mixed with astronomical observations his philosophical [physical] reasonings, which are altogether disparate in kind").[43] Moreover, bringing in physical considerations into astronomy was already a common response generally used *against* the Copernican theory. Many, including Clavius, pointed out the impossibility of the Copernican system since it postulated a moving earth, which was impossible under Aristotelian physics. So the official division between physics and astronomy was not consistently enforced. In addition, Kepler drew on an increasingly popular metaphysics to make sense of why it was permissible to use physics in astronomy. He argued that the world was created by a Platonic God, which means that God created the universe to express aesthetically interesting geometrical configurations. Given this, the essential nature of physical systems in motion *is* mathematical. Thus, in order to obtain knowledge about the causes of motion, one had to study motion mathematically.[44]

Kepler's justification, though clever, failed to persuade Maestlin. Maestlin had respect for Aristotle and Plato and appreciated Kepler's Platonic conception of reality. We don't know exactly why Maestlin rejected Kepler's method. He simply seems baffled that Kepler would subvert the standard approach and reproached him for going outside the method of astronomy.[45] To speculate, it seems reasonable that a Copernican astronomer would be especially committed to the distinction between the physical and mathematical disciplines. The Copernican system raised all sorts of physical problems but was extremely successful and appealing when considered from a mathematical perspective. Indeed, Maestlin's arguments for Copernicanism centre around the superior mathematical elegance of the Copernican system.[46] So perhaps Maestlin's objections were more pragmatic and strategic than philosophical.

Another way of reading this case is to tie it to Kuhn's notion of a paradigm (on one interpretation of paradigm). A Kuhnian paradigm is developed when, in a discipline, a particular method of approaching a problem achieves success. Continued success of this approach leads to the adoption of the procedure as the correct method of that discipline. Once adopted, the procedure defines disciplinary boundaries.[47] Thus, to use a different method takes one outside the discipline, and outside the debate.

Here again we have problems of interpretation that interfere with using the history of science as data for the philosophy of science. We cannot straightforwardly decide whether the dispute between Maestlin and Kepler is about the best way to achieve the goal of developing a true picture of the heavens, or about the best strategic position to take in defending Copernicanism. In other words, politics rather than questions of scientific rationality may be fuelling the debate, and it seems there is no way to settle the matter.

Fabricius, on the other hand, did not object in principle to Kepler's search for causes. But he, like many others of his day, did not hold out hope for a forthcoming physics that would be compatible with an empirically adequate astronomy. He even stated "I think that in fact we will never have true hypotheses without a thorough knowledge of the causes of motion,"[48] but he also called this the "astronomer's stone" (*Lapidem astronomorum*), something to which one aspired (without much hope) to find. The problem Fabricius had with Kepler was that he disliked Kepler's new physics. This was not unreasonable. Kepler's physics never really worked. In particular, he was unable to develop a satisfactory account of how the planets, since they travel elliptically, move closer and farther from the sun. Fabricius pointed out the unnaturalness of Kepler's physics, and that it seemed unlikely that the planets could move in the manner Kepler suggested.[49] This may not be a deep problem of incommensurability, but simply a cautious approach to an unconventional research program that hasn't yet shown itself to be workable.

This dispute was not resolved in Kepler's lifetime, perhaps because his physics was never successful. The story of this resolution is too long and complicated to go into in any detail here, so we will have to content ourselves with merely providing a taste of how the story goes. The key barrier to the acceptance of physics in astronomy was the official separation of the mathematical and physical disciplines. This barrier was crumbling in Kepler's time, in part due to the rising influence of Platonism and Neoplatonism. For example, Philip Melanchthon, a powerful Lutheran educational reformer who was instrumental in improving the status of mathematics, stated: "As Plato says, God always geometrizes, and vestiges of divinity can be exposed and interpreted through the use of beautiful geometry."[50] Clavius worked to improve the status of mathematics in Catholic institutions. Later, Descartes argued that the essential characteristic of physical bodies is their extension, which provided a philosophical foundation for his mathematical study of physical systems. And, of course, Newton's grand triumph was the successful unification of physics and astronomy.

As already mentioned, it would be too quick to conclude that Newton resolved the debate in favour of Kepler's position. Kepler and Newton had very different conceptions of what physics was, so different that Kepler would argue that Newton did not supply a physics of the heavens, but rather a kinematic account of the motions (for Kepler, any physics involved an account of causation).

Two brief comments before returning to our philosophical discussion. First, possibly Maestlin's and likely Fabricius's resistance to Kepler's research program was based on concerns about its probability of success. This issue, the issue of whether it is likely worth the time to understand another's position, will be key in our closing discussion. Second, one thing that is striking about the dispute about the relationship between physics and astronomy is that it becomes clear that there was no consistent monolithic tradition within that scientific community. For example, it was standard practice *both* to keep physics and astronomy separate *and* to rule out Copernicanism on physical grounds. Within the Aristotelian tradition, one could justify rigid disciplinary boundaries on the grounds of Aristotle's *Posterior Analytics*, or one could connect the two by appealing to some passages in Aristotle's *Physics*. This highlights how even in a relatively small subculture (Western-European astronomy), sufficiently diverse elements are available for renegotiation and reinterpretation of that subculture. This elasticity of culture tends to be glossed over by discussion of incommensurability in Kuhn and Laudan, yet it is this elasticity that may be at the root of many disagreements.

Another Way of Looking at Incommensurability

The previous remarks indicate a tension in the history and philosophy of science surrounding discussions of incommensurability. On the one hand, the *conceptual* arguments for incommensurability as standardly construed are lacking. Semantic incommensurability rests on a dubious philosophy of language and, were it to exist, it would be both omnipresent and potentially undetectable. Axiological incommensurability stands on somewhat firmer ground, but the evidence for endemic axiological disagreement in the history of science is shaky at best. As the case of Clavius and Kepler shows, we cannot determine whether a given disagreement is axiological or methodological on the basis of the historical data. On the other hand, as our case studies indicate, history abounds with cases that exemplify, if not standard incommensurability, then some failure of communication and/or resolution that closely resembles it. In this brief concluding section, we hope to reconfigure the idea of incommensurability (or to offer a surrogate concept) in a way that respects both the failure of the standard models and the prevalence of historical episodes that are suggestive of incommensurability.

Roughly our suggestion is this: for the most part we should regard incommensurability in terms of the *practical* difficulty that scientists from different theoretical outlooks face as they attempt to reach rational consensus. Consider this old chestnut. As they introduce the subject of incommensurability to their classes, instructors often ask students to consider the following question: "How in the world could Aristotle possibly understand quantum mechanics? Isn't the conceptual gulf between Aristotelian and modern science wide enough to make it virtually impossible for Aristotle to comprehend modern science?" Our deflationary answer to the question (which, incidentally, is also frequently offered by students) is that it would be very difficult for Aristotle to understand quantum mechanics, but not impossible in principle. It would be difficult for him, because, in order to understand where we are now, he might very well have to retrace the path we took to get here. Hence, it is possible that he would have to re-enact in his own head the battles fought by Copernicus, Galileo, Kepler, Newton, Maxwell, Planck, and a host of other physicists, not to mention biologists, chemists, philosophers, and theologians. And, of course, his difficulty would not be merely semantic. In addition to learning the meanings of the relevant theoretical terms, he would have to learn about both the history of experimentation that led to current science as well as the shifting ways in which experiments have been interpreted and deemed to be relevant. His task would be monumental because it would require him to reconsider nearly every facet of his perspective on science. However, "monumental" is not a synonym for "impossible." Perhaps, in this particular case, one could claim that it would be impossible for Aristotle, cursed with a merely human brain-pan and life-span, to come to grips with all of the necessary background material in a matter of a few decades; one could conclude from this that the opposition between sufficiently far-flung theories will lead to practical incommensurability for sufficiently finite beings. The case of Aristotle and quantum mechanics is obviously an extreme one. For the most part, we should grant that, given enough time and effort, one scientist should be able to understand the theories of another, especially for those cases in which the scientists are contemporaries of each other. The cases we discussed in the previous section more realistically instantiate the type and level of difficulty of communication and resolution that have occurred in the history of science.

Now, suppose for the sake of argument that Aristotle could come to understand quantum mechanics, but that it would take ten years of concentrated work for him to do so. We are now faced with the question of why he would want to bother to go through all that extra work in order to understand a new theory. What would his costs be? What would he stand to gain? His decision should be affected by at least the two following factors. First, there is the sacrifice that he would have to make: how much time and effort would he have to expend before being a fluent quantum thinker? What is important here is not so much that we should think of Aristotle as lazy or unwilling to work on something unless there is a quick payoff, but rather we should be aware of the massive sacrifice that Aristotle would have to make in order to devote a substantial portion of his finite intellectual life to the task of comprehending a new theory. In concentrating on learning quantum mechanics for ten years, work on his own program of research would have to stop, or at least be seriously attenuated. Aristotle's perceived net sacrifice is not simply a function of lost time. In assessing his potential loss, he would have to estimate the theoretical gains that he would achieve were he to spend those ten years in developing the theories he held prior to being offered the chance to learn quantum mechanics. Clearly, this sacrifice would be fairly minimal were Aristotle already in a desperate theoretical predicament, and it would be prohibitive were he to be in a period of high productivity and expectations.

If Aristotle were also able to assess the prospective gains to be derived from adopting quantum mechanics, then he would be able to determine whether devoting ten years of his life to learn quantum mechanics would be worth the trouble, all things considered. In that case, he would be able to calculate whether what he would lose by abandoning his old program is outweighed by what he would gain in the long run by learning and then working with quantum mechanics. However in order to decide whether to bother learning quantum mechanics, he would have to assess its likely benefits, and in order to assess its likely benefits, he would surely have to have already learned it. Aristotle is left in a circular or regressive predicament, from which he can escape only if there exists a rough and ready way of evaluating the prospects of a theory about which he has radically incomplete knowledge. Perhaps such ways exist. Maybe Aristotle could lend rational credence to the weight of public opinion: for instance he may think that if all the other scientists are doing it, then, surely it must be a good thing.[51] In most cases, however, such as the case-studies we have discussed, the proponents do have a fairly good idea of the potential benefits to be reaped from the rival programs, or at least of what their interlocutors take to be those benefits.

If we can resolve the circularity problem, we will have succeeded in providing a new analysis of incommensurability, according to which "incommensurability" stands for the practical issues involved in understanding people from different theoretical frameworks. Here, we mean to use "understanding" in the widest possible sense; we want it to include not just understanding the meanings of others' words and the propositional content of their theories, but also understanding the goals that drive them, the inferences they employ, what counts for them as a serious as opposed to a trivial problem, what counts as a solution to a problem, what counts as a problem that must be solved immediately vs. a problem for which the solution can wait, what counts as the procedural rules for their disciplines, in short understanding what makes them tick, epistemically speaking.

Semantic incommensurability, which entails the impossibility of understanding others is a limiting case of our form of incommensurability, for, in addition to countenancing non-semantic forms of incommensurability, our form tries to encompass different *degrees* of difficulty in understanding others. Value incommensurability, on the other hand, initially does not seem to fall under our concept of incommensurability. After all, scientists with different values can often understand each other perfectly easily, at least in principle. Their problem is that they cannot reach rational consensus. In order to retain value incommensurability (and the impossibility of rational consensus which it entails) we could widen our pragmatic notion of incommensurability to include all sources of difficulty in reaching rational consensus, rather than just all sources of difficulty in understanding and the ensuing difficulties in reaching rational consensus. For now, we will leave the matter open, partially because merely broadening incommensurability to degrees of comprehensibility provides us with the conceptual resources for our reconfiguration of incommensurability.

Given our revised concept, theorists who discuss incommensurability will have at least two jobs. First, they will have a descriptive job:

they will be responsible for cataloguing and diagnosing cases of lack of engagement in the history of science. Their second job will be prescriptive: they will be responsible for developing a theory of epistemic rationality and the appropriate formalism for deciding whether and when one should devote one's time to learning more about another radically different theory. In this paper, we have briefly tackled the first task. We shall pursue the second in future papers.

Because it centres on the transaction/opportunity cost of learning and/or pursuing another theory, our account shows how a rational community can be diverse without falling into Feyerabendian intellectual anarchy epitomized by the slogan "Anything goes." Furthermore, it attends to Kuhn's arguments in favour of dogmatism in science while showing that there are rational limits to that dogmatism. In this way, it strikes a reasoned balance between the radically different policies endorsed by the two most influential figures in the history and philosophy of science.

Our account also paves the way for the rational diversity of *types* of cognitive labour. Given the high transaction cost involved in coming to understand another theory from scratch, the scientific community could benefit by having a small number of agents who could best be described as "import and export specialists." These agents would be fluent in two or more theoretical outlooks, and, rather than being researchers per se, their job would be to help researchers minimize the cost of learning other theories.

We do not yet know whether our notion of incommensurability ensures an efficient epistemic market. As Kitcher has noted, an individual's epistemic goals may diverge from the goals of his or her community. For instance, an individual may have the goal of being on the research team that attains the community's goal, while the community merely aims at the goal being achieved, no matter by whom; or, an individual may have the goal of being the person who makes the big discovery, while the community is only concerned that the discovery be made. Our account adds substantially to Kitcher's analysis by factoring in the opportunity cost to a researcher of switching research allegiance in mid-stream. We are still left with some of the questions posed by Kitcher's analysis. For instance, what criterion/a of rationality should we employ in determining whether and when it is rational to give serious consideration to a comparatively alien way of thinking? Furthermore, we have yet to determine whether the sort of rational epistemic diversity provided by our account of incommensurability is such that it maximizes the attainment of community goals. In other words, we have to determine whether incommensurability plays the part of an invisible hand in the marketplace of ideas.

Most importantly, we think that our account of incommensurability has relevance, not just for science (e.g., for understanding the opposition between Kepler and Fabricius) but for all disciplines with a cognitive component. For instance, our account can be applied to our own discipline of philosophy. Analytic philosophers and continental philosophers spend relatively little time talking to each other. Their failure to communicate on a regular basis may not be a sign of intellectual closed-mindedness so much as an indication of workers in two healthy programs distributing their limited time in an optimal way. The same can be said for oppositions in other fields in the humanities: for instance, it may be neither in their own cognitive interests nor in the interests of their community for proponents of different schools of literary criticism to engage each other. Furthermore, since much artistic endeavour and innovation depend on finding new solutions to problems of technique and content, our approach should be generalizable to art, at least to the extent that it is a problem-solving activity with a rich cognitive component.

That said, the possibility of a rational lack of debate between analytic and continental thinkers does not entail that such a lack is automatically rational. There are other possible explanations: one could view analytic and continental philosophers as proponents of degenerating and unproductive programs, and could explain their lack of engagement with each other in brute terms of the will to hang on to whatever turf they have left, come what may. Our reconception of incommensurability offers a template for distinguishing rational from irrational refusals to engage, and we consider this to be one of its major selling points.

There are examples of bodies of literature where analytic and continental philosophers engage each other, for example, in the field of feminist philosophy. Even a cursory glance at feminist philosophy anthologies reveals that not only is there engagement, but there are also "cross-over artists." The reason this isn't blocked by problems of incommensurability, we believe, is in part because the proponents are motivated to engage (in this case there is a politically motivated desire to carve out a new conceptual space that is gender-inclusive) and in part because the root traditions are sufficiently flexible and contain enough conflicting elements to allow border crossings. This echoes Kepler's strategy of using conflicting elements within the received tradition to construct an approach to astronomy that opposes that tradition.

Since our examples have been drawn from academic subcultures, one question that needs to be addressed is whether our analysis can be applied to issues about cultures more generally. There is some reason to suppose that it can, at the very least, inform debates about and within cultures. Cultures as communities, cultures as social mechanisms, culture as problem-solving units, all of these ideas of culture crucially depend on the premise that cultures allow for the communication of information and, within certain bounds, the resolution of disagreements. Realistically speaking, cultures should be seen as perpetually bubbling cauldrons of debate, in which the resolution of one difference is often followed by the creation of several more. With the explosion in scientific knowledge of the last four hundred years, we have come to realize that no single person can hope to become acquainted with, let alone master all the debates in all the fields with substantial cognitive content. However, many people remain under the sway of the belief that *within* one's field, one should be aware of all of the major rival theories and able to participate in the major debates. A failure to engage with a rival is usually seen as a mark of disrespect and as a tacit acknowledgment of the rival theory's ultimate worthlessness; it means, in short, that if I'm not talking to you then I think that you are not worth talking (or listening) to. Since our theory is opposed to this dismissive interpretation of a failure to engage, it allows us to re-approach the concept of culture on several basic issues, such as the tolerance of difference within a culture, the epistemic responsibilities of intellectual workers within a culture, the basic nature of respect for other persons, and the connection between what a culture can be said to "know" and what individuals within it know. It is pretty obvious that there is a feedback system between what a culture "knows" and what an individual knows. We wish to emphasize that given various pragmatic considerations individuals can and do resist or abstain from embracing all beliefs of the culture or subculture they work in. This contributes to the sometimes contradictory nature of cultural trends and supplies some of the means for cross-cultural communication. Our account indicates when it makes sense for the individual to resist taking on certain cultural beliefs. At the very least, our account sheds some light on one of the most pervasive and perhaps important, but yet ignored, aspects of working within a diverse intellectual community, namely the issue of the rationality of simply ignoring others. In certain cases, not only would this failure to pay attention be rationally permissible, it would be obligatory, even for the most intellectually unselfish member of a community. However, our account places limits on the rationality of the failure to listen, limits that we feel are often sadly unobserved.

We are often motivated by political, economic, and ethical concerns to bridge the gap between cultures or subcultures. In some cases the concerns are large enough to outweigh the pragmatic difficulties inherent in reaching understanding. Our account of incommensurability does not even pretend to offer a means of accessing some universal set of standards that can be appealed to in bridging this gap. In some cases (especially those pertaining to human rights violations), this is unfortunate. If we are stuck with some form of incommensurability, then we are, however, better off with our pragmatic notion rather than with the axiological or semantic versions. Unlike these versions, pragmatic incommensurability allows, given a favourable cost-benefit analysis, the possibility of rational conflict resolution and communication.

Notes

1. Thanks to Bob Bright, Ben Caplan, Joyce Jenkins, Rob Shaver, and two anonymous reviewers for their helpful comments on earlier versions of this paper. Thanks also to Adam Muller for his careful editing and useful suggestions. Special thanks to Sylvia Wrogemann for collecting much of the source material used in this essay. This paper was funded in part by Social Sciences and Humanities Research Council of Canada.
2. I. Scheffler, *Science and Subjectivity* (Indianapolis: Bobbs Merrill, 1967).
3. Thomas Kuhn, *The Structure of Scientific Revolutions* (Chicago: University of Chicago Press, 1970).
4. David Bloor, *Knowledge and Social Imagery* (London: Routledge, 1974).
5. Roger Kimball, "When Reason Sleeps: The Academy vs. Science," *The New Criterion* 12, no. 9 (1994): 10–18.
6. Charles Taylor, "Rationality," in *Rationality and Relativism*, ed. Martin Hollis and Steven Lukes (Oxford: Blackwell, 1982), 87–105.
7. Paul Feyerabend, "Explanation, Reduction, and Empiricism," in *Minnesota Studies in the Philosophy of Science*, ed. H Feigl and G. Maxwell (Minneapolis: University of Minnesota Press, 1962), 28–97.
8. T.S. Kuhn, *The Copernican Revolution: Planetary Astronomy in the Development of Western Thought* (Cambridge, MA: Harvard University Press, 1985).
9. Feyerabend, "Explanation, Reduction, and Empiricism," 39.
10. For more on the foundations and plausibility of holism, see Gerry Fodor and Ernest Lepore, *Holism: A Shopper's Guide* (Cambridge MA: Blackwell, 1992).
11. Kuhn's use of "paradigm" is actually multiply ambiguous, but we need not concern ourselves with this issue for the purposes of this paper.
12. T.S. Kuhn, "Objectivity, Value Judgment, and Theory Choice," in *Philosophy of Science: The Central Issues*, ed. M. Curd and J.A. Cover (New York: W.W. Norton, 1998), 102–18.
13. For such a view of Kuhn, see Harold I. Brown, *Rationality* (London: Routledge, 1990).
14. Many philosophers and scientists would deny the incompatibility of quantum mechanics with the existence a true and unified description of the entire physical universe. However, a resolution of the debate over quantum reality is not within the scope of this paper. What is important is that Laudan takes the incompatibility seriously.
15. Larry Laudan, "Progress or Rationality: The Prospects for Normative Naturalism," *American Philosophical Quarterly* 24 (1987): 19–31.
16. Philip Kitcher, *The Advancement of Science* (Oxford: Oxford University Press, 1993).
17. Bas van Fraassen, *The Scientific Image* (Oxford: Oxford University Press, 1980).
18. Kitcher, *The Advancement of Science*.
19. Antonio Gramsci, "Culture and Ideological Hegemony," in *Culture and Society, Contemporary Debates*, ed. Jeffrey Alexander and Steven Seidman (New York: Cambridge University Press, 1998), 47–54.
20. Kepler suggested that the gravitational pull of the moon caused the tidal motion. Galileo was aware of Kepler's hypothesis and had the following to say: "But among all the great men who have philosophized about this remarkable effect, I am more astonished at Kepler than at any other … he has nevertheless lent his ear and his assent to the moon's dominion over the waters, to occult properties, and to such puerilities" (Galileo, *Dialogue*, 462).
21. Johannes Kepler, *Gesammelte Werke* (hereafter *KGW*), VII, 7, 9. Editor's note: this collection of works was produced over a long period of time, each volume with different translators. Subsequent entries identity the volume number, date of publication, and its relevant translator as per disciplinary convention.

22 Jardine compares Kepler's and Clavius's versions of realism in detail in N. Jardine, "The Forging of Modern Realism: Clavius and Kepler against the Sceptics," *Studies in History and Philosophy of Science* 10 (1979): 141–73.

23 Actually, prior to Kepler's work, the mean sun rather than the true sun was used in planetary models. The mean sun is an empty point in space a short distance from the sun.

24 J.M. Lattis, *Between Copernicus and Galileo: Christoph Clavius and the Collapse of Ptolemaic Cosmology* (Chicago: University of Chicago Press, 1994), 131–32.

25 Christoph Clavius, "Commentary on the 'Sphere' of Sacrobosco," in *Between Copernicus and Galileo*, ed. J.M. Lattis, 134–35.

26 *KGW* I, 15, translated by Duncan 1981, 75.

27 *KGW* XX, 1, 21, translated by Jardine 1984, 140.

28 Harper and Smith refer to this as "systematic dependencies" in W. Harper and G. Smith, "Newton's New Way of Inquiry," in *The Creation of Ideas in Physics*, ed. J. Leplin (Netherlands: Kluwer, 1995), 113–16.

29 In the writing of this paper, we encountered problems of incommensurability. One author holds that the presence of systematic dependencies is clear evidence for the evidential superiority of the Copernican system and the other does not! Philosophers of science still debate the virtues of predictions versus explanations, and the question of how seriously to take prohibitions on ad hoc modifications.

30 From the General Scholium added in the second edition of the *Principia*. As William Harper (personal communication) points out, a mere hypothesis is not deduced from phenomena.

31 R. Martens, *Kepler's Philosophy and the New Astronomy* (Princeton: Princeton University Press, 2000), esp. ch. 2.

32 Methuen focuses on this metaphor in the works of Maestlin, Kepler, and others in C. Methuen, *Kepler's Tübingen: Stimulus to a Theological Mathematics* (Aldershot, UK: Ashgate, 1998), ch. 4.

33 Maestlin taught Kepler astronomy at the University of Tübingen. Maestlin was a significant advocate of Copernicanism. He was impressed by the mathematical elegance of the Copernican system and argued that the comet of 1577 could only be accounted for by a heliocentric theory (Westman 1975, 333). In addition, Maestlin helped Kepler with technical matters in Kepler's first book, the *Mysterium cosmographicum*, and helped promote the work once published. They remained in contact throughout Keplers life. Fabricius was a well-known astronomer with whom Kepler maintained a friendly competition. Fabricius comments and criticisms of Keplers work significantly influenced the writing of Kepler's *Astronomia nova* (see Voelkel, *The Composition of Kepler's Astronomia Nova*).

34 J. Kepler, *New Astronomy*, trans. W.H. Donahue (New York: Cambridge University Press, 1992).

35 J. Barnes, *The Complete Works of Aristotle: The Revised Oxford Translation* (Princeton: Princeton University Press, 1984), 71b10–25, 73a3, 75a38–b20, 79a8–12, 81b4.

36 Martens, *Kepler's Philosophy and the New Astronomy*, ch. 5.

37 There are other violations of a more technical nature; see Kuhn, *The Copernican Revolution*, 69–77.

38 N. Jardine, *The Birth of History and Philosophy of Science: Kepler's a Defense of Tycho against Ursus with Essays on Its Provenance and Significance* (Cambridge: Cambridge University Press, 1984), ch. 7.

39 Westman, "The Astronomer's Role in the Sixteenth Century," 105–8.

40 Voelkl, *The Composition of Kepler's Astronomia Nova*, 322–27

41 Letter of Kepler to Fabricius, Nov. 10, 1608 translated in Baumgardt, *Johannes Kepler*, 81; *KGW* XVI, 205.

42 *KGW* XVII, 201–2.

43 *Apologia*, 177; *KGW* XX.1, 43.

44 Martens discusses this in more detail in Martens, *Kepler's Philosophy and the New Astronomy*, ch. 5.

45 Maestlin's letter to Kepler, September 21, 1616; *KGW* XVII, 186–88.

46 As Kepler observes [*KGW* I, 9].

47 Kuhn, *The Structure of Scientific Revolutions*, 10–23.

48 *KGW* XV, 378.

49 *KGW* XV, 379.

50 From *Novae planetarum*, translated in Methuen, *Kepler's Tübingen: Stimulus to a Theological Mathematics*, 83.

51 Whether or not there is a way out of the circle is a serious question, and we will provide some brief remarks concerning it later in the paper, but for the purposes of this paper let us merely say that it is a problem which must be addressed if our account of incommensurability is to be worked out in full detail.

CONTRIBUTORS

Born in France in 1907, JACQUES BARZUN came to the United States in 1920. After graduating from Columbia College, he joined the faculty of the university, becoming Seth Low Professor of History and, for a decade, Dean of Faculties and Provost. The author of some thirty books, he received the Gold Medal for Criticism from the American Academy of Arts and Letters, of which he was twice president.

CHRISTOPH BRUMANN did his undergraduate and graduate studies in anthropology, Japanology, and Sinology at the University of Cologne. In 1998–99 he was a research fellow at the National Museum of Ethnology in Osaka. Since 1999 he has been a Lecturer at the Department of Ethnology at the University of Cologne. His research interests include townscape and heritage disputes, communitarian groups, utopian communes, gift exchange, the concept of culture, and globalization.

GEOFFREY H. HARTMAN is Sterling Professor (Emeritus) of English and Comparative Literature at Yale University, and the Project Director of Yale's Fortunoff Video Archive for Holocaust Testimonies. His many books include *Scars of the Spirit* (2002), *The Longest Shadow: In the Aftermath of the Holocaust* (1996), *Easy Pieces* (1985), and *Saving the Text: Literature, Derrida, Philosophy* (1981).

METTE HJORT is Professor of Intercultural Studies at Aalborg University, Denmark, Visiting Research Associate with the Kwan Fung Cultural Research and Development Program, Lingnan University, Hong Kong, and Honorary Associate Professor at the University of Hong Kong. She is the author of *The Strategy of Letters* (1993) and *Small Nation, Global Cinema* (forthcoming), and, with Ib Bondebjerg, of an interview book entitled *The Danish Directors: Dialogues on a Contemporary National Cinema* (2001). She is the editor or co-editor of *Rules and Conventions* (1992), *Emotion and the Arts* (1997), *Cinema and Nation* (2000), *The Postnational Self* (2002), and *Purity and Provocation: Dogma 95* (2003). She has translated two books, *Food for Thought* (1989) and *To Destroy Painting* (1994), both by Louis Marin.

RHONDA MARTENS is an Associate Professor in the University of Manitoba's Philosophy Department. She was recently a Fellow at MIT's Dibner Institute for the History of Science and Technology. She is the author of *Kepler's Philosophy and the New Astronomy* (2000) and the articles "A Commentary on Genesis: Plato's 'Timaeus' and Kepler's Astronomy" in *Plato's* Timaeus *as Cultural Icon*, edited by Gretchen Reydam-Schils (2001) and "Kepler's Solution to the Problem of a Realist Celestial Mechanics," in *Studies in History and Philosophy of Science* (1999).

CARL A. MATHESON is Professor and Head of the Philosophy Department at the University of Manitoba. His areas of specializations include aesthetics, metaphysics, and the history and philosophy of science. He has published widely on topics including *The Simpsons*, historicist theories of rationality, chaos, and jazz in such publications as *The British Journal of Aesthetics*, *The Journal of Aesthetics and Art Criticism*, and *Philosophy and Literature*.

ADAM MULLER is an Assistant Professor in the University of Manitoba's Department of English and currently a Visiting Scholar in the English Department at Cornell University. His areas of research specialization include critical theory, cultural studies, modernism, South African literature, narrative film and film theory, and literary exile, and he has published in these areas in such places as *Cultural Critique, Semiotic Inquiry, Textual Studies in Canada,* and *The Johns Hopkins Guide to Literary Theory and Criticism.*

DAVID NOVITZ was a Reader in Philosophy at the University of Canterbury, New Zealand, where he taught the philosophy of art, ethics, and the history of philosophy. His many publications include *Pictures and Their Use in Communication* (1977), *Knowledge, Fiction and Imagination* (1987), and *The Boundaries of Art* (1992), as well as numerous journal articles. He also co-edited two well-known collections of essays on New Zealand society, *Culture and Identity in New Zealand* (1989) and *New Zealand in Crisis* (1992), together with sociologist Bill Willmott.

MARTHA NUSSBAUM is Ernst Freund Distinguished Service Professor of Law and Ethics at the University of Chicago. She holds appointments in the Law School, the Philosophy Department, and the Divinity School, and is an Associate Member of the Classics Department. Related publications include *The Quality of Life* (1993, edited with Amartya Sen), *Women, Culture, and Development* (1995, edited with Jonathan Glover), *Sex and Social Justice* (1998), and *Women and Human Development: The Capabilities Approach* (Cambridge, 2000). From 1986 to 1993, Professor Nussbaum was a Research Advisor at the World Institute for Development Economics Research, Helsinki (a division of the United Nations University), where she worked with Amartya Sen, directing a project on the measurement of quality of life.

JIM PARRY is former Head of the Department of Philosophy and the School of Humanities at the University of Leeds, England, and is a member of its Centre for Business and Professional Ethics and its Centre for Physical Education and Sport Science. His academic expertise is in applied ethics, and he has extensive experience of working with practitioners in many fields in considering the ethical implications of their professional activities. In the area of sport, this includes consultancy with the International Olympic Committee (Lausanne and Paris), the Football Association (London), the European Community's Group on Ethics (Brussels), the United Nations (Kosovo), and the

International Olympic Academy (Ancient Olympia). He is co-editor of the Routledge series *Ethics and Sport*, and co-author of *The Olympic Games Explained*.

MARTIN ROBERTS received a Ph.D. in French literature from Cambridge University and has been teaching at The New School since 1997. He has also taught at New York University, MIT, and Harvard University. His research interests centre on media and cultural studies, with a focus on globalization and popular culture. His publications include articles on ethnography and surrealism, world music, and the global documentary film *Baraka*. More recent publications focus on the role of media in the formation of national and transnational identities, including chapters for a recent anthology on cinema and nationalism and a forthcoming collection on the Danish Dogme 95 group. His current research focuses on globalization and subcultures.

ROBERT STECKER is Professor of Philosophy at Central Michigan University. He is the author of numerous papers on the philosophy of art, of mind, the history of modern philosophy, and ethics, as well as several books including *Artworks: Definition, Meaning, Value* (1997), *Interpretation and Construction: Art, Speech, and the Law* (2003), and *Aesthetics and the Philosophy of Art: An Introduction* (2005).

IMRE SZEMAN is Senator William McMaster Chair of Globalization and Cultural Studies at McMaster University. He is author most recently of *Zones of Instability: Literature, Postcolonialism and the Nation* (2003) and co-editor of the second edition of *The Johns Hopkins Guide to Literary Theory and Criticism* (2005).

BIBLIOGRAPHY

Mrs. Rupan Deol Baja and Another V. Kanwar Pal Singh Gill and Another, 309 AIR (1996).

Abu-Lughod, Lila. "The Interpretation of Culture(s) after Television." *Representations* 59 (1997): 109–34.

———. "Writing against Culture." In *Recapturing Anthropology: Working in the Present*, edited by Richard G. Fox, 137–62. Santa Fe: School of American Research Press, 1991.

———. *Writing Women's Worlds: Bedouin Stories*. Berkeley and Los Angeles: University of California Press, 1993.

Achinstein, Peter. *Concepts of Science*. Baltimore: Johns Hopkins University Press, 1968.

Adorno, Theodor. *Aesthetic Theory*. Translated by Robert Hullot-Kentor. Minneapolis: University of Minnesota Press, 1998.

———. "On the Question: 'What Is German?'" In *Critical Models: Interventions and Catchwords*, translated by Henry W. Pickford, 205–14. New York: Columbia University Press, 1998.

Agarwal, Bina. *A Field of One's Own: Gender and Land Rights in South Asia*. Cambridge: Cambridge University Press, 1994.

———. "'Bargaining' and Gender Relations: Within and Beyond the Household," *Feminist Economics* 3 (1997): 1–51

Ahmad, Imtiaz, ed. *Modernization and Social Change among Muslims in India*. Delhi: Manohar, 1983.

Ahmed-Ghosh, Huma. "Preserving Identity: A Case Study of Palitpur." In *Forging Identities: Gender, Communities, and the State in India*, edited by Zoya Hasan, 169–87. Boulder, CO: Westview Press, 1994.

Alexander, Jeffrey C. "Analytic Debates: Understanding the Relative Autonomy of Culture." In *Culture and Society: Contemporary Debates*, edited by Jeffrey Alexander and Stephen Seidman, 1–30. Cambridge: Cambridge University Press, 1998.

Amit-Talai, Vered. "Anthropology, Multiculturalism, and the Concept of Culture." *Folk* 37 (1995): 135–44.

Amit-Talai, Vered, and Helena Wulff, eds. *Youth Cultures: A Cross-Cultural Perspective*. London: Routledge, 1995.

Anderson, Perry. "Components of the National Culture." *New Left Review* 50 (1968): 3–58.

Angrosino, Michael V. "The Culture Concept and the Mission of the Roman Catholic Church." *American Anthropologist* 96 (1994): 824–32.

Appadurai, Arjun. *Modernity at Large: Cultural Dimensions of Globalization*. Minneapolis: University of Minnesota Press, 1996.

Arendt, Hannah. *Between Past and Future*. New York: Viking, 1961.

———. "The Crisis in Culture." In *Between Past and Future*, 197–226. New York: Viking, 1961.

———. *Essays in Understanding, 1930–1945*. Edited by Jerome Kohn. New York: Harcourt Brace, 1994.

Arnold, Matthew. *Culture and Anarchy*. Edited by J. Dover Wilson. 1869. Cambridge: Cambridge University Press, 1963.

Ascheid, Antje. "Speaking Tongues: Voice Dubbing in the Cinema as Cultural Ventriloquism." *The Velvet Light Trap* 40, no. 3 (1997): 32–41.

Ashcroft, Bill, Gareth Griffiths, and Helen Tiffin. *Key Concepts in Postcolonial Studies*. New York: Routledge, 1998.

Assmann, Aleida, and Jan Assmann. "Kultur und Konflikt: Aspekte einer Theorie des unkommunikativen Handelns." In *Kultur und Konflikt*, edited by Jan Assmann and Dietrich Harth, 35. Frankfurt-am-Main: Suhrkamp, 1990.

Auerbach, Erich. "La Cour et la Ville." In *Scenes from the Drama of European Literature*, translated by Ralph Mannheim, 133–79. Minneapolis: University of Minnesota Press, 1984.

Axford, Barrie. *The Global System: Economics, Politics and Culture*. Oxford: Polity Press, 1995.

Bachmann-Melik, Doris. "Weltweite Vogelperspektive: Anthropologische und postkoloniale Herausforderungen der Literaturwissenschaft." *Frankfurter Rundschau*, December 10, 1996.

Bacon, Francis, and G.W. Kitchin. *The Advancement of Learning*. London: Dent, 1973.

Balibar, Étienne, and Pierre Macherey. "On Literature as an Ideological Form: Some Marxist Propositions." In *Untying the Text: A Post-Structuralist Reader*, edited by Robert Young, 79–99. London: Routledge & Kegan Paul, 1981.

Bardhan, Kalpana. *Of Women, Outcastes, Peasants and Rebels: A Selection of Bengali Short Stories*. Berkeley: University of California Press, 1990.

Barnard, Alan, and Jonathan Spencer. "Culture." In *Encyclopedia of Social and Cultural Anthropology*, edited by Alan Barnard and Jonathan Spencer, 136–43. London: Routledge, 1996.

————, eds. *Encyclopedia of Social and Cultural Anthropology*. London: Routledge, 1996.

Barnes, J. *The Complete Works of Aristotle: The Revised Oxford Translation*. Princeton: Princeton University Press, 1984.

Barrett, Stanley R. *Anthropology: A Student's Guide to Theory and Method*. Toronto: University of Toronto Press, 1996.

Barth, Fredrik. "A Personal View of Present Tasks and Priorities in Cultural and Social Anthropology." In *Assessing Cultural Anthropology*, edited by Robert Borofsky, 349–60. New York: McGraw-Hill, 1994.

Bateson, Gregory. *Steps to an Ecology of Mind; Collected Essays in Anthropology, Psychiatry, Evolution, and Epistemology*. San Francisco: Chandler, 1972.

Baudrillard, Jean. *La Guerre du golfe n'a pas eu lieu*. Paris: Galilee, 1991.

Baumgardt, C. *Johannes Kepler: Life and Letters*. New York: Philosophical Library, 1951.

Beardsley, Monroe. *Aesthetics: Problems in the Theory of Criticism*. New York: Harcourt, Brace and World, 1958.

Beardsley, Monroe. "Art and its Cultural Context." In *The Aesthetic Point of View: Selected Essays*, edited by Michael J. Wreen and Donald M. Callen, 352–70. Ithaca, NY: Cornell University Press, 1982.

Becker, Ernest. *The Lost Science of Man*. New York: Braziller, 1971.

Becker, Gary S. "The Economic Way of Looking at Behavior." In *The Essence of Becker*, edited by Ramón Febrero and Pedro S. Schwartz, 647–48. Stanford, CA: Hoover Institution Press, 1995.

————. *A Treatise on the Family*. Cambridge, MA: Harvard University Press, 1981.

Bell, Bernard Iddings, and Cicero Bruce. *Crowd Culture: An Examination of the American Way of Life*. 4th ed. Wilmington, DE: ISI Books, 2001.

Bell, Clive. *Art*. London: Chatto and Windus, 1914.

Bellah, Robert N. *The Broken Covenant: American Civil Religion in a Time of Trial*. Chicago: Chicago University Press, 1992.

Benedict, Ruth. *Patterns of Culture*. Boston: Houghton Mifflin, 1989.

Benjamin, Walter. "The Work of Art in the Age of Mechanical Reproduction." In *Illuminations: Essays and Reflections*, 217–51. New York: Schocken Books, 1968.

Bernal, Martin. *Black Athena: The Afroasiatic Roots of Classical Civilization*. New Brunswick, NJ: Rutgers University Press, 1989.

Bernard, H. Russell, ed. *Handbook of Methods in Cultural Anthropology*. Walnut Creek, CA: AltaMira Press, 1998.

Blanchot, Maurice. *L'écriture du désastre*. Paris: Gallimard, 1980.

Bloom, Harold. *The American Religion: The Emergence of the Post-Christian Nation*. New York: Simon and Schuster, 1992.

Bloor, David. *Knowledge and Social Imagery*. London: Routledge, 1974.

Blumenthal, Albert. *The Best Definition of Culture*. Marietta, OH: Marietta College Press, 1937.

Boas, Franz. "Anthropology." In *Encyclopedia of the Social Sciences*, edited by Edwin R.A. Seligman, 73–110. New York: Macmillan, 1930.

Boas, Franz. "History and Science in Anthropology: A Reply." In *Race, Language, and Culture*, 305–11. Chicago: University of Chicago Press, 1982.

―――. *Race, Language, and Culture.* Chicago: University of Chicago Press, 1982.

Boddy, Janice, and Michael Lambek. "Introduction: Culture in Question." *Social Analysis* 41, no. 3 (1997): 3–23.

Bordwell, David. *Planet Hong Kong: Popular Cinema and the Art of Entertainment.* Cambridge, MA: Harvard University Press, 2000.

Borofsky, Robert. "On the Knowledge and Knowing of Cultural Activities." In *Assessing Cultural Anthropology*, edited by Robert Borofsky, 331–47. New York: McGraw-Hill, 1994.

―――. "Rethinking the Cultural." In *Assessing Cultural Anthropology*, edited by Robert Borofsky, 243–49. New York: McGraw-Hill, 1994.

Bourdieu, Pierre. *Acts of Resistance: Against the Tyranny of the Market.* Translated by Richard Nice. New York: The New Press, 1998.

―――. *Distinction: A Social Critique of the Judgement of Taste.* Translated by Richard Nice. Cambridge, MA: Harvard University Press, 1984.

―――. *La Distinction: Critique Sociale du Jugement.* Paris: Editions de Minuit, 1979.

―――. *The Field of Cultural Production: Essays on Art and Literature.* Edited by Randal Johnson. New York: Columbia University Press, 1993.

―――. *Outline of a Theory of Practice.* Cambridge: Cambridge University Press, 1977.

―――. *The Rules of Art: Genesis and Structure of the Literary Field.* Translated by Susan Emanuel. Stanford, CA: Stanford University Press, 1996.

Bourdieu, Pierre, and Jean-Claude Passeron. *La Reproduction: Eléments pour une théorie du système d'enseignement.* Paris: Minuit, 1970.

―――. "Literate Tradition and Social Conservation." In *Reproduction in Education, Society and Culture.* London: Sage, 1990.

Boutang, Pierre, and George Steiner. *Dialogues: Sur le Mythe d'Antigone/Sur le Sacrifice d'Abraham.* Paris: Lattès, 1994.

Breckenridge, Carol A., Sheldon Pollock, Homi K. Bhabha, and Dipesh Chakrabarty, eds. *Cosmopolitanism.* Durham, NC: Duke University Press, 2002.

Brightman, Robert. "Forget Culture: Replacement, Transcendence, Relexification." *Cultural Anthropology* 10 (1995): 509–46.

Bromwich, David. *Politics by Other Means: Higher Education and Group Thinking.* New Haven, CT: Yale University Press, 1992.

Brooks, Van Wyck. *America's Coming-of-Age.* New York: B.W. Huebsch, 1915.

―――. *The Early Years: A Selection from His Works, 1908–21.* Edited by Claire Sprague. New York: Harper and Row, 1968.

―――. *Letters and Leadership.* New York: B.W. Huebsch, 1918.

Brown, Donald E. *Human Universals.* Philadelphia: Temple University Press, 1991.

Brown, Harold I. *Rationality.* London: Routledge, 1990.

Brown, Wendy. *States of Injury.* Princeton: Princeton University Press, 1995.

Brudney, Daniel. *Reclaiming the History of Ethics: Essays for John Rawls.* Cambridge: Cambridge University Press, 1997.

Brumann, Christoph. "The Anthropological Study of Globalization: Towards an Agenda for the Second Phase." *Anthropos* 93 (1998): 495–506.

Buck-Morss, Susan. *Dreamworld and Catastrophe.* New York: MIT Press, 2001.

Bull, Martin. "Between the Cultures of Capital." *New Left Review* 11 (2001): 95–114.

Burtless, Gary, et al. *Globaphobia: Confronting Fears about Open Trade.* Washington: Brookings Institute, 1998.

Burton, Michael L., Carmella M. Moore, John M.W. Whiting, and A. Kimball Romney. "Regions Based on Social Structure." *Current Anthropology* 37 (1996): 87–123.

Calleo, David P. *Coleridge and the Idea of the Modem State.* New Haven, CT: Yale University Press, 1966.

Camper, Fred. "Out of the Shadows." *Chicago Reader,* 18 September 1998.

Canadian Multiculturalism Act (R.S. 1985, c. 24 [4th Supp.]).

Carl-Diem-Institut, ed. *The Olympic Idea: Pierre de Coubertin, Discourses and Essays.* Stuttgart: Olympischer Sportverlag, 1966.

Carroll, Noel. "Anglo-American Aesthetic and Contemporary Criticism: Intention and the Hermeneutics If Suspicion." In *Beyond Aesthetics,* 180–90. Cambridge: Cambridge University Press, 2001.

———. *Beyond Aesthetics: Selected Essays.* Cambridge: Cambridge University Press, 2001.

Cassirer, Ernst. *Logic of the Humanities [Kulturwissenschaften].* Translated by C.S. Howe. New Haven: Yale University Press, 1961.

Cavell, Stanley. *The Claim of Reason: Wittgenstein, Skepticism, Morality, and Tragedy.* New York: Oxford University Press, 1979.

Cerroni-Long, E.L. "Theory in Cultural Context." *Positions* 4 (1996): 173–81.

Cerroni-Long, E.L. "Insider or Native Anthropology?" In *Insider Anthropology,* edited by E.L. Cerroni-Long, 1–16. Arlington, VA: American Anthropological Association/NAPA, 1995.

Certeau, Michel de. *L'Écriture de l'histoire.* Paris: Gallimard, 1975.

Chambers, Iain. *Culture after Humanism.* New York: Routledge, 2001.

Chen, L., E. Huq, and S. D'Souza. "Sex Bias in the Family Allocation of Food and Health Care in Rural Bangladesh." *Population and Development Review* 7 (1981): 55–70.

Chen, Martha Alter. *A Quiet Revolution: Women in Transition in Rural Bangladesh.* Cambridge, MA: Schenkman, 1983.

Clausen, Christopher. "'National Literatures' in English: Toward a New Paradigm." *New Literary History* 25, no. 1 (1994): 61–72.

———. "Nostalgia, Freedom, and the End of Cultures." *Queen's Quarterly* 106, no. 2 (1999): 233–44.

Clavius, Christoph. "Commentary on the 'Sphere' of Sacrobosco." In *Between Copernicus and Galileo: Christoph Clavius and the Collapse of Ptolemaic Cosmology,* edited by J.M. Lattis, 134–35. Chicago: University of Chicago Press, 1994.

Clifford, James. *The Predicament of Culture: Twentieth-Century Ethnography, Literature, and Art.* Cambridge: Harvard University Press, 1988.

Clifford, James, and George Marcus, eds. *Writing Culture: The Poetics and Politics of Ethnography.* Berkeley: University of California Press, 1986.

Collective, Women of South Asian Descent. *Our Feet Walk the Sky: Women of the South Asian Diaspora.* San Francisco: Aunt Lute Books, 1993.

Coubertin, P. de "Forty Years of Olympism (1894/1934)." In *The Olympic Idea: Pierre de Coubertin, Discourses and Essays,* edited by Carl-Diem-Institut, 126–30. Stuttgart: Olympischer Sportverlag, 1934.

Cowie, Peter, ed. *World Cinema: Diary of a Day. A Celebration of the Centenary of Cinema.* Woodstock, NY: Overlook Press, 1994.

Crocker, David. "Functioning and Capability: The Foundations of Sen's and Nussbaum's Development Ethic, Part I." *Political Theory* 20 (1992): 584–612.

Culler, Jonathan, and Kevin Lamb, eds. *Just Being Difficult? Academic Writing in the Public Arena.* Baltimore: Johns Hopkins University Press, 2003.

Cultural Industries Sectoral Advisory Group on International Trade. *Canadian Culture in a Global World: New Strategies for Culture and Trade.* Ottawa: DFAIT, 1999.

Currie, Gregory. *The Nature of Fiction.* Cambridge: Cambridge University Press, 1990.

———. *An Ontology of Art.* Basingstoke: Macmillan, 1989.

D'Andrade, Roy. "Culture." In *The Social Science Encyclopedia*, edited by Adam Kuper and Jessica Kuper, 161–63. London: Routledge, 1996.

———. *The Development of Cognitive Anthropology.* Cambridge: Cambridge University Press, 1995.

———. "Moral Models in Anthropology." *Current Anthropology* 36 (1995): 399–410.

D'Souza, Dinesh. *Illiberal Education.* New York: Free Press, 1991.

Dahlén, Tommy. *Among the Interculturalists: An Emergent Profession and Its Packaging of Knowledge.* Stockholm: Almqvist & Wiksell, 1997.

Dale, Peter N. *The Myth of Japanese Uniqueness.* New York: St. Martin's Press, 1986.

Danto, Arthur. "The Artworld." *Journal of Philosophy* 61 (1964): 571–84.

Danto, Arthur. *The Transfiguration of the Commonplace.* Cambridge, MA: Harvard University Press, 1981.

Darnell, Regna. "The Anthropological Concept of Culture at the End of the Boasian Century." *Social Analysis* 41, no. 3 (1997): 42–54.

Das, V. "The Anthropological Discourse on India: Reason and Its Other." In *Assessing Cultural Anthropology*, edited by Robert Borofsky, 133–44. New York: McGraw-Hill, 1994.

Das, Veena, and Ralph Nicholas. "'Welfare' and 'Well-Being' in South Asian Societies." edited by Social Science Research Council. New York: ACLS-SSRC Joint Committee on South Asia, 1981.

Dasgupta, Partha. *An Inquiry into Well-Being and Destitution.* Oxford: Clarendon Press, 1993.

Davies, David. "Interpretive Pluralism and the Ontology of Art." *Revue Internationale de Philosophie* 50 (1996): 577–91.

Davies, Stephen. *Definitions of Art.* Ithaca, NY: Cornell University Press, 1991.

Davis, Robert Con, and Ronald Schliefer. *Contemporary Literary Criticism: Literary and Cultural Studies.* White Plains, NY: Longman, 1994.

Debord, Guy. *La Société du spectacle.* Paris: Bucliet/Chastel, 1967.

Dennett, Daniel C. *Brainstorms: Philosophical Essays on Mind and Psychology.* Sussex: Harvester Press, 1981.

Derrida, Jacques. *Glas.* Paris: Galilée, 1974.

———. "How to Avoid Speaking: Denials." In *Languages of the Unsayable*, edited by Sanford Budik and Wolfgang Iser, 3–69. New York: Columbia University Press, 1989.

————. "The Other Heading: Memories, Responses, and Responsibilities." *PMLA* 108 (1993): 89–93.

Derrida, Jacques. *Psyché: Inventions de l'autre*. Paris: Galilee, 1987.

Devereaux, Mary. "Beauty and Evil: The Case of Leni Riefenstahl's the Triumph of the Will." In *Aesthetics and Ethics: Essays at the Intersection*, edited by Jerrold Levinson, 227–56. Cambridge: Cambridge University Press, 1998.

Devi, Ganesh N. "The Multicultural Context of Indian Literature in English." In *Crisis and Creativity in the New Literatures in English*, edited by Geoffrey Davis and Hena Maes-Jelinek, 345–53. Amsterdam: Rodopi, 1990.

Devji, Faisal Fatehali. "Gender and the Politics of Space: The Movement for Women's Reform, 1857–1900." In *Forging Identities: Gender Communities and the State in India*, edited by Zoya Hasan, 22–37. Delhi: Kali for Women, and Boulder, CO: Westview Press, 1994.

Diawara, Manthia. *African Cinema: Politics and Culture*. Bloomington: Indiana University Press, 1992.

Dickie, George. *The Art Circle*. New York: Haven Publications, 1984.

Dilthey, Wilhelm. "The Human Studies." In *Culture and Society: Contemporary Debates*, edited by Jeffrey Alexander and Steven Seidman, 31–38. Cambridge: Cambridge University Press, 1998.

Dorfman, Ariel, and Armand Mattelart. *How to Read Donald Duck*. New York: International General, 1975.

Douglas, Mary. *Purity and Danger: An Analysis of Concepts of Pollution and Taboo*. London: Routledge & Kegan Paul, 1966.

Downey, Gary Lee, and Juan D. Rogers. "On the Politics of Theorizing in a Postmodern Academy." *American Anthropologist* 97 (1995): 269–81.

Drèze, Jean, and Amartya Sen. *India: Development and Participation*. New Delhi: Oxford University Press, 2002.

Driver, Harold. *Indians of North America*. Chicago: University of Chicago Press, 1961.

Dumézil, Georges. *Mythe et Épopée*. Paris: Gallimard, 1968.

Dumont, Louis. *German Ideology: From France to Germany and Back*. Chicago: University of Chicago Press, 1994.

During, B., and J.F. Brisson. "Sport, Olympism and Cultural Diversity." In *For a Humanism of Sport*, edited by B. Jeu et al., Ch. 19. Paris: CNOSF-Editions, 1994.

Dyzenhaus, David. "John Stuart Mill and the Harm of Pornography." In *Mill's on Liberty: Critical Essays*, edited by Gerald Dworkin, 31–54. Lanham, MD: Rowman and Littlefield, 1997.

Eagleton, Terry. *After Theory*. New York: Basic Books, 2003.

————. *The Idea of Culture*. Oxford: Blackwell, 2000.

————. *The Ideology of the Aesthetic*. Malden, MA: Blackwell, 1990.

————. "In the Gaudy Supermarket." *London Review of Books* 21, no. 10 (1999): 13.

————. *Literary Theory: An Introduction*. Minneapolis: University of Minnesota Press, 1983.

————. *The Significance of Theory*. Oxford: Blackwell, 1990.

Egoyan, Atom, and Ian Balfour, eds. *Subtitles: On the Foreignness of Film*. Cambridge, MA: MIT Press, 2004.

Eichberg, H. "Olympic Sport: Neocolonisation and Alternatives." *International Review for Sociology of Sport* 19, no. 1 (1984): 97–104.

Elias, Norbert. *The Civilizing Process*. Cambridge: Blackwell, 1994.

Eliot, T.S. *Notes Towards the Definition of Culture*. London: Faber and Faber, 1948.

Elkins, James. *Pictures and Tears: People Who Have Cried in Front of Paintings*. New York: Routledge, 2001.

Eller, Jack David. "Anti-Anti-Multiculturalism." *American Anthropologist* 99 (1997): 249–60.

Ember, Melvin. "Evolution of the Human Relations Area Files." *Cross-Cultural Research* 31 (1997): 3–15.

Enterline, Lynn. *Pursuing Daphne: Body and Voice in Ovid and Renaissance Ovidian Poetry*. Stanford: Stanford University Press, 1997.

Etlin, Richard A. *In Defense of Humanism: Value in the Arts and Letters*. Cambridge: Cambridge University Press, 1996.

Eyler, M.H. "The Right Stuff." *Proceedings of the International Olympic Academy* 20 (1981): 159–68.

Fanon, Frantz. "On National Culture." In *The Wretched of the Earth*, translated by Constance Farrington, 206–48. London: MacGibbon and Kee, 1965.

Feigl, H., and G. Maxwell, ed. *Minnesota Studies in the Philosophy of Science*. Vol. 3. Minneapolis: University of Minnesota Press, 1962.

Feinberg, Joel. "Liberalism, Community, and Tradition." *Tikkun* 3 (1988): 38–41, 116–20.

Ferenczi, Sandor. *Thalassa: A Theory of Genitality*. New York: Psychoanalytic Quarterly, Inc., 1938.

Fernandez, James W. "Culture and Transcendent Humanization: On the 'Dynamics of the Categorial.'" *Ethnos* 59 (1994): 143–67.

Feyerabend, Paul. *Against Method*. London: Verso, 1975.

———. "Explanation, Reduction, and Empiricism." In *Minnesota Studies in the Philosophy of Science*, vol.3, edited by H. Feigl and G. Maxwell, 28–97. Minneapolis: University of Minnesota Press, 1962.

Finkielkraut, Alain. *La Défaite de la Pensée*. Paris: Gallimard, 1987.

Firth, Raymond. "Contemporary British Social Anthropology." *American Anthropologist* 53 (1951): 474–89.

Fish, Stanley. "The Common Touch, or, One Size Fits All." In *The Politics of Liberal Education*, edited by D.J. Glad and Barbara Herrnstein Smith, 241–66. Durham: Duke University Press, 1993.

Fodor, Gerry, and Ernest Lepore. *Holism: A Shopper's Guide*. Cambridge, MA: Blackwell, 1992.

Fodor, István. *Film Dubbing: Phonetic, Semiotic, Esthetic, and Psychological Aspects*. Hamburg: Buske, 1976.

Ford, James Alfred. *Cultural Dating of Prehistoric Sites in Virú Valley, Peru*. New York: Anthropological Papers of the American Museum of Natural History, 1949.

Fornäs, Johan. *Cultural Theory and Late Modernity*. London: Sage, 1995.

Fortes, Meyer. *The Web of Kinship among the Tallensi*. London: Oxford University Press, 1949.

Foucault, Michel. *The Archaeology of Knowledge.* London: Tavistock Publications, 1972.

———. *The History of Sexuality.* New York: Pantheon Books, 1978.

Fox, Richard G. "Cultural Dis-Integration and the Invention of New Peace-Fares." In *Articulating Hidden Histories: Exploring the Influence of Eric R. Wolf,* edited by Jane Schneider and Rayna Rapp, 275–87. Berkeley: University of California Press, 1995.

———. "For a Nearly New Culture History." In *Recapturing Anthropology: Working in the Present,* edited by Richard G. Fox, 93–113. Santa Fe: School of American Research Press, 1991.

Fraser, Nancy. "Rethinking the Public Sphere." In *Habermas and the Public Sphere,* edited by Craig Calhoun, 109–42. Cambridge, MA: MIT Press, 1992.

Frege, G. "On Sense and Reference." In *Translations from the Philosophical Writings of Gottlob Frege,* edited by Peter Geach and Max Black, 56–78. Oxford: Blackwell, 1966.

Friedman, Jonathan. *Cultural Identity and Global Process.* London: Sage, 1994.

Frow, John, and Meaghan Morris, eds. *Australian Culture Studies.* St. Leonards, NSW: Allen and Unwin, 1993.

Fumaroli, Marc. *L'État culturel: Essai sur une religion moderne.* Paris: Fallois, 1991.

Fussell, Paul. *The Great War and Modern Memory.* New York: Oxford University Press, 1976.

———. *Wartime: Understanding and Behavior in the Second World War.* New York: Oxford University Press, 1989.

Gaita, Raimond. *A Common Humanity: Thinking about Love and Truth and Justice.* New York: Routledge, 2000.

Galileo. *Dialogue Concerning the Two Chief World Systems.* Translated by Stillman Drake. Berkeley: University of California Press, 1962.

Gans, Herbert J. *Popular Culture and High Culture: An Analysis and Evaluation of Taste.* New York: Basic Books, 1974.

Garcia Canclini, Néstor. *Consumers and Citizens: Globalization and Multicultural Conflicts.* Translated by George Yúdice. Minneapolis: University of Minnesota Press, 2001.

Gates Jr., Henry Louis. *Loose Canons: Notes on the Culture Wars.* Oxford: Oxford University Press, 1992.

Gates Jr., Henry Louis. "The Master's Pieces: On Canon Formation and the African-American Tradition." In *The Politics of Liberal Education,* edited by Darryl J. Gless and Barbara Herrnstein Smith, 95–117. Durham, NC: Duke University Press, 1992.

Gates Jr., Henry Louis. "Powell and the Black Elite." *New Yorker,* September 25, 1995, 64–80.

Geertz, Clifford. *The Interpretation of Cultures.* New York: Basic Books, 1973.

———. *Myth, Symbol, and Culture.* New York: Norton, 1974.

———. "Thick Description: Towards an Interpretive Theory of Culture." In *The Interpretation of Culture,* 3–30. New York: Basic Books, 1973.

Gellner, Ernest. *Nations and Nationalism.* Ithaca, NY: Cornell University Press, 1983.

———. "Relativism and Universals." In *Rationality and Relativism*, edited by Martin Hollis and Steven Lukes, 181–200. Cambridge, MA: MIT Press, 1982.

Gilbert, Felix. *History: Politics or Culture? Reflections on Ranke and Burckhardt.* Princeton: Princeton University Press, 1990.

Gingrich, A. "Toward an Anthropology of Germany: A Culture of Moralist Self-Education?" *Current Anthropology* 39 (1998): 567–72.

Ginsburg, Faye. "Aboriginal Media and the Australian Imaginary." *Public Culture* 5 (1993): 557–78.

Gittings, John. "Fire Kills 74 Locked in Porn Cinema." *The Guardian*, 1 April 2000.

Goldschmidt, Walter. "The Cultural Paradigm in the Post-War Period." In *Social Contexts of American Ethnology, 1840–1984*, edited by June Helm, 164–76. Washington: American Anthropological Association, 1985.

Goodenough, Ward. *Cultural Anthropology and Linguistics*. Vol. 9, *Language and Linguistics*. Washington: Georgetown University, 1957.

———. "Culture." In *Encyclopedia of Cultural Anthropology*, edited by David Levinson and Melvin Ember, 291–99. New York: Henry Holt, 1996.

———, ed. *Explorations in Cultural Anthropology*. New York: McGraw Hill, 1964.

Goody, Jack. "Culture and its Boundaries: A European View." In *Assessing Cultural Anthropology*, edited by Robert Borofsky, 250–60. New York: McGraw-Hill, 1994.

———. *The Culture of Flowers*. New York: Cambridge University Press, 1993.

Gourmont, Rémy de. *Decadence and Other Essays on the Culture of Ideas*. New York: Harcourt, Brace, 1921.

Graff, Gerald. *Professing Literature: An Institutional History*. Chicago: University of Chicago Press, 1987.

———. "Taking Cover in Coverage." *Profession* 86 (1986): 41–45.

———. "Teach the Conflicts." In *The Politics of Liberal Education*, edited by Darryl J. Gless and Barbara Herrnstein Smith, 57–73. Durham, NC: Duke UP, 1992.

———. "What Should We Be Teaching – When There Is No 'We'?" *Yale Journal of Criticism* 1 (1987): 189–211.

Gramsci, Antonio. "Culture and Ideological Hegemony." In *Culture and Society: Contemporary Debates*, edited by Jeffrey Alexander and Steven Seidman, 47–54. Cambridge: Cambridge University Press, 1998.

———. *Selections from the Prison Notebooks*. Translated and edited by Q. Hoare and G. Nowell Smith. London: Lawrence and Wishart, 1971.

Grant, R.A.D. "Culture." In *A Companion to Aesthetics*, edited by David Cooper, 99–104. Oxford: Blackwell, 1992.

Grice, Paul. "Utterer's Meaning and Intentions." *Philosophical Review* 78 (1969): 147–77.

Grossberg, Lawrence. "Speculations and Articulations of Globalization." *Polygraph* 11 (1999): 11–48.

Group, Chicago Cultural Studies. "Critical Multiculturalism." *Critical Inquiry* 18 (1992): 530–55.

Habermas, Jürgen. "Citizenship and National Identity: Some Reflections on the Future of Europe." In *Theorizing Citizenship*, edited by R. Beiner, 255–83. Albany: State University of New York Press, 1995.

————. "Dual-Layered Time: Personal Notes on Philosopher Theodor W. Adorno in the '50s." *Logos: A Journal of Modern Society and Culture* 2, no. 4 (2003): 52–57.

————. *The Structural Transformation of the Public Sphere: An Inquiry into a Category of Bourgeois Society.* Translated by Thomas Burger with the assistance of Frederick Lawrence. Cambridge, MA: MIT Press, 1991.

Hall, G. Stanley. *Adolescence.* New York: Appleton, 1904.

Hamilton, Annette. "Video Crackdown, or, the Sacrificial Pirate: Censorship and Cultural Consequences in Thailand." *Public Culture* 5, no. 3 (1993): 515–31.

Hannerz, Ulf. "Borders." *International Social Science Journal* 154 (1997): 537–48.

————. *Cultural Complexity: Studies in the Social Organization of Meaning.* New York: Columbia University Press, 1992.

————. *Över Gränser.* Lund: Liber, 1983.

————. *Transnational Connections: Cultures, People, Places.* London: Routledge, 1996.

Hansen, Miriam. "The Mass Production of the Senses: Classical Cinema as Vernacular Modernism." *Modernism/Modernity* 6, no. 2 (1999): 59–77.

Hanson, Alan. "The Making of the Maori: Culture Invention and Its Logic." *American Anthropologist* 91 (1990): 890–902.

————. "Reply to Langdon, Levine, and Linnekin." *American Anthropologist* 93 (1991): 449–50.

Haraway, Donna J. *Simians, Cyborgs, and Women: The Reinvention of Nature.* London: Free Association Books, 1991.

Hardt, Michael, and Antonio Negri. *Empire.* Cambridge. MA: Harvard University Press, 2000.

Hark, Ina Rae, ed. *Exhibition: The Film Reader.* New York: Routledge, 2002.

Harper, W., and G. Smith. "Newton's New Way of Inquiry." In *The Creation of Ideas in Physics,* edited by J. Leplin, 113–16. Dordrecht: Kluwer, 1995.

Harris, Marvin. *Culture, People, Nature: An Introduction to General Anthropology.* 2nd ed. New York: Thomas Y. Crowell, 1975.

————. *The Rise of Anthropological Theory.* New York: Thomas Y. Crowell, 1968.

Hartman, Geoffrey. "Art and Consensus in the Era of Progressive Politics." *Yale Review* 80 (1992): 50–61.

Hartman, Geoffrey H. *The Fateful Question of Culture.* New York: Columbia University Press, 1997.

Hasan, Zoya. *Forging Identities: Gender, Communities, and the State in India.* Boulder, CO: Westview Press, 1994.

Havel, Václav. "The Culture of Everything." *New York Review of Books* 34, no. 10 (1992): 30.

Heaney, Seamus. *Beowulf: A New Verse Translation.* New York: Farrar, Straus, and Giroux, 2000.

Hegel, G.W.F. "Vorlesungen über die Philosophie der Geschichte." In *Sämtliche Werke,* edited by Herman Glockner, 101. Stuttgart: Friedrich Fromann Verlag, 1971.

Hegel, G.W.F. *The Phenomenology of Mind.* Translated by J.D. Baillie. London: Allen & Unwin, 1949.

Heider, Karl G. *Indonesian Cinema: National Culture on Screen.* Honolulu: University of Hawaii Press, 1991.

Herder, Johann Gottfried. "Yet Another Philosophy of History." In *Herder on Social and Political Culture*, edited by F.M. Barnard, 181–88. Cambridge: Cambridge University Press, 1969.

Herder, Johann Gottfried. *Outlines of the History of Man*. Translated by T. Churchill. London: Johnson, 1800.

Herman, Edward S., and Robert W. McChesney. *The Global Media: The New Missionaries of Global Capitalism*. Washington: Cassell, 1997.

Herskovits, Melville J. *Man and his Works*. New York: Knopf, 1948.

Herzfeld, Michael. "Anthropology and the Politics of Significance." *Social Analysis* 41, no. 3 (1997): 107–38.

Hibbs, Thomas S. *Shows about Nothing: Nihilism in Popular Culture from the Exorcist to Seinfeld*. Dallas: Spence Pub., 1999.

Hirsch, E.D. *Cultural Literacy: What Every American Needs to Know*. Boston: Houghton Mifflin, 1987.

Hirst, Paul, and Grahame Thompson. *Globalization in Question: The International Economy and the Possibility of Governance*. London: Polity Press, 1999.

Hjort, Mette. *The Strategy of Letters*. Cambridge, MA: Harvard University Press, 1993.

———, and Scott MacKenzie, eds. *Cinema and Nation*. New York: Routledge, 2000.

———. *Small Nations, Global Cinema*. Minneapolis: University of Minnesota Press, forthcoming.

Hoberman, J. *Sport and Political Ideology*. London: Heinemann, 1984.

Hollis, M. "Is Universalism Ethnocentric?" In *Multicultural Questions*, edited by S. Lukes and C. Joppke, 27–43. Oxford: Oxford University Press, 1999.

Honneth, Axel. *The Fragmented World of the Social: Essays in Social and Political Philosophy*. Albany: State University of New York Press, 1995.

Horkheimer, Max, and Theodor W. Adorno. *Dialektik der Aufklärung: Philosophische Fragmente*. Amsterdam: Querido, 1947.

Hossain, Rokeya Sakhawat. *Sultana's Dream and Selections from the Secluded Ones*. Translated and edited by Roushan Jahan. New York: Feminist Press of the City University of New York, 1988.

Hozic, Aida A. *Hollyworld: Space, Power, and Fantasy in the American Economy*. Ithaca, NY: Cornell University Press, 2001.

Hroch, Miroslav. *The Social Preconditions of National Revival in Europe: A Comparative Analysis of the Social Composition of Patriotic Groups among the Smaller European Nations*. Cambridge: Cambridge University Press, 1985.

Huntington, Samuel P. *The Clash of Civilizations and the Remaking of World Order*. New York: Simon and Schuster, 1996.

———. "The Clash of Civilizations?" *Foreign Affairs* 72, no. 3 (1993): 22–49.

Huyssen, Andreas. *Twilight Memories: Marking Time in a Culture of Amnesia*. New York: Routledge, 1995.

Ingold, Tim. "The Art of Translation in a Continuous World." In *Beyond Boundaries: Understanding, Translation, and Anthropological Discourse*, edited by Gisli Pálsson, 210–30. London: Berg, 1993.

———, ed. *Companion Encyclopedia of Anthropology: Humanity, Culture, and Social Life*. London: Routledge, 1994.

International Food Policy Research Institute. "'Bargaining' and Gender Relations: Within and Beyond the Household." FCND Discussion Paper, 1997.

IOC. *The Olympic Charter.* Lausanne: International Olympic Committee, 2004.

Jameson, Fredric. *Postmodemism; or, the Cultural Logic of Late Capitalism.* Durham, NC: Duke University Press, 1991.

Jameson, Fredric. "Finance Capitalism and Culture." In *The Cultural Turn: Selected Writings on the Postmodern, 1983–1998,* 136–61. New York: Verso, 1998.

Jardine, N. "The Forging of Modern Realism: Clavius and Kepler against the Sceptics." *Studies in History and Philosophy of Science* 10 (1979): 141–73.

Jayawardena, Kumari. *The White Woman's Other Burden: Western Women and South Asia during British Rule.* New York and London: Routledge, 1995.

Jenkins, Henry. *Textual Poachers: Television Fans and Participatory Culture.* New York: Routledge, 1992.

Jeu, B., et al., ed. *For a Humanism of Sport.* Paris: CNOSF-Editions, 1994.

Johnson, Randal. "The Brazilian Film Industry." In *The International Movie Industry,* edited by Gorham Kindem, 257–72. Carbondale: Southen Illinois University Press, 2000.

Johnson, Thomas H., ed. *The Complete Poems of Emily Dickinson.* Boston: Little, Brown, 1960.

Johst, Hanns. *Schlageter, Schauspiel.* München: A. Langen/G. Müller, 1933.

Joppke, C., and S. Lukes, eds. *Multicultural Questions.* Oxford: Oxford University Press, 1999.

Kamboureli, Smaro. *Scandalous Bodies: Diasporic Literature in English Canada.* Oxford: Oxford University Press, 1999.

Kant, Immanuel. *Critique of Judgment.* Translated by Werner S. Pluhar. Indianapolis: Hackett, 1987.

———. *Was ist Aufklärung? Aufsätze zur Geschichte und Philosophie.* Edited by Jürgen Zehbe. Göttingen: Vandenhoeck and Ruprecht, 1967.

Karakasidou, Anastasia N. *Fields of Wheat, Hills of Blood: Passages to Nationhood in Greek Macedonia, 1870–1990.* Chicago: University of Chicago Press, 1997.

Karamcheti, Indira. "The Graves of Academe." In *Our Feet Walk the Sky: Women of the South Asian Diaspora,* edited by the Women of South Asian Descent Collective, 274–77. San Francisco: Aunt Lute Books, 1993.

Kaufman, Anthony. "Life Isn't Beautiful Anymore, It's Dubbed." In *Indiewire,* August 23, 1999. http://www.indiewire.com/biz/biz_990823_KaufEditorial.html.

Keesing, Roger M. *Cultural Anthropology: A Contemporary Perspective.* 2nd ed. Fort Worth: Holt, Rinehart and Winston, 1981.

———. "Theories of Culture Revisited." In *Assessing Cultural Anthropology,* edited by Robert Borofsky, 301–10. New York: McGraw-Hill, 1994.

Keita, S. O. Y., and Rick A. Kittles. "The Persistence of Racial Thinking and the Myth of Racial Divergence." *American Anthropologist* 99 (1997): 534–44.

Keown, Damien. *The Nature of Buddhist Ethics.* New York: St. Martin's Press, 1992.

Kepler, J. *Epitome of Copernican Astronomy: Books IV and V.* Translated by C.G. Wallis. Edited by R.M. Hutchins. Vol. 16, *Great Books of the Western World:* Encyclopaedia Britannica, 1952.

————. *Gesammelte Werke*. Edited by W.V. Dyck et al. Vol. I–XX. Munich: Beck, 1937.

————. *The Harmonies of the World: V*. Translated by C.G. Wallis. Edited by R.M. Hutchins. Vol. 16, *Great Books of the Western World*: Encyclopaedia Britannica, 1939, 1952.

————. *New Astronomy*. Translated by W.H. Donahue. New York: Cambridge University Press, 1992.

————. *The Harmony of the World*. Translated by A.M. Duncan with an Introduction and Notes by E.J. Aiton, J.V. Field: American Philosophical Society, 1997.

————. *The Secret of the Universe*. Translated by A.M. Duncan with notes by E.J. Aiton. New York: Abaris Books, 1981.

————. "Apologia Pro Tychone Contra Ursum." In *The Birth of History and Philosophy of Science: Kepler's 'A Defense of Tycho against Ursus' with Essays on Its Provenance and Significance*, translated by N. Jardine, 134–207. Cambridge: Cambridge University Press, 1984.

Kimball, Roger. *Tenured Radicals: How Politics Has Corrupted Our Higher Education*. New York: Harper & Row, 1990.

————. "When Reason Sleeps: The Academy Vs. Science." *The New Criterion* 12, no. 9 (1994): 10–18.

Kitcher, Philip. *The Advancement of Science*. Oxford: Oxford University Press, 1993.

Kitto, H.D.F. *The Greeks*. Harmondsworth: Penguin, 1951.

Kluckhohn, Clyde, and William Kelly. "The Concept of Culture." In *The Science of Man in the World Crisis*, edited by Ralph Linton, 78–107. New York: Columbia University Press, 1957.

Knauft, Bruce M. *Genealogies for the Present in Cultural Anthropology: A Critical Humanist Perspective*. London: Routledge, 1996.

Knowles, Harry, Paul Cullum, and Mark Ebner. *Ain't It Cool? Hollywood's Redheaded Stepchild Speaks Out*. New York: Warner Books, 2002.

Kottak, Conrad Phillip. *Cultural Anthropology*. 3rd ed. New York: Random House, 1982.

————. *Prime-Time Society: An Anthropological Analysis of Television and Culture*. Belmont, CA: Wadsworth, 1990.

Krieger, Murray. *Arts on the Level: The Fall of the Elite Object*. Knoxville: University of Tennessee Press, 1981.

Kroeber, A. L., and Clyde Kluckhohn. *Culture: A Critical Review of Concepts and Definitions*. New York: Vintage Books, 1952.

Kroeber, A.L. "The Superorganic." *American Anthropologist* 19 (1917): 163–213.

Kuhn, T.S. *The Copernican Revolution: Planetary Astronomy in the Development of Western Thought*. Cambridge, MA: Harvard University Press, 1985.

————. "Objectivity, Value Judgment, and Theory Choice." In *Philosophy of Science: The Central Issues*, edited by M. Curd and J.A. Cover, 102–18. New York: W.W. Norton, 1998.

Kuhn, Thomas. *The Essential Tension*. Chicago: University of Chicago Press, 1977.

————. *The Structure of Scientific Revolutions*. Chicago: University of Chicago Press, 1970.

Kuper, Adam. "Culture, Identity, and the Project of a Cosmopolitan Anthropology." *Man* 29 (1994): 537–54.

LaCapra, Dominick. *History in Transit: Experience, Identity, Critical Theory.* Ithaca, NY: Cornell University Press, 2004.

Landry, F. "The Olympic Games & Competitive Sport as an International System." *Proceedings of the International Olympic Academy* 24 (1984): 157–67.

Lang, Hartmut. "Kultur und Evolutionstheorie." *Zeitschrift für Ethnologie* 123 (1998): 5–20.

Langness, L.L. *The Study of Culture.* Novato, CA: Chandler and Sharp, 1987.

Lapiere, Richard T. *Sociology.* New York: McGraw-Hill, 1949.

Lattis, J.M. *Between Copernicus and Galileo: Christoph Clavius and the Collapse of Ptolemaic Cosmology.* Chicago: University of Chicago Press, 1994.

Laudan, Larry. "Progress or Rationality: The Prospects for Normative Naturalism." *American Philosophical Quarterly* 24 (1987): 19–31.

———. *Science and Values: The Aims of Science and their Role in Scientific Debate.* Berkeley: University of California Press, 1984.

Lawrence, Joseph P. "What Is Culture?" *Future: The Hoechst Magazine* 1 (1997): 10–17.

Lefebvre, Henri. *Le Langage et la société.* Paris: Gallimard, 1966.

Lenk, H. "Towards a Philosophical Anthropology of the Olympic Athlete." *Proceedings of the International Olympic Academy* 22 (1982): 163–77.

———. "Values, Aims, Reality of the Modern Olympic Games." *Proceedings of the International Olympic Academy* 4 (1964): 204–11.

Levin, Harry. "Semantics of Culture." *Daedalus* 94, no. 1 (1965): 1–13.

Levine, H. B. "Comment on Hanson's 'the Making of the Maori.'" *American Anthropologist* 93 (1991): 444–46.

Levinson, David, ed. *Encyclopedia of World Cultures.* 10 vols. Boston: G.K. Hall, 1991–95.

Levinson, Jerrold. *Art, Music and Metaphysics.* Ithaca, NY: Cornell University Press, 1990.

———. "Intention and Interpretatation in Literature." In *The Pleasures of Aesthetics,* 175–213. Ithaca, NY: Cornell University Press, 1996.

———. "Messages in Art." In *The Pleasures of Aesthetics,* 224–241. Ithaca, NY: Cornell University Press, 1996.

———. "Refining Art Historically." *Journal of Aesthetics and Art Criticism* 47 (1989): 21.

Linke, Uli. "Gendered Difference, Violent Imagination: Blood, Race, Nation." *American Anthropologist* 99 (1997): 559–73.

Linnekin, Jocelyn. "Culture Invention and the Dilemma of Authenticity." *American Anthropologist* 93 (1991): 446–49.

Linton, Ralph. *The Study of Man: An Introduction.* New York: D. Appleton-Century, 1936.

Lloyd, David, and Paul Thomas. *Culture and the State.* New York: Routledge, 1998.

Lotman, Y.M., and B.A. Uspensky. "On the Semiotic Mechanism of Culture." *New Literary History* 9, no.2 (1978): 211–32.

Lowie, Robert. *Primitive Society.* New York: Boni and Liveright, 1920.

Lubbock, John (Lord Avebury). *The Origin of Civilization and the Primitive Condition of Man.* London: Longmans, 1912.

Lukács, Georg. *History and Class Consciousness: Studies in Marxist Dialectics*. Translated by Rodney Livingstone. Cambridge, MA: MIT Press, 1971.

Lukes, S. *Liberals and Cannibals*. London: Verso, 2002.

———. "Moral Diversity and Relativism." *Journal of the Philosophy of Education* 29, no. 2 (1995): 173–80.

Lundberg, Shelly, and Robert A. Pollak. "Bargaining and Distribution in Marriage." *Journal of Economic Perspectives* 10 (1996): 139–58.

Lynes, Russell. "Highbrow, Lowbrow, Middlebrow." *Harper's Magazine* Feb. (1949). Reprinted in Lynes, *The Tastemakers*, 310–22, 331–33. New York: Grosset and Dunlap, 1954.

Lyons, Andrew P. "The Television and the Shrine: Towards a Theoretical Model for the Study of Mass Communications in Nigeria." *Visual Anthropology* 3 (1990): 429–56.

Lyons, Harriet D. "Television in Contemporary Urban Life: Benin City, Nigeria," *Visual Anthropology* 3 (1990): 411–28.

Lyotard, Jean-François. *The Postmodern Condition: A Report on Knowledge*. Translated by Geoff Bennington and Brian Massumi. Minneapolis: University of Minnesota Press, 1984.

———. "What Is Postmodernism?" In *The Postmodern Condition: A Report on Knowledge*, 71–82. Minneapolis: University of Minnesota Press, 1984.

Macedo, S. "Multiculturalism for the Religious Right? Defending Liberal Civic Education." *Journal of the Philosophy of Education* 29, no. 2 (1995): 223–38.

Maguire, J. *Global Sport: Identities, Societies, Civilisations*. Cambridge: Polity Press, 1999.

Malinowski, Bronislaw. *Crime and Custom in Savage Society*. Totowa, NJ: Littlefield, Adams, 1976.

———. "Culture." *The Encyclopedia of the Social Sciences* 4 (1931): 621–45.

———. "The Group and the Individual in Functional Analysis." *American Journal of Sociology* 44 (1939): 938–64.

Mankekar, Purnima. "National Texts and Gendered Lives." *American Ethnologist* 20.3 (1993): 543–63.

———. "Television Tales and a Woman's Rage." *Public Culture* 5 (1993): 469–92.

Mann, Elizabeth A. "Education, Money, and the Role of Women in Maintaining Minority Identity." In *Forging Identities: Gender, Communities, and the State in India*, edited by Zoya Hasan, 130–67. Boulder, CO: Westview Press, 1994.

Manuel, Frank. *Shapes of Philosophical History*. Stanford: Stanford University Press, 1965.

Marcuse, Herbert. "The Affirmative Character of Culture." In *Negations: Essays in Critical Theory*. Translated by Jeremy J. Shapiro, 88–133. Boston: Beacon, 1968.

———. *Negations: Essays in Critical Theory*. Translated by Jeremy J. Shapiro. London: Free Association Books, 1988.

———. *One-Dimensional Man: Studies in the Ideology of Advanced Industrial Society*. Boston: Beacon, 1964.

Margolis, Joseph. *Art and Philosophy*. Brighton: Harvestor Press, 1980.

———. *Interpretation Radical but Not Unruly*. Berkeley: University of California Press, 1995.

———. *What, after All, Is a Work of Art?* University Park: Pennsylvania State University Press, 1999.

Martens, R. *Kepler's Philosophy and the New Astronomy.* Princeton: Princeton University Press, 2000.

Martinet, Marcel. *Culture Prolétarienne.* Paris: Librairie du Travail, 1935.

Mattelart, Armand. *Networking the World, 1794–2000.* Translated by Liz Carey-Libbrecht and James A. Cohen. Minneapolis: University of Minnesota Press, 1996, 2000.

Mcfee, Graham. "The Historicity of Art." *British Journal of Aesthetics* 38 (1980): 307–24.

McGoogan, Kenneth. *Canada's Undeclared War.* Calgary: Detselig Enterprises, 1991.

McNeill, William. *Plagues and Peoples.* New York: Anchor, 1998.

Mead, Margaret. *Cooperation and Competition among Primitive Peoples.* New York: McGraw-Hill, 1937.

Menand, Louis. "The Culture Wars." *The New York Review of Books* (1994): 16–21.

Mendus, S. "Tolerance and Recognition: Education in a Multicultural Society." *Journal of the Philosophy of Education* 29, no. 2 (1995): 191–202.

Metcalf, Barbara. "Reading and Writing About Muslim Women in British India." In *Forging Identities: Gender Communities and the State in India*, edited by Zoya Hasan, 1–21. Delhi: Kali for Women, and Boulder, CO: Westview Press, 1994.

Methuen, C. *Kepler's Tübingen: Stimulus to a Theological Mathematics.* Aldershot, UK: Ashgate, 1998.

Mill, John Stuart. *The Subjection of Women.* Edited by S.M. Okim. Indianapolis: Hackett, 1988.

Miller, Mark Crispin. *Boxed In: The Culture of TV.* Evanston, IL: Northwestern University Press, 1988.

Miller, Roy A. *Japan's Modern Myth: The Language and Beyond.* New York: Weatherhill, 1983.

Miller, Toby. *Global Hollywood.* London: British Film Institute, 2001.

Mishra, Vijay. *Bollywood Cinema: Temples of Desire.* New York: Routledge, 2002.

Mitchell, W.J.T. *Against Theory: Literary Studies and the New Pragmatism.* Chicago: University of Chicago Press, 1985.

Miyoshi, Masao. "Ivory Tower in Escrow." *boundary 2* 27, no. 1 (2000): 7–50.

Mohanty, Satya. *Literary Theory and the Claims of History: Postmodernism, Objectivity, Multicultural Politics.* Ithaca, NY: Cornell University Press, 1997.

MoMA, and San Francisco Cinematheque. *Big as Life: An American History of 8mm Films.* San Francisco: Foundation for Art in Cinema, 1998.

Moody-Adams, Michelle. *Fieldwork in Familiar Places: Morality, Culture, and Philosophy.* Cambridge, MA: Harvard University Press, 1997.

Moore, Sally Falk. "The Ethnography of the Present and the Analysis of Process." In *Assessing Cultural Anthropology*, edited by Robert Borofsky, 362–74. New York: McGraw-Hill, 1994.

More, Thomas, William Rastell, William Edward Campbell, and Arthur William Reed. *The English Works of Sir Thomas More.* London: Eyre and Spottiswoode, 1931.

Morris, Meaghan. *Ecstasy and Economics: American Essays for John Forbes.* Sydney: EMPress, 1992.

Moya, Paula M.L., and Michael R. Hames-García, eds. *Reclaiming Identity: Realist Theory and the Predicament of Postmodernism.* Berkeley: University of California Press, 2000.

Muller, Adam. "American Theory and Criticism: 1970 and After." In *The Johns Hopkins Guide to Literary Theory and Criticism,* edited by Michael Groden, Martin Kreiswirth, and Imre Szeman, 44–50. Baltimore: Johns Hopkins University Press, 2005.

Murdock, George Peter. "British Social Anthropology." *American Anthropologist* 53 (1951): 465–73.

——, ed. *Studies in the Science of Society: Presented to Albert Galloway Keller.* Freeport, NY: Books for Libraries Press, 1937.

Nagel, T. *Equality and Partiality.* Oxford: Oxford University Press, 1991.

Narayan, Uma. "Contesting Cultures." In *Dislocating Cultures: Identities, Traditions, and Third-World Feminism,* 1–40. New York: Routledge, 1997.

——. "Cross-Cultural Connections, Border-Crossings, and 'Death by Culture.'" In *Dislocating Cultures: Identities, Traditions, and Third-World Feminism,* 81–118. New York: Routledge, 1997.

Nass, Matthias. "Unverkrampft im Reich der Mitte: Bundespräsident Herzog suchte eine neue Gesprächsbasis mit der aufsteigenden Weltmacht." *Die Zeit,* November 29, 1996.

Neumann, Erich. *Apuleius: Amor and Psyche, the Labors of the Feminine.* New York: Pantheon, 1965.

Niedermann, Joseph. *Kultur: Werden und Wandlungen des Begriffs und seiner Ersatz-Begriffe von Cicero bis Herder.* Florence: Libreria Editrice, 1941.

Niethammer, Lutz. "Konjunkturen und Konkurrenzen kollektiver Identität. Ideologie, Infrastruktur und Gedächtnis in der Zeitgeschichte." *PROKLA: Zeitschrift für kritische Sozialwissenschaft* 96 (1994): 377–99.

Nissiotis, N. "Olympism and Today's Reality." *Proceedings of the International Olympic Academy* 24 (1984): 57–74.

Nornes, Abé Mark. "For an Abusive Subtitling." *Film Quarterly* 52, no. 3 (1999): 17–34.

Norris, Christopher. *Against Relativism: Philosophy of Science, Deconstruction, and Critical Theory.* Oxford: Blackwell, 1997.

——. *The Truth About Postmodernism.* Oxford: Blackwell, 1993.

Novitz, David. "The Anaesthetics of Emotion." In *Emotion and the Arts,* edited by M. Hjort and S. Laver, 246–62. Oxford: Oxford University Press, 1997.

——. *The Boundaries of Art.* Philadelphia: Temple University Press, 1992.

——. "Disputes About Art." *Journal of Aesthetics and Art Criticism* 54 (1996): 153–63.

——. *Knowledge, Fiction & Imagination.* Philadelphia: Temple University Press, 1987.

——. "Messages 'in' and Messages 'through' Art." *Australasian Journal of Philosophy* 73 (1995): 199–203.

——. "Participatory Art and Appreciative Practice." *Journal of Aesthetics and Art Criticism* 59 (2001): 153–65.

——. "Ways of Artmaking: The High and the Popular in Art." *British Journal of Aesthetics* 29 (1989): 213–29.

Novitz, David, and Bill Willmott, eds. *Culture and Identity in New Zealand.* Wellington: GP Books, 1989.

Nowell-Smith, Geoffrey. *The Oxford History of World Cinema.* New York: Oxford University Press, 1996.

Nussbaum, Martha. "Aristotelian Social Democracy." In *Liberalism and the Good,* edited by R.B. Douglass et al., 203–52. New York: Routledge, 1990.

———. "Aristotle on Human Nature and the Foundations of Ethics." In *World, Mind and Ethics: Essays on the Ethical Philosophy of Bernard Williams,* edited by J.E.J. Altham and Ross Harrison, 86–131. Cambridge: Cambridge University Press, 1995.

———. "Capabilities and Human Rights." *Fordham Law Review* 66 (1997): 273–300.

———. *The Feminist Critique of Liberalism, The Lindley Lecture.* Lawrence: Dept. of Philosophy, University of Kansas, 1997.

———. "The Good as Discipline, the Good as Freedom." In *The Ethics of Consumption: The Good Life, Justice, and Global Stewardship,* edited by D. Crocker and T. Linden, 312–41. New York: Rowman and Littlefield, 1997.

———. "Human Capabilities, Female Human Beings." In *Women, Culture, and Development,* edited by M. Nussbaum and J. Glover, 61–104. Oxford: Clarendon Press, 1995.

———. "Human Functioning and Social Justice: In Defense of Aristotelian Essentialism." *Political Theory* 20 (1992): 202–46.

———. "Nature, Function, and Capability: Aristotle on Political Distribution." *Oxford Studies in Ancient Philosophy,* suppl. vol. 1 (1988): 145–84.

———. "Non-Relative Virtues: An Aristotelian Approach." In *The Quality of Life,* edited by M. Nussbaum and A. Sen, 242–69. Oxford: Clarendon Press, 1993.

———. "Public Philosophy and International Feminism." *Ethics* 108, no. 4 (1998): 762–96.

———. *Sex and Social Justice.* New York: Oxford University Press, 1998.

———. "Still Worthy of Praise: Comments on Richard Posner's the Problematics of Legal and Moral Theory." *Harvard Law Review* 111 (1998): 1776–1795.

———. "Why Practice Needs Ethical Theory: Particularism, Principle, and Bad Behavior." In *The Path of the Law in the Twentieth Century,* edited by S. Burton, 50–86. Cambridge: Cambridge University Press, 1998.

———. *Poetic Justice: The Literary Imagination and Public Life.* Boston: Beacon Press, 1995.

———. *Women and Human Development: The Capabilities Approach.* Cambridge: Cambridge University Press, 2001.

Nygard, Roger. *Trekkies.* Paramount Pictures, 1997.

Nzegwu, Nkiru. "Recovering Igbo Traditions: A Case for Indigenous Women's Organizations in Development." In *Women, Culture, and Development: A Study of Human Capabilities,* edited by M. Nussbaum and J. Glover, 444–66. Oxford: Clarendon Press, 1995.

Opler, Morris E. "Component Assemblage and Theme in Cultural Integration and Differentiation." *American Anthropologist* 61 (1959): 955–64.

Ozouf, Mona. *La Muse Démocratique: Henry James ou les Pouvoirs du Roman.* Paris: Calmann-Lévy, 1998.

Pace, Richard. "First-Time Televiewing in Amazônia: Television Acculturation in Gurupá, Brazil." *Ethnology* 32 (1993): 187–206.

Paleologos, K. "Hercules, the Ideal Olympic Personality." *Proceedings of the International Olympic Academy* 22 (1982): 54–71.

Panunzio, Constantinem. *Major Social Institutions: An Introduction.* New York: Macmillan, 1939.

Parry, J. "Globalisation, Multiculturalism and Olympism." *Proceedings of the International Olympic Academy* 39 (1999): 86–97.

———. "The Justification of Physical Education." In *Physical Education: A Reader,* edited by K. Green and K. Hardman, 36–68. Aachen: Meyer & Meyer, 1998.

———. "Olympism at the Beginning and End of the Twentieth Century." *Proceedings of the International Olympic Academy* 28 (1988): 81–94.

———. "Physical Education as Olympic Education." *European Physical Education Review* 4, no. 2 (1998): 153–67.

Parsons, Talcott, and Edward B. Shils. "Values and Social Systems." In *Culture and Society: Contemporary Debates,* edited by Jeffrey Alexander and Steven Seidman, 39–46. Cambridge: Cambridge University Press, 1998.

Peoples, James, and Garrick Bailey. *Humanity: An Introduction to Cultural Anthropology.* 3rd ed. St. Paul, MN: West, 1994.

Percival, Philip. "Stecker's Dilemma: A Constructive Response." *Journal of Aesthetics and Art Criticism* 58 (2000): 51–60.

Perec, Georges. *[La] Disparition.* Paris: Denoel, 1983.

Pippin, Robert B. *Modernism as a Philosophical Problem: On the Dissatisfactions of European High Culture.* Cambridge, MA: Blackwell, 1991.

Pitts, Leonard. "Gangsta Rap Represents Destruction." *Milwaukee Journal Sentinel,* November 11, 1999, sec. 18A.

Poovey, Mary. "The Twenty-First Century University: What Price Economic Viability?" *differences* 12, no. 1 (2001): 1–16.

Postrel, Virginia. "When It Comes to Enforcing Taste, It's Best to Tread Lightly." *New York Times,* July 13, 2000, 2.

United Nations Development Programme. *Human Development Report.* New York: United Nations Human Development Report Office, 1997.

Radcliffe-Brown, A.R. *A Natural Science of Society.* Glencoe, IL: Free Press, 1957.

———. "On Social Structure." *Journal of the Royal Anthropological Institute of Great Britain and Ireland* 70 (1940): 1–12.

Rawls, John. "The Law of Peoples." In *On Human Rights: The Oxford Amnesty Lectures 1993,* edited by S. Shute and S. Hunley, 41–82. New York: Basic Books, 1993.

———. *Political Liberalism.* New York: Columbia University Press, 1993.

———. *A Theory of Justice.* Cambridge, MA: Harvard University Press, 1971.

Raz, J. *Ethics in the Public Domain.* Oxford: Oxford University Press, 1994.

Readings, Bill. *The University in Ruins.* Cambridge, MA: Harvard University Press, 1996.

Rich, Frank. "The New Blood Culture." *New York Times,* 6 December 1992, sec.9.

Robbins, Bruce. *Secular Vocations.* London: Verso, 1993.

Robbins, Bruce, and Pheng Cheah, eds. *Cosmopolitics: Thinking and Feeling Beyond the Nation.* Minneapolis: University of Minnesota Press, 1998.

Roberts, John M. *Three Navaho Households*. Reports of the Ramah Project, Report No. 3. Cambridge, MA: Peabody Museum of American Archaeology and Ethnology, 1951.

———. "Within-Culture Variation: A Retrospective Personal View." *American Behavioral Scientist* 13 (1987): 266–79.

Roberts, Martin. "Variable Cinema: Portable Movies and the Pleasures of Reinvention." Paper presented at the Society for Cinema Studies Conference, Denver, CO, May 23–26, 2002.

Rodseth, Lars. "Distributive Models of Culture: A. Sapirian Alternative to Essentialism." *American Anthropologist* 100 (1998): 55–69.

Rofel, Lisa. "Yearnings: Televisual Love and Melodramatic Politics in Contemporary China." *American Ethnologist* 21 (1994): 700–722.

Romney, A.K., Carmella Moore, and C.D. Rusch. "Cultural Universals: Measuring the Semantic Structure of Emotion Terms in English and Japanese." *Proceedings of the National Academy of Sciences (U.S.A.)* 94 (1997): 5489–5494.

Romney, A. Kimball, William H. Batchelder, and Susan C. Weller. "Recent Applications of Cultural Consensus Theory." *American Behavioral Scientist* 31 (1987): 163–77.

Romney, A. Kimball, Susan C. Weller, and William H. Batchelder. "Culture as Consensus: A Theory of Culture and Informant Accuracy." *American Anthropologist* 88 (1986): 313–38.

Rorty, Richard. "On Analytic Philosophy and Transformative Philosophy: The Relation of Contemporary Philosophy to Humanities." Paper delivered at the *Humanities in the Two Hemispheres Conference*, Brisbane, Australia, June 5–7, 1999.

Rosaldo, Renato. *Culture and Truth: The Remaking of Social Analysis*. London: Routledge, 1993.

Rose, Kalima. *Where Women Are Leaders: The Sewa Movement in India*. New Delhi: Vistaar Publications, 1992.

Rosenbaum, Jonathan. "Fables of the Reconstruction." *Chicago Reader*, November 26, 1999. http://www.chireader.com/movies/archives/1999/1199/991126.html

———. "Internet Film Culture." In *Correspondence: An International Review of Culture and Society*, 4–15, 2001.

———. *Movie Wars: How Hollywood and the Media Conspire to Limit What Films We Can See*. Chicago: A Cappella, 2000.

Sahlins, Marshall. "Goodbye to Tristes Tropes: Ethnography in the Context of Modern World History." In *Assessing Cultural Anthropology*, edited by Robert Borofsky, 377–94. New York: McGraw-Hill, 1994.

———. *How "Natives" Think: About Captain Cook, for Example*. Chicago: University of Chicago Press, 1995.

Said, Edward W. *Culture and Imperialism*. New York: Knopf, 1993.

———. *Orientalism*. New York: Pantheon Books, 1978.

Sainte-Beuve, Charles Augustin. *De la Tradition en littérature, et dans quel sens il la faut entendre*. Vol. 15, *Causeries du Lundi*. Paris: Gamier Frères, 1857–62.

Sapir, Edward. *Selected Writings in Language, Culture, and Personality*. Edited by D. G. Mandelbaum. Berkeley: University of California Press, 1949.

———. "The Unconscious Patterning of Behaviour in Society." In *Selected Writings of Edward Sapir in Language, Culture and Personality*, edited by David G. Mandelbaum, 544–59. Berkeley: University of California Press, 1958.

Sarkar, Susobhan. *Notes on the Bengal Renaissance*. Edited by A. Gupta. Jadavpur, Calcutta: The National Council of Education, 1958.

Sartre, Jean-Paul. *La Nausée*. Paris: Gallimard, 1938.

Scarry, Elaine. *On Beauty and Being Just*. Princeton: Princeton University Press, 1999.

Scheff, Thomas J. "Toward a Sociological Model of Consensus." *American Sociological Review* 32 (1967): 32–46.

Scheffler, I. *Science and Subjectivity*. Indianapolis: Bobbs Merrill, 1967.

Schlesier, Renate. "Zauber der Unschärfe: Ein Plädoyer für einen Wandel der Fächer." *Die Zeit*, November 22 1996, 11.

Schneider, David. "Notes toward a Theory of Meaning." In *Meaning in Anthropology*, edited by K. Basso and H. Selby, 197–220. Albuquerque: University of New Mexico Press, 1976.

Schor, Juliet. "Towards a New Politics of Consumption." In *The Consumer Society Reader*, edited by Juliet B. Schor and Douglas Holt, 446–62. New York: The New Press, 2000.

Schwartz, Vanessa. "Le Fesitval de Cannes." *Liberation*, May 10, 2001.

Schwichtenberg, Cathy, ed. *The Madonna Connection: Representational Politics, Subcultural Identities, and Cultural Theory*. Boulder, CO: Westview Press, 1993.

Scruton, Roger. *The Aesthetics of Architecture*. London: Methuen, 1979.

———. "Emotion and Culture." In *The Aesthetic Understanding: Essays in the Philosophy of Art and Culture*, 138–52. London: Methuen, 1983.

Sedgwick, Eve Kosofsky. "Pedagogy in the Context of an Antihomophobic Project." In *The Politics of Liberal Education*, edited by D.J. Glad and Barbara Herrnstein Smith, 145–62. Durham: Duke University Press, 1993.

Sen, Amartya. "Capability and Well-Being." In *The Quality of Life*, edited by M. Nussbaum and A. Sen, 30–53. Oxford: Clarendon Press, 1993.

———. *Choice, Welfare, and Measurement*. Oxford and Cambridge, MA: Basil Blackwell and MIT Press, 1982.

———. *Commodities and Capabilities*. Amsterdam: North-Holland, 1985.

———. "Equality of What?" In *Tanner Lectures on Human Values 1*, edited by S. McMurrin, 353–69. Cambridge: Cambridge University Press, 1980.

———. "Freedoms and Needs." *The New Republic*, January 10–17, 1994, 31–38.

———. "Gender and Cooperative Conflicts." In *Persistent Inequalities*, edited by I. Tinker, 123–49. New York: Oxford, 1991.

———. "Gender Inequality and Theories of Justice." In *Women, Culture, and Development*, edited by J. Glover and M. Nussbaum, 153–98. Oxford: Clarendon Press, 1995.

———. "Human Right and Asian Values." *The New Republic*, July 10–17, 1997, 33–41.

———. *Inequality Reexamined*. Oxford and Cambridge, MA: Clarendon Press and Harvard University Press, 1992.

———. *Resources, Values, and Development*. Oxford and Cambridge, MA: Basil Blackwell and MIT Press, 1984.

————. "Well-Being, Agency, and Freedom: The Dewey Lectures, 1984." *Journal of Philosophy* 82 (1985): 169–221.

Sen, Amartya, and Jean Drèze. *The Amartya Sen and Jean Drèze Omnibus*. New Delhi: Oxford University Press, 1999.

Sen, Krishna. *Indonesian Cinema: Framing the New Order*. Atlantic Highlands, NJ: Zed Books, 1994.

Seymour-Smith, Charlotte. *Macmillan Dictionary of Anthropology*. London: Macmillan, 1986.

Shusterman, Richard. *Practicing Philosophy: Pragmatism and the Philosophical Life*. New York: Routledge, 1997.

Shweder, Richard A. "Cultural Psychology – What Is It?" In *Cultural Psychology: Essays on Comparative Human Development*, edited by J.W. Stigler, R.A. Shweder, and G. Herdt, 1–43. Cambridge: Cambridge University Press, 1990.

Simpson, David. *The Academic Postmodern and the Rule of Literature: A Report on Half-Knowledge*. Chicago: University of Chicago Press, 1995.

Slocum, David, ed. *Violence and American Cinema*. New York: Routledge, 2001.

Smith, Barbara Herrnstein. "Hirsch, 'Literacy, and the National Culture.'" In *The Politics of Liberal Education*, edited by D.J. Glad and Barbara Herrnstein Smith, 75–94. Durham: Duke University Press, 1993.

Sobchack, Vivian. "Nostalgia for a Digital Object: Regrets on the Quickening of Quicktime." In *Future Cinema: The Cinematic Imaginary after Film*, edited by Jeffrey Shaw and Peter Weibel, 66–73. Cambridge, MA: MIT Press, 2003.

Soyinka, Wole. *Myth, Literature and the African World*. Cambridge: Cambridge University Press, 1976.

Spiro, Melford. *Culture and Human Nature*. Chicago: University of Chicago Press, 1991.

Spradley, James P., ed. *Culture and Cognition: Rules, Maps and Plans*. San Francisco: Chandler, 1972.

Stecker, Robert. *Aesthetics and the Philosophy of Art*. Lanham, MD: Rowman and Littlefield, 2005.

————. *Artworks: Definition, Meaning Value*. University Park: Penn State University Press, 1997.

————. *Interpretation and Construction: Art, Speech, and the Law*. Cambridge, MA: MIT Press, 2003.

————. "The Constructivist's Dilemma." *Journal of Aesthetics and Art Criticism* 55 (1997): 43–51.

Steiner, Wendy. *Venus in Exile: The Rejection of Beauty in Twentieth-Century Art*. New York: Free Press, 2001.

Stevens, Wallace. *Notes toward a Supreme Fiction*. Cummington, MA: Cummington Press, 1942.

Stocking, George. "Matthew Arnold, E.B. Tylor, and the Uses of Invention." *American Anthropologist* 65 (1963): 783–99.

Stolcke, Verena. "Talking Culture: New Boundaries, New Rhetorics of Exclusion in Europe." *Current Anthropology* 36 (1995): 1–24.

Stone, Judy. *Eye on the World: Conversations with International Filmmakers*. Los Angeles: Silman-James Press, 1997.

Strachey, James, ed. *Civilization and Its Discontents.* New York: Norton, 1962.

Strauss, Claudia, and Naomi Quinn. *A Cognitive Theory of Cultural Meaning.* Cambridge: Cambridge University Press, 1997.

Suppe, Fred, ed. *The Structure of Scientific Theories.* Urbana: University of Illinois Press, 1977.

Tagore, Rabindranath. "Letter from a Wife." In *Of Women, Outcastes, Peasants, and Rebels: A Selection of Bengali Short Stories,* edited by Kalpana Bardhan, 96–109. Berkeley: University of California Press, 1990.

Taine, Hippolyte. *History of English Literature.* Translated by H. Van Laun. New York: F. Ungar, 1965.

Tamir, Y. "Two Concepts of Multiculturalism." *Journal of the Philosophy of Education* 29, no. 2 (1995): 161–72.

Taylor, Charles. *Hegel and Modern Society.* Cambridge: Cambridge University Press, 1969.

———. "The Politics of Recognition." In *Multiculturalism and the Politics of Recognition,* edited by Amy Gutmann, 25–73. Princeton, NJ: Princeton University Press, 1992.

———. "Rationality." In *Rationality and Relativism,* edited by Martin Hollis and Steven Lukes, 87–105. Oxford: Blackwell, 1982.

Taylor, Peter. *Modernities: A Geohistorical Interpretation.* Minneapolis: University of Minnesota Press, 1999.

Teo, Stephen. *Hong Kong Cinema: The Extra Dimensions.* London: BFI, 1998.

Therborn, Goran. "Into the 21st Century: The New Parameters of Global Politics." *New Left Review* 10 (2001): 87–110.

Thom, Paul. *Making Sense.* Lanham, MD: Rowman and Littlefield, 2000.

———. "Review of Michael Krausz, *Rightness and Reasons: Interpretation of Cultural Practices.*" *Literature and Aesthetics* 7 (1997): 183.

Thurnwald, Richard. *Der Mensch Geringer Naturbe-Herrschung: Sein Aufstieg zwischen Wahn und Vernunft.* Berlin: de Gruyter, 1950.

Tolhurst, William. "On What a Text Is and How It Means." *British Journal of Aesthetics* 19 (1979): 3–14.

Tomlinson, John. *Cultural Imperialism.* Baltimore: Johns Hopkins University Press, 1991.

———. *Globalization and Culture.* Chicago: University of Chicago Press, 1999.

Trilling, Lionel. *Beyond Culture: Essays on Literature and Learning.* New York: Viking, 1965.

Tsui, Amy O., Judith N. Wasserheit, and John G. Haaga, eds. *Reproductive Health in Developing Countries.* Washington: National Academy Press, 1997.

Turan, Kenneth. *Sundance to Sarajevo: Film Festivals and the World They Made.* Berkeley: University of California Press, 2002.

Turner, Graeme. *Film as Social Practice.* New York: Routledge, 1999.

———, ed. *The Film Cultures Reader.* New York: Routledge, 2002.

Tylor, Edward B. *Primitive Culture.* London: John Murray, 1871.

Ukadike, N. Frank. "African Video-Films: An Alternate Reality." *Correspondence: An International Review of Culture and Society* 8, no.3 (2001): 3–14.

Urban, Gregory. "Culture's Public Face." *Public Culture* (1993): 213–38.

————. "The Two Faces of Culture." *Working Papers and Proceedings of the Center for Psychosocial Studies* 49 (1992): 1–25.

Usai, Paolo Cherchi. "Origins and Survival." In *The Oxford History of World Cinema*, edited by Geoffrey Nowell-Smith, 6–12. New York: Oxford University Press, 1996.

Van Fraassen, Bas. *The Scientific Image*. Oxford: Oxford University Press, 1980.

Verow, Todd. "Mov: The First Philippines Digital Film Festival." *Res* 5, no. 3 (2002): 72–73.

Vidal, John. "Dicaprio Filmmakers Face Storm over Paradise Lost." *The Guardian*, 29 October 1999.

Voelkel, James R. *The Composition of Kepler's Astronomia Nova*. Princeton: Princeton University Press, 1994.

Wallace, Anthony F. C. *Culture and Personality*. New York: Random House, 1960.

Walsh, W.H. "Colligatory Concepts in History." In *The Philosophy of History*, edited by Patrick Gardiner, 127–44. Oxford: Oxford University Press, 1974.

Walton, Kendall. "Categories of Art." *Philosophical Review* 79 (1970): 334–67.

Walton, Kendall L. *Mimesis as Make-Believe: On the Foundations of the Representational Arts*. Cambridge, MA: Harvard University Press, 1990.

Walzer, M. "Education, Democratic Citizenship and Multiculturalism." *Journal of the Philosophy of Education* 29, no. 2 (1995): 181–90.

Warner, Michael. *The Letters of the Republic: Publication and the Public Sphere in Eighteenth-Century America*. Cambridge: Harvard University Press, 1990.

————. *Publics and Counterpublics*. New York: Zone Books, 2002.

Wasson, Haidee. "Blinking, Stammering, Stuttering, Gone: The Size and the Speed of Web Movies." Paper presented at the Society for Cinema Studies Conference, Denver, CO, May 23–26, 2002.

Weiner, Annette B. "Culture and Our Discontents." *American Anthropologist* 97 (1995): 14–40.

Weitz, Morris. "The Role of Theory in Aesthetics." *Journal of Aesthetics and Art Criticism* 15 (1956): 27–35.

Westman, Robert S. "The Astronomer's Role in the Sixteenth Century: A Preliminary Study." *History of Science* 18 (1980): 105–47.

Westman, Robert S. "Three Responses to the Copernican Theory: Johannes Praetorius, Tycho Brahe, and Michael Maestlin." In *The Copernican Achievement*, edited by Robert Westman, 289–305. Berkeley: University of California Press, 1975.

White, Leslie. "Ethnological Theory." In *Philosophy for the Future*, edited by Roy Wood Sellars, V. J. McGill, and Marvin Farber, 357–84. New York: Macmillan, 1949.

————. *The Science of Culture*. New York: Farrar, 1969.

White, Leslie, and Beth Dillingham. *The Concept of Culture*. Minneapolis: Burgess, 1973.

Wilk, Richard R. "'It's Destroying a Whole Generation': Capitalism and Moral Discourse in Belize." *Visual Anthropology* 5 (1993): 229–44.

Williams, Bernard. *Making Sense of Humanity and Other Philosophical Papers, 1982–1993*. Cambridge: Cambridge University Press, 1995.

Williams, Bernard Arthur Owen. *Truth & Truthfulness: An Essay in Genealogy*. Princeton, NJ: Princeton University Press, 2002.

Williams, Raymond. *Culture*. London: Fontana, 1981.

———. *Culture and Society, 1780–1950*. Harmondsworth: Penguin, 1983.

———. *Keywords: A Vocabulary of Culture and Society*. New York: Oxford University Press, 1976.

———. *Problems in Materialism and Culture: Selected Essays*. New York: Verso, 1980.

Wimmer, Andreas. "Kultur: Zur Reformulierung eines sozialanthropologischen Grundbegriffs." *Kölner Zeitschrift für Soziologie und Sozialpsychologie* 48 (1996): 401–25.

———. "L'héritage de Herder: Nationalisme, migrations et la pratique théorique de l'anthropologie." *Tsantsa: Revue de la Société Suisse d'Ethnologie* 1 (1996): 4–18.

———. *Transformationen: Sozialer Wandel in Indianischen Mittelamerika*. Berlin: Reimer, 1995.

Wollheim, Richard. *Art and its Objects*. New York: Harper and Row, 1969.

Woolf, Leonard. *Principia Politica: A Study of Communal Psychology*. London: Hogarth, 1953.

Worrall, John. "Fix It and Be Damned: A Reply to Laudan." *British Journal for the Philosophy of Science* 40 (1989): 376–88.

———. "The Value of a Fixed Methodology." *British Journal for the Philosophy of Science* 39 (1988): 263–75.

Wright, Susan. "The Politicization of 'Culture.'" *Anthropology Today* 14, no. 1 (1998): 7–15.

Yanagisako, Sylvia, and Carol Delaney. "Naturalizing Power." In *Naturalizing Power*, edited by S. Yanagisako and C. Delaney, 1–22. New York: Routledge, 1995.

Yoshino, Kosaku. *Cultural Nationalism in Contemporary Japan*. London: Routledge, 1992.

Ziff, Paul. "The Task of Defining a Work of Art." *Philosophical Review* 62 (1953): 58–78.

INDEX

eudaimonistic function of, 203
high arts, 116, 184
identity of an artwork, 215
meaning of a work, 217
messages "in," 205
messages "through," 205–6
ontology of, 210, 212, 214
paintings, 215
of and by the people, 113, 117
as product of culture, 220, 224
art, religion, and politics
contest among, 98–99
Asseya, Olivier, 258
assimilation, 162, 274, 276–77
astronomy, 347, 355
grounded in physics, 346, 354, 356–58
Auerbach, Erich, 95
Augustine, Saint, Bishop of Hippo, 4
authenticity, 104, 136
authors, 66
autonomy-based Liberalism (ABL), 266, 276
axiological incommensurability, 359

B

Bacon, Francis, 1
Balibar, Etienne, 166
Barrès, Maurice, 100
Barthes, Roland, 210
Barzun, Jacques, 31–32, 113–14, 130, 155, 210, 371
basic economic opportunities, 298
basic political rights and liberties, 298
basic skills and attitudes, 147
Baudelaire, Charles, 122
Baudrillard, Jean, 85
Beach, The (film), 245
Beardsley, Monroe, 203
beauty, 156, 168
Becker, Ernest, 2
Becker, Gary, 314–15
utilitarian model of the family, 292
Beijing Olympic Games, 270, 289
Bell, Bernard I., 115
Bell, Clive, 223
Bend It Like Beckham (film), 261
Benedict, Ruth, 28, 52
Bengal Renaissance, 300
Benigni, Roberto, 248
Benjamin, Walter, 171
Bennet, William, 146
Beowulf, 117

"Between Conflict and Consensus" (Conference), 132–33
Bhatt, Ela, 299, 316
Bicycle Thief (film), 201
biogenetic law, 10
biology, 2–3
Black, Stephanie, 262
Blair Witch Project, The (film), 245
Blake, William, 98, 100, 204, 205, 218
Blanchot, Maurice, 105
Blok, Alexander, 201
Boas, Franz, 11–12, 15–17, 25, 27, 52
Bollywood, 259–61
Book-of-the-Month Club, 122
Borofsky, Robert, 59–60
Boucher de Perthes, Jacques, 3
boundaries, 50, 55, 61, 146, 160
between common and other cultures, 145
boundedness, 44, 52–53, 58
Bourdieu, Pierre, 88, 166, 171, 176, 177, 210, 240
bourgeois public sphere, 151
bourgeoisie, 97
Brazilian film industry, 243
Brink, André, 200
British film culture, 261
Brooks, Van Wyck, 118
Brown, Brockden, 84
Brown, N. O., 93
Browne, Thomas, 116
Brumann, Christoph, 31, 42, 129–30, 155, 181, 371
Buck-Morss, Susan, 174
Buddhist beliefs, 309
Bugs Bunny, 140
Bull, Malcolm, 174–75
Burckhardt, Jacob, 99–100
Butler, Nicholas Murray, 121

C

California Newsreel, 247
Camp de Thiaroye (film), 243
Canadian Multiculturalism Act, 135
capabilities approach. *See* human capabilities
capitalism, 91, 158, 174–75
global, 167
carnality and brutality, 115, 118
censorship (film), 240, 243, 245–46
DVD editions, 257
foreign films, 244
Cervantes, Miguel de, 117
Chadha, Gurinder, 261

cultural identity, 182–84, 195–98, 201
  ethnic, 67, 69, 95
cultural imperialism, 28, 160, 162, 166, 261
Cultural Industries Sectoral Advisory Group
  on International Trade, 165
cultural integration, 30–31
cultural materialists, 23
cultural particularism. *See* particularism
cultural pluralism, 14
cultural power, 139
cultural relativism. *See* relativism
cultural studies, 6, 64, 69, 92, 97, 166, 172, 213,
  239, 338
  British cultural studies, 7
  Chicago Cultural Studies Group, 132
  exponential growth of, 101
  ideology, 235n21
  intellectual sources, 232–33
  interdisciplinarity, 231
  revivification, 35
cultural systems, 17
cultural turn, 164
cultural unity, 31
culture, 9, 44, 54, 58, 68, 167
  as abstract aggregate, 41
  affirmative, 156, 172, 237
  affluence or social climbing, 94
  antinomy between "a culture" and
    "culture," 79, 100–101
  arguments against (skeptical discourse),
    44–47
  of capitalism, 175
  circulation of, 163
  as civilization, 8, 13
  classic perspective, 49, 52–53
  colligatory account of, 31, 181, 189–92, 195,
    206
  demarcation of, 192–95, 197
  elasticity of, 359
  in the era of globalization, 159, 174
  gender, 67
  geographical demarcation, 159, 161, 198
  ghostly (or Idealist) or Hegelian accounts
    of, 186, 188–89
  Hartman's two senses of, 79
  ideologies of, 87
  imperialism and colonialism, 166
  leisure time activity, 91
  limits to, 66
  meta-culture, 146
  mobility of, 168

national (*See* nation-states; national
  heritage)
productivity of, 168
professional cultures, 67
radical rethinking of, 168
reasons for retaining, 6, 62–70
regional, 67
relationship to freedom, 94–95
relationship to religion and politics, 99
separation (into highbrow and lowbrow),
  94, 100, 119, 169, 173 (*See also* elite
  groups; highbrow; lowbrow)
"shreds and patches," 52
social reproduction of, 65, 143
space of, 159
tolerance of difference, 365
T.S. Eliot on, 107n23
as "war by other means," 150
what a culture "knows," 366
Culture-and-Personality Studies, 16, 52
culture-as-text interpretivism, 52
"culture" (as word), 79, 100–101, 181, 184
  anthropological meaning of, 90
  definitions, 49–51
  general, 79, 97, 100
  historical semantics of, 97
  linguistic development, 89
  proliferation of, 88, 90, 94
  shifting meaning of, 161
culture clashes, 338. *See also*
  incommensurability
culture concept, 3, 5–7, 20–21, 31, 47, 49, 52, 58,
  64, 70, 130
  constructed nature of, 53
  defence of, 41
  misapplications of, 44, 54
culture industry, 113
"culture of the feelings" (Wordsworth's
  poetry), 89
culture of wit, 95
culture politics. *See* politics of culture
culture production, 176
culture speech, 89, 101
culture wars, 129, 133–35, 142, 145, 155
culturology, 21

D

Danish People's Party, 132
Darwin, Charles, 3
Darwin, Erasmus, 93
Das, Veena, 308–9

decent illiberalism, 276
democracy, 28, 278, 302
democratic citizenship, 145–46
Demotica, 115
Dennett, Daniel, 187
Descartes, René, 88, 358
Devanny, Jean, 200
Dickens, Charles, 218, 311
Dickinson, Emily, 85
difference, 148, 150, 278
  tolerance of, 336, 365
diffusionism, 52
digital technology, 238, 241
  and the distribution of films, 252
  and martial-arts movies, 259
  media formats, 245, 246, 257
digitization (film preservation), 256
dignity of the person, 298
Dilthey, Wilhelm, 12, 14–15
diversity, 129, 274, 278, 281, 303. *See also*
  argument from the good of diversity
  rational epistemic diversity, 363–64
Doctor Zhivago (film), 258
Dorfman, Ariel, 160
D'Souza, Dinesh, 136, 144
Durkheim, Emile, 19, 113

E

Eagleton, Terry, 13, 35, 166
economics, 162
  basic economic opportunities, 298
education. *See also* universities
  "Back to Basics" reform of the schools, 125
  basic skills and attitudes, 147
  centralized system of, 130, 143
  free public schooling, 120, 122
  liberal education, 143
  and mass culture, 173
  multicultural, 134, 137–38, 140, 143, 149–50, 286
  national or provincial systems, 145–46
  public education, 114, 121, 126
  ruling caste in higher education, 126
  sport in, 270, 273
  state supported educational systems, 143–45
Eichberg, H., 287
Eigentlichkeit, 105
Ekberg, Anita, 258
Eliot, T.S., 98, 107n23, 122
elite culture, 181. *See also* "highbrow"

elite groups, 29, 63, 80, 97, 116
  academic and intellectual, 120
Elkins, James, 169
embodiment, 79, 86, 88, 93, 95–99, 101–2, 110n44, 111n45
  as "cure of the body," 106n9
  false embodiments, 87
Emerson, Ralph Waldo, 118
empathy, 32
empowerment, 102
Encyclopaedia Britannica, 124–25
Encyclopedia of World Cultures, 67
Enlightenment, 96, 104, 136
equal rights. *See also* human rights
  universalizability, 136
equality and dignity, 136
Erskine, John, 121
essentialism, 47, 52, 210, 213
  acontextual, 222–25
  compatibility with historical contextualism, 222
ethnic identity. *See under* cultural identity
ethnocentrism, 9, 270
ethnographic studies of media audiences, 239, 253
ethnographic writing, 52–53
Etlin, Richard, 32
Eurocentrism, 161
European art cinema, 240
European Charter of Human Rights, 132
European exploration and colonization, 3–4
European football, 268
European New Wave, 241
European Union, 289
Evans-Pritchard, E., 28
evolutionism, 5–6, 8–10, 20, 52
  biological evolution, 2–3
  inferiority-superiority dichotomies, 21
Eyes Wide Shut (film), 257

F

Fabricius, David, 336, 346, 354–58
Fadiman, Clifton, 114
  Arnoldine mission, 124
  awards, 126
  "Back to Basics" reform of the schools, 125
  condescension toward, 122
  as critic for the *New Yorker*, 121
  crusade for public education, 121
  early life, 124
  as host of *Information, Please*, 123

Honneth, Axel, 113
Horkheimer, Max, 103–4
human capabilities, 291–92, 319–28
  central capabilities, 319, 321–28
  universal norms of, 294
Human Development Reports (UNDP), 319
human evolution
  developmental model of, 5–6
human rights, 34, 67, 136, 279, 289, 338, 277
humanities, 155, 158, 169, 174, 364
  cultural turn in, 164
  decline of, 167
  as defender of truth and beauty, 168
  as guardian of the good, 176
  marginalization, 165
  postmodernism in, 224
  role of, 168, 176
Huntington, Samuel, 64, 68, 164
Hutchins, Robert Maynard, 125

I

idealism, 12, 88, 181–82
identity, 81, 102, 104, 181. *See also* cultural
    identity; embodiment
  collective, 67
  inwardly generated, 136
identity politics, 150. *See also*
    multiculturalism
  Charles Taylor's analysis of, 135–37
ideographic approach to culture, 11
ideology, 87, 232
iFilm movement, 252. *See also* Internet
imagination, 87
incommensurability, 33–34, 64–66, 225, 335,
    360, 362
  academic subcultures, 365
  in analytic philosophy, 337
  axiological, 359
  barriers to theory evaluation, 345
  definition, 338
  goal-based, 346
  methodological, 352
  practical difficulty and, 359
  pragmatic, 336, 363, 366
  rationality of ignoring others, 336, 366
  reconception of, 363–64
  relevance in culture studies, 338
  in scientific subcultures, 338
  in scientific theories, 337

transaction/opportunity cost of learning
    other theories, 358, 363
  values. *See* values incommensurability
India, 312
  cultural diversity, 301–2
  pluralism, 305
  rights and freedoms in, 297, 298
India Cabaret (film), 260
Indian *Constitution*, 306
Indian feminist movements, 296
Indian women, 206, 296, 328
  protest, 299
  traditions of modesty and purity, 296, 298,
    301, 303
indigenous peoples, 7–8, 10
  forms of moral governance, 34
individual, 16, 20, 308
  Buddhist beliefs concerning, 309
  focus on, 307
individual rights. *See* human rights
Industrial Revolution, 2, 119
industrial societies, 146
  dependence on common culture, 143, 145
  shared standardized education, 144
industrialization, 113
Information, Please (radio show), 123
instrumentality, 23
integrity of the body, 298
intellectual elite, 29. *See also* elite groups;
    universities
intentional fallacy, 229
intentional systems
  human societies as, 187–89
intercultural cooperation and peaceful
    coexistence, 266
international development projects
  attention to cultural variety, 297
  quality of life assessments, 311
international feminism, 293, 295
international human rights bodies
  enforcing norms, 305
international level
  inclusion and exclusion, 139
International Olympic Committee, 271–72
internationalism, 286, 288–89. *See also*
    Olympism
Internet, 117, 126, 256
  film culture and, 238, 252
  film distribution, 251–52
  film fan culture, 255